Adobe Acrobat 6: The Professional User's Guide

DONNA L. BAKER AND TOM CARSON

Adobe Acrobat 6: The Professional User's Guide

ISBN (pbk): 1-59059-232-8

Printed and bound in the United States of America 12345678910

Technical Reviewers: Donna Baker, Teresa Banman, Ricky Brown, Tom Carson, Pam McCallie

Editorial Board: Dan Appleman, Craig Berry, Gary Cornell, Tony Davis, Steven Rycroft, Julian Skinner, Martin Streicher, Jim Sumser, Karen Watterson, Gavin Wray, John Zukowski

Assistant Publisher: Grace Wong

Project Manager: Kylie Johnston

Copy Editor: Mark Nigara

Production Manager: Kari Brooks

Compositor: Susan Glinert Stevens

Proofreader: Linda Seifert

Indexer: James Minkin

Artist: Marian Hartsough

Cover Designer: Kurt Krames

Manufacturing Manager: Tom Debolski

Distributed to the book trade in the United States by Springer-Verlag New York, Inc., 175 Fifth Avenue, New York, NY 10010 and outside the United States by Springer-Verlag GmbH & Co. KG, Tiergartenstr. 17, 69112 Heidelberg, Germany.

In the United States: phone 1-800-SPRINGER, email orders@springer-ny.com, or visit http://www.springer-ny.com. Outside the United States: fax +49 6221 345229, email orders@springer.de, or visit http://www.springer.de.

For information on translations, please contact Apress directly at 2560 Ninth Street, Suite 219, Berkeley, CA 94710. Phone 510-549-5930, fax 510-549-5939, email info@apress.com, or visit http://www.apress.com.

The source code for this book is available to readers at http://www.apress.com in the Downloads section. You will need to answer questions pertaining to this book in order to successfully download the code.

For my traveling companions, Erin and Deena.

—Donna Baker

Dr. John Warnock made this all possible by inventing PDF. John had a vision and developed it to be the bridge from the paper to the digital world.

—Tom Carson

Contents at a Glance

Contents

About the Authors

Donna L. Baker has worked as a graphics designer, information developer, and instructor for many years. Donna is the author of a number of books, including *Acrobat 5: The Professional User's Guide* (Apress, 2002). She writes monthly articles on graphics and web applications for the online magazine *WindoWatch*. Donna can be found on any given day in her office doing something visually interesting. Donna lives in the heart of the Canadian prairies with her husband, Terry, her daughter, Erin, two dogs, and a cat. Donna can be reached by email at dbaker@skyweb.ca.

Hugh T. (Tom) Carson is a gray-haired professional engineer and Adobe Certified Expert on Acrobat 4.6. Tom formerly edited the *Handbook on Hazardous Materials Management* and was president of a forty-person hazardous waste remediation firm that he sold in 1996. Tom is an eighth-generation East Tennessean and shares this beautiful country with his wife Judy, sons John and Joe, and two wonderful grandchildren, Austin (Auggie) and Kyler. Tom has two dogs, a duck, and a bunch of koi. Tom can be reached at htcarson@comcast.net.

Acknowledgments

Soon after the first edition of this book was released I received a very nice email from some man in Tennessee who said he bought all the Acrobat books to use for his work as an Acrobat trainer, and mine was the best of the bunch. I couldn't argue with that! We communicated regularly and discussed all and sundry in the world of PDF. Did he know his stuff? Well, as they say, he wrote the book. I would like to thank my coauthor Tom for his diligence, hard work, and humor. In truth, the book wouldn't have been written without you.

I would like to thank the usual cast of characters—my husband Terry, and my daughter Erin, who thinks each time a book is complete she gets to go on another trip. It's true of course. Thanks also to Deena for our usual chats. A special thanks to Bev and Barb for helping out with my overloaded schedule from time to time.

Thanks to my agent at Waterside, Matt Wagner, for managing my life in his usual superlative way.

Finally, my thanks to Tom Waits for musically supporting me during my quest for the right words.

—*Donna Baker*

I have spent a small fortune over the last four years on Acrobat books. I believe I own every one that has been printed. All the books have one thing in common: They come from the graphics community. Acrobat will be used the most outside the graphics community. Donna is a graphics designer, but she also has a business and scientific background. Her book had a different twist. I learned a lot from it. Asking me to coauthor this edition was scary given my workload and lack of a graphics background. I could not have done it without Donna's wonderful attitude and ability.

I really have a special thanks to my wife Judy. For two months, I did nothing but work my regular job and write. You kept my spirits up and did several of my honey-dos. I could not have done it without you.

My regular job is with the Southeast Tennessee Development District. I get to help local governments and industries in East Tennessee, Northwest Georgia and Southwest North Carolina enter the digital age with Acrobat. I also transfer this information to the federal and state governments. The District was very supportive and overlooked my sometimes glazed expression from writing too long. I now follow this into an exciting new venture—The New Economy Institute. America's technical workforce is aging and we are getting more competitive pressure from a global economy. We are attempting to capture the existing knowledge in an easy-to-use format and become more competitive.

Rich Bailey approached me about eBooks. He got the honor of writing the draft for that chapter. Chad Latham of Mueller Companies helped me with the video and Steve Shamblin of March Adams Engineers helped me with the engineering projects.

Our thanks to the people at Apress. An interesting bunch! Thanks to Project Manager Kylie Johnston, our keeper of the schedule, and Production Manager Kari Brooks for getting the whole project finished. Thanks to Mark Nigara, our patient and masterful copy editor, and Susan Glinert, our layout wizard. Thanks also to Hollie Fischer for her interesting marketing ideas and support.

—Tom Carson

Introduction

Our book is written from multiple perspectives. As a writing team, we each bring different perspectives on Acrobat 6.0 from the design and engineering communities. We both bring business experience and requirements to the table. Much of the book, just as much of Acrobat in version 6.0, can be used by people with any sort of business background or requirements, including managing and use of information.

Who This Book Is For

This book was written for both businesspeople and designers of different backgrounds ranging from engineering to graphics. Acrobat's functionality applies to a broad cross-section of the business community.

This book is *not* written for the novice, which is why the title includes the word "professional." Our focus is Acrobat 6.0 Professional, although we consider the other components of the version 6.0 products as well. Our working assumption is that people reading our book have a computer background sufficient to understand what we are referring to. That doesn't mean we don't provide theoretical information. Quite the contrary! Our belief is that readers with the level of interest required to read our book also have an interest in understanding why they're using particular settings, workflows, and so on.

We don't assume that everyone reading this book has advanced knowledge in all areas such as print or web delivery. As you all know, print output and web output, for example, are as different as night and day. Regardless of your area of expertise, we've included a feature that we think you'll find very useful. Sprinkled liberally throughout the chapters are tips. These tips include headings (unlike generic tips) and identify information and ideas that can be immediately useful to you as you work with Acrobat. When you read through a chapter, you'll find that they describe ways to use a particular feature, teach you how to choose settings, and when to use one process over another, and so on. The purpose of the tips is to answer the burning question that so often arises when reading a book: "What can this do for *my* work?"

Our book appeals to designers and businesspeople alike. Many parts of Acrobat 6.0 have strong business applications, and they're addressed from that perspective. Review cycles, for example, can't be differentiated on the basis of the user. Our goal in addressing business needs flow from the capabilities of the program itself.

Real-Life Scenarios

Our book includes materials kindly provided from a number of sources. For tutorial material, our manual was provided by Kathleen Kotchon. Terry Dyck provided a chapter of his book to use for creating an eBook.

The heart of the project process in our book is the knowledgebase. A knowledgebase is an organized collection of information on a subject. The subject may be small or large as a city. We recently won a National Association of Development Organizations Innovation Award for Local Government Knowledgebases. The computer world hasn't had a common platform until PDF. You can now take the information from all the various programs and have it on one neat, easy-to-use package.

The materials for the knowledgebase are scanned minutes that are an exact copy, but nevertheless remain searchable by word. In addition, forms for permitting can be filled out online, CAD drawings for plan review can be reviewed and tracked, and interactive maps can be used. Acrobat gives the typical small city the tools to go digital without breaking the bank.

How This Book Is Organized

The chapters follow a logical process. We cover the common processes you can perform with Acrobat 6.0 as well as numerous specialty functions. In general, creating a specific form of output will require using specialized features. The chapters' content generally follows this model.

The first two chapters deal with new features and versions of Acrobat 6.0, discuss the interface, and describe processes used to create PDF files. The first section also introduces the master project used in the book. Acrobat 6.0 is task-based in its interface, and the first of the fundamental tasks, creating PDF files, is the subject of Chapter 3. Also in Chapter 3 is the first of the knowledgebase projects.

Chapter 4 introduces document structure and bookmarking. Chapter 5 starts the discussion on commenting and commenting tools, which continues into collaboration and review cycles in Chapter 6. Chapter 7 introduces security methods and processes. Chapter 8 is the first chapter that introduces forms; it discusses the fundamentals of PDF forms.

Chapter 9 covers indexing and document management. Chapter 10 explores accessibility issues and how to make a file accessible by using tagged PDF formats. Chapter 11 covers output issues, looking at using articles for reflow, web-output types, and metadata.

Chapter 12 turns to print and Acrobat Distiller. It includes watched folders and the new printing specifications and capabilities. Chapter 13 is devoted to eBooks—their creation, structure, security, and distribution. Chapter 14 is a collage of other Acrobat activities such as video, working with layers, and destinations.

Chapter 15 covers Acrobat JavaScript. Throughout the book we discuss Acrobat JavaScript in relation to specific functions or types of output. This chapter is designed to give you an overall understanding of how Acrobat JavaScript works. It's very powerful, and it can be used to extend your Acrobat PDF projects, but it isn't for everyone.

Chapter 16 is a comprehensive-project chapter. Through a series of projects and discussions, you complete the knowledgebase that is systematically built through the book's chapters. This final project chapter describes how to make decisions and build components designed to streamline information handling and workflow. That, after all, is the name of the game.

This book also has two appendixes. Appendix A lists the URLs referred to in the book as well as other sources for information, reference, and interest. At the time of this book's writing, all URLs were correct. Appendix B discusses the plug-ins shipped with Acrobat as well as those used in our book. This appendix describes what they are, who provided them, and how they are integrated into the product as a whole.

We included both tutorials and projects throughout the book. Tutorials are used to explain how a particular process or procedure works, whereas a project is a step-by-step description of how to complete a series of tasks that contribute to the finished master project, the knowledgebase.

About the Project Material

Our book has a companion web site at Apress. On the web site you'll find the materials needed to complete the chapters' projects. We also included materials used to create the tutorials, in case you want to follow along with them as well. The projects' files come in two forms: raw and complete. The raw files are those used at the start of a project. The complete ones are the finished output. You can use these completed projects in a number of ways. For example, you can use them for reference in order to see how Acrobat works. Use them instead of working through a project to see how the project is developed. And you can also use them for troubleshooting if you run into difficulties trying the projects yourself. Enjoy the book. We know you will enjoy Acrobat 6.0.

Chapter 1

Welcome to the Acrobat 6.0 Family

Everyone knows a PDF file is a file you read in a special reader. Everyone has Acrobat Reader on their desktop, but Acrobat Reader is only two percent of the power. Where do the PDF files come from and what else does Acrobat do? This introductory chapter will introduce you to both Acrobat 6.0 and the structure of this book.

Welcome to Acrobat 6.0

During our two-decade relationship with these amazing machines called computers, we've learned a few truths. First, they aren't scary and nothing will explode if you hit the wrong button. Second, they truly are machines. That is, we do actually know more than a computer, even if we don't always speak the same language. The goal has always been to reach the point where we work less and the machine works more. This goal is both the reason this book was written and why you're reading it. When we got our first computers in the early 1980s, everyone was talking about the paperless office. Twenty-plus years later, we're using more paper now than ever.

We have very sophisticated software available to us that can help us become much more efficient. Sadly, most people comprehend only a small portion of what a program is capable of doing. On the average machine, if you consider the number of high-tech programs installed, a whole lot of functionality is being wasted. And what a waste! Each time you have to physically redo a piece of work already completed because it won't import into another program, for example, you're doing your computer's work. If you've spent good money for computer equipment and software—and who hasn't?—wasting that kind of functionality doesn't make sense.

One of Donna's activities (maybe even a hobby) over the last few years has been figuring out how to integrate and combine information created in one program with that of another. Some of the results have been pleasing, some less so, but it has certainly been a learning experience.

Donna works in two separate realms: as a power user of both Office-type applications (word processing, spreadsheets, and databases) and graphics programs (web design, interactivity, illustration, image editing). Tom, as an engineer, works in computer-aided design (CAD) and Office-type applications. We've happily seen the edges blur between the different program types, but there are still edges. And then this one super-program came along. Welcome to Acrobat 6.0.

What's New in Acrobat 6.0

We are tickled pink with Acrobat 6.0. When Adobe referred to a designer in Acrobat 5.0, they were talking about graphics designers. In Acrobat 6.0 when you talk about designers, you also include the engineers, CAD designers, and architects. Acrobat 6.0 has made major leaps into the engineering arena.

On the graphics front, Adobe greatly increased the functionality for the print industry and the ability to dual-purpose files for web and print.

New Versions of Acrobat

To celebrate the tenth anniversary of Acrobat, Adobe is making quantum leaps forward with the product. The core product is divided into essentially four products. Each of these products fits a specific niche. It's very important that the role each products fills in the workflow be understood by the professional.

Nearly a half-billion copies of Acrobat Reader and Adobe Reader have been distributed in over 20 languages. The Reader software may well be the most widely distributed program in the world. *The half-billion copies of Reader distributed by Adobe has been a blessing and a curse.* The success of Acrobat Reader and Adobe Reader software has caused much confusion and in some ways hampered the implementation of Acrobat. Everyone knows the Acrobat or Adobe Reader; therefore, they think they know Acrobat. When Tom says he's an Acrobat trainer, people look at him like he's an idiot. Everyone has the Acrobat Reader and thinks they know Acrobat. As he often tells his students, Acrobat Reader is only two percent of the power.

Acrobat Reader 5.05 allowed the user to fill out a form and submit files over the Web or fill out and print files, but not digitally sign or save them. Acrobat Reader 5.1. had many people wondering why some of the tools on their toolbars are inactive. Reader 5.1 has many of the same tools as the full Acrobat program, but the tools are only active in PDF forms or documents created with Adobe Server using Reader extensions.

The use of server-activated tools carries over into Adobe Reader 6.0. Using Adobe Document Server with Reader extensions allows large form users to distribute forms that activate the ability to comment, sign, and save forms. Acrobat 5 Approval was an off-the-shelf version between Reader and Acrobat. It had most of the same functions of Acrobat Reader 5.1, but the forms didn't have to be server-activated. Adobe has chosen not to continue Acrobat 5 Approval into 6.0, which Tom believes is a mistake. Adobe Server is too expensive for smaller users.

To solve the confusion between Acrobat and Acrobat Reader, Acrobat Reader is now called **Adobe Reader**. The Adobe Reader 6.0 is more functional than its predecessors. The former Adobe eBook Reader is now part of Adobe Reader 6.0. The Reader is also the Adobe Photoshop Album viewer. The server-enabled functions are still available, but hidden unless the features are active. This will remove much of the confusion. The Reader will view files created with layers, manage digital signature profiles, and verify digital signatures. We discuss the new Adobe Reader, because it's part of the professional user's arsenal.

The suite of tools now contains four different elements. Their relationships are shown in Figure 1-1. As you can see, each product is a subset of Acrobat 6.0 Professional.

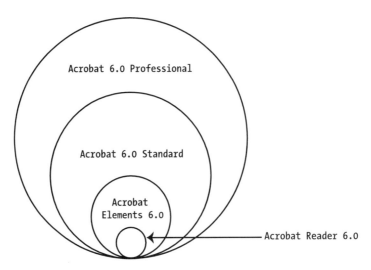

Figure 1-1
The four Acrobat 6.0 products

Acrobat Elements is a new member of the Acrobat family. Acrobat Elements, often called Acrobat "Lite" (probably to Adobe's chagrin) is a limited product designed for large corporate users and sold to companies purchasing a minimum of one thousand licenses. Acrobat Elements is used to create PDF files for distribution. It doesn't allow for combining PDF files or have the ability to create links for navigation. Acrobat Elements has all the functions of the Adobe Reader 6.0 in relation to server-enabled forms.

The mainline Acrobat product for version 6 is **Acrobat 6.0 Standard**. Acrobat 6.0 Standard provides most of the features of version 5.0 minus the Forms tool. We think the enhancements found in Acrobat 6.0 Standard more than make up for the loss of the Forms tool and certain other features to Acrobat 6.0 Professional. Acrobat 6.0 Standard raises the bar even higher for collaboration on document creation and review.

Acrobat 6.0 Professional is a dream. Adobe has listened well to the power users and added most of the features on their want lists. (Power users are, of course, already developing lists for version 7.0.) Acrobat 6.0 Professional has features especially designed for the engineering, architecture, and graphics communities. For the first time Acrobat 6.0 supports layers, known as optional content, in engineering documents created in AutoCAD or Visio. This will greatly expand the capabilities and give the developer geniuses more avenues to follow. There's expanded functionality for PDF/X, the standard for professional printing. Engineering tools allow for measurement of length and area inside PDF drawings.

New Features of Acrobat

Table 1-1 is a synopsis of the different Acrobat 6.0 versions' features.

Table 1-1   Comparison of Acrobat 6.0 Product Versions

Feature/Function	Adobe Reader	Acrobat Elements	Acrobat 6.0 Standard	Acrobat 6.0 Professional
View and print PDF documents	X	X	X	X
Macro-based Adobe PDF creation from MS Office products	--	X	X	X
128-bit encryption and password protection	--	--	X	X
Manage review and commenting tools	--	--	X	X
Combine documents from multiple sources	--	--	X	X
Macro-based PDF creation from AutoCAD, Visio, and MS Project (Windows)	--	--	--	X
Forms creation	--	--	--	X
Working with layers in technical drawings	--	--	--	X
Working with large-size documents	--	--	--	X
Preflighting tools for print production	--	--	--	X

Writing this book is like writing three books in one. We'll explain which features are found in a specific version and let you know when the features are common to all. The professional truly needs to know this information to adequately design workflows. Speaking of features, let's have a look at what's new in Acrobat 6.0.

A Completely New User Interface

The first time you open Acrobat 6.0, you'll wonder if you've opened the wrong program! As you can see in Figure 1-2, the user interface is completely different. After working with it for a short period, it's obvious that the changes are for the better. The interface is discussed in detail in Chapter 2.

Figure 1-2
What program did you say this was? Acrobat 6.0 has an all-new interface.

New Help Options

Adobe created a Windows Explorer-based Help function in version 6.0, as shown in Figure 1-3. The new Help format is easier to use than the book format in Acrobat 5.0. The Help interface opens on the right side of the program's interface, and is easy to search and navigate.

Figure 1-3
Looking for Help has never
been easier.

PDF Standard 1.5

PDF stands for Portable Document Format. The format was created by
Adobe Systems; version 1 was released in 1992. PDF is built on the Post-
Script (PS) printer language, also created by Adobe. PostScript is used to
describe documents. PostScript runs on both Windows and Macintosh
platforms. Acrobat 6.0 uses version 1.5 of the PDF file format. PDF 1.5
includes standards for layering, which are referred to as optional content.

Warning About Document Features

As hard as it may be to believe, there are people still using Acrobat 3.0.
Documents created with Acrobat 6.0 display a warning box in earlier
versions stating that the file may contain features that the older version
of Acrobat may not fully utilize, as shown in Figure 1-4. You're recommended to go to www.Adobe.com and download the latest version. Using
a current software version sure prevents customer complaints when the
form didn't work on Acrobat Reader 3.0 or Acrobat 4.0 will not open
files with 128-bit Acrobat 5.0 encryption.

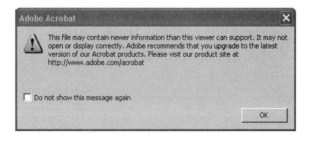

Figure 1-4
Documents generated in
Acrobat 6.0 display a
warning when the
document is opened in
earlier versions of the
product or Reader.

Automatic Conversion

Acrobat 5.0 introduced automatic conversion of documents through the PDFMaker macros that loaded into Microsoft Word, Excel, and PowerPoint. The macros allowed for much of the "intelligence" developed in these programs to be converted to PDF. If document formatting or tagging is correctly done, PDFMaker will make and link your bookmarks and links from the table of contents and the index will be converted. The conversion functions continue in an expanded version 6.0. All three versions have the macros for Office products. Both Professional and Standard versions now include PDFMaker macros for Microsoft Outlook and Internet Explorer. In Internet Explorer you can now right-click on a web page and create a PDF.

Rounding out the conversion improvements, the Professional version generates PDFMaker macros for Microsoft Visio, Microsoft Project, and AutoCAD.

Combining Content

Binder is a powerful new tool available in Standard and Professional versions. Binder allows you to arrange a series of files from different programs and automatically convert them into one PDF file, as you can see in Figure 1-5. In Standard this works for Word, Excel, PowerPoint, PDF, and most image files. In Professional, AutoCAD, Visio, and Microsoft Project files are also converted in the Binder process. If Binder had existed a few years ago, there would have been fewer gray hairs.

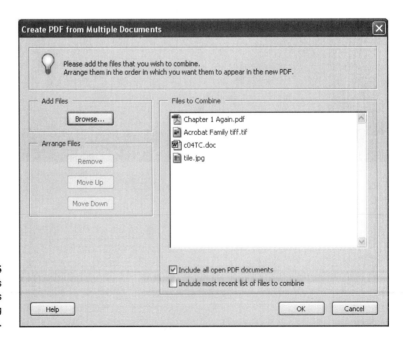

Figure 1-5
Combine documents from different sources into a single PDF using the Binder tool.

Tagged Adobe PDF and Accessibility

Logical tagging of document structure and the ability to reflow text was a major new feature of Acrobat 5.0. Tagged content killed two birds with one stone. PDF files were cumbersome to read on the small screens and on personal digital assistants (PDAs). Reflowing makes the text easy to navigate and displays it at readable sizes.

The second major advantage of tagging and reflowing is the ability to make files accessible for the visually impaired. Screenreaders can read tagged text in a logical order. With reflowing and the ability to set custom screen-color preferences, shown in Figure 1-6, people with reduced vision can often read PDF files. The Make Accessible plug-in in version 5.0 tagged existing PDF files to create a logical reading and reflow order. An accessibility checker evaluated the document according to customizable accessibility standards. Reading order was set with another tool.

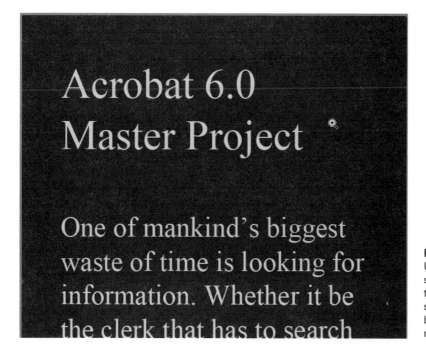

Figure 1-6
Users can configure their screen using preferences to display a custom color scheme. The text has also been reflowed at a higher magnification.

Both Standard and Professional versions have enhanced Make Accessible features. The enhanced Accessibility Checker and an enhanced structure touch-up tool are only found in Acrobat 6.0 Professional.

Adobe Reader 6.0, Acrobat Elements, and Acrobat 6.0 Standard and Professional versions have the ability to read documents aloud with synthesized speech. The View menu contains a new feature named Read Aloud.

Enhanced Collaboration

In Acrobat 5.0 collaboration is where Acrobat left the rest of the pack in the dust. Collaboration is one of the many home runs in 6.0. The advances are amazing. You can now use Review Tracker for incoming or outgoing email and web-based review and commenting workflows. The process makes it easy for people to work together on documents, as you can see in Figure 1.7.

Version 6.0 offers several new Comments tools. One of the most interesting is Insert Text. The comments in a PDF file import into the source Word file (Word XP only). The inserted or struck-through text can then be accepted or rejected and the changes automatically made in the Word document. This works only on tagged files created with the PDF-Maker macro because Acrobat Distiller doesn't tag files.

Figure 1-7
Make comments in a PDF document and export them to a Word document for editing.

A minor feature Tom really loves in Acrobat 6.0 is the ability to set the opacity of the drawing tools. You can put big lines on engineering drawings and make the lines transparent to reduce screen clutter.

Recycling Content

A bone Tom always had to pick with version 5.0 was the problem of converting a document back into Word. In version 5.0, documents could be exported as Rich Text Format (RTF) files and then laboriously touched up when reopened in Word. Version 6.0 offers a direct Save As command to save in Word format. The command works best with Word XP, but also works in Word 2000. Scanned documents converted to searchable text using Paper Capture also converted well.

Screen Capture, shown in Figure 1-8, is one of the new and neat features. You can capture screens in Windows by selecting Ctrl+PrtScrn. In Acrobat, use the new command Create PDF ➤ From Clipboard to convert the screen shot to a PDF image. The figure is an example of a screen shot marked up with Acrobat's commenting tools.

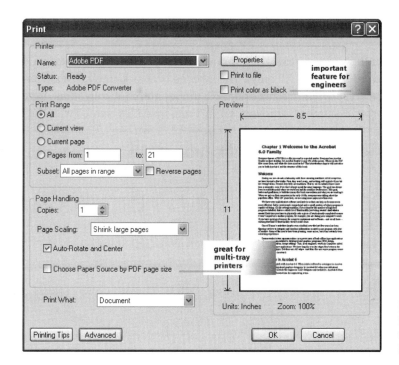

Figure 1-8
Printing capabilities and customizations are greatly enhanced.

Forms

The Forms tools are available only in Acrobat 6.0 Professional. The JavaScript is enhanced; the JavaScript Manual *Building Forms in Acrobat* is enhanced.

Adobe has introduced a stand-alone product called Adobe Forms Designer. The program combines a graphical creation environment with a more powerful Forms Creation tool as well as back-end tools for processes such as database connectivity. Adobe Forms Designer makes both XML and PDF forms. Adobe Forms Designer sells for about $1,500.

New Search Functions

Adobe put a six-liter, fuel-injected, turbocharged search function under the hood of Acrobat 6.0. The ability to search uncataloged documents is enhanced. The Boolean search ability of cataloged collections is greatly improved. You can search bookmarks and more document metadata.

Printing

Acrobat 6.0 Professional is crammed full of features for graphics and printing professionals as well as the regular user. There are preflight tools, support for PDF/X, color separation, rulers and guides, support for auto-tray sensors for high-end printers, and advanced printing controls for color management and job tickets. This expansive range of functionality leaves the engineering designer scratching his head at the complexity. As you can see in Figure 1-8, there are a couple of new features for engineers. In previous versions the color drawings printed as grayscale on engineering plotters. This was a major problem when yellow lines became too faint to see.

You Can't Use Acrobat Without PDF

The PDF file format is integral to the functionality of Acrobat. Most people know what a PDF file is: a file that has to be read in a special viewer and shows images and page layouts as well as text. But what actually is PDF and where did it come from? PDF was the brainchild of John Warnock, cofounder of Adobe Systems. John and Chuck Gieske developed the PostScript (PS) printer language. PS allowed for the development of the laser printer. PDF is a modification of PS, printing to an electronic space instead of paper.

The beauty of PDF is that files created in the PDF format can be viewed on essentially any modern computer platform; the files can be created from essentially any program with a Print command, by scanning or in some cases opening them directly.

In today's business world, the only common media is paper. As you can see in Figure 1-9 with PDF you print to interactive electronic paper. Adobe calls this e-paper. E-paper is WYSIWYG (what you see is what you get), which is why the printing industry is standardizing on PDF. This is the real power. Everything comes together for the first time in the virtual world.

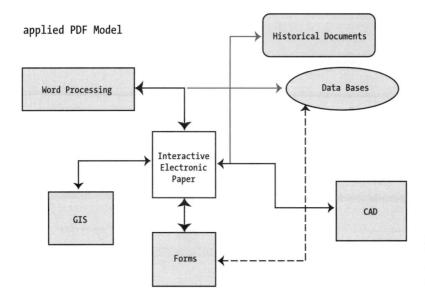

applied PDF Model

Figure 1-9
The appliedPDF model
demonstrates the extent
of PDF capabilities.

How PDF Files Work

As mentioned previously, you can't use Acrobat 6.0 without PDF. The file
format is based on how the PS language works. Different components of
the language interpret different parts of a file. Together, they make up
the PDF documents you use. PDF version 1.5 describes a document's
structure and metadata. Some of the "behind-the-scenes" information
from the PDF file made from this chapter's file is shown in Figure 1-10.

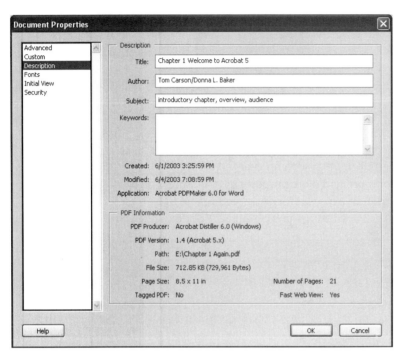

Figure 1-10
A view of the metadata created when this chapter's Word doc is converted to PDF. Changes in the Document Properties dialog box distribute metadata between several tabs.

Here is a brief rundown of the basic components that make up PDF files:

- Text and graphics are converted to a page description.

- A cross-reference table is used to locate and access pages. This process is almost independent of the total number of pages in a document.

- PDF files store font name and characteristics. When a document is viewed, the font used in the document will appear if it resides on the viewing computer or if it's embedded in the file. If neither of these applies, PDF uses a Multiple Master font to simulate the missing fonts (for Type 1 and TrueType font formats).

- PDF uses both binary and ASCII data. Because of this, the PDF output is portable across many different environments.

- Transparent objects created in Illustrator 9.0, Illustrator 10.0, and Photoshop 6.0 and later can be described.

- PDF can use a number of industry-standard compression filters, including JPEG, ZIP, and LZW.

- PDF is designed to be extensible. Plug-ins can extend the file format.

- PDF 1.5 has the ability to handle layers. This is currently just for engineering drawings, but will soon expand to graphics programs.

Publishing—What a Concept

Information is just so much stuff, all of it packed into little compartments conforming to the particular requirements of the type of stuff. So how do you unpack information? It may be a systematic process of building a specific document for a specific project; a more general document that may be modified as required; or a multipurpose, multifunctional document that can be used in a variety of projects in a variety of formats.

We're all standing knee-deep in information with an ever-increasing need to use that information for more and more purposes at faster and faster speeds. Unpacking information to use it efficiently requires a system. Let's have a look at the whole concept of publishing information.

Publishing, as you know, has been around since the time of Mr. Gutenberg. In a more modern sense of the word, the progression in publishing sophistication can be viewed as a continuum, as shown in Figure 1-11.

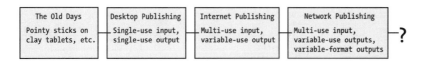

Figure 1-11
Publishing as a continuum

Let's jump right over the "old days" and start with the revolution that was desktop publishing.

Desktop Publishing

Some time ago, *desktop publishing* was hailed as the best of the best. PCs first became affordable in the early 1980s, and sometime soon thereafter Donna discovered something called a desktop publishing program. This was, of course, revolutionary. There was no longer a need to use a professional printer to set a formatted page and its elements. Granted, the output was less than stellar, but the idea of being able to do the design and layout was wonderful. If it was something really important, content could be copied to a floppy—a real floppy—and taken to a production house.

Some years later, with the advent of laser printers and color printers (or more correctly, when these printers became economically practical), the revolution went mainstream. This approach had one big problem (which certainly still exists): Somebody always had to print the output.

Setting up a document usually required several draft prints as the masterpiece was being designed and went through its approval process.

The more sophisticated the work, the more revisions were required. When it was finally complete, a copy of the material was stored on a disk or on the hard drive as space became more affordable. Of course, there was usually a printed copy stored someplace as well.

Then there was distribution. Mail worked, and of course a letter would also be required to explain what stuff was enclosed. Later this could be done by fax, but the early faxes used strange and smelly paper rolls, and they weren't always reliable, so a paper copy was often mailed as well. More paper. And now the person receiving the stuff would have to file it someplace.

Now suppose that several months later there was a need to reuse some portion of that earlier work. When the storage floppy was located, opened, copied, and pasted, the design process could continue. Of course, when the design was complete the approval and draft processes would start all over again, culminating, of course, in the same printing and distribution processes.

This idea can be summarized best by considering the relationships involved. Basically, we're describing a one-to-one relationship. For each effort made, a single medium is being used to produce a single message. The message is then distributed to a single recipient. Things started to change with the advent of the Internet.

Internet Publishing

The Internet, the World Wide Web, and email have become extremely powerful forces in the last decade. From a publishing perspective, these forces heralded change. Suddenly your work could be freely distributed for the entire world to marvel over—whether or not it should be wasn't the issue.

Remember the days when a browser was black text on a gray background? We remember the days before that, when the only way to access information was using UNIX on a black screen with yellow lettering. Advances in both technology and design software have yielded some amazing works, which will continue to improve. It's now possible to integrate a variety of materials from numerous sources into a web page.

The outputs are still limited and depend on the designer's input. For example, a page of wonderful information might or might not be available in a printer-friendly format. Barring that, it's the old copy-and-paste activity, or saving the entire page—ads, multiple tables, and all.

More and more downloads are becoming available as PDF-formatted files. Finally, the recipient has more control in terms of layout as well as security.

The freedom of the Internet has also resulted in the freedom to copy and download anything you can find. How do you know if your work is being copied and used by others ostensibly as their own? There's no way to tell unless you stumble across something by chance, which isn't likely to happen. You can attach a digital signature to an image, but that still doesn't guarantee security.

Acrobat has been around since the mid-1990s. Using this program has progressively given you both more security and more freedom. You can finally preserve the integrity of your work and create works that stand on their own as created.

Internet publishing is akin to a one-to-many relationship. The outputs are controlled by the creator. Whether or not there are different outputs depends on what decisions are made and the options provided. However, production of a single type of output might be used by numerous recipients (many).

Offering recipients an option to download information of various types from a site has been a commonplace activity for the past several years. But what if you could finally compose something from a number of inputs, manipulate the same material in a variety of ways, and distribute it to many users? Well, you can do that using network publishing.

Network Publishing

Acrobat 5.0, in conjunction with several other forces, ushered in a new era—the realm of *network publishing*. You can now publish to an extensive and ever-growing array of outputs. In addition to using monitors and printers, you can now output information to handheld devices and eBooks. These outputs are used in conjunction with the Internet, intranets, and extranets. Acrobat 6.0 continues and expands the trend.

The whole idea of network publishing is just so doggone cool. Imagine this: Using a variety of inputs, information can be shared (in numerous ways, including online) as it's being developed. The *same* information can be modified and formatted for output on some incredibly interesting devices and formats. And not only can the same information be reformatted depending on output requirements, but the entire pool of information held within an enterprise can be indexed, cataloged, and archived. Such a wonderful idea for a paper file-phobic people like us.

Influences

Things that were unknown half a decade ago are now becoming mainstream. It seems everyone has an Internet connection and bandwidth is becoming more accessible. Many of you now have broadband satellite connections at home while the idea wouldn't have occurred to you several years ago. E-commerce is commonplace. Server and network software is more friendly, widespread, and compatible with an ever-growing number of devices.

The outcome is a demand for content. The content must be personalized, available on a variety of devices, and available anytime. Acrobat 5.0 rose to the challenge admirably, and Acrobat 6.0 pushes the envelope even further. As you'll see in the next section, you can collect material from a number of sources, reuse content, and deliver it via different outputs.

Functioning as a workgroup team member has become commonplace and network publishing expands the functionality of workgroups. Rather than simply routing emails and comments, members of a workgroup can simultaneously review and add comments in a browser and then upload them to a shared web or network server for simultaneous viewing. An entire reviewing and commenting process is built-in to Acrobat 6.0, making collaborative processes function seamlessly. In conjunction with various security settings, digital and electronic signatures for online approval and processing completes the document-cycle process.

So now you've seen that what we do has changed and that it will continue to change. Also, by knowing some of the advancements and changes that are occurring around you on a daily basis, you gain a better understanding of how to use Acrobat 6.0 in your work. Now you have a context with which to approach the information in this book. Using that context, the information can be divided into a series of processes.

What Can Acrobat 6.0 Do for You?

The Adobe PDF file format used by Acrobat is becoming the workflow standard in many industries, ranging from publishing to financial services to government. This happened because users need to use information more intelligently and they need to be able to share that information more effectively.

If You're a Graphics Designer...

Consider this common graphics design scenario: You spend the better part of a week working on a layout for an important document for a client, complete with text, graphics, spreadsheets, charts, and tables. You send a draft to the client and he has problems. He doesn't have the application used to create the document, so you rebuild the thing in a program he has. Then he says he doesn't have the fonts you used and the layout is skewed. You send him the fonts or reset the entire project using fonts he's sure to have. (After all, every computer *must* have Times New Roman and Arial installed!)

Finally he can open the document. But when he prints it, it doesn't look the same at all due to printer differences. So you reset it again to meet his printer's requirements. At last the client can print it, but the original design is so distorted it could have been written in Notepad for all the style that is left. (A slight exaggeration, but you know how it feels.)

The client calls again and now wants the document available on his company's web site. You start all over again, this time in a web layout program. As a bonus, he wants to use the document in other document formats for some of his clients who don't use the same program for viewing and printing that he does. Oh yeah, and one of the board members uses a screenreader, so can you configure a copy that can be used with a reader? And please make a couple of changes to all the versions created so far.

Chilling, isn't it? By now, if this were a real scenario, there would be some gnashing of teeth and spewing of threats, and grocery bagging as a career move starts to sound very tempting.

Consider the same scenario using Acrobat. First, you can create the document in one or several different programs and then combine all the works into a single PDF file. Shipping a draft to a client for review and approval would be no problem. The client can open the file using free Adobe Reader software. When the file is displayed, all your lovely formatting, fonts, and graphics are displayed exactly as you created them.

The client wants a printed copy? No problem. The document prints on any printing device. Repurposing content? Well, that might or might not cost extra, depending on the desired output. Transferring some of the document's information to a web page is a simple matter. Transferring some of the content to a handheld device would require tagging the document, as would making the document work with a screenreader.

Finally, moving the document from one program to another for others to work on? Easy. Export the document as a Word document or into RTF and many programs can then import and use the information. As for making changes, it would still require some effort on your part, but at least it would be consistent types of changes.

If the client had access to a full version of Acrobat, he can add comments, request changes and the like before the draft got to the finished stage. And you could lock the document to prevent others from making changes to it until it was finally ready for delivery.

What a difference a piece of software can make! Along with stream-lining many of the work processes and saving time, you can preserve your sanity and your career.

If You're an Engineer, Architect, or Other Designer…

One of the biggest frustrations Tom experienced as an engineer and the reason he jumped all over Acrobat was paper (many might call it a midlife crisis). He was drowning in paper! During the fall of 1992 and the prequel to the big floods in St. Louis, he was running a large environmental remediation project. His partners had underbid it and he was trying to make up for the low bid and avoid penalties for late completion. This was an Engineered Job, but by an inexperienced young engineer. In essence it was a Design Build.

On receipt of the plans and specs, his partners broke them up and made numerous copies to send to potential subcontractors ($1,000 in reproduction costs.) Problems arose when items were missed by some of the subs who had not received complete sets. The bid was submitted on a paper bid form and the engineer had to transfer all the lines to a spreadsheet to look for bid unbalancing.

Even though everything was designed, six sets of shop drawings and catalog cuts of all items used in the project had to be submitted for approval. The company purchased two small copiers for the job and paid FedEx a small fortune. Once the documents arrived at the engineers, they were routed to the designers and the owner for approval. Approval took ten working days for the documents to arrive, be distributed, have the comments reviewed, and get approval on the components. Ten days seems like an eternity when you're away from home for four months and there are $1,000-per-day penalties if you're late.

Another requirement of the project was a "redlined" set of drawings. Any changes made in the design were marked up with a red pen. These became the as-builts unless the engineer reentered them in the CAD program and created a revised set.

The final product of the project was to provide the owner and engineer with two sets of owners' manuals and an operations manual consisting of four three-ring binders for each set. Moreover, when he went back eight months later to fix a problem, they had lost the manual for that piece of equipment. This was an environmental project, but a small forest was sacrificed for the paper.

Tom's reaction when he saw Acrobat for the first time? "This is **the solution** for engineering and construction." As you'll see throughout the book, a logical and practical workflow for accomplishing the entire engineering process can be readily managed from within Acrobat.

If You're Involved with Government...

One of Tom's current partners recently retired after 16 years as County Executive running the only debt-free counties in Tennessee. He met him right after he had just purchased an old shopping center to move staff and papers out of the courthouse and was spending $1 million to remodel the courthouse to handle the rest of the staff and their papers. All because of paper.

Acrobat is used to control and manage information within governments of all levels. Tom's partner Ron saw what could be done with Acrobat, and the appliedPDF Project at the Southeast Local Development Corporation was started in 2002 to transfer the technology to cities and counties in the region. The project also consults for distant counties and states to implement a PDF workflow into their information management processes.

If You're Involved with Industry...

Tom has a current client who makes large valves. During their many years in business, the client has had to deal with numerous regulatory required plans. The plans need to be developed and updated due to their industry's level of regulation as well as ISO certification. Tom developed a Unified Hazardous Materials Management plan for the plant in paper, but gave them a copy of the plan in PDF. The plan had CAD drawings, Word text, Excel spreadsheets, scanned color maps, and color photographs. They were amazed! He was asked to make a presentation to the plant managers. From that, he trained ten employees from across the plant. Now the company has an online knowledgebase for the plant. Any employee can find any drawing, policy, or procedure, equipment manual, interactive form, and so on in just a few mouse clicks. The costs to the company? Approximately $7,000 in Acrobat software, three additional Raid 5 hard drives, $3,000 for training and employee hours to organize the information. The plant is much more efficient, downtime is minimized, and time formerly spent on searching for information is applied to production.

If You're Involved with _____...

Anyone using paper as a means of communication can become more efficient. Just fill in the blank.

From the Inbox to the Outbox and Beyond

You may have the sense that Acrobat's scope is extensive. Not all of its features will be used by everyone all the time. The "problem" is that the program can do so much. How do you sort out what you want to do or could do from those things that will never apply to your work?

We mentioned earlier that this is complex software. With the exception of these early chapters—which use somewhat of a show-and-tell format to describe how the program physically works—we've taken a processes approach to Acrobat 6.0. Why? To help you make sense of it all. The processes are summarized into the set of interrelated operations shown in Figure 1-12. The program's uses are broken into three major components: document creation (input), document management (processes), and document distribution (output). At the core of the matter is the PDF document. A whole range of inputs can be used to create the document. Once the document has been built, it can be modified, shared, stored, and made secure. Finally, the document can be distributed in a range of different forms of output. Let's explore these processes a bit further.

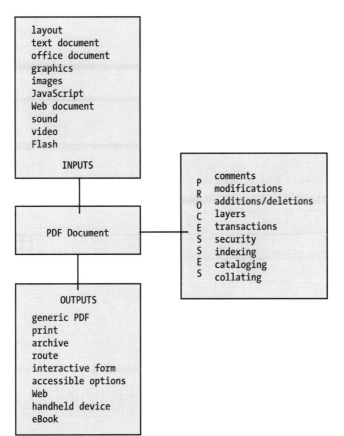

Figure 1-12
Using a document
management model to
understand Acrobat's
scope

Document Creation

In Figure 1-13, the central element is a PDF document. The document is
created from a collection of different inputs that range from text images
to JavaScript. Rudimentary inputs are familiar to anyone who has ever
used Acrobat. Lay out a document and save it as a PDF file.

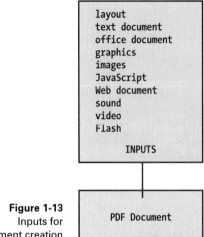

```
layout
text document
office document
graphics
images
JavaScript
Web document
sound
video
Flash

        INPUTS
```

PDF Document

Figure 1-13
Inputs for
document creation

As you can see in Figure 1-14, the list is quite a bit more extensive than that. We consider how the basic PDF document is created and will spend a considerable amount of time looking at some of the specialized types of input. Some are used for fairly generic effects, such as sound clips. Others, such as JavaScript, can be used in conjunction with XML to create interactive forms that can streamline many data input processes.

Document Management

There are two subsets of the document-management process; the process as a whole is shown in Figure 1-14. Some of these management processes refer to an individual document, while others are used for managing a number of documents. You'll look at the particulars of each of these functions, both from the technical aspects of performing the function as well as the use and place of each in managing your workflow. As with the inputs, some of these processes are fairly generic; others are more specialized.

```
┌─────────────────────────────┐
│ P   comments                │
│ R   modifications           │
│ O   additions/deletions     │
│ C   layers                  │
│ E   transactions            │
│ S   security                │
│ S   indexing                │
│ E   cataloging              │
│ S   collating               │
└─────────────────────────────┘
```

Figure 1-14
The document
management process

Document Distribution

Finally, let's consider the distribution of PDF documents, or outputs. As you can see in Figure 1-15, a substantial number of differing outputs are available. The list is organized in a specific way. First is the generic PDF you're all familiar with, which is most often printed. Next is archiving and routing outputs, which follow along from the indexing and cataloging processes referred to earlier. Then a number of specialized outputs are listed.

```
┌─────────────────────────┐
│         OUTPUTS         │
│                         │
│   generic PDF           │
│   print                 │
│   archive               │
│   route                 │
│   interactive form      │
│   accessible options    │
│   Web                   │
│   handheld device       │
│   eBook                 │
└─────────────────────────┘
```

Figure 1-15
Document distribution
options

Remember that these specialized outputs all start from the generic PDF file. However, each of these areas is sufficiently complex and requires enough intelligent decision-making to warrant thorough discussion.

Let's review. So far, we've described both new functionality and major processes available in Acrobat 6.0, established some context for using the program, and discussed processes for creating, managing, and distributing PDF documents.

Who Should Read This Book

We would like to say that this book is for everyone, well almost everyone. Certain parts of the book can be used by large portions of the population, but other areas are specific to particular industries. We think, though, that there's something here for everyone who is in any kind of business that requires management and use of information—which is an awful lot of people!

Here is a high-level list of what can be done using Acrobat 6.0. Do you do any of these things on a regular basis?

- Import documents and export documents in a variety of formats

- Repurpose content for different forms of output, including eBooks

- Attach security features to a document

- Share and collaborate on documents

- Attach different forms of communications to documents

- Create forms

- Repurpose content for Web deployment

Just as importantly, do you recognize your circumstances in this list?

- You waste lots of time searching for documents.

- You spend lots of money on document storage.

- You're looking for ways to plan work more efficiently and effectively.

Our book won't teach fundamental graphical or engineering design skills. We assume that everyone using this book will be at an intermediate level or higher. The focus is on helping you apply your skills to work more efficiently and securely. Print designers and publishers will appreciate the sections on printing and output. To an engineer, most print information is of little value unless she wants to become an Adobe Certified Expert (ACE) on Acrobat. As an engineer who failed the Acrobat 4.0 ACE the first time he took it, Tom knows what he's talking about.

There are several groups of people who stand to gain the most from using this book. They are the primary focus of our efforts:

- General graphic designers working in a variety of media, especially print, web, and interactive media

- Web designers responsible for management of information across a variety of platforms (intranet, extranet, Internet, network)

- Publishers and document-management enterprises, particularly those who are responsible for knowledge-management activities

- Business professionals (regardless of the size of the enterprise), given the collaborative nature of this version of Acrobat as well as its ability to repurpose information

- Engineers, architects, and contractors designing and building projects

- Medical records managers having to deal with the Health Insurance Portability and Accountability Act of 1996 (HIPPA)

- Trainers wanting to create interactive training material

Document management is taking more of a role in this book than it did in the first edition. We believe this emphasis brings Acrobat 6.0 closer to the masses. Collaboration and workflow are key concepts in this book. As such, these topics are applicable to all groups. Regardless of whether you're the person who is responsible for understanding how and why to tag a document or you're the person who says, "Make this thing work," there's something for you in these pages. Enjoy!

Up Next

If you're one of that rare breed who reads a book from cover to cover, you must be wondering when we're actually going to get down to business. That time is now. In this chapter we looked at the new functionality added to Acrobat 6.0, and some context for using the program. Up next, you'll jump into Acrobat 6.0 and see how to make it work. Chapter 2 looks at how Acrobat functions, and you'll get acquainted with the interface. Let's go!

What's Under the Hood?

In Chapter 1, we said people generally take advantage of only a very small portion of a program's capabilities. Since you're reading this, we assume you don't want to be one of those people. Good for you.

The simplest way to start to learn how a program works, and what its capabilities are, is to go through the menu items and toolbars. Open everything, read what it says, look around. Go through dialog boxes and see where they lead you. Remember, you really can't break it. A word of advice—perform these exploratory functions without an important document loaded into the program just to be on the safe side! In this chapter, we open the program and have a good look around.

A Look at the Interface

First things first: the interface. Figure 2-1 shows the entire Acrobat 6.0 work area as it appears in Acrobat 6.0 Professional; the Standard version is similar minus a few features. The work area looks cluttered in the figure. The help pane is open on the right, comments display at the bottom in the Comments panel, and the Bookmarks panel is shown in the navigation pane open on the left. It's rare that all three pane elements would be active at one time. Let's have a brief look at the components.

Tip

Why Did We Pick This Page as an Example?

Shooting an image of the introductory page to the program's Help files wasn't accidental. Most of what you need to do your work efficiently and intelligently is in these pages. And using Help files is just like any other skill—the more you use it, the more adept you become.

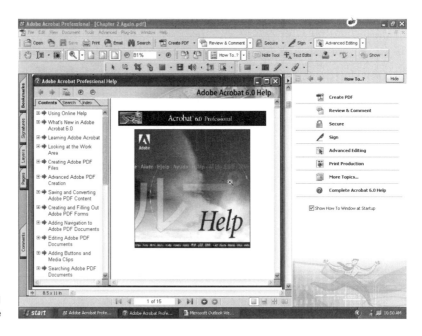

Figure 2-1
The Acrobat 6.0 interface

Menus

Acrobat 6.0 offers eight (nine if you have plug-ins) drop-down menus, and its layout is common to most programs. The sequence starts with File and Edit options, then moves to specific program functionality options and ends with Window and Help menus. Above the menu bar is the title bar, showing both the program's name and the name of the file in brackets. You'll look at the menu options later in this chapter.

Taskbars

Below the menu bar in Figure 2-2 you'll see most of the taskbars. The interface is now task-oriented, and includes the Create PDF Taskbar. Acrobat 6.0 includes a set of eight taskbars and numerous toolbars and subtoolbars. You can rearrange and combine them at will, and they may be docked or floating. Toolbars displaying a small arrow indicate that you can expand and collapse the contents, as shown in Figure 2-2. You'll look at the toolbars in detail in each section.

Figure 2-2
The default layout displays several toolbars and taskbars.

Document Pane

The document pane houses the document itself. Several menu and toolbar items control how the document is displayed. At the top right of the document pane's scroll bar is an arrow. Click the arrow to open a small selection of command options. Right-clicking on the document pane opens a tool-specific menu as shown in Figure 2-3.

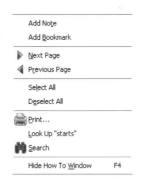

Figure 2-3
Right-click in the document pane with the Hand tool active to activate this menu.

Status Bar

The status bar is located at the bottom of the program's interface below the document pane. The status bar shows the number of the current page, and it contains some simple navigation controls and page-scrolling options. When you apply security settings, a small gold key will appear to the right of the page-scrolling options. The page display options are shown at the bottom right.

The status bar configurations are shown in Figure 2-4. The Page Size indicator is next to a horizontal scroll bar. Tom makes sure to point out this display when he shows a class a 76.5-inch × 67.9-foot engineering drawing.

Figure 2-4
The status bar components. The document displayed is page 1 of 47, the page is 8.25 inches × 11 inches, and the pages one at a time.

Navigation Pane

Borrowing from a standard web page layout, Adobe has placed a navigation pane to the left of the document pane. This pane consists of a series of tabs used to control movement throughout a document based on function. There have been considerable changes in the navigation pane in Acrobat 6.0. The Comments panel has been moved to the bottom of the display as shown in Figure 2-1.

The default set of navigation tabs are shown in Figure 2-5. In a newly created document, the four tabs shown—Bookmarks, Pages (formerly Thumbnails), Layers, and Signatures—display at the top left, and the Comments tab displays further down the left side of the screen. Clicking one of the top four tabs opens a vertical display for the panel as you can see in Figure 2-5. Clicking the Comments tab opens the Comments panel horizontally.

Acrobat 6.0 renames the thumbnails pane as the Pages panel, an adjustment made for those of you accustomed to earlier versions of Acrobat. In previous versions, the Thumbnails panel showed small thumbnail images of each page in the document and highlighted the page (or portion of a page) displayed in the document pane.

Figure 2-5
The default navigation
pane with the Pages panel
displayed. Each tab has an
Options menu.

Each tab has a drop-down menu at the top of the palette. Click the drop-down menu to display a list of commands. The commands for the Pages panel are shown in Figure 2-6.

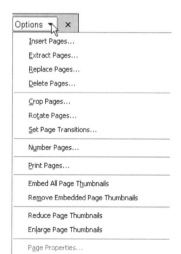

Figure 2-6
The Pages drop-down
menu options are a
convenient way to add
and subtract from the
document. Many of the
functions here were under
the Document menu in
Acrobat 5.0.

Making Your Way Through the Program

Finding the right tool—and finding it again—has to be one of the most annoying dilemmas known to humans in this computer-centric era. The more sophisticated the program, the more pervasive the problem.

Here are a few more tips for finding what you want, courtesy of the program's design.

- In addition to labeling the tools, Acrobat 6.0 labels the entire toolbar. The actual name of the tool collection will appear.

- Not sure if you've selected the right tool? Try the context menu options. With a tool selected, click the page and then right-click (Windows) or Ctrl+click (Mac OS). Don't forget that you'll have to actually select something on the page in order to make the context menu appear.

- Don't have each and every toolbar open and expanded. This has always been one of the most interesting things we've observed over the years teaching software to students. Many are of the opinion that if a toolbar exists it should be open, regardless of whether there's even the remotest possibility that it will be used. Removing some of the visual clutter may help you find what you're looking for more readily.

- If you're working along with this book, check the index.

- Still can't find what you want? Save your work and go for a walk. Amazing what a bit of distance and time can do.

Menus and Palettes

Acrobat 6.0 produces some very sophisticated output, requiring quite a range of tools and functions to perform PDF magic.

The Major Menu Items

Acrobat 6.0 offers eight major menus. Rather than mindlessly listing the content of each item (which would be sleep-inducing), let's look at some of the functionality available to you. First, have a look at the menu setup, shown in Figure 2-7.

Figure 2-7
The Acrobat 6.0 menu bar

File   Edit   View   Document   Tools   Advanced   Plug-Ins   Window   Help

File Options

Some of the File menu options are familiar. For those experienced in Acrobat 5.0, you won't find some of the functions under the File menu, such as Document Security (moved to Document Properties) and Batch Processing (moved to Advanced Tools, and available only in Acrobat 6.0 Professional.) Import and Export commands have been split up and moved to several new functions.

Some new commands appear on the File menu. For example, there are now several new commands related to document review and revision control. Document Properties have undergone a complete makeover as Acrobat moves into the document management arena, as you can see in Figure 2-8.

Note
This isn't an exhaustive examination of these program segments and their contents, but rather an additional orientation and background for working through this book. Please use the Help functions within the program for detailed information. A number of URLs are listed in Appendix A, including links to discussion groups, mailing lists, and web sites that you can visit to access more information on using Acrobat 6.0.

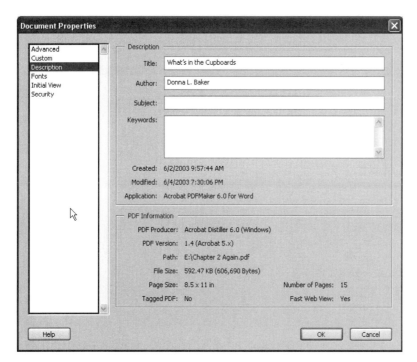

Figure 2-8
The Document Properties command is greatly expanded and changed. The Document Properties dialog box shows the addition of security and more features for search and advanced document management.

Edit Options

The Edit menu commands are fairly straightforward—the usual functional editing and searching options remain. The Spell Check command is under the Edit menu in version 6.0. An interesting new feature is Look Up Definition. You can highlight a word with the Text Select tool and it will take you to www.Dictionary.com and www.Thesaurus.com, which offers you the option to search the top ten hits on Ask Jeeves.

The most important menu item is the Preferences submenu. There are so many configurable options that modify the way Acrobat 6.0 functions to meet your needs and style of work. It's surprising how many advanced beginners and even intermediate users are unaware of the offerings here.

View Options

The View menu commands are the old standbys: zooming, rotating, and scrolling. View has a wonderful new feature called Read Out Loud. After several tests we're impressed. The View menu is where the first differences between the Standard and Professional versions exist. Professional has grids, rulers, and guides that Standard doesn't have.

Document Options

The Document menu, shown in Figure 2-9, has undergone a complete makeover, going from a 98-pound weakling to Mr. Atlas. Again the emphasis has changed from navigating the document to enhancing the document creation and management processes.

The following are three of the most powerful new features:

- Add Headings & Footers

- Add Watermarks & Background

- Export Comments to Word

Figure 2-9
The Document menu
contains several
powerful new options.

The new tools are discussed in detail in later chapters. A number of functions have been moved to the Document menu from the Tools menu, most noticeably Paper Capture. In Acrobat 5.0, Paper Capture was a plug-in that provided a very good Optical Character Recognition (OCR) program. Paper Capture converts the images of scanned documents to formatted text and graphics, or makes an exact copy with hidden text. Capture and OCR are cornerstones of document management.

Acrobat 5.0 was initially released without Paper Capture. However, when the masses stormed the bastions with lit torches, the plug-in was added as a free web download and as a bonus item on the program's CD. We're still amazed at how many people don't know about Paper Capture. Paper Capture in Acrobat 5.0 was restricted to capturing 50 pages at a time.

Acrobat 6.0 Professional has the added feature of Preflight, or preparing a document for printing. Printing is covered in Chapter 12.

Tools Options

What is software without tools? This area has been completely restructured. Most of the online tools have been removed from Acrobat 6.0. The major tools and their functions are described in Table 2-1.

Note

Adobe has a product called Acrobat Capture 3.04. Capture 3.04 is the industrial strength version for processing large quantities of documents. Capture 3.04 is complex software, but you can define workflows. For example, you can scan documents all day and the computer can capture the content all night.

Table 2.1　Major Tools in Acrobat 6.0 and Their Primary Purposes

Toolbar Name	Looks Like…	Function
Commenting		Contains the Note tool (electronic sticky notes). Text Edit tools, Stamp tools, and Highlighting tools are menu-only. The Stamp tools have dynamically generated stamps with login name and date.
Attach Tools		The Paper Clip is the Attach File tool (Push Pin in Acrobat 5.0). The Speaker is still the Attach Sound tool. The Attach Clipboard tool pastes images from the clipboard into the file—a real timesaver.
Highlighting		This bar opens from the drop-down menu at Text Edits and is a good graphical representation of function.
Advanced Commenting		Contains a greatly enhanced set of Drawing tools, Text Box tools (formerly called Free Text), the Pencil tool, the Pencil Eraser tool, and the Attach tool.
Drawing Tools		Polygon and Polygon Line have been added to both. Arrow and Cloud have been added to Acrobat 6.0 Professional.
Basic		This includes the Hand tool, Selection tools (Text, Table, and Image) and the Snapshot tool. The Image and Snapshot are similar, but the Snapshot selects both text and graphics with one marquee selection.

Table 2.1   Major Tools in Acrobat 6.0 and Their Primary Purposes (Continued)

Toolbar Name	Looks Like...	Function
Select		There is only Select Text in a marquee in Acrobat 6.0. This eliminated a lot of confusion.
Zoom		Acrobat 6.0 Standard uses the same tools as Acrobat 5.0. The Professional version has two new Zoom tools. The Loupe tool works like a magnifying glass on a large drawing; the Pan and Zoom tool works like a thumbnail and shows a portion of a drawing visible in the document pane.
Advanced Editing		Acrobat 6.0 Standard includes the Signature tool, but the Professional version doesn't. The Professional version also includes the Forms, Movie, Sound, and Touchup Object tools.
Forms		The Forms tool's icons are new and very logical. The Forms tool is in Acrobat 6.0 Professional only.
Measuring		In Acrobat 6.0 Professional only. Measure Length, Perimeter, and Area.

Advanced Options

Advanced options are what their name implies—a collection of features available to intermediate and advanced users only. The Advanced options separate the Standard and Professional versions of Acrobat. Both versions have a range of options ranging from Accessibility to Distiller, to eBook, to JavaScript as you can see in Figure 2-10.

Acrobat 6.0 Professional contains several functions not available in Acrobat 6.0 Standard, such as Batch Processing, Catalog, and PDF Optimizer. In addition, Acrobat 6.0 Professional has many more options than those found in Acrobat 6.0 Standard. Advanced options are described in detail throughout the book.

Figure 2-10
The Advanced options menu is expanded in the Professional version.

Plug-ins Options

You're looking at your program, and you don't have this option. As discussed in the master project, Adobe encourages the development of third-party plug-ins that enhance the ability of Acrobat. Purchase one of these plug-ins and the option is displayed on the menu bar as shown in Figure 2-11.

Figure 2-11
The plug-ins are added to the menu bar after installation. The LGIView Zoom-to-Search zooms and highlights a search in oversized documents.

Window Options

Many of the former Window options have been moved to View options, but two very powerful features are added to make up for the loss. Window is identical in both Standard and Professional. Split is one of the powerful new features. This splits the screen horizontally. As you can see in Figure 2-12, another new feature on the Window menu is the Clipboard Viewer.

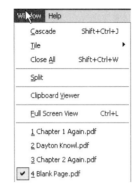

Help Options

Help is divided into a quick How To shown in Figure 2-13 and a Complete Acrobat 6.0 Help option. Acrobat 6.0 supports extensive JavaScript binding, which means you can use the program to customize forms and documents by expanding their utility and interactivity.

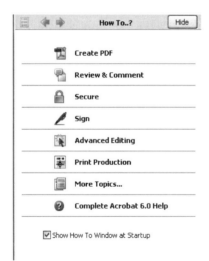

Acrobat 6.0 contains multiple subtoolbars, and sub-subtoolbars. As we cover different functions we'll show the applicable tools.

You've taken a first look at navigating the new workspace. We'll go into it in great detail in the following chapters. We've developed a real-world project to follow through much of the book and tie everything together. The project is introduced next.

Acrobat 6.0 Master Project

One of the most time-consuming efforts in today's society is looking for information. Whether it be the clerk that has to search 20 years of records to find a historically determined awning color or the maintenance person spending half a day looking for drawings and manuals for a piece of equipment.

The master project for this book is derived from Tom's work. People pay him to develop knowledgebases for their government, industry, research facility, and so on. Now we're including the processes as part of this book.[1] The creation of local knowledgebases has met with less-than-uniform success because the various formats used for materials weren't accessible by everyone using the information.

Acrobat 6.0's tools let us make a knowledgebase complete and easy to navigate. Paper Capture in Acrobat 6.0 brings historical documents to life in the electronic world. Catalog makes collections of thousands of documents searchable in ways never imagined. Commenting lets the information be constantly updated. Forms are everywhere and Acrobat 6.0 admirably conquers that beast.

---

appliedPDF Knowledgebase

An appliedPDF knowledgebase is the orderly assembly of information known on a subject in the PDF format. The term "applied" refers to the application of various Acrobat 6.0 functions to the task at hand. Tom wanted to call it an applied Acrobat knowledgebase, but Adobe has too many lawyers.

We're presenting several subprojects that come together by the end of the book. The book's knowledgebase is derived from a real-world project that Tom's clients are implementing and developing daily.

One of the major market thrusts for Acrobat 6.0 is engineering. Many of the people reading this book aren't engineers, architects, or contractors and frankly don't want to be engineers. We're going to teach you how to convert an engineering drawing to PDF and assemble it with other information. This is good experience for converting files from a wide range of programs.

Getting Ready

The book's web site contains a set of folders and subfolders that contain project information. A named chapter folder is available for many chapters from Chapter 3 on. Each folder contains material for the projects

---

1. Giving away secrets may not be a common business practice, but Tom hopes more organizations will want him to help implement what he refers to as an appliedPDF knowledgebase after reading our book.

and tutorials outlined in the chapter. Materials include source files to work with as well as samples of the finished projects and tutorials you can use for reference.

The master project is completed over the course of the book. The entire project uses material from a number of sources with a variety of processes and activities applied in different chapters. It isn't necessary for you to complete each project from the beginning to the end of the book in order to have a complete project. If you've worked through the book from Chapter 1, use your files to work on the master project in Chapter 8, for example. If you only want to do the project in Chapter 8, use the source files from the Chapter 8 file on the web site, which contains project files and content complete to that point.

You work with Acrobat 6.0 Professional as well as some viewers and plug-ins to complete the book's projects.

Plug-ins are small programs that fit into Acrobat 6.0 to enhance the program's functionality. Some of the features you see today were originally plug-ins. Adobe encourages the development of plug-ins through the Software Development Kit (SDK) and by publishing the PDF standard.

VoloView Express 2.01 is a viewer for AutoCAD drawings. AutoCAD uses the DRW file format. Unfortunately, the free VoloView Express 2.01 doesn't support conversion and saving of layers. We'll use examples of drawings with converted layers. Download the VoloView Express 2.01 viewer from AutoDesk at www.autodesk.com.

Arts PDF Splitter is a tool that lets you split your PDFs using several different methods. You can split a document using specific page values, by bookmarks, individual pages, or fragments. A demo version of the program can be downloaded from PlanetPDF, at www.planetpdf.com. While you're at PlanetPDF, a favorite site of PDF users, look through some of the other third-party software and plug-ins available. The scope of options is quite remarkable.

Project Overview

Imagine an icon on everyone's desk in your office that says XYZ Company Knowledgebase. An employee can click the icon and a menu pops up that includes the following:

- Corporate minutes (Boolean searchable)

- Policy and procedure manuals with links to areas such as human resources, environmental, purchasing, and travel

- Forms repository (active and many are connected to databases)

- Advertising materials

- Financial statements (password-protected)

- Plant drawings and equipment manuals that are constantly updated with comments and contain cross-linked drawings and manuals

- Product quality-control program

- Movies of company history

Using a combination of Windows file structure and Adobe Acrobat 6.0 you can develop this knowledgebase. Tom currently has clients with thousands of pages of information organized in this manner and these dynamic knowledgebases are growing daily as employees across the facility enhance their sections.

Tutorials

The book also contains a number of tutorials. We differentiate between tutorials and projects based on content. Projects are used to develop portions of the knowledgebase master project. Tutorials use a range of material. They show how to use some features and processes not incorporated into the master project. They also provide an opportunity to work with some different types of material and topics.

Up Next

Acrobat 6.0 is complex software because it can do so much. In this chapter you were introduced to the program's component parts and where they're located. The first part of the journey requires developing PDF files. Chapter 3, here we come.

Chapter 3

Creating PDF Files

In the previous chapter, we looked at the overall program and introduced a master PDF project for you to use throughout the book. But how does a file become a PDF file, and what kinds of files can be used? Inquiring minds, read on.

Where Do the Files Come From?

We recall the first time we opened Acrobat 3.0. By that time, we had been working with software for years and thought this was just one more weapon to add to our digital arsenal. Didn't work out so smoothly right from the start. We (1,472 miles apart) nonchalantly opened the File drop-down menu and moved the mouse over to click New. It wasn't there. Tried the usual shortcut keys. Nothing.

After looking through all the menu options and cursing the gods for creating such a devilish piece of software, Donna decided to track down this strange mystery and went to the Help files. Tom tried to find someone that understood the beast. Whereupon we both learned that we couldn't create a new blank file in Acrobat, but we could convert and import all kinds of things. Of course, with time and understanding, we learned we could make a Blank Page command and even a Blank Page menu item with JavaScript.

The moral of this tale? You still can't directly create a new blank file in Acrobat 6.0, but you can do a whole lot of fancy stuff with files from darn near anywhere else. Acrobat 6.0 is a wizard's bag of programs that all work together because Adobe published a standard and developed a Software Developers Kit (SDK) to allow great computer minds to make the program better. Every version brings new features from the wizards at Adobe and from all over the world.

Some of the options are truly one-click easy. Some applications, such as Adobe's FrameMaker, PageMaker, InDesign, and Photoshop have a Save As PDF option. Adobe now has three-click production of PDF files from many applications from within Acrobat 6.0.

Acrobat 6.0 has taken much of the pain out of creating PDF files. You have options of creating PDF files internal and external to the program. In Acrobat 5.0, production was external to the program. Let's have a look at that first.

Creating PDF Files Outside of Acrobat

There are three basic ways to generate PDF files external to Acrobat, as follows:

- Exporting a file as a PostScript (PS) file and converting it with Acrobat Distiller

- Printing to Acrobat Distiller from the native program

- Using the Adobe PDFMaker 6 macro in Word, Excel, and PowerPoint in all versions

You can also generate PDF files in Outlook and Lotus Notes in both Acrobat 6.0 Standard and Professional. In addition, you can produce PDF files from AutoCAD 2000, Microsoft Project, and Microsoft Visio using the macro provided by Acrobat 6.0 Professional.

Creating PostScript Files

What happens if the application you're using doesn't let you create a PDF file? Fear not. If you can create a PS file, you can create a PDF file from it with Distiller. PS files require an AdobePS driver and an Acrobat Distiller PostScript printer description (PPD), both of which are autoinstalled when you install Acrobat 6.0. Creating PS files is different in Windows than in Mac OS systems. We'll outline the process for each. Creating PS files is becoming rare and is used mainly for print work. With all the files Tom deals with in consulting and training, he only had to convert to PS twice in the last year.

Creating a PostScript File in Windows

First, let's look at how to create a file from a Windows application. In some applications, it might take a bit of configuring. The printer file format generated from Windows is recognized by Distiller.

1. Make sure the document is open in the application it was created in.

2. Select File ➤ Print. The Print dialog box will open.

3. From the list of printers, select Adobe PDF printer.

4. Click Print To File.

Tip

Depending on the program, you may have to open the Setup dialog box to select the printer from the list.

5. In the Save As dialog box, name the file and storage location. The default format is the .prn (printer file) format.

6. Click Print or OK. The file is saved.

Now let's have a look at the same process on a Mac.

Creating a PostScript File in Mac OS

As mentioned, the process is a bit different on a Mac. Here's how to do it:

1. You must have a default PostScript printer set up with the AdobePS printer driver. If you don't, select Chooser ➤ AdobePS Printer Driver ➤ PostScript Printer. Click Setup, click Select PPD, and then choose Acrobat Distiller from the list. Click Select, and then click OK. Close the Chooser.

2. With the document open in its original application, select File ➤ Page Setup. Select the PostScript printer from the Format For menu and click OK.

3. Select File ➤ Print and select Save As File.

4. From the Format menu, select PostScript Job. Click Save.

5. In the Save As dialog box, name the file and storage location. Use the .ps (PostScript) file extension.

Creating Adobe PDF Files from PostScript Files

Once your file has been converted to a PS or prn file, the second stage is to run it through Distiller. Here's what you do:

1. Launch Acrobat Distiller.

2. Select File ➤ Open and browse to the location of the file to be converted.

3. Click Open and enter a name and location for the file.

4. Click Save. If you hold down the Shift key (or Option on the Mac) and click Save, the PDF file output will have the same name as the file and will be stored in the same folder.

Tip

I Can't Print to File. What's the Deal?

If you're printing to Acrobat Distiller, you must send the fonts to Distiller. Click Properties in the Print Setup dialog box for the Acrobat Distiller printer. Then, verify that the option Do Not Send Fonts To Distiller is cleared on the Adobe PDF Settings tab of the Acrobat Distiller Properties dialog box.

5. Alternatively, just drag the file to the Distiller icon.

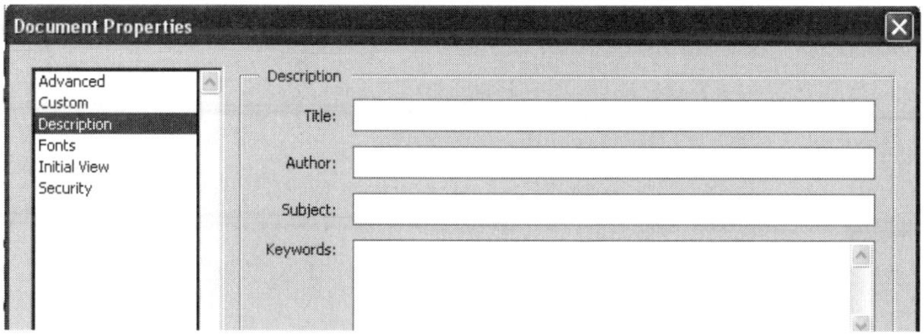
Document Properties
Advanced
Custom
Description
Fonts
Initial View
Security
Description
Title:
Author:
Subject:
Keywords:

Figure 3-1
The Document Properties dialog box. It's more important now than ever that this be used. This is a key part of document management. A poor example is shown. How would you ever file this?

Creating PDF Files Using PDFWriter

Ding dong the wicked witch is dead. PDFWriter was based on PDF 1.2 and was designed for use for simple documents with little or no graphics. It was a useful function in a time when computers were slow, had little hard disk space, and RAM was at a premium. In Acrobat 5.0 you had to manually install PDFWriter—it wasn't automatic. In Acrobat 6.0, you will not find it. Tom has been telling his students for four years not to use PDFWriter.

Why Bother to Edit Optional Information?

Because it can save you a lot of time. Suppose you have a series of files all with similar names. If you take a few seconds when saving the file originally to add a subject in the Document Properties dialog box, as shown in Figure 3-1, this information is displayed when you're browsing for the file. A Windows Explorer layout is shown in Figure 3-2. Because we added a subject to the document information, by placing the mouse over the file name, we can access the information we need and don't have to open all the files to find the one we need.

Acrobat has the makings of a great small- to medium-sized document management system. If everyone is faithfully inputting document information, untold hours will be saved in the business environment.

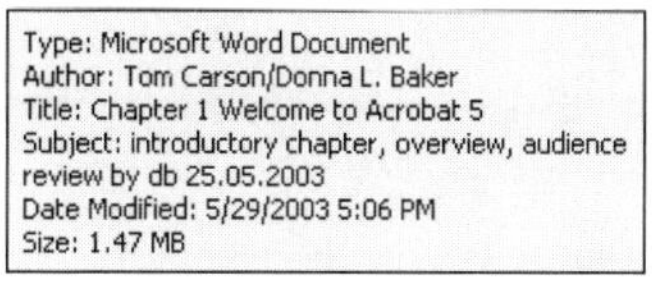
Type: Microsoft Word Document
Author: Tom Carson/Donna L. Baker
Title: Chapter 1 Welcome to Acrobat 5
Subject: introductory chapter, overview, audience review by db 25.05.2003
Date Modified: 5/29/2003 5:06 PM
Size: 1.47 MB

Figure 3-2
Information displayed for a file in Windows Explorer

Creating PDF Files Using Distiller

Acrobat Distiller is essentially a printer that prints to an electronic space identical to a paper space, and is the method used to create most PDF files. In Acrobat 6.0, Distiller is shown as both an Adobe PDF printer icon and it's listed under Advanced Tools.

The first major change is the Distiller settings. Adobe has taken away eBook, screen, and print and replaced them with qualitative terms, as shown in Figure 3-3. Settings have been added for PDF/X in Acrobat 6.0 Professional.

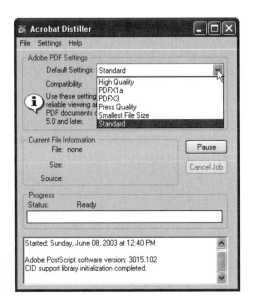

Figure 3-3
Default Distiller settings
in Acrobat 6.0

The key to Distiller is to THINK PRINT. You don't usually print a 36-inch × 48-inch engineering drawing on letter-size paper. You cannot read it! Remember that when you distill. Adobe made great strides in making the whole process easier by adding many more paper sizes, as you can see in Figure 3-4.

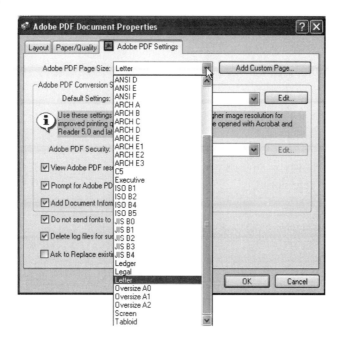

Figure 3-4
Distiller has numerous new built-in sizes.

Save Time Using Preferences

Set several preferences in Acrobat Distiller to save yourself a great deal of time. Choose Advanced ➤ Acrobat ➤ Distiller ➤ File ➤ Preferences. Look for these settings, as shown in Figure 3-5:

- Select Ask for PDF file destination to save time searching and choosing locations manually.

- Select View PDF when using Distiller. This option lets you see the output while you're still working in your source program, and it can be a timesaver. This option may add time for opening Acrobat, but the time is well spent as you can instantly check the output.

- Select Delete Log Files for successful jobs. You don't need to store the files.

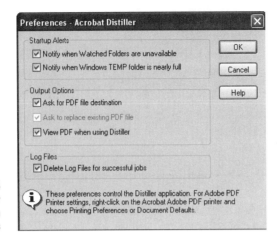

Figure 3-5
Acrobat Distiller
Preferences with
recommendations

THINK PRINT

Adobe has made it easier to think print with Acrobat 6.0. In version 3.0 the largest print size was 11 inches × 17 inches. In Acrobat 4.0 and 5.0 the page size increased to 200 inches × 200 inches, but the largest printed page size was still Tabloid (11 inches × 17 inches). You had to create PostScript Custom Pages to create the larger files. Most users never figured this out and printed large engineering drawings to letter-size space and wondered why the lines ran under fonts and the drawing was unusable. It wasn't easy to THINK PRINT, which hurt the implementation of Acrobat in engineering.

Converting Microsoft Office Files

For the ultimate in luxurious file conversion, try the custom macro, Adobe PDFMaker 6. This is one slick little option. Between us we have Windows 2000 ME, Windows 2000 Professional, XP Home, and XP Pro systems, and with alternate versions of the Microsoft Office applications as well. Acrobat 6.0 doesn't officially support Windows ME and you're probably asking for problems running it on ME. Like a fool, Tom runs ME on one of his computers and it crashes more than it should (Donna doesn't use ME for any purpose aside from testing other software.) When Acrobat is installed in Windows, a macro is autoinstalled into the standard Microsoft Office applications, including Microsoft Word 97/2000/XP, Excel 97/2000/XP, and PowerPoint 97/2000/XP, Internet Explorer 6.0, and Microsoft Outlook in all versions. The PDFMaker macros appear in MS Visio, MS Project, and AutoCAD.

Conversion Options

The Autoinstall feature adds an Acrobat drop-down menu to the main menu bar as well as three icons to the Office products, Visio, Project, and AutoCAD. The icons are shown in Figure 3-6. The icon on the left makes a PDF. The icon in the center makes a PDF and attaches it to an email. The icon on the right makes a PDF and implements the review cycle.

Figure 3-6
The set of PDFMaker icons

In Internet Explorer, Acrobat 6.0 adds an icon to the toolbar. Just click the icon, and the web page is converted to PDF with all the links maintained. Any links that aren't downloaded are signified by a hand with the mouse finger and a +. Click the icon and Acrobat reopens the web page, downloads, and attaches the file.

Outlook now has an Attach as Adobe PDF icon that can convert many types of files to PDF, as shown in Figure 3-7. Click the icon, navigate to the file you want to convert and attach, and voilà, an attached PDF. It can't get much easier than that.

But it does get a bit easier. The neatest conversion option is accessed through the shortcut menus. Right-click a file name or icon in Windows Explorer. Up pops a wonderful menu with the option to Convert to Adobe PDF or Combine in Adobe Acrobat. If the file is a native to a program with a PDFMaker macro, you're also given the option to Convert to Adobe PDF and EMail.

Figure 3-7
Shortcut menu options
for non-Office file with
Acrobat 6.0 installed

To get the most out of PDFMaker, you must know how to use Word to the fullest. Mainly you need to set the heading levels. Then Word can make your table of contents and PDFMaker can make your bookmarks. We aren't going to teach you Word! That costs extra.

The PDF Maker menu in Figure 3-8 shows the commands installed as part of the macro. As you can see, the menu contains the commands for the two conversion functions as well as an option to view the file in Acrobat as well as a selection for the Change Conversion Settings dialog box.

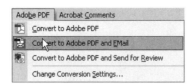

Figure 3-8
The PDFMaker
menu options

Using the Conversion Settings Dialog Box

Choose Acrobat ➤ Change Conversion Settings to access conversion settings for modifying how a file is converted to PDF. This section shows the options using the Word XP dialog box. With the exception of the XP Bookmarks tab, the dialog box is the same in Excel and PowerPoint. Because neither of the two programs uses bookmarks, no settings are required. Let's look at the available options.

The Settings Tab

The dialog box opens with the Settings tab, as shown in Figure 3-9. On this tab, you can select a general set of conversion settings from the drop-down menu. The other important feature is the Restore Defaults button. If you've made changes to any of the settings and want to revert, click the Restore Defaults button.

The Security Tab

Next is the Security tab, shown in Figure 3-10. Use this tab to set passwords and permissions. One feature of note is the level of encryption. As you can see in the figure, you're limited to a 40-bit encryption level. If you're converting a document that requires a higher level of protection, you have to use custom settings.

Unless you're certain you've finalized the document, it's better not to set security here.

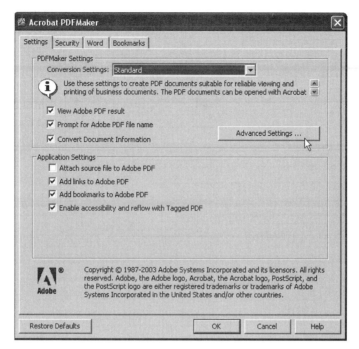

Figure 3-9
The Settings tab showing the default Standard Conversion Setting

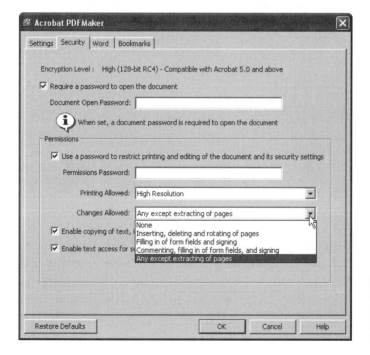

Figure 3-10
Security tab settings in PDFMaker. Set both passwords and permissions here.

The Office Tab

The third tab lists a number of options, both general and specific to the application you're working with. As shown in Figure 3-11, the first section lists a number of general options and the next section is specific to the program. For example, four Microsoft Word features are listed; Microsoft PowerPoint has only one feature listed.

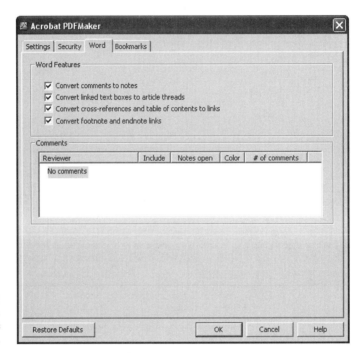

Figure 3-11
Office tab options.
The content is specific
to the host program.

The Bookmarks Tab

The fourth tab is specific to Microsoft Word. As shown in Figure 3-12, it's used to set Bookmark options. Optional settings include using either headings or styles as bookmark sources. The optional conversion settings allow you to readily convert a document and maintain all the advanced settings you've created. Figure 3-12 shows the default settings for this tab.

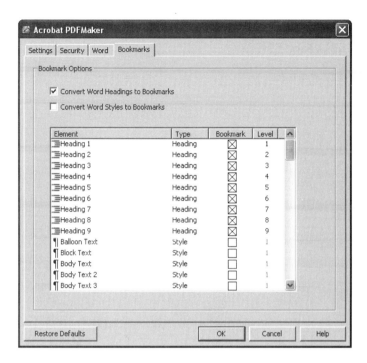

Figure 3-12
The Bookmarks
tab options. This tab
is exclusive to
Microsoft Word.

Customizing the PDFMaker Conversion Process

Once you've made your changes in the dialog box, click OK to process and convert your file. You might be wondering where the custom settings appeared from and how they're created. Earlier you saw the Settings tab, with custom settings displayed in the drop-down menu. What you couldn't see in that figure was a button named Edit Conversion Settings hidden behind the drop-down menu. If you click that button, an entirely new dialog box opens, complete with its own set of five tabs to customize the job options. Rather than go through each tab and discuss its contents, we've condensed the information into Table 3-1.

Table 3.1 Custom Job Options

Tab Settings	Means...
General	This tab lets you set compatibility with previous versions, Object Level Compression, Auto Rotate Pages, Binding, Resolution, Pages to Convert, Embed Thumbnails (not needed as Acrobat 5.0 and 6.0 generate on the fly), Optimize for Fast Web View, and Page Size.
Images	This sets downsampling for Image type. Adobe went to great lengths in designing the new Qualitative Settings, so resetting downsampling isn't often necessary.

Table 3.1   Custom Job Options (Continued)

Tab Settings	Means...
Fonts	This lets the user choose to Embed All Fonts (very wise), Subset Embedded Fonts when percentage used is less than (xx%), Choices for Failed Embedding, User Defined List of Fonts to Always Embed and the list of fonts to Never Embed. Acrobat now carries 40 fonts that don't require embedding, but the list applies only if the recipient is using Acrobat 6.0 or Adobe Reader 6.0.
Color	This tab allows the user to choose from several predefined color settings, color management practices, working spaces, and device-dependent data.
Advanced	This tab contains options such as PostScript type and gradient conversion. It also contains several Document Structuring Convention options.
PDF-X	This tab is in Professional only and allows the user to determine compliance with either PDF/X-1a or PDF/X-3.

In Table 3-1, we mentioned that the Fonts tab of the Job Options dialog box is used to control embedding. A portion of the tab is shown in Figure 3-13 to illustrate an important point (and present a segue into the sidebar.) As you can see in the figure, some of the fonts cannot be embedded due to licensing restrictions.

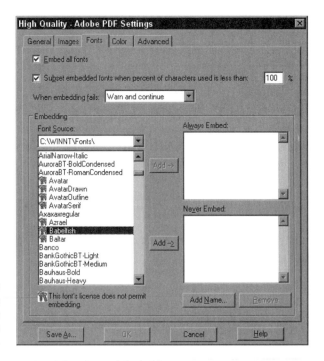

Figure 3-13
The Fonts tab of the
Custom Conversion
Settings dialog box
showing locked fonts.

Take some time when planning your work to review any font restrictions. What's the point of designing beautiful work if the font you have your heart set on isn't commonly available or can't be embedded?

That covers the ways to create a PDF externally to Acrobat. In the next section, you'll create a PDF file from within the program.

To Embed or Not to Embed

Why embed a font? Quest for perfection, of course. When fonts are embedded, anyone accessing the file can see and print your work as you intended it. If you're using Distiller to convert a file containing PostScript fonts, the fonts can always be embedded. The same can't be said of other types of fonts.

What happens if fonts aren't embedded? Acrobat 6.0 has substitute sets of Multiple Master serif or sans-serif typefaces. Depending on how the PDF file is defined, the master fonts can be reconfigured to fit and will maintain your line and page breaks. The whole plan can break down with decorative or script fonts, however.

What's the solution? Previewing and good decision making. You can readily preview a file to determine your course of action. With the file in question open, select View ➤ Use Local Fonts. You can then preview and print your document using substitute fonts. Any font that can't be substituted will display bullets and an error message. Try again after embedding the missing fonts. Remember, it will always be a trade-off between visual perfection and file size.

Creating PDF Files Inside Acrobat 6.0

You can create PDF files internally now, meaning you don't leave Acrobat to convert the file. Acrobat 5.0 had some of these internal conversion features scattered under a variety of different places. All the options have now been combined into a task button called Create PDF, shown in Figure 3-14, as well as a File menu option.

Internal conversion doesn't mean you can convert any program's file format whether you have the program or not. It means Acrobat opens the program in the background and makes the conversion.

PDFMaker was and is a nifty new feature, but Create PDF is niftier. This is almost the new file icon that Donna wanted. It's now extremely easy to create PDFs straight from Acrobat. This puts a 90-degree bend in your workflow, and should save you hours of work time each year.

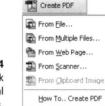

Figure 3-14
Create PDF is a new task
button containing several
conversion choices.

Internal Conversion Methods

There are five methods used to create a PDF from within Acrobat:

- From File. Acrobat executes a macro that opens the file in the native program and converts it to PDF. If the file is in a program with a PDF Maker, it will use the PDFMaker with its current settings. If the file is in a program without a PDFMaker, it opens the program and prints the file through the Adobe PDF Converter.

- From Multiple Files (a.k.a. Binder.) This is a wonderful new feature in Acrobat 6.0 Standard and Professional used to assemble and organize files from a variety of programs.

- From Web Pages (formerly known as Web Capture). Web Capture was a neat feature in Acrobat 5.0, but it was hidden under tools. A lot of pretty savvy users never found the feature. It's now out for the whole world to see and work with. The tool has been improved and now supports Flash media.

- From Scanner (formerly File ➤ Import ➤ Scan). The scan process is improved. You have more control of compression and Acrobat will remove the edge shadows from the scanned objects.

- From Clipboard Image. This is a completely new process and a boon to authors.

Let's have a look at the options.

Create PDF From File

This file conversion process is really simple. You never have to leave Acrobat. Select Create PDF ➤ From File. An Explorer window opens; navigate to the desired file, and click to select it. The file is converted if you have a program that can open and print the file or if it's a graphics file.

If you're in Windows Explorer you can also right-click the file and select the Convert to Adobe PDF option from the shortcut menu items. This option also replaces File ➤ Open Adobe PDF for graphics images.

Create PDF From Multiple Files

Imagine this scenario: It's time to create the annual budget. All the departments sent you a Word file with the text, PowerPoint with the current organizational chart, Excel with the budget figures and pie charts, and a department cover page created in Publisher complete with photos and graphics as well as a few PDFs. Twenty-three different departments averaging 5 files per departments equals 115 different files to manage. The accounting law states no blank pages are allowed in the document. You're printing to a duplex laser color printer. It's a nightmare.

By putting the content in a PDF, it's easy to insert pages with the city seal for blank pages. The finished document is ready to print. By redistilling to an eBook and with Fast Web Optimizing the same document goes straight to the Web.

Sounds easy, but in Acrobat 5.0 each document had to be opened in the native program, distilled, and added to the collection.

Untold hours would have been saved last year making a 422-page document from a series of Word, Excel, PowerPoint, PDF, Publisher, and JPEG files. With Binder, all you would have needed was to put them all in binder in the order you wanted (Binder allows you to change order) and click OK.

In a short time your unified PDF would appear. From a practical standpoint, there are a couple of minor problems in this solution. Publisher files aren't supported by Binder (come to think of it what does support Publisher?), and there may be problems with the way Excel spreadsheets are set to print, or how oversized documents tile. Overall, the process saves a great deal of time. It's much easier to fix these small problems than compile the report one file at a time.

Create PDF From Web Page

It's simple to get web pages into Acrobat. In fact, there are a number of ways to incorporate files, depending on circumstances. As you look at Create PDF ➤ From Web Page, we'll show you the different options and explain how to download HTML files we've stored locally.

Note

Create PDF From File is not a panacea. It's great in a business environment, but when we selected a CAD file and only had VoloView (the free AutoCAD Reader) on our computer, a D-Size drawing became 12 letter-size pages.

When a web page is downloaded, many elements are incorporated, including the following:

- HTML pages

- JPEG, Flash, and GIF animation

- Elements such as tables, links, frames, background colors, text colors, and forms

- Cascading Style Sheets (CSS) information

- Some JavaScript

Let's start from nothing.

1. Click Create PDF (either the task button or File ➤ Create PDF ➤ From Web Page.) The dialog box, displaying the default URL shown in Figure 3-15, will open. Enter the URL you want to capture, select a previous URL from the drop-down list, or click Browse to locate a file locally.

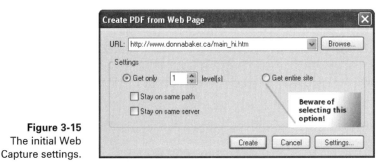

Figure 3-15
The initial Web Capture settings.

2. Click Conversion Settings to open the dialog box shown in Figure 3-16. As you can see in the figure, the Web Page Conversion Settings dialog box includes both general and page layout options. Most of these items are self-explanatory. Make any setting changes and click OK to close the dialog box.

3. Back in the Open Web Page dialog box, click Download to start the conversion process. As the file is being downloaded and converted, Acrobat displays a Download Status window indicating the progress of the conversion, as shown in Figure 3-17. Click Stop to abort the download process at any time.

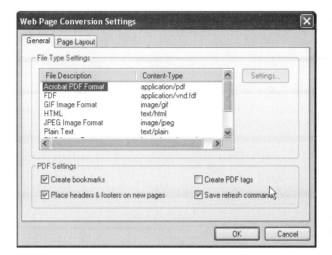

Figure 3-16
The Web Page Conversion Settings dialog box for customizing Web Capture settings.

Figure 3-17
The Download Status window. Note the local URL of the file being downloaded and converted to PDF.

4. When the download is complete, the Download Status dialog box closes and the file is loaded into Acrobat. Select File ➤ Save to save the file.

You can test this process on your own. We aren't using a sample of a downloaded file in the book. I would recommend you try this with www.Adobe.com. There is usually some nice animation on the first page that will demonstrate the enhanced ability to deal with animation. Download the first page, save it, close it, and reopen it. The animation will run from your local machine the same as it does on the web page.

Tip

Convert web pages by clicking the icon in Internet Explorer. It doesn't get any simpler than this. Suppose you're scrolling through Internet Explorer and spot a file you want to use. Just click the Acrobat icon on the Internet Explorer toolbar and you have an instant PDF.

Create PDF ➤ From Scanner

Note

Even if you install a TWAIN driver after installing Acrobat, the new driver will appear in the menu.

PDF is the de facto standard for storing scanned documents. The International Standards Organization (ISO) Committee is currently developing PDF-A or Archival ISO standard. Several U.S. and numerous international agencies have mandated PDF for records submissions and archival.

Nearly all scanners have TWAIN drivers. If you have a TWAIN scanner on your computer, creating PDF files from paper is a quick process.

Here's how to add a scanned paper document:

1. In Acrobat, choose Create PDF ➤ From Scan. The dialog box shown in Figure 3-18 opens.

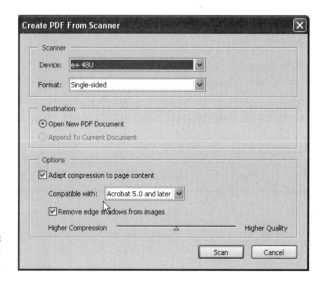

Figure 3-18
The Create PDF From Scanner dialog box.

2. Choose the scanner device and page format from the drop-down lists.

Note

If you have a scanner that scans both sides at once, leave Acrobat set on Single-sided and let the scanner drivers handle the duplex. Canon did not pay Tom to say this but the Canon DR-2080C is the best smaller scanner he has worked with, and he has worked with a lot.

3. Select a destination. You may either add the scanned pages to the end of an open PDF document or open a new file. As you can see in Figure 3-18, since you had no open file, you don't have the second destination available.

4. Choose either Single- or Double-sided format. Acrobat allows you to scan a stack of documents with a sheet feeder that only scans one side at a time, turns them over, and scans the other side. Acrobat then puts them in order.

5. Click Adapt Compression to Page Content and select a version-compatibility option. You can select from Acrobat 4.0, 5.0, or 6.0. The newer the Acrobat version, the smaller the created file without sacrificing quality.

6. When your scanner's interface launches, set the options you require.

7. Follow the process for your scanner to complete the scan.

8. Click Done (this button will appear in the dialog box after the first page is scanned).

9. Save your PDF file.

The PDF images you scanned are just images. You'll learn how to convert them to text later in the chapter using Optical Character Recognition (OCR), a process whereby bitmap images of text are interpreted as letters and characters to become actual text.

Create PDF From Clipboard

A fantastic new feature is Create PDF ➤ From Clipboard Image. The name says it all, but implementing it has several nuances. In any program, or from the desktop, press Ctrl+PrtScn (usually upper-right area on the keyboard) to place a copy of the screen on the clipboard. Now open Acrobat and click Create PDF ➤ From Clipboard Image. The screen shot appears in the document pane.

Use the Create PDF ➤ From Clipboard Image command or use the Attach tool and attach the clipboard content to another PDF or paste the clipboard content into another program as a graphic file.

Using the Snapshot Tool

A neat new Snapshot tool allows you to isolate a portion of the screen and capture only that area. Follow these steps to use the tool to move content out of a document to create a separate document.

1. Open the document you want to copy from.

2. Zoom in to the part of the screen you want to use.

3. Click and drag the tool to draw a marquee around the selected area. Release the mouse. A message appears that the screen shot has been placed on the clipboard as shown in Figure 3-19.

4. Choose Create PDF ➤ From Clipboard Image. The clipboard content is pasted to a new file.

5. Save the new document.

Tip

Scanning for Paper Capture

We recommend 300-400 dpi (in some instances up to 600), black-and-white bitmap. In some instances the better recognition is worth the reduction is scanning speed. Acrobat uses several compression algorithms to compress the files.

Tip

Zoom in to the snapshot area before you attach the image to the clipboard. Zoom in as large as possible, but stop when the image or area starts to appear distorted.

Note

At this point, the image is copied to the clipboard and can be pasted into other programs like Word. The clipboard image can also be inserted into a PDF using the Attach Clipboard command.

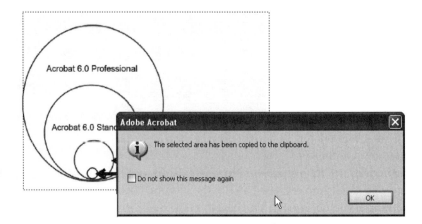

Figure 3-19
Fence an area with
the Snapshot tool to
copy it to the clipboard.

Figure 3-20 shows a PDF created using the clipboard process. You also see an information window describing the PDF as picture-based and some of the image options you can use in Acrobat.

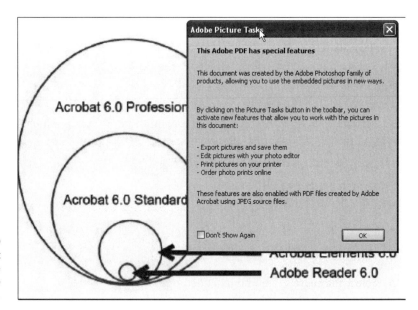

Figure 3-20
The clipboard content
is pasted to a new file
and displays the
Picture Tasks list.

You've looked at the ways to create a PDF file. It's time for the first project. You create the first elements of the knowledgebase, a set of captured minutes.

Project Project 3.1: Preparing Minutes for the Knowledgebase

Text isn't text unless you can manipulate it, tag it, index it, change it. Until then, it's just an image of text. To make what looks like text in fact behave as text, it must be captured.

The first element for the knowledgebase project is a set of school board minutes. On the book's web site you'll find scans of one year of school board minutes for a small community in Tennessee. These are PDF images. In this project, you capture the content. Once the set of files is captured, you go through the set and make conversion corrections.

What You Need

You need the contents of the Chapter 03 Source folder on the web site, which contains these files:

- Knowledgebase Main Page.pdf

- Minutes Main Page.pdf

- PDF Scan of 1 Years Minutes.pdf

Test the Files

1. In Acrobat, choose File ➤ Open and select Scan of 1 Years Minutes.pdf.

2. On the Basic toolbar, choose Select Text. Try to select text on the page. The content is an image of text, not actual selectable text, so you can't select any words or letters.

3. Select Tools ➤ Paper Capture. The dialog box shown in Figure 3-21 opens.

4. Click Edit to open the Paper Capture Settings dialog box.

5. Select the Searchable Image (Exact) option.

6. Click OK to close the Paper Capture Settings dialog box and return to the main Paper Capture dialog box.

7. Click OK to start the capture process. The plug-in will rasterize the page and then perform a number of page recognition and structure processes. Be patient!

8. When the process is complete, the dialog box closes and Acrobat redraws the page.

9. Save the file as 1999.pdf in your knowledgebase folder.

Note

Create a folder on your hard drive to store the knowledgebase files as they're prepared. Download the files from the book's web site and store them in your folder.

Note

Each project contains a set of source files for you to work with. You also find a set of completed files for each session as well. For example, in this project, use the files in the Chapter 3 Source folder. If you want to check your results against our results, the completed files are the Chapter 3 Complete folder.

Note

Minutes are converted using the Searchable Image (Exact) option. The Clerk might be required to swear before a judge that the minutes are a true and exact copy; pages captured using Searchable Image (Exact) cannot be modified in Acrobat 6.0.

Tip

Convert several pages and then test using the Search function to make sure the capture is satisfactory.

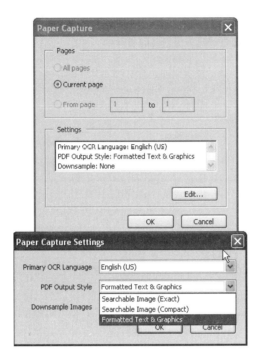

Figure 3-21
The Paper Capture
dialog box

Check for Suspects

Before the page is ready for final output, you have to check the content. The OCR capture process "reads" bitmaps of text and tries to substitute words and characters for the bitmaps. Acrobat will mark any words as suspect when it isn't sure of the translation. In the final part of this chapter's project, you check the converted files for suspect characters.

1. Open1999.pdf, and then open the Pages panel and extract one page.

2. Select Documents ➤ PaperCapture ➤ TouchUp Text ➤ Show Capture Suspects. Any words flagged as suspect will be outlined by a red box.

3. Select Documents ➤ PaperCapture ➤ TouchUp Text ➤ Find First Suspect. The first suspect word is highlighted on the page and its original bitmap image appears in the Suspect Image window as shown in Figure 3-22.

4. Click Accept to accept the change, or click Next to skip to the next suspect. To change the spelling, select the TouchUp Text tool and edit the word on the page. Then click Next to move forward.

Figure 3-22
The captured 1998.pdf file
showing suspect text

5. When you've finished, click Close to close the Find Element
    dialog box.

6. Choose File ➤ Save. The file has been corrected.

You have a set of school board minutes that are converted from scans
and corrected. In the next chapter, you add navigation to the set of files.
Later you'll develop a catalog from the files.

Before the chapter ends, let's look at the TouchUp Text tool.

Touch Up the Text

Here are a few hints for using the TouchUp Text tool:

- The TouchUp Text tool makes changes line-by-line only.

- Text attributes can be modified (except for the Font and Embedding
  attributes).

- If a font is installed on your system and isn't embedded, you can
  change characters.

- You can unembed an embedded font.

- You can set text appearance, including font, size, fill and outline
  colors, scale, baseline shift, tracking, and spacing.

Tip

**When You Suspect
There Are Too Many
Suspects**

Whenever possible, get
a PDF version of the
original document. Not
only will it have all its tags
attached, but also the
suspect correction
process will be moot. In
those circumstances in
which you cannot get the
original document,
however, it can sure beat
re-creating it from scratch!

Tip

Line by Line Can Be a Drag

The TouchUp Text tool is used to edit text. This is true. It's also true that it only works one line at a time. Editing a large amount of text isn't an efficient use of your time. Instead, edit the document in the program where it was created originally, then re-create the PDF file or part of the file. If a segment of the PDF file you created initially is fine, just regenerate the corrected pages and insert them as required.

Up Next

In this chapter, you looked at PostScript files and the various PDF printer options. You looked at importing files from different sources, including Microsoft Office applications, web pages, and scanned pages. Once a file is safely into Acrobat, you can apply many functions, and it can be converted to numerous types of output.

You completed the first part of the knowledgebase project, converting and capturing a set of minutes. You converted the files using Paper Capture, and then made corrections using the Suspect evaluation process.

In the next chapter you'll look at how to navigate files and collections of files. In the electronic world it's very important that files navigate like web pages, thereby making information much easier to find than in a printed document.

Chapter 4

Linking, Navigating, and Repurposing

Never lead someone into the forest unless you blaze a trail they can use to return without you.

What Is This Supposed to Mean?

How often have you opened a PDF file only to find it has all the same problems and advantages as a paper book? You can flip through the pages, look up sections in the table of contents, type in the page number only to get the wrong page, and click the Bookmark tab only to find it empty?

What you've seen is repurposing at its worst. The document was designed for paper and repurposed for electronic media without taking advantage of the features available and expected of a good electronic document.

To correctly repurpose a document you must first identify the following:

- Intended uses of the document

- Requirements for repurposing

- Features currently in the document

- How to make the necessary modifications

- How to skillfully add the necessary features to the document

We've said throughout this book that our intention isn't to create a click-this, click-that guide to using Acrobat but rather to give insight into how to use the program to work more efficiently. We never said this route would be easy. But wouldn't you rather be a Picasso than a paint-by-numbers artist?

This chapter's project repurposes several documents and adds them to the knowledgebase. We're going to look at how to change the documents from their original formats and bring them into the electronic world. We're also going to develop documents for print that can be easily repurposed into electronic formats.

Planning Your Workflow

You just learned a multistep process for repurposing content. Let's have a look at its components and see what they mean.

Tip

What we're discussing is referred to as cross-media publication. You can sign up for a free subscription of CrossMedia magazine at www.crossmediamag.com. The magazine contains some state-of-the-art articles that may help you in your work.

Identify Uses of the Document

Identifying uses of a document isn't as easy as it seems. Many documents were originally created with the sole purpose of printing them either on a printer or a press. A major concept to remember is that Acrobat will downsize to meet a purpose, but once a document is downsized, its resolution cannot be successfully upsized. For example, if you create a document for the Web and repurpose it for print, you have a problem. Acrobat downsizes graphics for web usage to 150 dpi. Even if the layout is appropriate for the new purpose, your graphics resolution is too low for print quality.

Not only must you consider the obvious problems inherent in repurposing material, but you must also identify what the source materials contribute to document structure.

Understand What Is Required for the Various Uses

There are PDF standards for print, yet a common complaint of printers is that the PDF files "aren't good enough." Adobe has taken a major step with Acrobat 6.0 Professional by adding PDF/X-1 and PDF/X-3a settings. A document that is compliant with PDF/X standards carries all the information required for print. Now suppose you've created a document that meets printing standards—what does it take to make a good electronic document?

Inventory What You Have

An inventory follows from understanding what you need, and you should have an inventory of the available components in a document. Suppose you've assembled the perfect document for print. The images you have are at very high resolution and will downsize perfectly for electronic usage. However, the reverse isn't true, as you can see in Figure 4-1.

The text and layout will look good in an electronic format. Will the document reflow? That is, will it resize and wrap to make it more readable? Another consideration for repurposing is will it meet accessibility requirements for the visually challenged?

To be useful, the document must be tagged. Examining the overall document, ask yourself how the user can navigate the document electronically.

Figure 4-1
In the left image, the painting and text is very clear; in the right image, after decreasing resolution for online use and then increasing resolution again, the quality has suffered tremendously.

Make the Necessary Modifications

You've determined both the uses for your document and what is required for its transformation as well as made an inventory of what you have. Now you must make the necessary modifications. Modifications are the subject of much of this book and can be completed in a variety of ways. Some modifications are automatic in Acrobat 6.0 with a well-planned workflow.

Create the Output Skillfully

Creating output isn't a job for amateurs! Just because you can finish something doesn't necessarily mean that it's a good piece of work. When Tom developed his first knowledgebase, he knew that he wanted to develop a system that made a wide range of documents available in a format that was easy to access and navigate.

One of Tom's early shortcomings was leading people into the forest only to realize that they couldn't find their way back without his help. Why? Experience and understanding. With enough forethought and planning, some of the work involved in producing multiple outputs can be streamlined.

All of the elements of a repurposing plan are based on understanding how a document is made and how people utilize documents in different formats. That is, it's not what you see, but more important, what you don't see. It's the underpinnings of a document that allow for manipulation and the ability to repurpose the content.

What's in a Document?

In earlier chapters, we briefly looked at the content of converted documents. This is where we get into the heart of the matter. Look at a printed document. Notice the content, whether it's text or tables or images. Take note of the pagination elements, such as the page numbers and header and footer elements. Examine the layout elements, such as the figures.

Imagine that you could see the manuscript as we were editing it. You would see editing functions, such as text and graphic markups and comments. Now imagine that you could see the pages laid out for printing. What else do you see? Crop marks, print notations, and the like.

This is a basic document. This is also a description of an unstructured document. Not that there isn't a lot of visual structure, because there certainly is. However, this structure doesn't have to be programmed, nor can its source be reused automatically. Sure, you could copy and paste to your heart's content, but it's still unstructured.

The key to repurposing content lies in structure. In a PDF document, there are two levels of structured document: structured and tagged. Look at it as a continuum. At one end is a simple text document, at the other end is a tagged document, and somewhere in between lies a structured document.

Like Leaves on a Tree

If you consider content to be the leaves of a tree, the structure would be twigs and tags would be the branches and trunks. In the case of structured and tagged documents, all contain content, but there are additional components.

Structured Documents

Structured documents contain a structure tree in addition to the content. Content is referenced in a logical reading order, just as the pages of a book are structured. For example, this book uses a structured layout in that different levels of headings are used. So, when you read this paragraph, which has a lower-level heading than this subsection, you know that it's part of the larger heading, which in turn is part of the main headings. Have a look at Figure 4-2. This is a screen shot of a portion of this chapter's preliminary outline view. You can easily see how the levels branch out from the main level—that is, the chapter title.

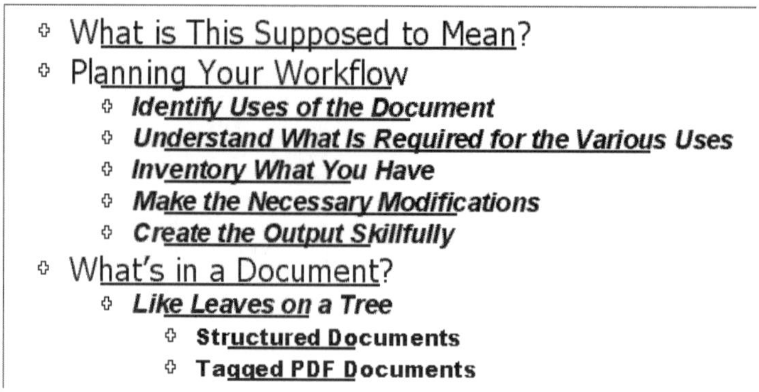

What is This Supposed to Mean?
Planning Your Workflow
Identify Uses of the Document
Understand What Is Required for the Various Uses
Inventory What You Have
Make the Necessary Modifications
Create the Output Skillfully
What's in a Document?
Like Leaves on a Tree
Structured Documents
Tagged PDF Documents

Figure 4-2
A structured document's layout uses a hierarchy to arrange elements.

> **Note**
> Some authoring applications, such as Adobe FrameMaker 6, can produce structured PDF files. In FrameMaker, for example, you save the file by selecting File ➤ Save As and choosing settings. You can also print to PostScript and convert to PDF using Acrobat Distiller. We'll look at that process a bit later in the chapter.

A similar structure is in place from Acrobat's perspective. Some of the elements contained in a regular, unstructured document aren't used. For example, comments or page numbers aren't translated into a structured format because they aren't considered useful structures in terms of formulating outputs.

A basic structured document is one that contains elements such as bookmarks. If the document you're writing were converted to a PDF and opened in Acrobat, the bookmarked structure would look like the outline structure. As you can see in Figure 4-3, we did convert the document, and the same structure is outlined in Acrobat.

Options
Bookmarks
Signatures
Layers
Pages
What is This Supposed to Mean?
Planning Your Workflow
Identify Uses of the Document
Understand What Is Required for the Various Uses
Inventory What You Have
Make the Necessary Modifications
Create the Output Skillfully

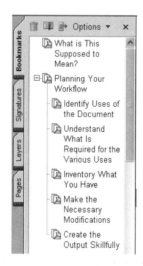

Figure 4-3
A structured document in Acrobat uses bookmarks corresponding to the outline levels initially set in Word.

Tagged PDF Documents

The most advanced form of document we look at in this chapter is the tagged document. Other elements are defined in addition to the content and structure already described. These other elements also relate to content, but from a different perspective. Content, as described earlier, relates to the words, tables, images, and so forth. In a tagged document, additional content information includes word spacing, hyphenation, and Unicode character values.

As you can see in Figure 4-4, although the Tags Root heading is present and the headings displayed in the earlier two images appear, the tags don't have anything in the document assigned to them. On the other hand, if you had chosen to have the bookmarks tagged, the document's elements would appear here.

Tip

Don't Use an Elephant Gun to Hunt a Fly

I'll bet that got your attention. Sometimes, depending on the source materials you have available, it can take a good deal of time to plan and produce a tagged file and finesse components such as line breaks. But what if you don't need the tags? Don't use them. Again, the situation boils down to what you need, which was outlined in the master plan at the start of this chapter.

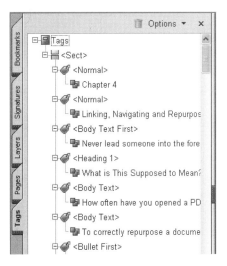

Figure 4-4
The logical structure tree in the Tags panel defines objects in a hierarchy.

Tagging has become critical in the world of repurposing documents. If a document isn't tagged, it will not currently reflow for the smaller screens of personal digital assistants or for use with screenreaders for the visually impaired.

As we've described, depending on the characteristics of your document, you can repurpose the content in different ways. Table 4-1 lists the three document types and summarizes the features each can support.

Note

Tagging is such an important method of structuring a document that it's the basis for the discussion of accessibility in Chapter 10. A tagged document can move straight from the paper world to special uses in the digital world.

Table 4-1   Repurposing Capabilities of Different PDF Document Types

Characteristic	Unstructured	Structured	Tagged
Save to RTF	Yes	Yes	Yes
Paragraph recognition	Yes	Yes	Yes
Text formatting	No	Yes	Yes
Lists/tables	No	No	Yes
Reflow ability	No	No	Yes
View on screenreader	No (unreliable)	Yes (unreliable)	Yes

Working with Bookmarks

Any desktop publishing program that can generate a table of contents or an outline can have the table converted to bookmarks in Acrobat.

As with all other elements, bookmarks in Acrobat can be customized and manipulated. Bookmarks can be

- Added and deleted

- Edited

- Reorganized (in their hierarchy)

You access bookmarks by opening the Bookmarks tab on the navigation pane or selecting Window ➤ Bookmarks. Remember that commands are available for each of the areas you look at through either the context menu or by using the drop-down menu on the Bookmarks panel.

Rather than a simple list of instructions or commands, we included a tutorial to show you how to manipulate bookmarks.

Tutorial: Manipulating a Set of Bookmarks

Note

The tutorial file is an article originally published in *WindoWatch* magazine, Vol. 7, No. 2, February 2001. (Copyright © 2001 by Donna L. Baker. Used with permission.)

Let's have a look at bookmarking functions using a sample file named satellite.pdf. The file used in the tutorial is available in the Chapter 4 Projects folder.

Adding and Deleting Bookmarks

A common bookmarking activity is adding and deleting bookmarks. For example, if you're using a heading or style structure as the basis for converting a PDF file from a Microsoft Word document, you might have a structure similar to the one shown in Figure 4-5. This doesn't mean that you're necessarily satisfied with the locations and numbers of bookmarks once you have the file converted. In this example, we used a Word document and selected the headings as the basis for the bookmark structure.

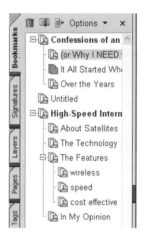

Figure 4-5
The bookmark hierarchy from the satellite.pdf document is based on the Word document's heading structure.

The document has a small bio attached at the end. Because the file was converted using headings as bookmarks, the bio wasn't added. Follow these steps to add an additional bookmark:

1. Click the bookmark above the desired location for the new one. In the example, the new bookmark is to be added at the end, so the *In My Opinion* heading is selected.

2. Navigate to the correct location in the document where the bookmark is to be linked—in this case, the last page (page 5).

3. Click the Create New Bookmark icon at the top of the Bookmarks panel or select Bookmark ➤ New Bookmark from the Bookmark drop-down menu.

4. Select some text in the document to serve as the label, such as *Donna Baker.*

Note

If you didn't select a location, it would be added automatically to the end of the list, which is where you want it anyway.

5. Press Enter.

6. Test the bookmark by clicking a different bookmark and then clicking the new one. The first revision to the Bookmarks tab is shown in Figure 4-6.

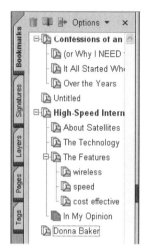

Figure 4-6
The Bookmarks panel can include converted bookmarks as well as new ones; a new bookmark is shown in the figure.

The top two bookmarks in the list are actually a title and a subtitle. To delete the subtitle, click the bookmark to select it and then press Delete. A confirmation window opens; click Yes to confirm the deletion and remove the bookmark permanently. The bookmark list now appears as shown in Figure 4-7.

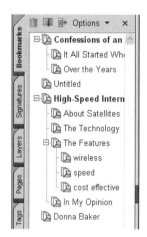

Figure 4-7
You can readily delete unwanted bookmarks from the Bookmarks panel.

Now let's look at editing bookmarks.

Editing the Bookmarks' Content and Appearance

Next you'll edit text in the *In My Opinion* bookmark (shown in Figure 4-7) and change the appearance of the two main headings. Follow these steps:

1. Double-click the *In My Opinion* bookmark and change the text to *My Opinion*. (You can also right-click the bookmark and select Rename).

2. Click the first bookmark to select it and then choose Bookmark Properties from the context menu or the Bookmark panel's menu.

3. In the Bookmark Properties dialog box, select the color and text style for the bookmark in the Appearances tab.

4. Click Close to save the changes.

The modified bookmarks are shown in Figure 4-8. If you look at the satellite.pdf file, you'll see that the headings are now the same color and font as the headings in the document.

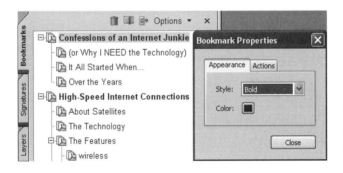

Figure 4-8
The text of your bookmarks can be customized to coordinate with the document.

Setting Bookmark Destinations

The destination settings are the last of the editing functions you'll look at. Be careful when you use these settings; we'll explain why as you go along.

1. Select the bookmark to be edited. Move to the location you want to specify as the new bookmark destination in the document pane.

2. Adjust the magnification. Set destination.

Note
The destination for a bookmark is a particular magnification of a specific area of a specific page. This isn't the same as using Destinations. Destinations, although they still use bookmarks and specific locations and magnifications, are used with more than one document.

Here is where the caution comes. You can choose from several magnification options. The options are listed by name, along with their effect, in Table 4-2.

Table 4-2   Magnification Options

Option	Displays This
Fit Page	Current page in the destination window
Actual Size	Displays on the screen as printed size
Fit Width	Width of the current page in the destination window
Fit Visible	Width of the visible contents of the current page in the destination window (usually without margins)
Inherit Zoom	Magnification level the reader is using when the link or bookmark is clicked

You aren't restricted to using this method for setting how a bookmark is displayed. The sidebar describes a way to create consistent bookmark displays.

The last stop on the bookmark trek is a look at the hierarchy structure and how it can be modified.

Using Magnification Options Correctly

As with many other settings, a magnification option will apply until you change the option. This means that each time you add a new bookmark, it inherits the magnification last specified. This may or may not be a problem. Suppose you're adding several bookmarks to a document. If the setting you use is different from the ones used with the other bookmarks, readers will find their progress through your document quite jumpy and distracting.

On the other hand, the inherited magnification options can streamline your bookmarking processes. Select the first bookmark and set the magnification options to whatever you desire. To set all subsequent bookmarks, select a bookmark, which will move the document to the appropriate place in your document, right-click the bookmark, and select Set Destination. Click OK to confirm the bookmark's destination.

Establishing the Bookmark Hierarchy

Bookmarks come in a nested arrangement. There are relationships between the levels of bookmark (you can change those relationships, of course). Look at Figure 4-9 as we go through these points.

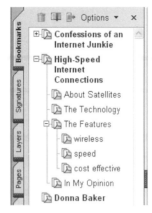

Figure 4-9
The finished hierarchy for the satellite.pdf document shows the custom appearance and arrangement of the bookmarks.

- One of the bookmark groups is open and one is closed, indicated by the plus sign (+) or minus sign (-). The second group is expanded to show all the subtitles. This is referred to as *nesting*. The subtopics are considered children of the parent title.

- A new set of bookmarks is added under *The Features*. These are the concepts outlined in the bullets in the document. They have a parent/child relationship with *The Features* subtitle, which in turn has a parent/child relationship with the *High-Speed Internet Connections* heading.

- In case you were wondering earlier why the main heading colors and text attributes were assigned to the author's name, here's why. The name is promoted to a first-level position.

- When all the nested groups are collapsed, the set of three headings are listed. Also note the author's name isn't nested—that is, there are no dependencies on this heading.

- Due to the parent/child relationship of the bookmarks, if you deleted *The Features*, for example, the bookmarks set for the bullets would also be deleted.

Other Tools to Repurpose Documents

Two other tools figure prominently in creating repurposed documents. Links and forms buttons both help to direct your user's path through your documents.

Note

To move a bookmark, click the name to select it, and then drag it slowly to the left (promoting it to a higher level in the hierarchy). A black bar shows the location of the icon. When you release the mouse button, a confirmation dialog box will appear. Click OK to move the bookmark.

Tip

We love Acrobat 6.0, but have trouble with the Link tool's logic. In Acrobat 5.0, all you had to do was draw a box around where you wanted to create a link and then navigate to the location where you wanted the link to go. In Acrobat 6.0, you have to know where you're going before you draw the box, making for a more difficult workflow. If you forget the destination location, for example, you can't set the link but have to back out of the process and start over. If you're upgrading from Acrobat 5.0 to 6.0, keep this difference in mind.

The Link Tool

The Link tool (aka Hyperlink tool) is a major tool for the author to make a document work in different types of media. In the paper world, a URL can be in italics or even in color, but you cannot click on the link and have the designated web page open. In the electronic version, all you need is one click on a link and voilà, the web page appears.

In the upcoming project, you'll look at creating links in documents that make the user's experience with a document pleasant and easy.

The Forms Button

Tom's three-year old grandson is an expert on buttons. Auggie pushes every button he sees because pushing buttons cause an action. Buttons in PDF are no different. You can make form buttons do a wide variety of actions. In the following project you'll use buttons as part of the navigation processes.

In the first part of the chapter, we discussed how to repurpose documents for a specific use—mainly converting documents intended for the print world to the electronic world. A knowledgebase is an organized collection of information about a subject. Now we're going to look at simple ways to organize the information so that the user can both find what they need to know and make their way out of the woods.

Project Project 4-1: Creating a Navigation Strategy for the Knowledgebase

Acrobat offers links, bookmarks, and buttons to aid in navigating a document collection. These are your primary tools. They allow you to lead the user in and out of the knowledgebase. In this project, the knowledgebase is given a face. The completed project from this chapter is available in the Chapter 4 Projects folder.

What You Need
You need these files from the Chapter 4 folder:

- interface.pdf file

- 1999 Minutes captured.pdf

- Help.pdf

Start from the Interface Page

A knowledgebase needs an interface. Like other applications, you must have a central starting point for the user to see what the application contains, and how to proceed. There are three methods of navigating to material in your knowledgebase. With experience you'll develop a strategy of using the methods in combination based both on the material and your users.

Tom is an engineer and as such isn't known for his artistic design ability. His usual interface or navigation-page design method uses a PowerPoint slide in a table format. He adds a background and puts in a dash (-) as a placeholder for text. Tom's theory is "keep it simple." Donna is a graphic artist. Not only must the interface be functional, but it also must be pleasing to the eye. The final choice for the book is her design—not a PowerPoint slide in sight.

Adding Links to Page

Open the interface.pdf document. It's a one-page layout for the interface. The first step is to add text to the interface to use for linking.

1. Select Advanced Editing ➤ TouchUp Text tool. Figure 4-10 shows the Advanced Editing toolbar.

2. Click the document where you want to add the text using the TouchUp Text tool. The dialog box shown in Figure 4-10 opens.

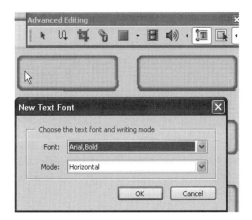

Tip

Tom always used Free Text (now Text Box) to put in the text for a link. This worked fine with Acrobat 5.0, but there was a problem with Acrobat Reader 5.0. Free Text is a comment. Comments are on a layer above the base. Links are also above the base layer. In Reader 5.0, the layers are flipped, so the text box was over the link box. You could only use the link where the link box was larger than the text box. Adobe fixed this in Reader 5.1, but you'll still have problems with people who haven't downloaded the latest reader. Moral of the tip—it's safer to insert text.

Figure 4-10
Click the document with the TouchUp Text tool and use the New Text Font dialog box to add additional text to a document.

3. The phrase *New Text* is added to the document at the point where you clicked. Type **Minutes** and then select the word, right-click to open the context menu, and choose Properties to open the Properties dialog box.

4. People view blue text as links, so you should select blue for Fill. Figure 4-11 gives you the choices for text.

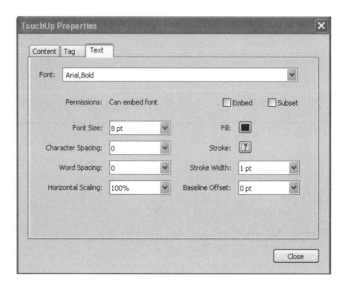

Figure 4-11
You can choose a full range of options to customize text you insert into a page.

5. Select the Link tool on the Advanced Editing toolbar.

Draw a link box around the *Minutes* text. Release the mouse, and the Create Link dialog box will open, as shown in Figure 4-12.

Figure 4-12
Use the Create Link dialog box to choose link action settings.

6. We're going to link to a new file. Click on Open a File and Browse to 1999 Minutes captured.pdf. Select the file and click Open in the Browse dialog.

7. The Browse dialog box closes and another dialog box named Specify Open Preference opens, as shown in Figure 4-13. Select Window Set By User Preference and click OK.

Figure 4-13
Once you choose a document to link to, you have to specify how the document is displayed.

8. The final step is to set the initial view for the document. Choose File ➤ Document Properties ➤ Initial View. Select Bookmarks Panel and Page as shown in Figure 4-14. Click OK to close the document properties. Save the document.

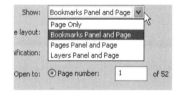

Figure 4-14
The choices for the page opening under initial view

Adding Bookmarks to a Captured Document

The 1999 Minutes captured.pdf file is an exact copy of the original scans with searchable text. There are no bookmarks. In this part of the project, you learn how to bookmark documents the fast way.

1. Go to page 1 dated January 5, 1999. Click the Select Text tool on the Basic toolbar.

2. Highlight January 5, 1999 with the Select Text tool, and then right-click and select Add Bookmark as shown in Figure 4-15. A bookmark titled *January 5, 1999* is created and linked to the current view. Because it's easier to see, we usually keep the view to Width, but many people prefer Full view. You'll need to make this choice based on your users.

3. Repeat with the first page for each meeting's minutes.

The set of minutes are now bookmarked. The process continues in the next section.

Tip
It's less disorienting to allow the user to use their regular settings. Some people prefer to work in the same window while others prefer each new document to open in a separate window.

Tip
A properly designed document for the e-world includes bookmarks that display when the document opens.

Making Our Way Out of the Forest

There are two different ways to return from lower levels of the knowledgebase to the start. The first is with bookmarks leading back to higher-level documents and the other is with Forms buttons. This section starts up where the last ended with the 1999 Minutes captured.pdf file captured and bookmarked.

Adding a Bookmark Home

1. Select Options from the Bookmarks menu and choose New Bookmark (Ctrl+B).

2. Drag the bookmark to below the first bookmark.

3. Drag the first bookmark below the second. The downward-pointing red arrowhead means it will be on the same level as the first. An angled red line and arrow shows it will nest under the bookmark.

4. Name the Bookmark. We usually use *Navigation*, but you can choose a term based on your situation. Use a word that everyone will understand.

5. Right-click the bookmark and choose Properties from the context menu. Figure 4-16 shows that we've selected blue and bold for the bookmark to make it stand out.

Figure 4-16
Select options for the return bookmarks that make them clearly visible.

6. Next set the destination for the bookmark. Click the Actions tab and select Go to a Page in Another Document as shown in Figure 4-17. Click Add.

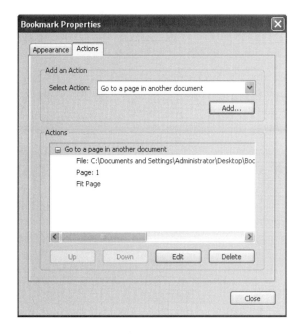

Figure 4-17
Set the action to go to another page to return to the interface.

7. A Go to a Page in Another Document dialog box opens as shown in Figure 4-18. Click Browse and select the interface page in the Target Document section. Click OK to close the dialog box and set the bookmark action.

8. Test the new bookmark trail.

9. Add return bookmarks from the remaining minutes pages.

In the last part of the project, add a button to use for navigation in the knowledgebase.

Figure 4-18
Set the action to return
to the original
interface page.

Adding a Button for Navigation

As part of your knowledgebase, you'll need to make directions. Here's how to make a button from the Click for Help text on the interface page. A link would work just as well, but this is a convenient place to learn how to use a button.

Buttons have several advantages for navigation. The primary one is you can create your graphics and navigation link at the same time. This example doesn't show this since the text is already there. Buttons can also be duplicated throughout the whole document. In large manuals, we often make a button linking to the table of contents and duplicate it throughout the manual. Buttons are another important tool in your trailblazing bag of tricks.

Tip

Buttons are covered in detail in Chapter 8 when you'll look at forms.

1. Select Tools ➤ Advanced Editing ➤ Forms ➤ Button tool. Draw a box around the Click for Help text. The Button Properties dialog box opens.

2. On the General tab, choose Visible but Doesn't Print in the Form Field drop-down menu (see Figure 4-19). You can leave the default name Button1.

3. On the Appearance tab, select no for Border Color and no for Fill Color (see Figure 4-20).

4. On the Options tab, in the Layout drop-down box, choose Label Only (see Figure 4-21). Leave the Label field blank since the page already contains text.

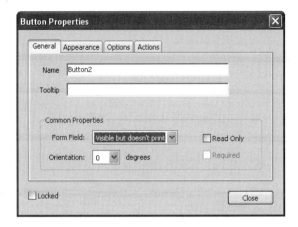

Figure 4-19
Choose options to make the Form Field visible.

Figure 4-20
The form field is technically visible, but uses no color.

Figure 4-21
Leave the Label Only option selected and don't add text to maintain invisibility.

5. On the Actions tab, select On Mouse Up from the list of Triggers. Choose Go to a Page in Another Document. Click add to open the Go to a Page in Another Document dialog box.

6. Click Browse and select the Help.pdf document in the Chapter 4 documents. You have options of Open In. We suggest the Window Set by User Preference. You also can put in a page number or select a destination.

7. Click OK to close the dialog box and set the button. Click the Hand tool on the Basic toolbar and test the button.

Up Next

In this chapter, you learned that a PDF document with a little enhancement is as good in the electronic world as the print world. You started with a game plan for planning and organizing workflow. As you saw at the very end of this chapter, this approach makes sense.

We've discussed in some detail bookmarks and tags, which are both key elements in using Acrobat intelligently. These two ideas will reappear in the next several chapters.

In the first four chapters, you learned how to create PDF documents from a wide variety of sources, including scanning and capturing documents. In Chapter 5 you're going to look at the Commenting tools and in Chapter 6 you're going to apply these tools to collaborating on documents.

Chapter 5

Commenting and Advanced Editing Tools

In the new task-oriented Acrobat world, tools are separated into Review & Commenting tools and Advanced Editing tools. In this chapter you'll work with the tools and look at the new functionality. There have been some exciting changes based on the input of interface experts and cranky old users alike.

Examining the Tools of the Trade

Comments in Acrobat are equivalent to the notes scribbled on margins and the doodles and arrows you see as a paper document makes the rounds. Comments can take a variety of forms, depending on a number of factors:

- Your mood

- The toolbars you have opened

- Your method of working and communicating

- Any corporate policies or procedures you may be bound to

In addition to attaching notes or comments to a document, you can include images or sound files. One interesting feature you'll be looking at in an upcoming chapter is the ability to import and export comments. As you'll see, this is a handy, space- and time-saving feature.

As listed in Table 2-1, Acrobat 6.0 groups the tools into Commenting, Advanced Commenting, and Review Functions. You'll look at the Commenting and Advanced Commenting tools here. The Review Functions are discussed in "Collaboration and Review Tracking" in Chapter 6.

Commenting Tools

There are several Commenting tools, including the Note tool (electronic sticky notes), Text Edit tools, Highlighting tools, and Stamp tools. Click the Review & Comment Task button, and open the Commenting toolbar, as shown in Figure 5-1. The Stamp tools have dynamically generated stamps with login name and date. Before we get into specifics, here are some general commenting concepts:

- Comments can be customized.

- Comments can be used to navigate through a document.

- Comments can be imported and exported.

Figure 5-1
A collection of different types of comments are grouped together on the Commenting toolbar

In other words, when it comes to workflow, comments are a good way to organize your work.

Adding a Note

In Figure 5-2, a simple text comment is added to a page. The color bar and the icon for the note are yellow. Adding a comment is like inserting any type of object. Select the Note tool and click the document page where you want to add the note. To deselect the Note tool, click the Hand tool (on the Basic toolbar), or select another tool or function.

Note
You can double-click a comment to open a Note box.

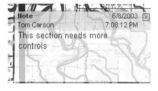

Figure 5-2
A simple text comment on a page. Note that the text box is semitransparent.

Comment properties can be modified at any time. Suppose you're in a lavender mood. Right-click the Text Comment icon (the dark overlay on the icon indicates that it's selected), and select Properties from the context menu. The Note Properties dialog box shown in Figure 5-3 opens. Change the color and opacity as desired. Click Close and your new color is ready for use.

Acrobat 6.0 has totally changed the philosophy behind the simple Note tool. The note takes the appearance of its intended comment function. If the comment is intended to be a key idea, the icon for the comment can become a key, like that shown in Figure 5-4.

Note
Your mood is set once. That means once you've specified a color scheme, all the insertion icons will change to the same color. Subsequent insertions will also be the same color, until you change the scheme again.

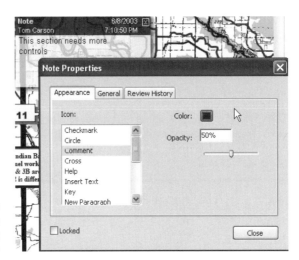

dem, of course, and

Figure 5-4
Using a key icon to
specify a note's purpose.

Vhen...

gave me a most wor

The opacity is also easier to set. Instead of having to reset the opacity in the Comments preferences, opacity is right there on the Properties dialog box. The author can also be reset under this section for computers with unusual login names like *administrator*.

Let's have a look at the other types of commenting that can be added. This discussion doesn't describe how to create and modify each of the types in depth, rather the discussion on notes can be applied to most of the other types as well, with a couple of exceptions. Remember that you can access any customizations by right-clicking and opening the context menu.

Using the Text Editing Tools

Editors love these new features. Text editing has numerous new features that import into Word XP and will apply the selected Text Edit commands. Figure 5-5 lists the options for text editing. You can use File ➤ Export Comments to Word or Document ➤ Export Comments to Word to export comments.

Text Editing tools are somewhat passive. You select the area or text first and then select the action.

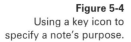

Tip

In the Real World, Would Custom Colors Ever Be Used?

Absolutely. There's more to this than a visual expression of mood! A good example: Suppose you're a member of a multidisciplinary project team. One way to coordinate processes is to color-coordinate the members. For example, database people may be coded yellow, programmers red, writers blue, program managers green, and so on.

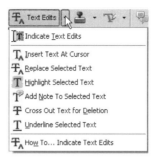

Figure 5-5
Use the Text Editing options to mark up a document for exporting comments.

Highlighting with Text Highlighting Tools

The three Text Highlighting tools are essentially the same as their counterparts under Text Edits. The highlighting tools are like your college teacher with a red pen. Select the tool then start the action.

After you've zapped a line of text with a Highlighting tool, you can add a note. Right-click the highlighted text and choose Properties to add a note to the comment. The Text Highlighting tools are described in Table 2-1 and shown in Figure 5-6. Also in the figure, you can see the Strikethrough tool in action and the highlighting of the *I* to show it requires caps.

Note

Highlighting tools work in an opposite fashion to the Text Edit tools. Select the tool first, and then select the text.

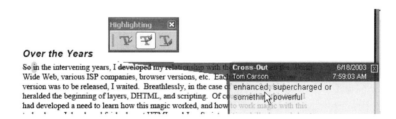

Figure 5-6
Text highlighting— just like in college

Which Tool to Choose?

Some of the tools on one toolbar look strangely like the same tool with the same name on another toolbar. For example, highlighting appears both on its own toolbar and on the Text Edit toolbar. If you want to point something out in a PDF document, use the Highlighting tool on the Highlighting toolbar. If you want the highlight exported to a source document created in Word XP, use the Highlight Selected Text on the Text Edit toolbar. The same differentiation applies to the Strikethrough and Underline tools.

Adding a Stamp

Remember the old days when nearly everyone had a stamp or two to use for various purposes? Some people had so many stamps they needed racks to hold them. Well, those days are back, in a digital way. Stamps are added like other comments. They come in quite an assortment; a common choice is shown in Figure 5-7. Adobe greatly reworked this functionality and made it a true business tool. A set of dynamic stamps have been added to the tools. Dynamic stamps imprint the login name of the user, time, and date on the stamp.

Figure 5-7
Dynamic stamps are a
powerful new business
feature in Acrobat 6.0.

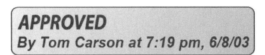

Creating and Managing Stamps

Before Acrobat 6.0, creating and managing stamps required knowledge and persistence. Donna spent five pages in the first edition of this book describing how to create and manage stamps—we're spending about a page showing how to do it in Acrobat 6.0. Figure 5-8 shows the Stamp tool menu. The bottom three menu choices simplify what required five pages in the last book.

Figure 5-8
The final three menu
items make it easy to
create and manage
groups of stamps.
Great Pointers and
Fancy Words are stamp
groups created from the
Acrobat 5.0 stamps.

You can create stamp categories and then add and name stamps. Stamps can be created from Adobe Illustrator (AI), Adobe Photoshop (PSD), JPEG, GIF, PDF, and bitmap files. In the first project for this chapter, you add a custom stamp to use for the knowledgebase.

Project

Project 5-1: Creating a Custom Stamp

Creating custom stamps is *much* easier in Acrobat 6.0. On the web site in the Chapter 5 projects folder, we've included two TIFF images used to create two stamps. The files are named tom.tif and db.tif. You're going to make custom stamps from the images.

Create the First Custom Stamp

Follow these steps to create the first custom stamp. Once the stamp is created, you add it to a custom stamp category.

1. Click the arrow next to the Stamp tool on the Commenting tool-bar to open a drop-down menu. Click Create Custom Stamp from the drop-down menu. The Create Stamp dialog box opens, as shown in Figure 5-9.

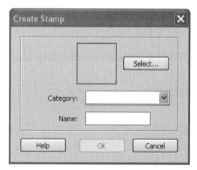

Figure 5-9
Create a custom stamp starting from the Create Stamp dialog box.

2. Click Select to open the Select dialog box, as shown in Figure 5-10.

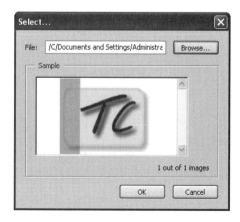

Figure 5-10
Locate the file you want to use for the stamp.

3. Click Browse. In the Browse dialog box, navigate to tom.tif and click Select.

4. The Browse dialog box closes and the image is displayed in the Sample window.

5. Click OK to close the Select dialog box and return to the Create Stamp dialog box.

6. In the Category field, type **Authors** as shown in Figure 5-11.

7. In the Name field, type **Tom**.

Figure 5-11
Name both a stamp
category and the
individual stamp.

8. Click OK to close the dialog box and save the new stamp.

Create the Second Custom Stamp

You've created Tom's stamp, now let's create Donna's. Some of the process is the same as for the first stamp; saving the second stamp is simpler. Follow these steps:

1. Click the arrow next to the Stamp tool on the Commenting toolbar to open a drop-down menu. Click Manage Stamps to open the Manage Stamps dialog box.

2. Click the arrow to open the Category drop-down list and select Authors.

3. Click Create. Repeat Steps 3 to 5 in the previous set of instructions. Select the db.tif file and name the stamp "Donna Baker". The new stamp is added to the Authors category as shown in Figure 5-12.

4. Click OK to close the Manage Stamps dialog box.

You added another custom stamp (see Figure 5-13).

Figure 5-12
Using the Manage Custom Stamps feature to add Donna's stamp.

Where Did the Pictures Go?

Adobe took the fun out of using stamps in Acrobat 6.0. They just didn't convey the business image of 6.0. Grumpy was a lot of fun. If you still have Acrobat 5 on a computer, find the fun stamps at \Program Files\Adobe\Acrobat 5.0\Acrobat 5.0\Acrobat\Plug_ins\Annotation\Stamps\ENU. The fun stamps are the Faces, like Grumpy in Figure 5-14, Pointers, and Words.

Tom was unable to figure an easy way to add them back into 6.0, but came up with a solution. Follow these steps:

1. Paste the stamps into this folder: \Program Files\Adobe\Acrobat 6.0\Acrobat 6.0\Acrobat\Plug_ins\Annotation\Stamps\ENU.

2. In Acrobat, click the Stamp tool's drop-down menu and choose Create New Stamps.

3. Name a new category, for example, *Words* becomes *Fancy Words.*

4. Add the stamps by name.

5. Close the Create Stamps dialog box.

It takes some time, but the stamps are a lot of fun. As you can see in Figure 5-14, it would take a lot of words to convey the meaning expressed in one simple image.

Figure 5-13
Add stamps from Acrobat 5.0 to Acrobat 6.0.

Figure 5-14
Grumpy—the face
says it all.

Advanced Commenting Tools

Acrobat 5.0 contained some drawing tools, which have been greatly enhanced in Acrobat 6.0. The tools now include the Text Box tools (formerly called the Free Text tool), an Attach tool, and both Pencil and Pencil Eraser tools.

Note

Adobe HIGHLY recommends AGAINST having two versions of Acrobat on the same machine unless the machine has a dual boot.

Adding a Text Box

The Text Box tool, formerly the Free Text tool, is a major change in Acrobat 6.0. Text boxes are similar to notes, except that a text box is always visible, as you can see in Figure 5-15. Text Boxes have a full range of text configuration options and are easy to edit. As a certified techie, Tom is ecstatic about the Super- and Subscript options. After drawing the box and inserting text you can double-click to open the Text Box Text Properties toolbar. You have choices of boxes, opacity, and color.

Tip

Ctrl+E also opens the Text Box Property toolbar depending on where you are in the process.

Figure 5-15
A free text comment. This type of comment remains visible.

Printing Text Boxes

Text boxes are a comment. Comments only print if Print Document and Comments is turned on in the Print dialog box. Tom forgot this when he published an eBook using a mixture of text and free text. Some recipients were not pleased with the results. One workaround is to flatten the text box to the base layer.

There are flattening options for layers and transparencies in Acrobat 6.0, but we've been unable to find any mention of flattening comments.

The ARTS Tools plug-in offers a flattening solution. For each page of comments you want flattened to the background, choose File ➤ Flatten Current Page. The comments are flattened to the background and will always print.

You can visit www.planetpdf.com and purchase the ARTS Tools. Figure 5-16 shows a view of the extra tools added to Acrobat by ARTS Tools. A few of the tools aren't needed in Acrobat 6.0 and we expect replacements will be made in the upgrade. If you talk to Tom's good buddy Sean down there in Australia tell him G'day!

Figure 5-16
Tools added to
Acrobat 6.0, available
by purchasing the ARTS
Tools plug-in from
www.planetpdf.com.

Using the Attach Toolbar

The Attach toolbar is a subtoolbar of the Advanced Comments toolbar. To open it, choose Tools ➤ Advanced Commenting ➤ Attach ➤ Show Attach Toolbar. You can use three different types of attachments—a file, sound, or the contents of the clipboard.

Attaching a File

The File Attachment tool enables you to embed a file at a specific location in a document. An attached file is managed as part of the main document. For example, if you're creating a general business document, you can attach spreadsheets in areas of the document referencing specific data. A symbol appears on the document as shown in Figure 5-17; the document name serves as a description for the comment. If you email the main document, the embedded files are attached to it and emailed as well.

Click the Attach File tool on the toolbar, and then click the location on the page you want to display the icon. A Browse dialog box opens. Locate the file you want to attach and click Attach.

am requestın

'?).

Acrobat Family tiff.pdf

Figure 5-17
Embed documents into
other documents using
the Attach tool.

The File Attachment Properties dialog box opens. You can set the appearance of the Attach File icon as shown in Figure 5-18. Choose an optional icon that represents the type of file attached. Click Close to close the File Attachment Properties dialog box.

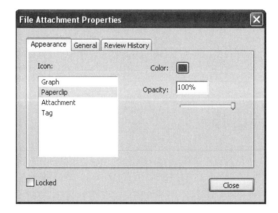

Figure 5-18
The File Attachment
Properties dialog box is
used to configure an
external file attachment.

Tip

**Using External
File Icons**

When developing a communication system within a workgroup, you may want to use the icons on a regular basis for specific types of attachments. Just as comment colors may be assigned, so may the attached file icons. For example, my comments and attached files may be colored red, and other members of my group can use other colors.

You can modify a file attachment. Simply right-click on the icon to open the context menu. Select Properties (or type **p**) to open the File Attachment Properties dialog box. Set the appearance options and click Close.

Attaching Sound

The ability to record a sound file into a PDF file is still somewhat of a novelty to most people. From experiments Tom ran with Acrobat 5.0, a one-minute recording was about 1 MB in size. The experiment was repeated with Acrobat 6.0 and a one-minute recording was only 292 KB. You can record sound directly or attach a sound file. Click the Sound tool on the Attach toolbar; click the document to open the Sound Recorder, shown in Figure 5-19.

Figure 5-19
Use the Sound Attachment tool to record or attach a sound file.

To record and attach a sound, follow these steps:

1. Click the red Record button. (The black Play arrow changes to a black square indicating that recording is active.)

2. Record your attachment.

3. Click the black Stop icon to stop recording. Click OK when finished.

4. The Sound Attachment Properties dialog box opens. Choose an optional icon for the sound attachment. You can use an Ear, Speaker, or Microphone icon. Choose the icon and click OK to close the dialog box.

5. Double-click the icon on the page and listen to how bad your Southern drawl sounds (where applicable). Donna's British-Canadian accent sounds really interesting.

To attach a sound from a file, follow these steps:

1. Click Browse on the Sound Recorder dialog box. In the Browse dialog box, locate the file you want to use and click Attach. The dialog box closes.

2. Click OK in the Sound Recorder dialog box. The dialog box closes and the Sound Attachment Properties dialog box opens.

3. Select an icon for the attachment and click OK. The dialog box closes and the sound file is attached to the page.

Tip

Scroll your mouse over the icon on the document to display the file size.

Note

In a test, we attached a 42 KB QuickTime sound file to the document. The resulting file was 24 KB.

Novel Today, Commonplace Tomorrow

A few physicians that have seen the Sound Attach tool in action aren't so sure about the novelty. Tom is working with one hospital to convert their files into PDF; the long-term plan is to have the patients' files in PDF. The staff will access the files using wireless tablets. The present-day paper forms will be replaced by PDF forms attached to databases. The medical staff will dictate their notes directly into the PDF documents.

Attaching a Clipboard Image

Attaching a clipboard image is a solution to many problems. It was difficult to place an image in Acrobat 5.0. You could use an image as an icon on a Form button or pasted as an object. The icon could be sized within Acrobat, but the object had to be sized externally to the program.

Now it's simple. You just copy the image to the clipboard, click on the Attach Clipboard tool and draw a box on the page where you want the new content.

Follow these steps:

1. Select the Snapshot tool on the Basic toolbar.

2. Click the image or drag a marquee around the image you want to copy to the clipboard. When you release the mouse, an Information dialog box states that you've copied the content to the clipboard.

3. Select Paste Clipboard Image tool on the Attach toolbar (see Figure 5-20).

Figure 5-20
The Paste Clipboard Image tool is a powerful addition to Acrobat 6.0 that replaces inferior workarounds. Both images to create this illustration were clipboard images pasted into a PDF with the tool.

4. Drag a marquee box where you want the clipboard image to be placed. Release the mouse and the clipboard content is pasted.

5. Click on the image to select it, and adjust the image box to the size you desire.

Adding Graphic Comments

Some people simply can't communicate with words. Science and technology people communicate with lines, boxes, and circles every day. Acrobat 6.0 has greatly expanded the tools available for drawing.

Polygons, polygon lines, clouds, arrows, and so on enhance the ability to communicate. Figure 5-21 is a drawing done with Acrobat's drawing tools. The tools aren't meant to replace CAD files, but with grids and snap, you can do some good basic drawings. Being an engineer, Tom loves the Super- and Subscript options in the Text Box Text Properties toolbar.

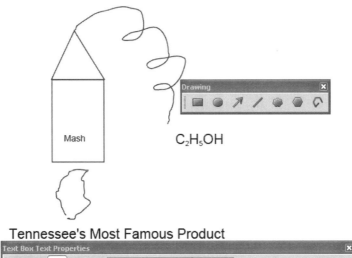

Mash

C_2H_5OH

Tennessee's Most Famous Product

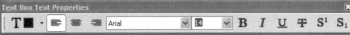

Note

Acrobat 6.0 Standard doesn't have the Cloud tools, and arrows are a little more difficult to draw.

Figure 5-21
A drawing done with the Drawing tools and the new Text tools, including subscripts

The Comments Pane

Comments are stored in the Comments panel. Unlike the panels that are arranged as tabs down the left side of the interface, comments are listed horizontally at the bottom of the page, as shown in Figure 5-22.

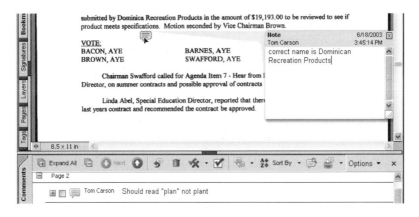

Figure 5-22
Comments display in the Comments List arranged horizontally under the document pane.

Here's how comments behave:

- Click a comment in the list. The page on which the selected comment is located appears in the document pane, and the highlighted comment scrolls into view.

- Navigate between comments by clicking another one in the Comments panel.

- Click a sound comment. It will play to the end and stop automatically.

- Launch attached files by double-clicking the file attachment; the method for closing the file depends on the file format and program used to create the file.

Project **Project 5.2: Attaching Comments to Knowledgebase Components**

Note

You'll catalog the minutes in a later chapter to make them easy to search.

In Chapter 3 you captured one year of minutes of the Dayton Tennessee School Board. You history buffs will remember this for the famous Scopes Monkey trial in 1925, the basis for the movie *Inherit the Wind*. By the way, the minutes used in the project are not the minutes from 1925.

Minutes of a government body are public record and are not to be changed. In the knowledgebase project you're using Paper Capture to capture the minutes in Searchable Image (Exact) format.

Occasionally you may want to put notes or other comments on these documents for future researchers. As we've said several times, comments are on a layer above the document, and do not print unless you choose Print Document and Comments in the Print dialog box. Therefore, you can add comments to the documents without changing the documents.

No matter how thoroughly minutes are proofed, there will often be a few typos. Figure 5-23 shows the commenting on typos and the Comments list at the bottom.

This isn't a structured step-by-step project. Instead, download and open the 1999 Minutes with comments.pdf file in the Chapter 5 project folder on the book's web site. Add more comments using a variety of Comment tools.

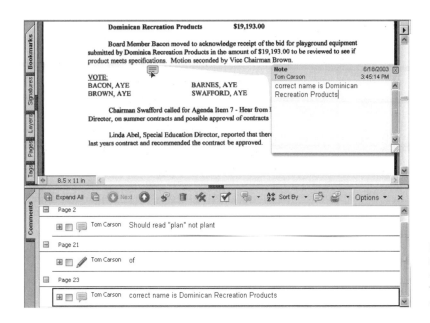

Figure 5-23
Click a comment on the
Comments list to display
the comment on the
document pane.

The Advanced Editing Tools

Acrobat 6.0 has a set of Advanced Editing tools. To open the toolbar,
click the Advanced Editing Taskbar button and select Advanced Editing
Toolbar. You can also open the tools by choosing Tools ➤ Advanced
Editing ➤ Show Advanced Editing Toolbar.

Table 5-1 lists the eight editing tools and their primary functions. As you
can see, these tools are used for quite a range of functions. Some of the
tools are prominent players in other chapters, so we'll simply give you
an overview of them now. If a function figures prominently in another
chapter, we've referenced that chapter in the table.

Table 5-1   The Advanced Editing Tools

Icon	Name	Function
	Object Select tool	Selects all objects of the same type in the document
	Article tool	Lets you create linked rectangles to connect sections of a document and control its flow (see Chapter 10)
	Crop tool	Crops the margins of a page
	Link tool	Inserts a link into a document (see Chapter 4)

Table 5-1   The Advanced Editing Tools (Continued)

Icon	Name	Function
▣	Form tool	Inserts form elements into a page (see Chapter 8)
▤	Movie tool	Inserts a movie into a document (see Chapter 12)
◀»	Sound tool	Slightly different variation of sound tool described in previous section
〖T	TouchUp Text tool	Allows you to make minor changes to a document's text
▣	TouchUp Object tool	Allows you to export, alter, and import graphics from Acrobat

In this chapter, you'll work with the two TouchUp tools and the Crop tool as you continue with the project. Let's start with the TouchUp tools.

Project Project 5-3: Correcting Minor Errors Using the TouchUp and Crop Tools

Note

The Chapter 5 Projects folder contains a copy of the "clean" interface named interface.pdf. This is the original PDF created without errors.

In this project, you'll learn how to modify the interface file used for the project's knowledgebase. Use the interface_bkgd.pdf file located in the Chapter 5 Projects folder. Open the file and follow along.

The original interface is shown in Figure 5-24. Donna is a perfectionist and Tom had to plead with her to make some simple errors for you to correct in Acrobat—a text error, a graphics error, and an inappropriate layout on the page. Coincidentally, these are the touch-ups we want to discuss. First, let's look at the text error and how to correct it.

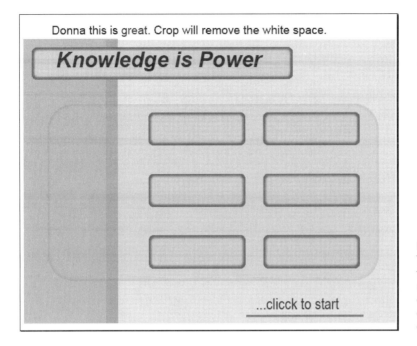

Figure 5-24
The document before touch-ups are done. The note isn't part of the original file, but an added comment used in the development process.

Touching Up Text in Acrobat

The most important thing to remember is that you can make changes in either the program you created the original document in or in the Acrobat PDF version. If you're making minor changes, use the tools. If, on the other hand, the changes required in a document are substantial, it's more practical to return to the source program. Acrobat 6.0 has improved the TouchUp Text tool as well; you can edit a paragraph at a time instead of a line at a time.

As you can see in Figure 5-24, the text contains a typo: "cclick". Here's how to correct the error using the TouchUp Text tool:

1. Click the TouchUp Text tool on the Advanced Editing toolbar to activate it.

2. Click the row of text to select it. A blue box (shown in Figure 5-25) surrounds the line.

Figure 5-25
The selected row of text is identified.

3. A cursor appears in the line. Click to position the cursor at the correct position in the line. Delete the extra letter.

4. Click the Hand tool on the Basic Tools toolbar to deselect the text line.

You can also make changes to text attributes for the line. If you right-click the selected text line and select Properties from the context menu, the palette shown in Figure 5-26 opens. The settings in the dialog box are especially helpful if the fonts used in the document aren't embedded.

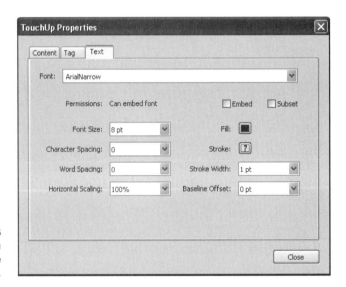

Figure 5-26
Text properties you can alter using the TouchUp Text tool.

Other text touch-ups you can do in Acrobat include the following:

Note
You have to assign an image editor in Acrobat 6.0. Select Edit ➤ Preferences ➤ General ➤ TouchUp. In the resulting dialog box, click Choose Image Editor and browse to the location of your preferred application. Click OK to select it. You can also set a preference for a page-editing application in the same way by clicking Choose Page/Object Editor.

- Create a new line of text in a document by using Ctrl+click (Option+click on a Mac).

- Remove or add embedding from a font by clicking the Embed check box on the Text Properties palette.

- Touch up rotated text (the baseline shift will be left and right instead of up and down as for horizontal fonts).

Now let's have a look at the TouchUp Object tool.

Touching Up Graphics in Acrobat 6.0

Acrobat has limited object-editing capabilities. What you can do though is access the original authoring application directly from Acrobat. You can use this technique with line art and images.

The project's Interface page contains a layout error: There is a line under "click to start".

Here's how to correct the problem using the TouchUp Object tool. Follow these steps to correct a graphic error:

1. Click the TouchUp Object tool on the Advanced Editing toolbar. The entire object is selected.

2. Click the Select Object Tool on the Advanced Editing toolbar and click the line element to select it. A bounding box will appear around the object (as shown in Figure 5-27).

3. Press Delete to remove the line.

Tip

The line isn't really an error; Tom just doesn't like it.

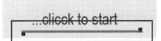

Figure 5-27
The line selected with the Object Select tool.

Now let's move on to page layouts and cropping.

Cropping a Page in Acrobat

The Crop tool is a handy feature. If you look back at Figure 5-24, you can see that the layout of the page is uneven, with margins different on all sides and too much extra space around the page. You can't see the extra space clearly in the book so we added a text box at the top of the page to use for demonstration.

Follow these steps to crop the page correctly:

1. Select the Crop tool from the Editing toolbar. Click and drag a cropping rectangle on the page.

2. Double-click inside the rectangle to open the Crop Pages dialog box, as shown in Figure 5-28.

3. Set required margins by entering a value in the margin's box or using the arrows. The location of the margins is shown on the thumbnail. Other options are available as well:

   • Click Set to Zero to restore margins to 0; click Revert to Selection to return to the values of the original cropping rectangle; or enable the Remove White Margins option to trim the page to content.

   • Select page ranges as required. The demo document has only one page.

Note

The cropping rectangle includes resizing handles along the edges you can use for resizing visually.

Note

You can crop pages in Single Page layout. Select View ➤ Single Page to display the document in single-page layout, or click the single page icon on the status bar at the bottom of the page.

Note

The Crop function in Acrobat is a hidden problem for engineers and others who use large-sized images. If you crop a large color map with the Crop tool, there's no effect on the file size as the entire map is still in the document. To crop permanently, open the content in another program, such as Photoshop.

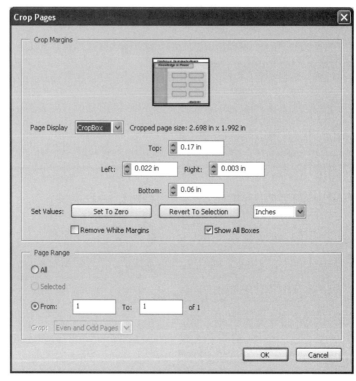

Figure 5-28
Use the Crop Pages dialog box for precise settings or multiple pages.

4. Click OK to set the new margins.

5. Save the interface.

Cropping isn't absolute in Acrobat. As you can see in Figure 5-29 the text box is still there after cropping and saving. You can reopen the crop box and reset the crop margins to zero and the white space returns.

Figure 5-29
Illustrates a cropped file but still shows the original area. The Crop function in Acrobat doesn't delete content, it only hides it.

Donna this is great. Crop will remove the white space.

Up Next

The idea behind this chapter was to describe how commenting and advanced editing are performed on an Acrobat document. Along the way we demonstrated the editing tools and briefly discussed reusing materials.

In the next chapter you'll put the Commenting tools together with the new Review Tracking features in Acrobat 6.0. You'll investigate the advantages of web and email review. You'll also review the new Comment Exporting to Word XP feature. In other words, we'll show you how Acrobat puts a dent in overnight delivery.

Tip

What About Other Objects?

You can select anything on a page with the TouchUp Object tool. That doesn't mean it will do you much good. If you select a word or title and then right-click and choose Edit Object from the context menu, a temporary file consisting of many pages of code and symbols opens. So how is this a tip? If you aren't familiar with a document and you're trying to evaluate the amount of work you have to do, you can try this technique on something that may be either text or an image. Making small corrections to text is much faster than modifying embedded images.

Chapter 6

Collaboration

"Mr. Bright, it has come to my attention from Mr. Sly that your recent progress report was highly creative. When we hired you, we relaxed our dress code because of your creative reputation but we will not relax our standards for reporting. Creative accounting like 76 percent reduction in overnight delivery, while increasing output by 26 percent in a department that lives on collaboration among multiple offices is unacceptable. What do you have to say for yourself?"

It's amazing to us that such improvement in a department should not be meritorious. Mr. Bright initiated electronic review and collaboration on documents. He reduced turnaround time by eliminating overnight delivery and the manpower to manually sort the comments. He did this with Adobe Acrobat 6.0. Maybe if the noose was removed from Mr. Sly's neck, sufficient oxygen might go to his head and he could be creative too.

That's Collaboration with a Capital "C"

Acrobat 6.0 adds a whole new meaning to what we call collaboration. In the past Acrobat had somewhat informal features for collaboration, but they weren't intuitive. They're formalized in Acrobat 6.0 and have Review Tracking subprograms to make it a powerful collaboration tool.

Our goal in writing this book is to explain to you how to use Acrobat and ways we have used it over the years that have saved both time and money. We'll show you how to use the Review Tracker using both email and web delivery. We'll further apply the Review & Commenting tools to work smarter.

Coming Up

In Chapter 1, we introduced the idea of network publishing. Here, in this chapter, we want to show you some of the processes that are tailor-made for networks. In this chapter, we'll discuss a number of topics:

- Review Tracking

- Using Acrobat with networks

- Setting up and using network folders

- Using online commenting

Just a note before we start. Some of these topics are a bit more technical than others, for good reason: The information is sophisticated. We're doing it for a particular purpose, however. If you're a designer, it isn't necessary to also be a network administrator. That isn't our goal. But we think it's important to have an understanding of why and how the environment works the way it does to be a *great* designer of any type. The more general understanding you have of what your IT colleagues do, the better you're able to design within that system and convey advanced requirements of your software to others. Also, because you work with a specific goal in mind, knowing what is possible is a great advantage in communicating your requirements to others.

Knowledge is power, after all! So here comes a heaping spoonful of power.

Review Tracking in Acrobat 6.0

Reviewing documents and sharing them with a group isn't new. In Acrobat 5.0, you could comment and share, but it was primarily a manual process. In Acrobat 6.0, most of the process is automated.

Sending Email for Review

The ability to conduct email reviews was available in Acrobat 5.0 but was only used by the most advanced Acrobat users. With Acrobat 5.0, you emailed the file to a list of reviewers. They reviewed the documents. The comments were exported from the file using the File ➤ Export ➤ Comments command. The comments used the forms data format (FDF) extension. You had to open the email program and manually attach the FDF file. The receiver had to save the attachment and open the desired PDF. The FDF files were added by using the File ➤ Import ➤ Comments command. It's easy to see why it wasn't used.

Tip

You can also open the same dialog box from Acrobat by choosing Review & Comment ➤ Send by Email for Review or File ➤ Send by Email for Review.

Acrobat 6.0 makes email-based commenting an easy task. If you're in a program with a PDFMaker macro, click the Email Review icon.

The Send by Email for Review dialog box seen in Figure 6-1 opens. Enter the email address for the recipient, and click OK.

If you haven't set up your Email Identity under Edit ➤ Preferences ➤ General ➤ Identity, you'll be asked to enter your email address. The dialog box has places for email addresses of the reviewers and instructions for the reviewers. Unlike the email process under Acrobat 5.0, the process in Acrobat 6.0 is automated. If your email system doesn't allow you to send email automatically due to security reasons a warning message shown in Figure 6-2 will appear.

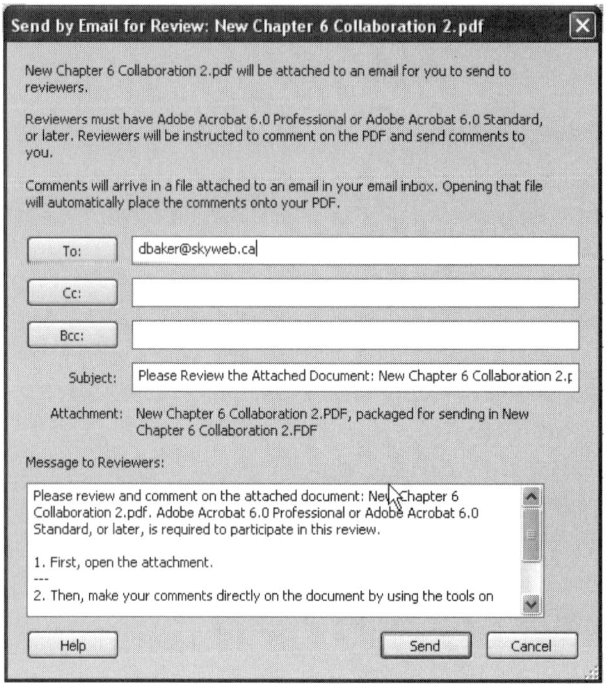

Figure 6-1
The Send by Email
for Review dialog box
opens when you
initiate a review cycle.

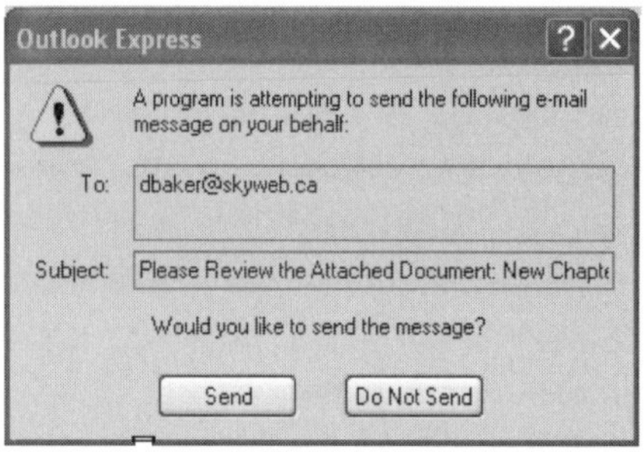

Figure 6-2
A warning message
appears on email systems
that don't allow email to
be sent automatically.

Sending the email automatically starts Review Tracking for the document.

Receiving Email for Review

The Review Tracker generates an .fdf file extension on the PDF sent for review. The FDF contains the data and computer instructions for the review process. The message sent to the recipient contains information about the document as well as instructions for working in the review cycle as shown in Figure 6-3.

Please review and comment on the attached document: STC_workshop_dbaker.pdf. Adobe Acrobat 6.0 Professional or Adobe Acrobat 6.0 Standard, or later, is required to participate in this review.

1. First, open the attachment.

---

2. Then, make your comments directly on the document by using the tools on the Commenting toolbar.

---

3. After you have finished making your comments, click the "Send Comments" button on the Commenting toolbar to email your comments to me.

Figure 6-3
The recipient receives instructions as well as the review document.

The attachment is a PDF wrapped in an FDF. When you open the file, it's still an FDF. Figure 6.4 displays the warning that the file is still temporary and urges you to save it. When saved, the file becomes a PDF with the FDF instructions attached. Remember that exported comments are FDF files.

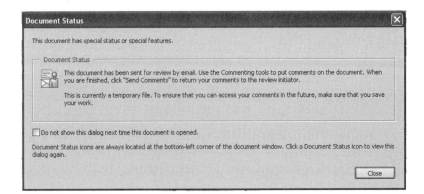

Figure 6-4
The document used by the recipient has special Document Status properties.

A Send Comments icon appears in the taskbar each time a file in the review process is opened.

Each time you open a PDF file received in a review process a Document Status dialog box similar to Figure 6-4 opens explaining the status. The process couldn't be simpler. Even if the reviewer is totally untrained in Acrobat, the Help menu for commenting opens with the file.

If the reviewer determines that more people need to be added to the email-based review, the person who initiated the review process should add the new names. The reviewer uses all the Commenting and Advanced Commenting tools at their disposal to make the comments. When finished, they click the Send Comments icon and the process is automatic.

Note

Only the comments are sent back—not the whole file.

Note

If you filter comments before sending them, all the comments may not be sent. We'll look at filtering comments a bit later in the chapter.

In Chapter 5 and earlier in this chapter we said that comments are on a layer above the PDF. Unless the comments are flattened with a tool like ARTS Tools Flattener, comments don't change the PDF file. The Send Comments command takes the FDF information that came with the file and adds the comments. The original FDF information contains the directions on how to automatically send the comments, and once received by the initiator, it says how to automatically add them to the original document.

Even if the reviewer wakes up in the middle of the night and wants to add more to the document, she can add more comments and send them. The Review Tracker handles the duplicates.

Tracking the Review Process

The Review Tracking process is a major reason the business world will adopt Acrobat 6.0. The first time Tom told his customers about this feature in Acrobat 6.0, one customer purchased 30 licenses, sight unseen.

The customer, the building permit department of a midsized city, reviews approximately 100 sets of building plans per month. Contractors, engineers, and architects are required to send 6 sets of plans and specs for review. The coordinator determines all the necessary reviewers and sometimes may need to make even more sets. The plans are delivered to the reviewers and are manually tracked. The city is legally required to maintain copies for at least 50 years or until the destruction of the building. Some plans must be kept in perpetuity.

Enter Acrobat 6.0 and Review Tracking. Many engineers and architects already have Acrobat and are using it to share drawings with clients without CAD. A set of plans and drawings costs around $100 to produce. In the example described here, if the submitter could submit electronically, he would save more than the cost of a copy of Acrobat 6.0 on each project. The city would save untold amounts of money in reproduction, storage, and review if the plans and specifications were submitted, stored, and reviewed electronically.

The Review Tracking process can be accessed by choosing either Review & Comment ➤ Track Reviews or View ➤ Review Tracker. When you institute an email or browser-based review the Review Tracker starts working. Figure 6-5 shows an open review case in the Review Tracker.

When you click on a file, the Review Tracking status is shown in the bottom panel.

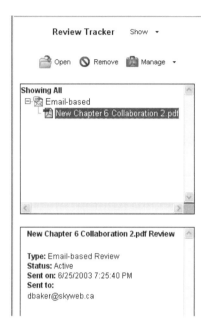

Figure 6-5
The Review Tracker panel allows instant status review of documents in the process.

The initiator can manage the process by emailing different groups of reviewers to remind them of the review cycle, or she can invite more to an email-based review. The Manage menu is grayed out for the recipient. If the recipients want to add more people to the review process, they must email the initiator and have her add more recipients to the review process. Figure 6-6 shows the Manage menu options. Again you must remember that the initiator is the only one to add reviewers to an email review.

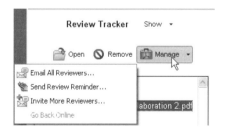

Figure 6-6
The Manage commands allow the initiator to manage an email-based review.

A coordinator of numerous reviews would soon have a Review Tracker panel that would be unmanageable. The Show menu under Review Tracker in Figure 6-7 allows the initiator to filter the files displayed.

Figure 6-7
The Show menu allows the initiator to filter files in the Review Tracker panel to manage numerous projects under review.

The initiator in an email review can respond to any comment by simply clicking the comment and clicking the email reply comment as shown in Figure 6-8. The comment is typed in the box that opens and is emailed to the appropriate person.

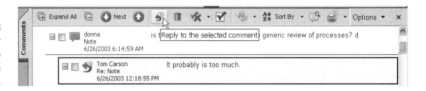

Figure 6-8
The Review Tracker makes it very easy to reply by email to a specific comment.

Filtering Comments (Plus a Bonus: Working with Acrobat 5.0 in a Tracked Review)

You were introduced to Mr. Sly at the start of this chapter. Due to his oxygen deficiency caused by the noose around his neck, Mr. Sly's comments aren't worth reading, but they're still cluttering up everything. Even though you aren't going to use his comments, he has to be given the opportunity to speak due to office politics. You know that Mr. Sly isn't going to authorize the purchase of Acrobat 6.0. Here is how you work with Mr. Sly.

1. Save the PDF document you receive in the Tracked Review email to your hard drive.

2. Manually attach the PDF file to the email being sent to Mr. Sly.

3. Mr. Sly receives the email and makes his comments as shown in Figure 6-9.

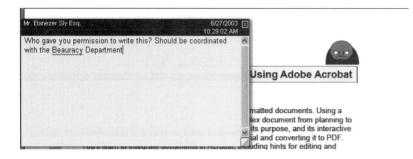

Figure 6-9
Mr. Sly usually generates pretentious, obnoxious, and meaningless comments. As you see he can't even spell his own department's name.

4. Mr. Sly manually attaches the document to an email to return to you. He uses this chance to tell you of his self-worth.

5. You open the attachment, which is the whole PDF file, and Acrobat 6.0 gives you the choices listed in Figure 6-10.

Tip

This tip is rather tongue in cheek—if problems ever come up from the initiator not receiving the comments, blame it on Mr. Sly not having Acrobat 6.0.

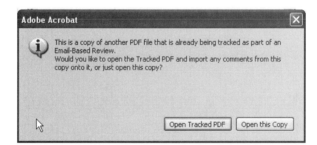

Figure 6-10
Acrobat 6.0 allows you to reenter a tracked document into the review process even though the comments come from a machine using Acrobat 5.0.

6. You click Open Tracked PDF. Mr. Sly's Comments are now littering the document as shown earlier in Figure 6.9.

7. Click the Comments Tab and click Show ➤ Show by Reviewer. Select everyone but Mr. Ebinezer Sly Esq. You'll notice two Mr. Ebinezer Sly Esq. entries in Figure 6-11.

Once Mr. Sly is deselected you have the nicely reviewed file shown in Figure 6-12. Remember what we said earlier about Send Comments with some filtered. Click Send Comments and the comments are returned to the initiator.

Note

Donna wasn't about to change her login name, so she changed the author under each individual comment in Comment Properties. If you see this in a workflow, someone is trying to cheat and you've caught them.

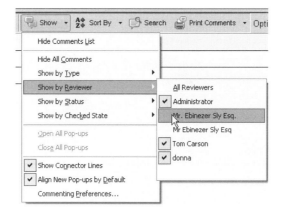

Figure 6-11
Deselecting (Filtering)
Mr. Ebinezer Sly Esq.
from visible comments
is an effective way of
limiting the screen clutter.

Figure 6-12
You can create a
neatly commented
document received by
the initiator with Mr. Sly's
ranting removed.

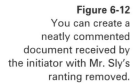

Creating Multipurpose Documents Using Adobe Acrobat

Description of Workshop:

Adobe Acrobat is a widely used tool for sharing formatted documents. Using a sample project, you'll learn how to develop a complex document from planning to production. You'll learn how to plan the document, its purpose, and its interactive options. You'll learn tips for choosing source material and converting it to PDF. You'll learn to integrate documents in Acrobat, including hints for editing and modifying content in your PDF document. You'll learn how to create a user path through your document, and how to add the elements that provide interactivity. You'll see how to create a multi-purpose document that can be used on screen.

Network and Online Reviews

This is the area where most of you must become diplomats and work with the foreign power known as Information Technology (IT) or Information Services (IS) or Information Management Services (IMS). Even though many may feel that IS departments are power-hungry robots, they control your success. They control the access to the servers that makes web-based review and collaboration possible. Most IS people are actually nice. Working with computers all day may deprive them of people skills. Remember that they catch the most grief when the system goes down or is compromised. To them, your web-based commenting is just another unknown that may cause them more problems. Try to grant them partial ownership and give them part of the credit for the success. As Grandma Carson used to say, "Sugar catches more flies than vinegar."

We mentioned in previous chapters of this book that online commenting can be used by multiple users. Commenting is the essence of collaboration—reviews can take place either online, in real time, or offline, with the comments uploaded to a server storage location for use by others. The latter process uses a storage process of some type.

If you recall from Chapter 5 when we introduced commenting, and later in Chapter 5 when we looked at commenting from a security perspective, the original document isn't altered by users as they're commenting. The comments for a group of users can be saved in a different location and appended to the original document. In Acrobat, this external location, called a *repository*, can be a database, a network folder, or a web folder.

Although Acrobat can be used with four repository types, we'll discuss only one in detail and give you briefer information on the other types. The available repository types are as follows:

- Network folder

- Database

- Web Distributed Authoring and Versioning (WebDAV)

- Web discussions

Regardless of which system you're working within, there are common functions. Because online commenting is one of the most common types of collaboration over networks, let's look at these commonalities from that perspective. We'll examine identification, security, and data structures first. We'll also add a sprinkling of tips.

Acrobat 6.0 uses online commenting and browser-based review. Online commenting is essentially the same as in Acrobat 5.0. Online commenting has no Review Tracking abilities and requires the participants to be more knowledgeable about computers and networks. We'll discuss both methods.

Initiating a Browser-based Review (Windows Only)

This powerful new feature is, regrettably, available only in Windows and only to users of Acrobat 6.0 Standard and Professional. Mac users will have to use the email-based review or set up for online commenting like in Acrobat 5.0. The Review Tracker isn't available for nonbrowser-based review.

There are at least two ways to start the browser-based review. Click Review & Comment ➤ Upload for Browser-based Review or File ➤ Upload for Browser-based Review. If the PDF file is already uploaded to a server, open the file in the browser and choose Review & Comment ➤ Invite Others to Review This Document.

If you haven't set preferences you'll receive a friendly tip like the one shown in Figure 6-13.

Note

Browser-based reviews are a Windows-only function. To participate in a browser-based review the reviewer must use Acrobat 6.0 Standard or Professional in Windows. Acrobat 5.0 users cannot participate, because of limited reviewing capabilities.

Tip

Determining where to place the repository isn't to be taken lightly. Will it be inside or outside the firewall? Will all the participants be able to access the file? These are issues that you need to explore thoroughly with your IT department. A false start with browser-based review can do permanent damage to implementation and your reputation.

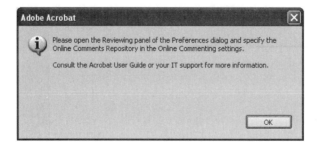

Figure 6-13
This informational warning appears for those who haven't set up Comments Repository preferences.

Remember what we said about the importance of IT people; even Adobe suggests that you see IT for support. If you're on a network of any size, you'll need help unless you are the administrator. To set up the preferences, go to Edit ➤ Preferences ➤ General ➤ Reviewing. Figure 6-14 shows the selection of the storage site and the type of storage sites supported.

Figure 6-14
The drop-down list has been moved to show the place for the server settings or the address to where the comments are stored.

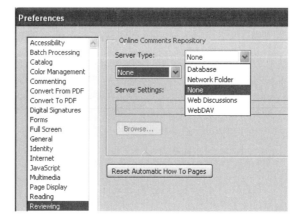

When you initiate a browser-based review, you automatically send an FDF file to the reviewers by email. Opening the FDF automatically opens the browser, configures the review process, and opens the PDF file ready for review. This removes much of the system knowledge requirements of the reviewers.

The reviewer has the option of commenting in real time online. By using the upload or download icons, the progress of the review can be seen by all reviewers. Reviewers can comment on the comments of other commentators but cannot delete the comments of fellow reviewers. The reviewers can save the PDF to their computer, comment outside the browser, and once it's complete, can open the file in the browser and send the comments back as an FDF.

The browser-based review adds another dimension to the review process. The recipients are now empowered to add people to the review process. This will open a new dimension in computer manners. Do you add people based on your ideas or do you ask for permission from the initiator?

Online Review and Commenting for the Rest

Browser-based review works only for users of Acrobat 6.0 Standard and Professional using Windows. What about the rest of the Acrobat world, those that use Macs or have a mixed workflow with Acrobat 5.0 and 6.0? Online commenting is still possible, but it puts a higher burden of knowledge on the users.

Network Folders

A network folder repository is the simplest to set up. Material is saved to a network volume or hard drive instead of to a web server or database. Users open and comment on a document. Acrobat then creates a version of the document and saves each user's comments as a separate FDF file.

Following our earlier discussion, in order for this to work, the server must have a network folder to store comments that is accessible and allows write-access to users, and it must allow access to the location the document is stored in.

Web Discussions

You can set up a different type of commenting system using Microsoft Web Discussions. This system is similar to a threaded discussion. Users can both create topics and reply to others.

In order to use this system, the server must have Microsoft Office Server Extensions installed. All users must have access to the server being used as the discussion server.

Database Repository

The database repository is the enterprise-strength solution for online activity. Users communicate directly with an SQL database using a new technology called Acrobat Database Connectivity (ADBC). This is similar to Open Database Connectivity (ODBC), and it allows Acrobat JavaScript access to an SQL database.

Note

A thorough search of the Adobe information in the Acrobat 6.0 *Help Manual* and the 415-page *Adobe Acrobat 6.0 Professional Help* (on the CD) sheds no light on methods other than Browser-based Review and Email-based Review. This leaves you on your own. You'll find information on the Acrobat 5 installation disk. Look for Collaboration ➤ Online Comments.

Web Distributed Authoring and Versioning

Finally, you have the WebDAV option. WebDAV is a protocol that allows for remote collaborative authoring of web resources. WebDAV can use a Microsoft FrontPage Extended Server or an FTP server to serve comments as long as the users are running Windows 2000. This system can also be used with Apache servers or Internet Information Server (IIS) 5.

Up Next

Networked workplaces are pervasive. In this chapter, we've shown you the neat new features of Acrobat 6.0 that work together in the virtual world. The uses for these new features in the business world are really exciting, but if they aren't secure, they're of little benefit to the business world. In the next chapter we'll look at securing documents and the ability to transact commerce with electronic documents.

Chapter 7

Making Your Documents Secure

Tom is a collector. Over the years he has bought and sold the autographs of numerous famous people. You might wonder how he verified that the signature of Abe Lincoln, George Wythe, or James Buchanan were genuine since forging signatures has been prevalent for years. Contemporary forgers steal money from a checking account or alter documents to pass them off as historically significant documents. Documents are verified by comparing a signature known to be genuine on a signature card or by verifying the document in question. Information on the usage can also help with verification. Verifying the George Wythe document was easy. Wythe was a judge in Virginia. The document has the Virginia court seal and an impressed federal tax stamp.

As we move into the electronic age, documents come from people from all over the world. There's no such thing as unique handwriting. How can we ever know if a document hasn't been altered? How can we know if a person simply used a pasted scan of their signature?

This chapter will cover how to protect your work from being altered and verify that the person who signed the document actually did the work. This process is complex but easier to verify than handwritten signatures.

Protecting Your Work

The processes for document security in Acrobat 6.0 are the same as in Acrobat 5.0, but the names have been changed and the security enhanced. In this chapter, you'll examine all the security features at your disposal and learn how they work. You'll encrypt files, lock documents, build and share signatures, and create and share certificates. Sounds like a lot of work, and it is.

Acrobat 6.0 takes advantage of the security features of Windows XP. Because a number of security systems integrate with Acrobat, we'll mention those at the end of the chapter as well. You'll find more information on the third-party security systems on the Acrobat 6.0 installation CD.

Basically, we cover four separate processes:

- Protecting a document using passwords—attaching password protection to a file

- A document with rights assigned with certificates—granting different recipients different levels of permission to modify a document

- Adding signatures to a document—identifies creation or modification of a document after creation

- Certifying documents—a new process identifying the initial signature on a document

Acrobat 6.0 uses the same 128-bit RC4 encryption technology as Acrobat 5.0, a format created by RSA Data Security, Inc. This is a good thing because you can provide varying levels of control over access to the document's components. Acrobat 5.0 security caused problems with a search of secured documents and with creating templates from secured documents. Acrobat 6.0 solved the template problem by creating changes under the filling in of form fields and signing options. A new Acrobat 6.0 security level fixed the search problem. The new security level enables plain text metadata to be searched.

Note

Documents created with Acrobat 6.0 security cannot be opened by earlier versions.

Digital signatures and corresponding certificates allow for three different means of security. Adobe no longer uses the .apf file extensions for the private keys in the default Certificate Security (formerly Adobe Self-Sign Security.) Windows key extensions are .pfx (personal information exchange format, aka PKCS12) and Mac OS uses the .p12 file extension. A document can be signed with either an Adobe or third-party plug-in.

Note

A third-party plug-in is a commercial process. A key is generally provided by a trusted third party that verifies your identity, issues the private key, protects the public key, and maintains integrity of the system.

A system of signature authentication between creator and users monitor document authenticity. This applies to the original document as well as different versions. In addition to enhancing overall document security, you can view different versions of a document based on the signature. Information about your digital signature can be shared with a select list of people who can, in turn, read the protected files you send them.

Digital signatures also allow the creation of certified documents. A certified document has user permissions set and validated with the digital signature. As long as recipients only perform functions assigned to the document by the creator, the document retains its certification.

The third use for the digital signature keys involves the encryption of documents and assigning user permissions based on rights.

You'll dive headfirst into each of these areas. But first, we'll give you a few explanations on security concepts in general.

What Does a "Secure Document" Really Mean?

Security in a digital world is akin to home security. Just as you lock your doors or have passwords for your alarm system, so too do you lock a file or encrypt it. Acrobat 6.0 can protect documents by using two levels of passwords. Depending on which version of the software you're using, you have access to different levels of protection. Let's have a look at them.

Versions 3.x and 4.x of Acrobat used 40-bit RC4 encryption. Using a few different methods (you'll look at this later), you can protect a document at this level giving it a level of security akin to a locked door. Table 7-1 lists the options for 40-bit RC4 encryption.

Table 7.1   Protection Available Using 40-Bit RC4 Encryption Settings in Acrobat 3.x and 4.x

Encryption Setting	Prevents the User From...
No printing	Cannot print the file
No changing the document	Includes form-field creation
No content copying or extraction	Disallows extracting content or selecting content for copying
Disable accessibility	Disables text and graphics copying or using the Accessibility interface
No adding or changing comments	No adding or changing comments or form

Acrobat 5.0 used a more powerful 128-bit RSA encryption algorithm. As you can see in Table 7-2, the rights given to a recipient can be defined more precisely.

Table 7.2   128-Bit RC4 Encryption Settings in Acrobat 5.0

Encryption Setting	Functions Allowed
Full access	Allows access to any component of the document, printing, copying, extraction, full access to content
Enable content access for the visually impaired	Allows document contents to be copied (required to support the Accessibility feature)
Allow content copying and extraction	Allows selecting and copying of contents
Changes allowed—None	Locks down the file so that users cannot do anything with it.
Changes allowed—Document assembly only	Allows users to manipulate pages (insert, delete, rotate) as well as create bookmarks and thumbnails
Changes allowed—Only form-field fill-in or signing	Allows users to sign and fill in forms
Changes allowed—Comment authoring, only form-field fill in or signing	Allows users to do everything in the previous two options, plus add comments
Changes allowed—General editing, comment, and form-field authoring	Users can access the document for any purpose except content extraction or printing
Printing not allowed	Allows no printing rights
Printing low resolution	Allows users to print each page as a bitmapped image
High resolution or fully allowed	Allows users to print as desired

Acrobat 6.0 uses the same 128-bit encryption as Acrobat 5.0, but a few additional choices correct past problems.

Table 7.3   128-bit RC4 Settings in Acrobat 6.0

Encryption Setting	Functions Allowed
Enable text access for screenreader devices for the visually impaired	Allows screenreaders access to the text
Enable copying of text, images, and other content	Allows selecting and copying of contents
Enable plain text metadata	Makes information available for search engines.
Changes allowed—None	Locks down the file so that users cannot do anything with it
Changes allowed—Inserting, deleting, and rotating pages	Allows users to manipulate pages (insert, delete, rotate) as well as create bookmarks
Changes allowed—Filling in form fields and signing	Allows users to sign and fill in forms
Changes allowed—Commenting, filling in form fields and signing	Allows users to do everything in the previous option, plus add comments
Changes allowed—Any except extracting pages	Users can access the document for any purpose except content extraction or printing
Printing not allowed	Allows no printing rights
Printing low resolution	Prints page at 150 dpi
High resolution or fully allowed	Allows users to print as desired

Choosing Security Settings

Thousands of times all over the world people are asking the same question: What security setting should I use? Tom likes to take an aggressive stand. For the first time, Acrobat 6.0's documents have a box warning users of earlier versions of Reader or Acrobat that unless they download Acrobat 6.0, the file may have features unavailable to them. The ONLY problem is that if you have the security set to 6.0, the earlier versions cannot decrypt the document far enough to reach the warning.

If you aren't creating files using the features of 6.0 and pushing them to move to 6.0, you're doing your clients a disservice. However, we definitely don't recommend this if you're using workflows with clients using Acrobat 5.0 Approval. Adobe chose not to continue Approval. This decision leaves small governments who cannot afford the $70,000+ for Acrobat Server with Reader extensions out in the cold.

The other problem comes with clients that are still using full Acrobat 4.0 or 5.0. (Heaven forbid that anyone still uses Acrobat 3.0.) They'll likely have problems with the full program and Adobe Reader 6.0 on the same machine. Adobe strongly recommends that none of Acrobat 6.0's family be installed with earlier versions.

Every professional will need to make this decision based on the workflow of their client. There's no easy answer here. Since the only real advantage of Acrobat 6.0's security is added search, using Acrobat 5.0 or higher security will likely be the norm for at least the next year. Adobe has unintentionally set 5.0 as the default by making it the default for standard conversion settings in the PDFMaker macros.

By Definition

We spend a considerable amount of time in this chapter discussing signatures: how to make them, how to use them, and how to share them. Before you plunge into the world of Acrobat security settings, a couple of definitions are in order.

First, *passwords*. As everyone knows, a password is a secret word or phrase that allows a user access to a program, system, or file. Passwords are the weakest link in security.

Next, *encryption*. Encryption is translation of data into a secret code. In order to have access to a file and also be able to read it, you must first have access to a key or password that will decrypt it. Encryption is done using mathematical algorithms.

Finally, *public-key encryption*. This isn't so much a separate definition as a subset of encryption in general. Acrobat uses the RC4 algorithm, developed by RSA Data Security, Inc. This encryption device is based on the fact that there's no simple way to factor very large numbers. As a result, deducing an RSA key is extremely time consuming and uses a lot of processing power. The RSA algorithm is the de facto standard for encryption, especially for data transmitted by Internet methods.

Public-key encryption, as you'll see later, requires two keys: a public key and a private key. If you wanted to send a secure message, you would use your public key to encrypt the message. When you wanted to decrypt the message, you would use your private key. With the public-key system, only a public key can be used for encryption, and only a corresponding private key can be used for decryption.

Now let's see how to actually do some of these things in Acrobat.

Password Security Settings

Passwords can be set at the open document or permissions levels. They can be added to a file through Distiller, PDFMaker macros, or Acrobat. Coming up, you'll look at the processes.

First, a few rules on passwords:

- Passwords can be added at any time—either at file creation or whenever you save the file in Acrobat. As a workflow suggestion, it usually saves time if you do the password when you're finishing the file. It takes time to unset passwords to make changes.

- A PDF file can have two passwords: one to open the document and one to change permissions or security settings.

- Opening security with a permissions password allows the person to change what can be done to the file.

- Passwords may NOT use ! @ # $ % ^ & * , | \ ; < and all the other characters are case-sensitive. (Didn't your mother tell you not to cuss in public?)

Let's look at an example of how these rules work, and then we'll show you how to add passwords.

Adding Security to a PDF File

We mentioned that security can be set in Distiller, a PDFMaker macro, or in Acrobat. Here's how:

1. Open the Adobe PDF-Security dialog box. The dialog box shown in Figure 7-1 opens.

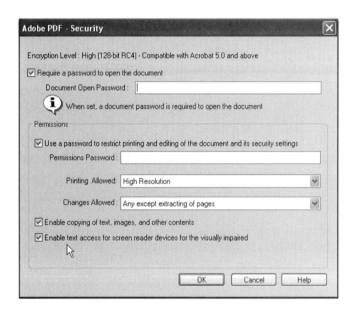

Figure 7-1
You can set password security settings in Distiller, a PDFMaker macro, or in Acrobat.

- From Distiller: Open Distiller, then select Settings ➤ Security.

- From PDFMaker macros: Click Adobe PDF ➤ Change Conversion Settings ➤ Security.

- From Acrobat: Select File ➤ Document Properties ➤ Security ➤ Password Security. The dialog box shown in Figure 7-2 opens. Select Password Security from the Security Method drop-down list to open a dialog box nearly identical to that shown in Figure 7-1.

Note

The encryption level (compatibility) is set under Settings ➤ Edit Adobe PDF Settings.

Note

Encryption level is set under the Settings tab ➤ Advanced Settings. When you change the setting to a different compatibility level, you create a custom conversion setting.

Note

You can also set security with batch processes, which will be discussed in Chapter 15.

Figure 7-2
Select security settings
in Acrobat through the
Document Properties
dialog boxes.

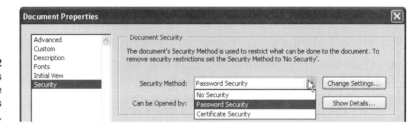

• The Password Security option in Acrobat also includes compatibility options, as shown in Figure 7-3.

Figure 7-3
You can also choose a
version compatibility from
the Compatibility drop-
down list in Acrobat.

Note

The Document Open
Password and
Permissions Password
fields must be different.
Permissions Password will
override the Document
Open Password field.

Note

The password security
is installed as part of
the default Certificate
Security with the typical
installation of Acrobat.
It's the program's default
security handler. If you're
running Windows XP the
Windows Certificate
Security will install as the
default. We'll look at the
Certificate Security
functions later in the
chapter.

2. Choose Password Security in the Adobe PDF - Security dialog box (shown in Figure 7-1.)

3. Enter your passwords in the Document Open Password (only if you want a password to open the document) and Permissions Password fields. Click the check box in the Permissions area to activate the option.

4. Choose the security settings desired based on encryption level. The options were listed earlier in Tables 7-1, 7-2, and 7-3.

5. Choose the permissions for the document viewer.

6. Click OK to close the dialog box and then save the file. Security isn't set until you save and close the file. If you've added security to a document that was previously unsecured, the dialog box shown in Figure 7-4 will open. Click OK to dismiss the message dialog box.

7. The Confirm Permissions Password dialog box shown in Figure 7-5 opens. Type your password, and then click OK to open the document.

8. Retype your password. Since most people use the permissions password the most frequently, it will now override the document open password. A new warning box opens stating that security isn't set until the document is saved and closed.

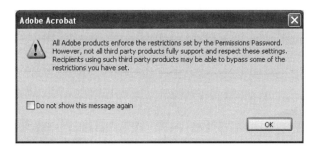

Figure 7-4
If you attempt to open a file using a different level of encryption than you're capable of using, you'll see this warning message.

Figure 7-5
You have to enter a permissions password in order to open a protected document.

Checking Your Settings

Not sure if you set the right permissions on the file? Select File ➤ Document Properties ➤ Security to open the Document Security dialog box. Click Display Setting. The summary window shown in Figure 7-6 opens.

Review the settings and click OK to close the dialog box.

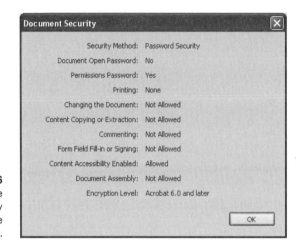

Figure 7-6
You should use the
Document Security
summary to review the
settings attached to a file.

Project Project 7.1: Setting Custom Security on a Document

Tip
Protecting Your Work

Many of us are quite
protective of our work.
It's not that we don't
want people to see it; we
just don't want anyone
else wrecking it, right?
The solution is to use two
levels of password
protection. When you're
sharing a file with team
members, give them the
document open
password so they can
access your file. Set
security restrictions on
the content and add a
permissions password.
Your permissions
password is yours. Your
client or team member
can admire your work
without changing it,
unless you give them
permission to make
certain changes.

This project demonstrates how to use the password and security functions and their effects. It's only a project in the loose definition of the word. We think it's important, though, because next we're moving into encryption—which is a whole new ball game.

You'll need the file called project1.pdf, which is in the Chapter 7 folder. This is a page from an eBook of which Tom is coauthor. There are over 1,000 color illustrations. This note is rare and valuable. We don't want someone trying to make replicas to fool uninformed collectors.

Start with the Basic File

Let's start with the unprotected file.

1. Open project1.pdf in Acrobat.

2. Open the Document Security dialog box by selecting File ➤ Document Properties ➤ Security. As you can see in Figure 7-7, this document is free for the taking, so to speak.

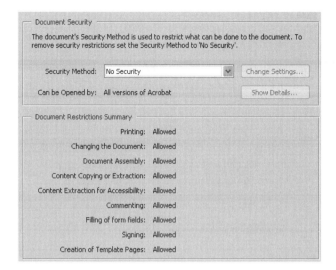

Figure 7-7
The document has no security and the information is free to be changed or taken at will.

3. Test some of the features to see how an unrestricted file works.

4. Using the Touchup Text tool on the Advanced Editing toolbar, select a line of text (as shown in Figure 7-8).

Figure 7-8
In an unprotected document you can select and modify content. The file actions are functional—for example, selecting text for alteration.

320 3rd NE **Chattanooga Ch2559 1875**

5. Extract the title image by selecting File ➤ Export ➤ Extract Images As ➤ JPEG/JPEG2000/PNG/TIFF (select one). You'll be asked where to save the file. Save and look at the images. Close the dialog box.

6. Test-print the file. Because this is a completely unrestricted document, it should print clearly.

Can you see how an unscrupulous person could extract the images and make a decent copy that would fool an unknowledgeable collector?

Note
When exported as a JPEG the front image displays an unusual bug. It appears in color, but looks like a color separation without the cyan layer. Adobe is working to fix this.

Add the Settings

Now add the security settings to the file.

1. Select File ➤ Document Properties. When the Document Properties dialog box opens, select Security ➤ Password Security from the Security Options drop-down list.

2. In the Password Security dialog box, set compatibility to Acrobat 5.0 and later. We aren't going to release the book with a password to open it. However, for this exercise check Require a Password to Open the Document and type **OPEN.**

3. In the Permissions section, Check the Use a Password to Restrict Printing and Editing of the Document and Its Security Settings box. For Permissions Password type **saysme**. You see that the dialog box now has different selections.

4. Choose one of the following:

   • Check the Enable Text Access for Screen Reader Devices for the Visually Impaired box.

   • Clear the Enable Copying of Text, Images and Other Content box.

   • Click the drop-down menu for Printing Allowed and select Low Resolution (150 dpi).

   • Click the drop-down menu for Changes Allowed and select None.

5. Click OK. You'll be notified as in Figure 7-4 that not all PDF applications honor all the restrictions.

6. You'll be asked to enter the passwords again. Since one is all caps and the other one is in lowercase, we expect you to get at least one wrong password warning.

7. You'll be advised that for the warnings to take place, you must first save the file and close it.

Test the Document

Finally, let's test out the password settings.

1. Open the file. You'll be prompted for your password. Enter the user password (in our case, **OPEN**).

2. Test the same functions as listed earlier. You'll note that there are no options for exporting images, the editing palettes are nonfunctional and print output is typically low resolution.

3. Attempt to change the document's security settings. Right-click the padlock and choose Document Security. When the dialog box opens, click Change Settings. A password entry box is displayed. Try entering the user password again. After each incorrect attempt at entering passwords, you will see the warning in Figure 7-9.

4. Try again by entering **saysme** in the Permissions Password field. Acrobat will accept the password and display the Standard Security dialog box. The settings are now active.

5. Close the dialog box without making changes.

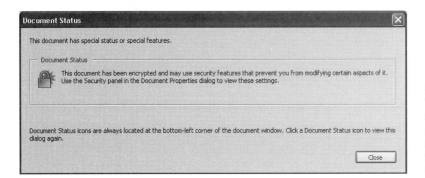

Figure 7-9
The Document Status dialog box warns that the document is encrypted and may have security features that prevent you from modifying certain aspects.

Document Status

When the file opens, you'll see a small, gold, closed padlock in the status bar at the bottom left of the window. This indicates that security settings have been attached to the file. If you click the padlock a Document Status dialog box like in Figure 7-9 opens stating that the document is encrypted.

If you right-click the padlock, a pop-up menu allows you to choose between the Document Status, Document Security, and Document Property dialog boxes. (Document Security and Document Property open the same screen since the Document Security is now under Document Properties.)

The aim of this project was to show you how the different security settings function as well as how the passwords work. Remember that a file can be opened using either password. Unless you log in to a file using the permissions password, however, the security settings are disabled. And that ends the discussion of "simple" password protections for a PDF file. Now it's on to signatures.

Figure 7-10
You'll see this
password error
message. It's not a
Caps Lock issue;
the wrong password
was entered.

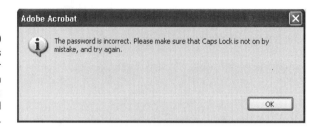

Certificate Security

Default Certificate Security is a signature handler plug-in for Acrobat that is installed with a typical install of the software. Acrobat 6.0 also has the option of Windows Certificate Security. Windows Certificate Security is a major addition to the Acrobat workflow. These plug-ins are used for signing documents.

Signing documents is a process, not a singular event. When you sign a check or other official document, you add your signature to validate it. When you originally opened the account, you signed a signature card to verify your signature. In a similar way, a digital signature identifies you as the person signing a document. Your public key is the signature card that is used to verify the signature. Your hand is the private key. Digital signatures store additional information about both the signer and the state of the document when it was signed (almost like a snapshot.)

Note

Password Security is referred to as symmetric security. The Passwords are the same on both ends. Certificate Security is referred to asymmetric security. The private and public keys are different.

Certificate Security uses a private/public key (PPK) system that verifies both the authenticity of a signature and the integrity of a signed document version.

Author's Opinion

Self-Sign Security with Acrobat has been a toy for most. Made legal shortly before the release of Acrobat 5.0, the tools were for most people nothing more than a plaything. Admittedly smaller workgroups used the digital security and so did a few large companies. This has got the rest of the business world thinking and we're going to see the implementation rapidly escalate.

Once you create a signature, it's associated with a profile. Each profile contains two keys. You use the private key to sign a document. When you attach a signature, the public key is embedded in the signature and is later used to verify your signature. How? An encrypted checksum is stored when you sign, and a public key decrypts the checksum when a signature is verified.

Don't verify your own document. You already know who you are and the state of a document when you signed it. Only recipients of the document need to verify it. In order for other users to do this, you must provide them with your public key, contained in a certificate. They must have trust that the certificate is yours. Certificates that you know are genuine and add to your files are referred to as *trusted certificates*.

The process sounds complicated, and it is. However, once you go through the different aspects of the process, you should have a good understanding of the whole concept. You'll start with how Acrobat uses signatures.

Using Signatures

Along with allowing you to sign a document to indicate completion of some process, Acrobat uses the signature process in a number of other ways. These include the following:

- *Version control.* Once you've signed a document, changes you've made are preserved. You can also return to a different signed version.

- *Verification.* It's often important to know who has done what when you're working in a workgroup. You can verify signatures to ensure the authenticity of what you've received.

- *Management.* By using the Signatures palette in Acrobat, you can locate any version of a document that has been signed. You can also compare two versions of a signed document.

- *Encryption.* You can encrypt a PDF document to distribute securely to specific recipients.

Let's look at the first part of this process. The first thing to do is to create a profile.

Creating Your Signature Profile

A signature handler profile stores a number of items. Each profile consists of several elements, stored in different ways. They are as follows:

- Your private key, which is encrypted.

- Your public key, which is wrapped in a certificate.

Note

Acrobat 6.0 comes with two signature handlers and you can add more. You can set preferences to ask each time which handler to use. You can optionally set a default signature handler in the Selection dialog box.

- A list of trusted certificates, which are certificates others share with you.

- A timeout value, which is a time set to determine when you must enter a password before signing.

Starting the Process

The first thing to do is start a new user profile. This can be done at any time, whether or not you have an open document. As with other features in Acrobat 6.0 there are multiple ways to do this. The easiest method is to have a document open. The process is very different from what it was in version 5.0. Fortunately, you don't have to memorize a lot of steps as the program holds your hand as you create a signature. You'll first follow the track to create a signature.

1. Click the Sign Document icon. The Alert dialog box shown in Figure 7-11 opens.

Figure 7-11
In an unsigned document, the program alerts you to different methods of securing the document. You'll continue by signing the document.

2. Click the Continue Signing to open the Create Signature as shown in Figure 7-12. Click the Show Certification on Document radio button to display the signature.

Figure 7-12
Acrobat allows you to select either a visible or an invisible signature.

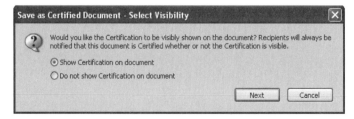

3. Click Next to open the dialog box shown in Figure 7-13 instructing the user on the next step, which is to draw the signature box. Click OK to close the dialog box.

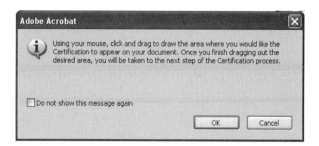

Figure 7-13
The next step is to draw the signature box; the dialog box instructs you on how to proceed.

4. The cursor is an active form tool. Draw the Signature Box and click OK.

5. The Apply Digital Signature dialog box shown in Figure 7-14 opens. In an electronic workflow, a person may have numerous digital signatures depending on function. An engineer might have one from each state where he holds a professional engineering license. You may have one that your bank gave you for electronic banking purposes and different signatures for different workgroups.

Note
Acrobat and Windows Certificate Security will help you manage the private keys and the trusted certificates and public keys of your workgroup.

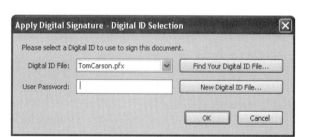

Figure 7-14
Select a Digital ID file in the dialog box or create a new one. In this discussion, a new Digital ID is created.

6. Click New Digital ID File. The Acrobat Self-Signed Digital ID Disclaimer dialog box, as shown in Figure 7-15, opens.

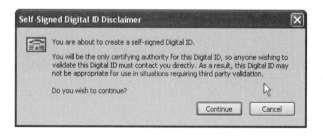

Figure 7-15
The Digital ID disclaimer describes the limitations of using a self-sign security process.

Trust—Third Party and Otherwise

At this point we really need to discuss trust in more detail. How do you trust? In the 1800s, a lot of trust was based on image and reputation. You had to maintain an image so people believed that you were who you say you were. Identity theft was as prevalent then as now.

Unless you use a third party, the recipient of your certificate and public signature is completely responsible for verifying the authenticity of your signature. This is a risk to you and them. How is it a risk to you? Well, someone could make up a certificate claiming to be you and trick someone into accepting the certificate. We would bet a steak dinner that this disclaimer was developed by the Adobe attorneys.

Note

We got a warning on the organization name used in the signature shown in Figure 7-17 due to the "&". We corrected it, and the box didn't open. Remember what your mother said: ! @ # $ % ^ & * , | \ ; < shouldn't be used in public.

7. Click Continue to open the Create Self-Signed Digital ID dialog box where you actually create the digital signature shown in Figure 7-16.

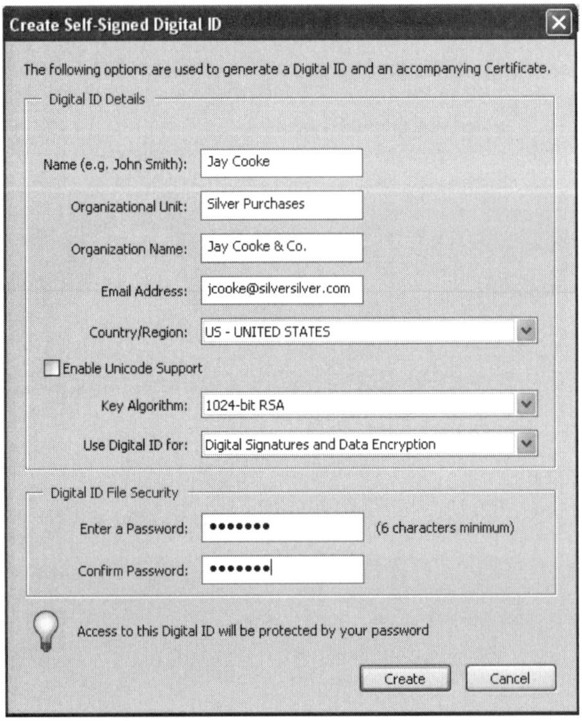

Figure 7-16
You build a non-third party Digital ID in the Create Self-Signed Digital ID dialog box.

8. Click Create. The Apply Digital Signature - Digital ID Selection dialog box opens as shown in Figure 7-17. This dialog box also shows the expiration date of the signature.

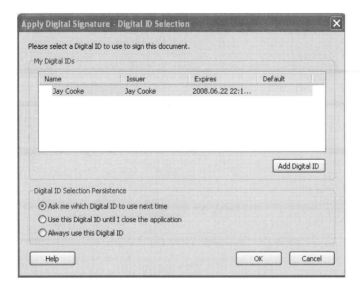

Figure 7-17
This dialog box displays the results of the new signature, including the name of the certificate, issuer, and expiration date.

9. Double-click Jay Cooke's name to customize the signature in the Configure Signature Appearance dialog box shown in Figure 7-18.

10. Click the Imported Graphic radio button. Click PDF File; select the Jaye Cooke & Co.pdf document from the Chapter 7 folder. The thumbnail of the image is displayed in the Preview area on the dialog box.

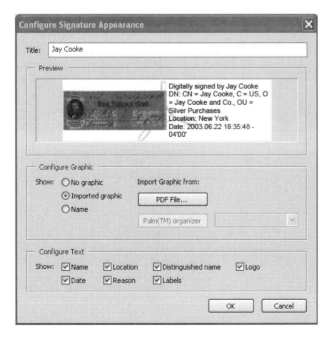

Figure 7-18
You can set the properties for a custom signature, including a graphic image.

11. Click OK to sign the document. Figure 7-19 shows the verified signature from a signed document.

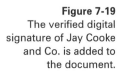

Figure 7-19
The verified digital signature of Jay Cooke and Co. is added to the document.

Digitally signed by Jay Cooke
DN: CN = Jay Cooke, C = US, O = Jay Cooke and Co., OU = Silver Purchases
Reason: Wealthy Silver Purchaser
Location: New York
Date: 2003.06.22 18:18:04 -04'00'

About Jay Cooke and Co.

The certificate in this demo was named for Jay Cooke. Jay helped finance the Civil War and was a much-respected financier. In the 1800s fancy checks meant you were wealthy and helped develop trust. They were sometimes used to intimate wealth that didn't exist. The graphic image is a check for $200,000 in silver.

Five months after this check was written, Jay Cooke and Co. went bankrupt, sending the U.S. economy into the Panic of 1873. Cooke died in 1905. You have a digital signature verified with a public certificate. Would you trust this?

Choosing a Signing Method

Tip

Managing Digital Security

Numerous whole books could be written on Digital ID and managing digital security in the workplace. Setting up the system for your company is going to take careful planning from a team. The legal implications are huge. Test everything thoroughly before the rollout. If you need legally defensible security, you may want to consider the third-party expert vendors.

As we discussed earlier, Acrobat 6.0 comes with the ability to use the default Certificate Security, Windows Certificate Security or third-party authorities. To select a signing method, choose Edit ➤ Preferences ➤ Digital Security to display the options shown in Figure 7-20.

An Advanced Preferences button is at the bottom of the dialog box shown in Figure 7-20. Click Advanced to open the dialog box shown in Figure 7-21. As you notice certain choices under the Windows Security store can cause certificates to be wrongly trusted.

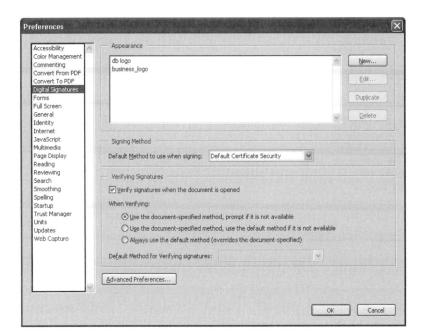

Figure 7-20
Choose a signing method according to your work requirements.

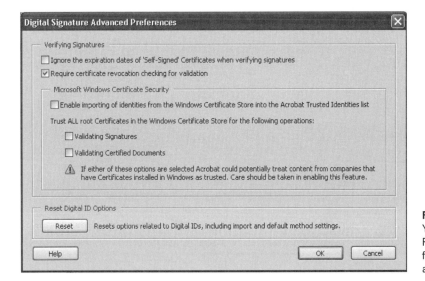

Figure 7-21
You can use the Advanced Preferences dialog box for validating signatures and documents.

Managing Digital IDs

Managing Digital IDs in Acrobat 6.0 is greatly expanded over version 5.0. Many of the features to manage the signatures have been moved to Advanced ➤ Manage Digital IDs as shown in Figure 7-22.

Trusted IDs

You develop a list of trusted IDs over time or use a third-party source to provide you with the IDs. It's especially important that you remember the trust aspect. Figure 7-23 shows a list of trusted IDs that we've added to our list. Three of the four IDs are fictitious.

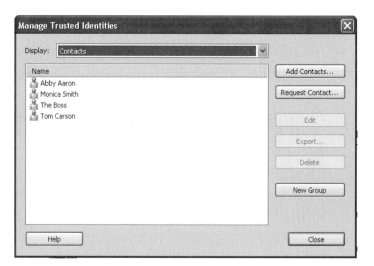

Your Digital ID Files

As we said earlier, you may have several digital signatures. Acrobat 6.0 allows you to choose between the options shown in Figure 7-24 to manage your signatures. You can change your signature as you would any other user settings.

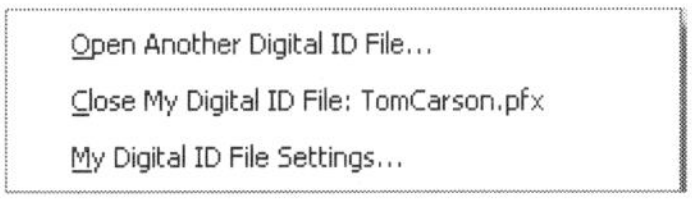

Open Another Digital ID File...

Close My Digital ID File: TomCarson.pfx

My Digital ID File Settings...

Figure 7-24
You have several
selections for managing
your digital signature.

Configure Identity Search Directories

This is an *important* new feature. A key to bringing digital signatures to
the forefront in a workgroup is having a way to develop a trusted key
storage and verification area for the group. Acrobat 6.0 allows you to
configure a series of identity search directories as shown in Figure 7-25.
There's a built-in link to the VeriSign Internet Directory Service.

Figure 7-25
Create a directory listing
to store and collect trusted
certificates.

Click New to configure a new directory as shown in Figure 7-26. Companies
and governments will use this to develop signature vaults for the certificates they have authenticated. One or two people will act like a notary
and issue private keys while storing and protecting the private keys. The
keys must be stored on a Lightweight Directory Access Protocol (LDAP)
server. If you check the Internet there are shareware versions of this protocol. Given the implications, make sure you know what you're doing.

Figure 7-26
The Edit Identity Search Directory dialog box gives you options for setting up a search directory for public keys.

Project Project 7-2: Creating a Personalized Signature with a Graphic

Note

You could create the signature block in any program capable of performing the functions, then export it or print it to Distiller. However, Donna likes the automatic features available in Photoshop and Illustrator. The only restriction is that the file ends up as a PDF file, with the image centered on the page. Tom is simple again—just do it in Acrobat.

Perhaps this project title is a bit of a misnomer. After all, every signature is just that—personalized. In this project, you'll use a scanned signature and a graphic to create a custom signature file. There are no files for this project.

Sign Here

First you need a signature. We created the PDF file from within Photoshop. Follow the same steps if you're using Illustrator.

1. Write your signature on a piece of paper.

2. Open Photoshop or Illustrator. Select File ➤ Import ➤ Scan x (depending on your hardware). In Acrobat, select Create PDF from Scan.

3. Follow your scanner's import method. It's best to preview and crop before you scan.

4. Crop the image as necessary.

5. Save the file as a Photoshop, Illustrator, or Acrobat PDF file, and close the program.

Figure 7-27
This figure shows the signature of someone who missed their calling to be a doctor.

Create the Custom Signature

Now you have a signature block to be imported into Acrobat for a custom signature block. Let's set up the signature appearance.

1. Open a document to sign in Acrobat.

2. Click the Signature tool and choose Sign This Document. You'll be asked to draw a box where you want to sign. You'll be asked to choose which signature to use. After you select Signature, the Apply signature box will open.

3. Under Signature Appearance in the Apply signature box, select Edit.

4. When the Configure Signature Appearance dialog box opens, enter a title for the new signature, click Show Imported Graphic, and then click Import Graphic from PDF File.

5. Browse to the location where the image file is stored and select it. It will appear in a sample window.

6. Click OK to select the image and return to the Configure Signature Appearance dialog box, as shown in Figure 7-28.

7. In the Configure Text area at the bottom of the dialog box, select text items you want to appear with your picture. By default, we've left the entire list selected.

8. Click OK to close the dialog box. Leave the User Settings dialog box open.

Figure 7-28
This figure shows
the completed
custom signature.

One last item, and then the project is done. Remember to create a certif-icate for your signature (more on that coming up soon). For now, follow these steps:

1. Click the User Information option in the left pane of the dialog box. The user information you entered earlier is listed.

2. The signatures will be stored based on the security handler you've chosen.

Now you've created this lovely signature. Alternatively, you also have the option to use a generic signature. Which begs the question, what do you do with a signature? Read on.

Using Signatures, Custom or Otherwise

Using signatures in Acrobat is the same as routing a document around an office. Each person who receives a document can add comments and sign the document. Same with digital signing. The good thing about a

Note

You can edit or delete pictures, change the graphic, or change text items from the User Settings dialog box. Click Select Signature Appearance in the left pane and then click Edit. Click Delete to remove a custom signature completely.

digital signature is that its changes can be attributed directly to the person making them, removing the guesswork. Another nice feature of digitally signing a document is that you can look at different versions of the same document sorted by who signed the document and when.

You use signatures in a number of ways and for a number of purposes. In this section, you'll learn the following:

- Signing a document

- Signing a document in a browser

- Deleting signatures

- Verifying a signature

- Viewing versions

All this can be done with just one object!

Document Signing Alternatives

Documents may be signed either in Acrobat or in a browser. Here's how to do both. We'll start with basic signing. (We'll assume that you're already logged in to your signature profile.)

Adding a Signature

To add one more level of complexity, Acrobat allows a signature to be either visible or invisible. The only difference is that an invisible signature doesn't appear in a block on the document's page. It is, however, visible in the Signatures panel.

Note

Don't delete a signed page. This will also delete the signature.

1. Select Sign tool ➤ Sign This Document ➤ Choose Visible or Invisible ➤ Instruction to Drag Box.

2. When the cursor changes to crosshairs, click and drag to place the signature on the page.

3. The Select Method dialog box will open. Choose between default, Windows, or a third party.

4. The Sign Document dialog box will open, as shown in Figure 7-29.

5. Re-enter your password. Select the options for the signature from the selections in the dialog box.

6. Click Save. Use Save As to save the file with a different name.

Note

If you're already logged into the signature profile, you won't see the Password Entry dialog box. Also if you're using Windows Certificate Security you won't see the request for password very often.

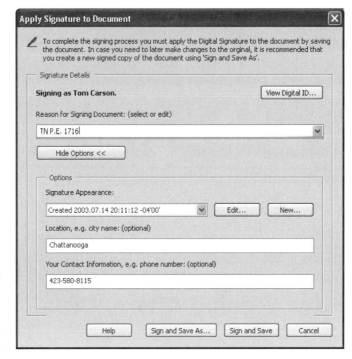

Figure 7-29
Adding information and
selecting the signature
appearance from the
Apply Signature to
Document dialog box

7. To save the entire file, click the Save icon on the Acrobat toolbar, and save the file.

Tip

Why Are There Signature Removal Options?

It depends on what you want to do with a signature. If you've added a signature, and then see that it was added too hastily, for example, you can delete it completely. If you want to add a number of signatures to a document to coordinate it with different functions, you may want to add a number of signature fields that correspond with the different processes. That way, when the signature fields are full, your work is done.

Removing Signatures

Sometimes you have to take signatures out. You have two options: Either remove a signature completely or remove the contents from a signature field. Both can be handled the same way:

- *Remove one signature or clear a field.* Click the signature to select it. Right-click the signature and select Delete Signature or Clear Signature Field.

- *Remove all the signature fields in a document.* Select Signature Tab ➤ Options ➤ Clear All Signature Fields.

So these are the options for actually getting a signature into or out of a document. In the next section you'll learn how to prove that you are who you say you are—better known as *signature verification*.

Verifying Signatures

You can verify signatures in one of two ways. Look at Figure 7-30, which shows a portion of a document's signature in the Signature panel. Notice that one of the signatures has a green check mark next to it indicating that it's valid. A question mark would mean the signature hasn't been verified. Here's how to verify a signature:

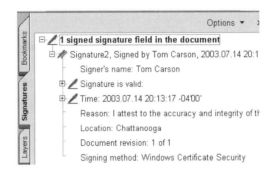

Figure 7-30
Valid signatures are identified in the Signature panel in the Signatures tab.

1. Log in to your profile, and then right-click the first signature in the Signature panel. Choose Verify Signature from the context menu. The same right-click method applies if you select a signature field in the document pane. (Use Control+click on a Mac.)

2. Once the program checks the document and signature to make sure nothing had been changed since the document was signed, the check mark replaces the question mark.

The signature is verified. But what if the signature comes from someone else? This is the second validation method, and it requires user certificates. The next section covers certificates and verifying them.

Viewing Signature Information

All the signatures attached to a file are displayed in the Signatures panel. Their status and the order in which they were added are also shown. For any signature, you can click the plus sign (+) to expand the signature and see other information entered when the signature was added.

More information is available on signatures right there for the viewing. Click a signature to select it. Click the Signatures panel drop-down menu and choose Properties. The dialog box shown in Figure 7-31 will open.

Note

If you don't log into your profile first, you'll be prompted when you right-click a signature.

Tip

Watch Out for Those Signatures

Don't use the Save As command in the regular course of working with a document. If you use it at any time except when attaching a new signature, all other signatures attached to the file will be deleted. If you have to change the name of a file at another time, do it from outside Acrobat in Windows Explorer (or by choosing Find on the Mac.)

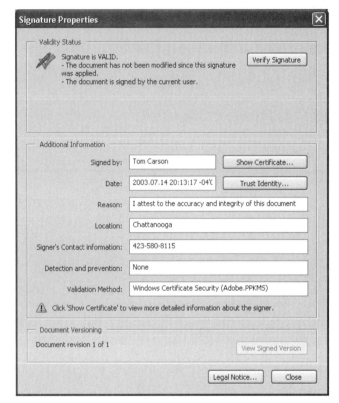

Figure 7-31
You can read the
particulars of a signature
in the Signature
Properties dialog box.
Everything you could
possibly want to know!

Note

You can get information
on a specific signature on
a page using context
menu options. Right-click
a signature (Control+click
on a Mac) and select
Properties from the
context menu.

Note

None of this information
can be changed in these
windows. You can copy
and paste it to alternate
locations if desired.

From the Signature Properties dialog box, you can verify signatures and
view different versions of the document. You can also see the text information entered when the signature was created. Click Show Certificate
to display the signer's user certificate. Click Verify Identity to open another
dialog box showing more information, including the fingerprints for the
user identification.

Viewing Alternate Document Versions

In Figure 7-31 shown earlier you can see a listing at the bottom of the
dialog box regarding document versions. In this last topic (and hasn't it
been l-o-n-g?), we'll explain how to view different versions of a document.
A signature is used to create a "snapshot" of a document at the time it is
added. This ensures that each version is unique and unalterable.

To view the version corresponding to a particular signature, select
Document ➤ Compare Documents. Acrobat will open the selected
version in a new file.

Finally, if you want to see a written summary of changes made to a document between versions, select a signature by clicking it. Then select Compare Signed Version to Current Document. A summary window similar to that shown in Figure 7-32 is displayed in a new file.

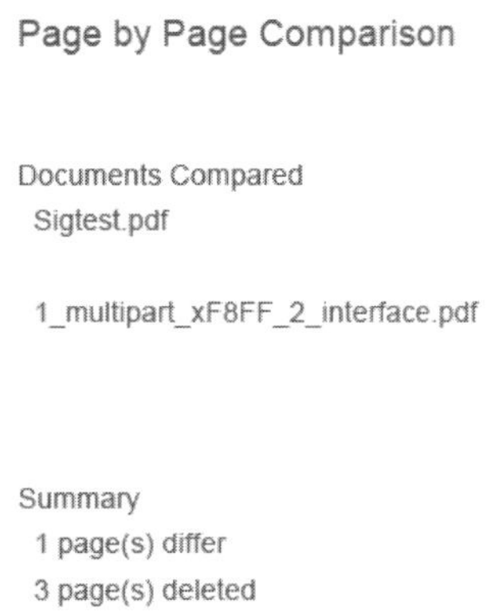

Page by Page Comparison

Documents Compared
Sigtest.pdf

1_multipart_xF8FF_2_interface.pdf

Figure 7-32
A summary of changes made to a document between versions is displayed in a new window after comparison.

Summary
1 page(s) differ
3 page(s) deleted

And that, in a nutshell, is how signatures work in Acrobat. Okay, maybe a giant clam shell.

Sharing Is a Good Thing

We should swap keys for this?

This final section is about sharing certificates and the key (no pun intended) to making the public/private key (PPK) encryption process work. Earlier in this chapter we introduced the idea of PPK encryption. You use a public key to encrypt the message, and you use a private key to decrypt it.

You'll look at a number of events and activities surrounding sharing and encryption, including the following:

- Importing trusted certificates and creating a list of recipients

- Managing your recipient list

- Sharing your certificate with others

- Importing a certificate from a signature on a document

First up is importing certificates, and then building a recipient list.

Importing Certificates

Tip

Why Does a File Need Fingerprints?

The purpose of fingerprints is to verify the identity of a signature holder. Because you can share certificates easily and recipients can extract certificates directly from a signature, you should copy and paste the fingerprints into a text file and keep them for reference. The next time someone needs verification of your identity, simply send them a copy of the fingerprint file. The recipient can check the content of your file against the fingerprint strings extracted or received.

You cannot add someone to a list unless that person's certificate resides on your computer and is available to the signature handler. Otherwise, unless the certificate is available, like those shown in Figure 7-23, it's like hosting a party and not sending out the invitations.

But where do the trusted certificates come from? Like most things digital, a certificate is nothing more than a specific type of file. This file can be emailed to you, or you can access it through a network file process. You can extract it from a signed document. You can even walk a copy on a floppy over to someone—how archaic.

Certificates are stored on your hard drive. When you receive a file, it's saved with a .pfx extension, (.p12 on Mac OS.) Store it with your other files. Storage is a function of your digital security method.

Adding a new certificate is a two-dialog box process. Select Advanced ➤ Manage Digital IDs ➤ Trusted Identities to open the Manage Trusted Certificates dialog box shown in Figure 7-33, and click Add Contacts to open the Select Contacts to Add dialog box.

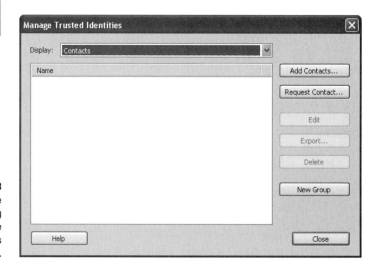

Figure 7-33
Start from the Manage Trusted Identities dialog box to organize the certificates and contacts in your computer.

In the Select Contacts to Add dialog box, shown in Figure 7-34, click Browse for Certificates to search for additional certificates.

Click Request Contact (shown at the top of the dialog box in Figure 7-33) to open an Email a Request dialog box, as shown in Figure 7-35. You're emailing your certificate and asking the recipient to return hers. Adding the return certificate to your list is an automated process.

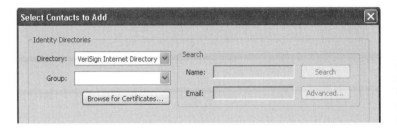

Figure 7-34
Click Browse for
Certificates to search for
additional certificates you
can add to your list.

Figure 7-35
You can request an email
transfer of your certificate
and a returned certificate.

Selecting a Signature Handler

At the beginning of the chapter, we noted that there were a number of different signature handlers. Each of these is a plug-in, and Acrobat supports all of them. What we've used in this chapter is either the default Certificate Handler or the Windows Certificate Handler. You've seen how to add, verify, and manage signatures using Acrobat's tools. The individual plug-in will determine how the signatures are used and managed. The signature handler used will vary depending on your work environment. For example, the VeriSign Signature Handler is verified online.

Certificate-based Document Security

In Acrobat 5.0 the process was referred to as Self-Sign Security; now it's Certificate Security. If you choose File ➤ Document Properties ➤ Security, you can choose a document security method. Choose Certificate Security from the drop-down list to open the Restrictions dialog box, as shown in Figure 7-36.

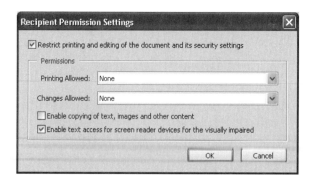

Restrict Opening and Editing to Certain Identities

Identity Directories

Directory: Trusted Identities

Group: All

Browse for Certificates...

Search

Name:

Email:

Search

Advanced...

Name	Email	
Abby Aaron		
Adobe Root CA		
Monica Smith		
The Boss		
Tom Carson	tcarson@sedev....	

Add to Recipient List

Recipients

Name	Email	
The Boss		
Tom Carson	tcarson@sedev....	

Recipient Details...

Remove from List

Set Recipient Permissions...

☐ Enable plaintext metadata (compatible only with Acrobat 6.0 and later)

Help   OK   Cancel

Figure 7-36
You can define the rights assigned to users in the Restrict Opening and Editing to Certain Identities dialog box.

Note

When teaching this in class the first things Tom's students always do is send a document with these encryptions to people whose public keys aren't on them. We think they just like to imagine what the recipient will say when the get the notice that they don't have permission to open the document.

Select a certificate in the upper window and click Add to Recipient List. In the bottom portion of the dialog box, select a recipient and click Set Recipient Permissions. We selected The Boss and clicked on Set Recipient Permissions to open the dialog box shown in Figure 7-37. The boss has a real problem with messing things up, so we give him no rights other than opening the document.

The security is set by the recipient's public key. If someone other than the intended recipients receives the documents, they'll receive an alert that they don't have permission to open the document.

Recipient Permission Settings

☑ Restrict printing and editing of the document and its security settings

Permissions

Printing Allowed: None

Changes Allowed: None

☐ Enable copying of text, images and other content
☑ Enable text access for screen reader devices for the visually impaired

OK   Cancel

Figure 7-37
You can set a range of restrictions for your certificate holders.

Certified Documents

Bet you thought we were through with security. Well, almost! Acrobat 6.0 introduced one final new feature, the Certified Document. A certified document is one that carries a certification that it's genuine as long as designated functions only are performed. An example is a multiple page form. The certification is set where only the form can be filled out and signed. As long as no other changes are made, the document retains its blue ribbon (certified) status.

Certifying a document is a lot like signing a document. Click the Sign tool and the Alert box in Figure 7-38 appears. Instead of signing (discussed earlier in the chapter) you click Certify Document.

Figure 7-38
Choose either a certification or a signature for an unsigned document.

Click Certify Document. You're warned by a dialog box to get a third-party certificate as shown in Figure 7-39. Why do you need a Digital ID from an Adobe partner? The verifying party will need to verify your public key in order to verify the document.

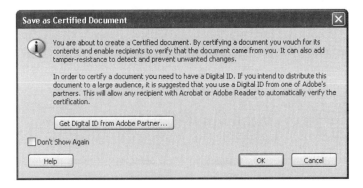

Figure 7-39
Acrobat gives you a reminder that you need a Digital ID from a trusted source for recipients to verify the certification.

After clicking OK you choose the allowable action as shown in Figure 7-40. You'll notice that we checked the Lock the Certifying Signature so that It Can't Be Cleared or Deleted by Anyone option.

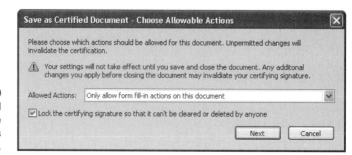

Figure 7-40
Choose actions allowed
for the users of the
document after it has
been certified.

Next, you have a series of dialog boxes asking if it's visible or invisible, telling you to draw the box and asking if you want to sign, following the same sequence of events as a regular signature application. When the process is complete, your signed blue seal is placed on the document as shown in Figure 7-41.

Figure 7-41
The blue seal of approval
is added to the document
to certify the document.

We'll end this chapter with a blue ribbon: first place.

Up Next

This chapter has certainly been complex, hasn't it? A lot is involved in dealing with security, as you've certainly seen. You looked at passwords, both user and master types. You examined different ways to protect content in a document and restrict access to functions. You learned about signatures and created a custom signature; you explored the process of sharing documents and ways to distribute certificates. You looked at several ways to use the certificates in security.

It's time for more sharing. In Chapter 8, you'll look at a function that only professionals can use: Acrobat Forms. The Forms tool is only in Acrobat 6.0 Professional, but after all, this is a guide for Acrobat 6.0 Professional users.

Creating Forms
with Acrobat

"Fill out this form in triplicate and go to the next line. They will have more forms for you." —A slice of modern life

Forms, Forms, Everywhere. . .

Forms are one of the least understood business costs. Take a simple plumbing permit. Thousands of plumbers go to the local building permit offices every day to "pull" a permit. After filling out a form, standing in line, and chatting with the permit clerk, they are finally issued a permit. Everyone knows what plumbers cost, but not everyone knows that part of that cost is the 2 hours, 40 miles, and lost productivity involved with the permit form process.

Let's put a price on a plumber of $30 per hour. Although the permit itself is only $26, its actual cost includes an additional $60 for the plumber's time, $14.60 in mileage and an extra $15 in lost productivity, making the permit's actual cost $89.60. A conservative SWAG (Scientific Wild "Donkey" Guess) would be that 10,000 permits are issued in the U.S. per business day, and that these permits cost $896,000 per business day or $224,000,000 per year in nonproductive expenditures. This estimate doesn't even include the city's cost to handle the form.

Warning to Acrobat 6.0 Standard Users

If you're using Acrobat 6.0 Standard or an earlier version of Acrobat, DO NOT READ THIS CHAPTER, unless you can afford $150 for the upgrade to Acrobat 6.0 Professional. Reading without $150 will cause a severe case of the "I Needs."

One medium-sized city has decided to cut these costs using the computer. All its permit forms are now electronic in PDF. The plumber, the electrician, the building contractor, the electrical contractor and the owner can download the active form from the city web site. They fill out the form, digitally sign it, and email it back using Acrobat or Acrobat Approval. If they have Adobe Reader they can fill it out, print it, and then fax it. A payment mechanism has been prearranged, and the approved permit is returned by email.

We're just beginning to look at how to save time and money on the city side. Eventually, the form data will be linked to a database. The ability to retrieve the permits with Search is already in place.

Now that we're on the way to converting you into an eForm zealot, let's see what the big deal is.

So What Is a Form?

At the risk of stating the obvious, a *form* is a means of communicating specific types of information in specific formats. In database terms, a form is nothing more than an organized front end for collecting data to add to tables.

For example, if you're filling in a tax form, your information is input into the form in a specific way. Of course, since the tax collection process doesn't end with filling out the form, the data collection process becomes something larger. If you're filling in a form to enter a contest at your local supermarket, the data collected is nothing more than the data collected. Unless the contest organizers use the information you provide, it's wasted information.

Let's see what we have here.

Online Forms

There are millions of forms online. Many online forms are HTML-based and use server-side scripting to collect data, which is then transmitted to databases. You might wonder, "What's wrong with that?" We're glad you asked. Nothing is particularly wrong with it, except for the fact that these forms must have an Internet connection to be filled out successfully.

Some situations can take a very long time to complete—for example, submitting an online résumé. Even though you think you're prepared, depending on how the site's forms are structured, you often end up back in a word processor composing or revising a segment, and then copying it and pasting it into the appropriate field in the form.

Think about the last time you were doing something online and your Internet connection was interrupted for some reason. Unless it was something very important, the odds are pretty good that you left the site. Just one of those online things.

To prevent interruptions in the process, sites make forms available for download. But what kind of forms?

Tip

Try to web capture the form to PDF. In the browser window, click on the URL to select it, and then right-click and choose Copy. In Acrobat 6.0 choose Create PDF ➤ From Web Page; right-click and paste the URL into the URL line. Choose the Get 1 Level option in the Settings and click Create. There is a good possibility that the PDF form that appears will let you complete it offline and when you press Enter, it will upload it to the database. Tom once successfully submitted a abstract to a conference in this manner.

Forms vs. Smart Forms

Although you can download files online, not many of these forms are smart. That is, aside from providing a specific layout and other elements that the PDF file format does so well, the form is static. In all likelihood, the form was created from a paper document. Once the form is down-loaded, you have to print it, fill it in, and then mail or fax it back to the source, a process that leads to dead trees and high labor costs. The information from this form will in all likelihood have to be reconverted into an electronic format.

Not an efficient way of working.

Now imagine a form that could be downloaded, completed offline, and then uploaded back to the site where you originally found it. Once the file was uploaded, the form data could be parsed and processed by submitting either the form data or HTML format (depending on the form's design). In other words, it's a smart form.

In this chapter, you're going to look at smart forms. Creating a regular fill-in-the-blank-and-mail-it-to-me form is not the focus here. That is design and layout. This is doing more than that. Earlier in the book, we discussed the difference between a scanned document and one that was converted into a searchable PDF file. This is much the same idea. On the one hand, you have what looks like a form. On the other, you have a form that can be used to both configure user responses and communicate with whatever data storage processes you want to use. Cool. (We think we just heard your little geeky propeller-beanie start up.)

What Makes a Form Smart?

A form becomes smart when it can be used electronically for more than one stage of the collection and processing cycle. And it can get smarter and smarter. Table 8-1 shows some examples of smart functionality from the user's perspective, along with benefits to the author or designer from the same concept.

Table 8.1 User Benefits vs. Designer Benefits: Two Sides of the Same Coin

The Users...	Author and Designer Benefit
Can fill it out electronically.	Provides overall control of users' responses.
Are guided in their responses by different options for data entry.	Provides options for the user to select from, and will decrease errors and confusion.
Are assisted by having fields configured to accept only specifically formatted responses.	Ensures that the responses are entered in a format usable by the receiving system.
Navigate through the form directly (control or administration form fields are hidden).	Saves troubleshooting time in assisting users with completion problems; saves processing time by submitting calculated data.
Can submit the form electronically.	Information can be entered directly into the receiving system; saves time and labor. The form can be scanned for completion prior to acceptance, saving even more time and effort.

If you look down the list, you can see a progression from filling out the form, to specific ways to collect data, to submitting the completed form. As you can see from the table, it's smart to be smart! In some circumstances, you might need analog signatures or hard-copy documents for one purpose or another. Even so, by providing smart form capability, the user can store backup copies electronically rather than having to print or copy extra files for storage.

So how do you create a form that is smart? Let's have a look. Along the way, we'll provide a few projects so you can get a good handle on some of these concepts.

Go to the Source

Like virtually anything else in Acrobat, forms based on PDF files are created elsewhere. Also, as you do when converting files from other programs for other purposes, you must plan carefully before designing and converting a file with forms creation in mind.

Tip

Image-Intensive Forms

If you're using a scanned image for a form background with smaller images superimposed, use a vector-based program such as Adobe Illustrator or Macromedia FreeHand to create the file. Doing so will make for a smaller file size than if you use either a pixel-based program or a Microsoft Office application. On the other hand, if your form is text intensive, use a layout application such as FrameMaker or InDesign instead.

Source Programs for Forms Creation

If you're doing a complex form, you should use a layout program. You'll be working with a form in a few minutes that Bubba's secretary did in Word. Word is a word-processing program, not a layout program.

Adobe FrameMaker is probably the best program around for making forms that must be accessible and reflow. Everything in FrameMaker is tagged. InDesign 2.0 also makes some good forms. Adobe has a new product redesigned from the Accelio acquisition. If you have to make many complex forms the Adobe Forms Designer is the way to go. It's not cheap, but it will pay for itself for serious forms creators. It costs $1,695 and is for Windows only.

You may find that you have to do some experimentation to create the form output you want. When you create forms in your source application, think also of how you'll be working with the basic layouts once you get into Acrobat. For example, you may want to add a frame structure in the source application that will have the form fields overlaid for a 3D effect. Plan this in advance. Modifications can be done using the TouchUp tool in Acrobat. As with other types of file conversion, however, it depends on how much work there is to do.

The second way to convert a source document is from a scanned copy. Again, there are variations in how this can be done and what type of program a scanned file should be imported into. It may or may not be necessary to scan using Optical Character Recognition (OCR) capabilities. The form elements are added over the document in any case.

About Bubba

Let's get started on Bubba's project. Bubba is a good ole boy. Talking to him you would think he just came out of the backwoods, but don't let that fool you. Bubba has a BE in Engineering from the University of Utah and an MBA from Vanderbilt. Yankees tend to underestimate good ole boys. Bubba's people spend a couple man-weeks per month filling out all the applications and certificates for payment for all his companies. You're going to make one form that will save them a lot of time, cut down on errors, and work for all the companies. Open the form described in the tutorial and follow along. You learn best by doing—not reading.

Tutorial: Creating and Customizing Text Box Form Fields

For this tutorial, you're using a file in the Chapter 8 folder named Bubba's Form.pdf. Bubba hired you to make him a workable form from the original his secretary created in Word. We made a PDF that will work just fine on a computer and later link to his database. There is a copy of the form in the Chapter 8 folder named Bubba's Form done.pdf, which is the completed form with all its fields and scripts attached.

Note

There are a lot of Acrobat Professional users that don't work with forms. We're going to start from the beginning and mix in advanced concepts along the way.

Let's get down to the heart of the matter. You have a document that has been converted and is now in Acrobat. How do you take it from this point and make it into a slick, smart application? First things first! You have to build the form fields.

Creating Form Fields

Note

In Figure 8-1 the field is already named; the field is named in step 3.

The form is converted to a PDF from the source Word document. To start the process, choose Tools ➤ Advanced Editing ➤ Forms ➤ Show Forms Tools. Float the toolbar to where it best fits your style of working.

Create the First Text Box

Let's start at the top of the form and add text box fields.

1. With the magnifying tool, zoom in on the upper portion of page 1 of the form. You need to make a text box field for the owner's name.

2. Click the Text Box tool on the Forms toolbar and drag a marquee to the right of the word "OWNER" as shown in Figure 8-1. Make the box roughly the same size as shown in the figure; it's resized later.

Figure 8-1
Draw the first text box at the top right of the form. In the figure the field is already named.

3. When you draw the box and release the mouse the text box is outlined in color, and the Text Box Properties dialog box opens.

4. Every Form Field must be named. Acrobat 6.0 Professional gives them default names but you're going to use a hierarchy for the names—the purpose will be evident later in the chapter. Figure 8-2 shows the General tab in the Text Fields Properties dialog box. Name the field Owner.name.

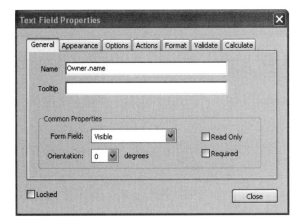

Figure 8-2
Name the form field in the General tab—each form field requires a name.

5. Click Appearance to display the Appearance tab. The form field is a white area; unless the user is familiar with the form, they wouldn't realize the fields existed. Unless someone knew the form, they wouldn't realize where the fields are. Figure 8-3 shows the appearance options selected. We used a thin underline in pale gray, and a Times Roman 8 point font.

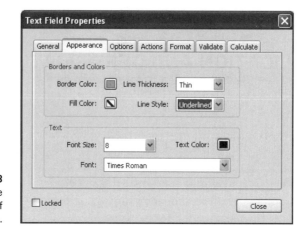

Text Field Properties

General | Appearance | Options | Actions | Format | Validate | Calculate

Borders and Colors

Border Color: ▢   Line Thickness: Thin ∨

Fill Color: ◩   Line Style: Underlined ∨

Text

Font Size: 8 ∨   Text Color: ■

Font: Times Roman ∨

☐ Locked   Close

Figure 8-3
Set the field's appearance according to the rest of the form.

Tip
Creating Multiple Copies of Fields

In Acrobat 5.0 you could name a field "name.1" and then press the Ctrl key and drag a copy of the field to a new location. This still works in Acrobat 6.0. In Acrobat 5.0, you could then hold Shift and press the + key to rename the file "name".2. The Shift+ method doesn't work in Acrobat 6.0. In Acrobat 6.0, you use the Create Multiple Copies of Fields feature.

6. Click Close to close the dialog box.

7. With the Text Box tool still selected, drag a resize handle on the sides of the form field to approximate the size of the field shown in the figure.

8. Click the Hand tool on the Basic toolbar to deselect the form field. You've created your first form field—pat yourself on the back.

Create Multiple Copies of the Text Box

Now you'll use a super neat new feature.

1. Right-click the Owner.name text box and select Create Multiple Copies from the context menu. The Create Multiple Copies of Fields dialog box shown in Figure 8-4 opens.

2. Choose copy amounts. Type **1** for the copy across and **2** for the copy down values.

3. Click OK to close the dialog box and add the additional fields.

4. Click the Hand tool on the Basic toolbar. The fields are named using a hierarchy, that is, .0, .1, .2.

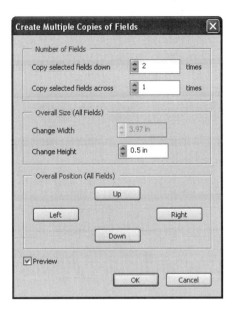

Figure 8-4
Use the Create Multiple
Copies of Fields dialog box
to quickly duplicate a field
on the form.

Creating Default Text in Text Box Fields

Next up, add some default text to the form. You can easily add text
using the Text Box form tool.

1. Click the Text Box form tool and drag a form box beside the
   Contractor label below the Owner label (you can see the location
   at the bottom of Figure 8-1).

2. Right-click the field and select properties to open the Text Field
   Properties dialog box. Name the field Contractor.name. Check
   Read Only as shown in Figure 8-5.

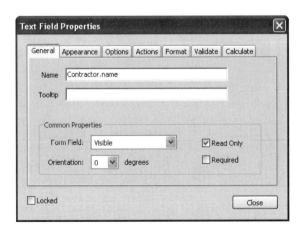

Figure 8-5
Set the Form Field to Read
Only—form fields don't
always have to have user
input to serve a purpose.

Tip

Although the field is Read Only, setting a font sizes the field to coordinate with others on the page.

3. Click Appearance. Set the font to 8 point Times Roman.

4. Click the Options tab and type **Bubba's Excavating** in the Default Value field, as shown in Figure 8-6.

Figure 8-6
Create the first text field for the contractor information.

5. Click Close to close the Text Box Field Properties dialog box.

6. Click the Hand tool and see the finished form field, shown in Figure 8-7. Using a default value and making the form Read Only makes the text permanent.

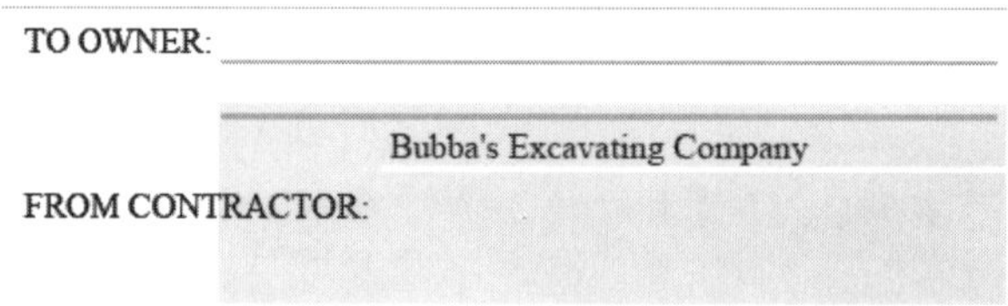

TO OWNER: _____

Bubba's Excavating Company

FROM CONTRACTOR:

Figure 8-7
Create the first text field for the contractor information.

7. Right-click the Contractor.name field and select Use Current Properties as New Defaults from the context menu. The structure of the field you added is now used as a default, which saves a lot of time when creating multiple fields that are the same.

8. Right-click the field and choose Create Multiple Copies. Use the same settings as earlier, that is, set the copies for one across and three down. Click OK.

9. Double-click the second field to open the Text Field Properties dialog box. Click the Options tab as shown in Figure 8-8, and type Bubba's company address, **1 Bulldozer Path.** Click Close to close the dialog box and set the field.

Note

Bubba has three companies. You're going to apply a bit of forms magic later and you'll use this field to ensure the form works for all three companies.

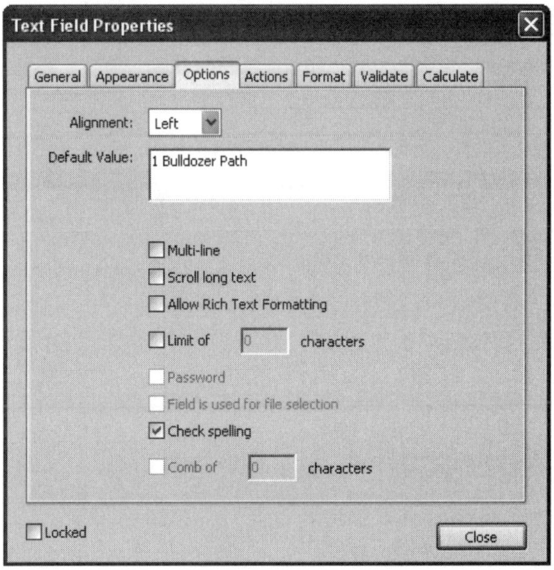

Figure 8-8
Enter the text for Bubba's company address in a simple text field.

10. Repeat with the third text box field, this time entering the rest of his address, **Dirt Track, TN 00000** as the Default Value in the Option tab of the Text Field Properties dialog box.

To the right of the contractor information is an area to enter engineer information. Set three fields; these must be active fields to enter data.

1. Draw a Text Box field and name it Engineer.name. Clear Read Only on the General tab as shown in Figure 8-9. The option is part of the defaults you set in Step 7. Click Close to close the dialog box and set the field.

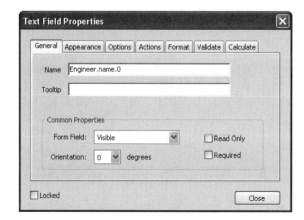

2. Right-click and choose Use Current Properties as New Defaults from the context menu to create a new default using active (not read-only) fields.

3. Duplicate the field twice for a set of three fields, as shown in Figure 8-10.

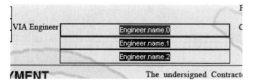

Figure 8-10
Create a set of three fields
to use for the engineer's
information.

So far the form contains a set of numbered fields for Bubba's company, some of the fields are active, that is, you can enter text, while others are read-only and are used for adding content to the form page.

Let's carry on with more form building.

Tutorial: Using Multiple Line Text Boxes and Aligning Fields

This tutorial picks up immediately where the last one left off. Continue with the same Bubba's form.PDF document. At this point the form contains numerous text box fields, some are active and others are read-only fields.

Multiple Line Text Boxes

Bubba's projects have a wide variety of names and some of the owners, architects, and engineers have very long titles.

1. With the Text Box tool, draw a text box beside the Project title on the form. When the Text Field Properties dialog box opens, name the field **Project**.

2. Click Options. Click Multi-line.

3. Click Close to close the dialog box and set the field.

The user can add text to the field, and when they get to the end of the field, it wraps to the next line. Figure 8-11 shows some sample information added to the Project field.

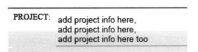

Figure 8-11
Create a multiline field on the page for long titles and blocks of text.

Cleaning Up Field Sizes and Distribution

You now have a set of fields in a variety of areas that are both active and read-only. Some of the fields aren't neatly aligned or distributed. You can use tools to quickly correct alignment issues.

Depending on how you drew the fields, your layout is going to be slightly different. However, the concept is the same.

The principle is that you select one field and size it as you wish, and then select all the others that you want to apply the same sizes to. Right-click the group and choose alignment, distribution, and sizing options, the sizing options are shown in Figure 8-12. The goal is to have an evenly sized and distributed set of fields.

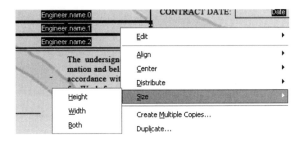

Figure 8-12
Use the alignment and distribution options to organize your fields on the form.

There are still several fields that need creating. However, the fields require specific types of input. Rather than merely dropping in a field, the fields are formatted to minimize wrong answers or data type. That's what's coming in the next tutorial.

Tutorial: Adding Formatted Fields

Our mission is to produce a smart form. That means some forms must contain a specific type of entry or a specifically formatted entry in order to be accepted. This tutorial carries on from the last. You add four fields in this tutorial and format their data type. You also add two fields that are duplicated to the second page of the form.

Formatting Form Field Content

In the center top of the form is an area for numbers and dates. You add four fields in this area of the form.

1. With the Text Field tool, draw a box for the Application No field. The field is highlighted and the Text Field Properties dialog box opens.

2. In the General tab, name the field **Application No**. Use the default settings used throughout for the appearance.

3. Click the Format tab. Select Number from the format category drop-down list. The Number Options area is shown in Figure 8-13. Set the decimal places to 0. Choose a separator style.

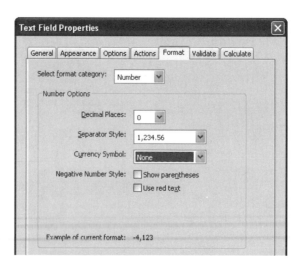

Figure 8-13
Choose a numbering format for fields using numerical input.

4. Click Close to close the dialog box and set the field. The numbers shown are our picks, but you might like to choose a different separator style.

5. Test the field. Click the Hand tool and try to enter a decimal number in the field. You can see the number and its decimal value as long as the field is active, as shown in Figure 8-14a. As soon as you click out of the field, the number is rounded off, as shown in Figure 8-14b.

(a)   (b)

122.33333   NO: 122

Figure 8-14
You can enter a decimal value into a field, but with the values set at 0 decimal places, the value is rounded off when you click another field.

Duplicating Fields on Different Pages

The Application No, Period To, and Project No fields are on both pages. When the three fields are configured, you can duplicate them to the second page.

1. With the Text Box tool, draw a field for the Period To field. Name the field **Period To**, and use the default settings (the settings set when you created the engineer fields.)

2. Draw another field for the Project Nos. label, and name it **Project No**.

You have a set of three fields so far, as shown in Figure 8-15. Align, distribute, and size the fields.

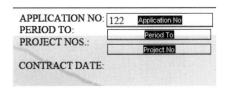

Figure 8-15
The next set of fields is almost complete.

1. Press Shift+click to select the three fields—Application No, Project No, and Period To fields.

2. Right-click and select Duplicate from the context menu. In the Duplicate Field dialog box, click From, and type **2**. Click OK to close the dialog box.

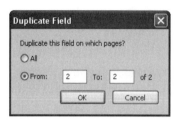

Figure 8-16
Select the fields and set
their page locations in the
Duplicate Field dialog box.

3. Go to page 2 of the form. The set of three fields is duplicated in the same location on the second page as it appeared on the first page. By the way, if you have any sample or test numbers added when you select the fields, the duplicates contain the test values as well.

Figure 8-17
The selected fields are
duplicated and display in
the same location on the
second page as they
appeared on the first page.

APPLICATION NO.:	Application No
APPLICATION DATE:	Period To
PERIOD TO:	Project No

Setting Date Formats in Form Fields

Tip

You can set date and time under date options. To set time alone, select Time from the Select Format Category drop-down list.

A few years back the world economy got a tremendous boost due to a problem called Y2K. In the early days of computers, years were limited to two digits to conserve storage space. All of a sudden, we needed four spaces to adequately describe the year. To make sure that your form works correctly with your database, you must specify the date format.

1. Using the Text Field tool, draw a field for the Contract Date. In the Text Field dialog box, name the field **Contract Date** in the General tab.

2. Click the Format tab and choose Date from the format category drop-down list. Choose the date form required for your database, as shown in Figure 8-18.

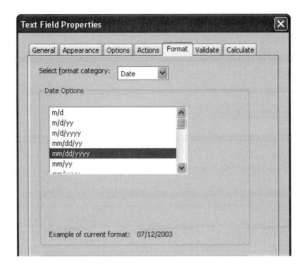

Figure 8-18
Select a data format to match your needs. You can choose from a list of options or create a custom alphanumeric date format.

3. Click Close to close the Text Field Properties dialog box.

4. Click the Hand tool and then click the new date field to test it. Enter a two-digit year date. You receive an error message as shown in Figure 8-19.

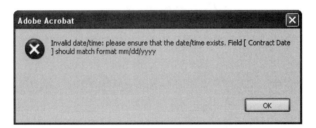

Figure 8-19
Incorrect entries result in display of an error message and description of how data should be entered in the field.

It's time to take a break from designing forms and discuss form-field naming.

Field Naming Theory 101

We identify four distinct influences on naming fields. The option you choose depends on the purpose of the form and how important the names are to the performance of the form. The four options are as follows:

- Stand-alone form

- Database-connected form

- Parent-child naming hierarchy

- Implementation of a Personal Field Naming (PFN) system

The Stand-Alone Form

Note

Take it from experience: You get sloppy calling form fields by any name that comes to you. Although you may understand what you're doing the day you construct the form, it's hard for someone else to upgrade your forms if needed.

In today's PDF forms environment, probably 95 percent of the active forms (a term that means there are active fields—not just an image) fall into this category. They're just replacing a paper form that can be filled out and printed instead of typed. Naming in a stand-alone form is simple. Call the field almost anything you want. As long as the names don't conflict, you're okay.

Database Connected Forms

A lot of your choices for naming and attributes have been determined by the database. Your field formats must match and the naming must be the same or convert through an intermediate table.

Parent-Child Naming Hierarchy

Parent-child isn't new to you, since we did it in an earlier tutorial on Bubba's pay form. If you create a field, and then right click and choose Create Multiple Copies, you add "grandchildren" to the mix by adding the .0, .1, and .2 suffixes to the end of the field names. If we had not used the Create Multiple Copies command, we would have named the second one Owner.address and the third one Owner.citystate.zip. The latter is easier to follow for updating, but the former works. In fact, before the chapter is finished, the fields are renamed using a more descriptive name when we add variable addresses that display in response to button clicks.

Figure 8-20
The Create Multiple Form Fields command creates a parent-child naming structure automatically.

Why should you use parent-child naming? Naming with a parent-child hierarchy allows you to perform a task on all fields at once. You'll look at that a little later in the chapter.

Personal Field Names

Adobe had a wonderful idea for forms in a small group environment called Personal Field Names (PFN). The Acrobat 5.0 installation CD contained both a template and the information to set it up. The Acrobat 5.0 help manual only had a fleeting mention of PFN and as a result, in most enterprise environments, IT loads the program without allowing the users to see the bonus info on the installation CD.

PFN allows you to develop your forms with a common naming format. All employees fill out a template containing fields that are commonly on forms. The employee fills them out once and pushes a Submit button. The Submit button executes a File ➤ Export ➤ Form Data command. The data is saved as a forms data format (FDF) file on the employee's hard drive. When the employee opens a PFN-compliant form, there is an Import button. They click the button, and the PFN data automatically populates the identical fields.

Adobe left PFN out of Acrobat 6.0, probably because of the changes in location of menu items. An Acrobat 6.0 PFN system would need a Submit button with action Advanced ➤ Forms ➤ Export Data. The Input button would need to have Advanced ➤ Forms ➤ Import Data. In a mixed Acrobat workflow (5.x and 6.0), you'll need dual buttons. You'll work through a good PFN tutorial later in the chapter.

Tip
Storing Resource Material

Develop a resource storage area and keep the bonus information from the Acrobat 5.0 CD. If you're in an enterprise environment, have the IT staff put the information, especially the batch, database, and forms folders in a shared resource storage folder. There is also lots of good information on www.planetPDF.com and the Adobe web site. Store the information in your resource storage area. Finding and sharing the information will save your group time and improve the effectiveness of your program.

Using Actions and Triggers on Forms

Before we continue with the tutorial, we want to look at triggers and actions, because they're going to figure prominently in the next tutorial.

Triggers are events that are used to invoke an action. You use triggers with mouse commands primarily, although they can also be used with key strokes. Actions can be used with a variety of activities, such as triggers, links, bookmarks, and document actions. We use triggers in the form; Table 8-2 summarizes the various triggers and when to use them.

Table 8.2   Triggers Available to Use with Form Fields

Trigger	Description	Uses
Mouse Up	Action happens when mouse released.	Gives user time to change mind after clicking. Drag out without releasing.
Mouse Down	Action happens instantly on clicking.	Good for functions like games requiring instant action.
Mouse Enter	Assigned actions occur when mouse enters the field.	Great for rollover pop-up instructions.
Mouse Exit	Assigned Action when mouse leaves field.	Sets action on leaving rather than selecting Next. Without this, actions may not happen until next field is selected.
On Focus	Action happens when tab or mouse enter field.	Initiate rollover pop-up on tabbing into field.
On Blur	Action happens when tab or mouse exit field.	Calculation happens when you leave field.

You can choose any of 16 actions. Most of the actions are self-explanatory. Several of these are new and offer new innovations for the creative forms designer. Table 8-3 is a summary of the actions that aren't readily understandable.

Let's get back to work.

Table 8.3   Summary of Actions that Are Not Self-Evident

Action	Results
Go to snapshot view	Interesting new tool. Use the Snapshot tool and copy desired part of PDF to clipboard. Select Go to Snapshot View and click Add. It will take the clipboard image and make the action. A substitute for Go to View used in Acrobat 5.0.
Read an article	Follows an article thread thorough an article (described in Chapter 11).
Execute a menu item	Executes command like Advanced ➤ Forms ➤ Import Data. (Be careful, because of changes of menus from 5.x to 6.0).
Set layer visibility	Right now, it's only useful for engineers, but it will have tremendous powers once it expands to the graphics community.
Run a JavaScript	Powerful tool that can make an Acrobat form anything you can imagine.

Tutorial: Creating Form Fields Using Radio Buttons

Bubba has three companies that use the same paper form. Bubba wants you to make one PDF form that works for all companies.

Making Fields Appear and Disappear with Radio Buttons

We'll create some form fields using radio buttons, and a little forms magic.

1. Zoom in to the upper-right corner of the first page. The name of Bubba's Excavating Company is already present on the text layer of the page.

2. Add two text fields above the Excavating Company name. Name one Bubba's Brick Laying Co and Bubba's Concrete Co as shown in Figure 8-21. For each field, do the following:

   - Set the properties to read-only on the General tab

   - Set the appearance to no fill or border color

   - Set the text to Times Roman 11 point

   - Add default text to the field using the names of the companies (that is, Bubba's Brick Laying Co and Bubba's Concrete Co).

Note

When Tom was young, car and house radios had a set of mechanical buttons to select the station. Push one button and another pushed out. These were called radio buttons. The same concept applies to forms.

Tip

We could have added these other companies three ways. We chose default value on the forms tools to give you exercise with forms. You can use the Text Box tool or use the TouchUp Text tool, press Ctrl+click to add a new line of text.

Figure 8-21
Name the fields Bubba's
Concrete Co and
Bubba's Brick Laying Co.

Bubba's C⟨Bubba's Concrete Co⟩pany

Bubba's B⟨Bubbas Brick Laying Co⟩ompany

Bubbas Excavating Company

Figure 8-21
Name the fields Bubba's
Concrete Co and
Bubba's Brick Laying Co.

3. Click the Radio Button tool and draw a box next to Bubba's Concrete Company. The Radio Button Properties dialog box opens.

4. In the General tab, name the field **bubbabutton.** Set the Form Field visibility to Visible but Doesn't Print as shown in Figure 8-22.

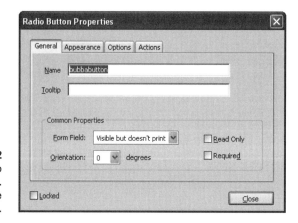

Figure 8-22
The form field is set to
visible, but it doesn't print.
Bubba's buttons will use
company colors.

5. Bubba wants the buttons to use company colors to make it easier for employees to choose the right forms and also to instill brand identity. Figure 8-23 shows the color selections of Bubba's Concrete selected in the Appearance tab. Each company uses one light fill color and one dark border color.

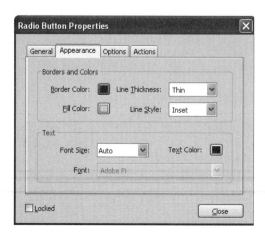

Figure 8-23
Set custom colors for the
radio buttons according to
the company the button is
associated with.

6. Click the Options tab. Select Circle from the Button Style drop-down list. Type an export value of **BCC** as shown in Figure 8-24. Radio buttons have the same name (they're all named bubbabuttons) but different export values.

Tip

If you were using this with other form fields and calculations this could be a number.

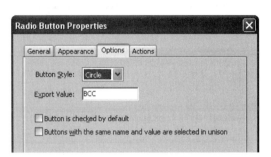

Figure 8-24
Create a button to use for selecting a company.

You're going to add JavaScript to this form field. The script activates when the mouse is released. Ron works with Tom. Ron is a firm believer that all he needs to know about JavaScript he learned in kindergarten— copy, cut, and paste. This script originated in an employee status change form in a JavaScript tutorial on the Adobe web site. Figure 8-25 shows the fields after the JavaScript is applied and the named altered. You copy, paste, and change the field names. Type it in EXACTLY as written. You'll understand it shortly.

7. Click the Actions tab. Select Mouse Up from the Select Trigger drop-down list.

8. Click the Select Action drop-down list and choose Run a JavaScript as shown in Figure 8-25.

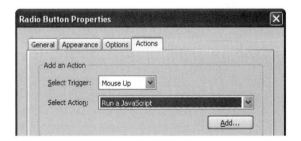

Figure 8-25
Choose a trigger and an action to start the button activity.

9. Click Add. The JavaScript Editor opens as shown in Figure 8-26. Type this code into the Editor exactly as written in Listing 8.1.

Listing 8-1. Code for creating visible and hidden fields for the Concrete company.

```
this.getField("Concrete").display = display.visible;
this.getField("Brick").display = display.hidden;
this.getField("Excavation").display = display.hidden;
```

Figure 8-26
Type the JavaScript into the JavaScript Editor to use as an action for the button.

10. Click OK to close the JavaScript Editor and return to the Radio Button Properties dialog box. You see the trigger and action are added to the Actions section of the dialog box as shown in Figure 8-27. Click Close to close the dialog box and set the button.

Now the first button is built and coded. Create two additional buttons.

Multiplying and Modifying the Buttons

You can duplicate button fields just as you did to the text fields earlier.

1. With the Radio Button tool, right-click the bubbabutton to open the context menu and choose Create Multiple Copies of Field. Choose 3 down and 1 over. Click OK.

2. Voilà, you have three radio buttons, although they don't work correctly.

Note

Radio buttons MUST have the same name, but different export values. You must make two corrections to make them work.

Figure 8-27
The trigger and action are set for the button.

3. Right-click the second radio button and select Properties from the context menu. The Radio Button Properties dialog box opens. Make these changes:

- In the General tab, delete the numerical suffix, .1 that Acrobat added when the multiples were created.

- In the Appearance tab, set the border color to orange; fill to white; and text to orange.

- In the Options tab, change the Export Value to BBC (Bubba's Brick Company).

4. Click the Actions tab. Run a JavaScript will be listed in the Action section of the tab (as shown in Figure 8-27.)

5. Click Run a JavaScript to select it, and then click Edit to open the JavaScript Editor.

6. Modify the first two lines of the script, and leave the third line as is to read as shown in Listing 8-2.

Note

In order to use a set of buttons that are mutually exclusive (that is, only one can be clicked at a time) name the fields the same thing and change the export values.

Listing 8-2. Code for creating visible and hidden fields for the Brick company.

```
this.getField("Concrete").display = display.hidden;
this.getField("Brick").display = display.visible;
this.getField("Excavation").display = display.hidden;
```

7. Click OK to close the JavaScript Editor and then click OK to close the Radio Button Properties dialog box.

8. Right-click the bottom radio button and select Properties from the context menu. The Radio Button Properties dialog box opens. Make these changes:

   • In the General tab, delete the numerical suffix .2 that Acrobat added when the multiples were created.

   • In the Appearance tab, set the border color to green; fill to brown; and text to green.

   • In the Options tab, change the Export Value to BEC (Bubba's Excavating Company).

9. Click the Actions tab. Run a JavaScript will be listed in the Action section of the tab (as shown in Figure 8-27).

10. Click Run a JavaScript to select it, and then click Edit to open the JavaScript Editor.

11. Modify the first and third lines of the script, and leave the second line as is to read as shown in Listing 8-3.

Listing 8-3. Code for creating visible and hidden fields for the Excavation Company.

```
this.getField("Concrete").display = display.hidden;
this.getField("Brick").display = display.hidden;
this.getField("Excavation").display = display.visible;
```

If you're familiar with JavaScript, you know where this is heading. If not, you're going to perform some interesting maneuvers in the next tutorial.

Tutorial: Creating Hidden Sets of Fields

So far you have one set of text fields for one of the companies. You need sets of address fields for the other two companies as well.

1. With the Text Tool selected, press Ctrl+click to select the set of three Contractor text boxes.

2. Right-click and select Create Multiple Copies of Field. Choose 1 across and 3 down as the multiplying options, and click OK to add the fields.

3. The fields are renamed using default names, but we rename them to use meaningful names as shown in Figure 8-28. The sets of names change to Excavation.name, Excavation.address, and Excavation.citystate.zip; make similar changes to the Brick Company's and Concrete Company's fields.

Figure 8-28
Rename the sets of fields with meaningful names.

4. Click the Hand tool and click the radio buttons. The proper fields are visible according to each selection.

5. Stack the sets of fields on top of one another. Don't worry about their appearance when the fields are deselected.

6. Test the buttons one more time. Only those fields belonging to the clicked radio button are visible at any one time.

Next up, some more form fields, this time different boxes such as check and combo boxes.

Tip

Organizing Form Fields

When maneuvering form fields and organizing them on a page, zoom in to a high magnification. Save your eyes. Acrobat uses vectors and the magnification is your friend.

Tutorial: Creating More Form Fields

Now you add even more types of form fields to the form. You add a set of check boxes to define recipients on a distribution list, and also create a combo box to select signatories for the form.

Adding Check Boxes

Check boxes are the easiest of all form fields to create, especially since everything a check box will do, you've already done.

1. Click the Check Box tool on the Forms toolbar. Draw a box matching the one in front of Distribution to Owner. The Check Box Properties dialog opens.

2. In the General tab, name the field **CB** (for check box).

3. In the Appearance tab, choose Auto for the font size. The check mark will size itself to the dimensions of the check box.

4. Click the Options tab and select Check from the Check Box Style drop-down list.

5. Click Close to close the dialog box and set the field.

6. Right-click the field and choose Create Multiple Fields to create a set of five check boxes. You must manually drag the created check boxes over the existing boxes (see Figure 8.29).

Distribution to:

OWNER
ARCHITECT
CONTRACTOR
ACCOUNTANT

Figure 8-29
Create a set of check box fields to use for distributing the form.

7. Test the check boxes. You can select multiple check boxes (Figure 8-30) because the entry isn't restricted like the radio buttons.

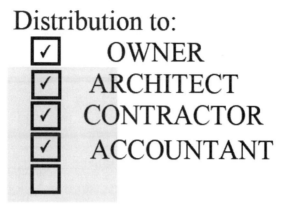

Figure 8-30
Select recipients on the distribution list using check marks.

Creating Combo Boxes aka Drop-down Lists

The application and certificate for payment legally requires that the document be signed by a person with signatory authority in the company. Bubba got in trouble with that once. He wants a combo box with a list of names of people with signatory authority.

1. Click the Combo Box icon and draw a box besides the By field above the Notary area as shown in Figure 8-31. The Combo Box Properties dialog box opens.

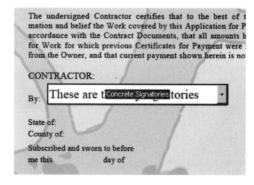

Figure 8-31
Draw a box to contain the list of signatories for the form.

Tip

If you want, you can create a separate box for each company like we did with the radio buttons. You're using one box in the tutorials that activates with the Concrete Company button.

2. In the General tab name the field Concrete.signatories.

3. On the Appearance tab, choose a black border, pale gray fill, thin line, and font size 12 point as shown in Figure 8-32.

Figure 8-32
Configure the combo box appearance to coordinate with the rest of the form.

4. Click the Options tab. One by one, type items in the Item field and click Add to move them to the Item List (Figure 8-33).

5. Check the Sort Item box to alphabetize the entries.

6. Click "These are the only signatories" to highlight it and make it the default value. Click Close to close the dialog box and set the field.

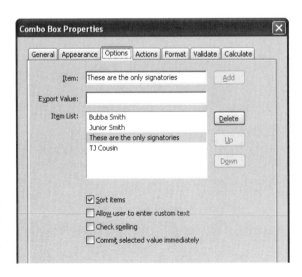

Figure 8-33
Add a list of signatories to the combo box to use for Bubba's Concrete Company.

7. Click the Hand tool and give it a try. If the Concrete button isn't pushed, you will not see the field! (See Figure 8-34.)

Figure 8-34
Test the signatories combo box. Unless you choose the Concrete company's radio button, the combo box is hidden.

Creating Buttons

Buttons have one purpose and that is to initiate an action. Bubba's form needs a Clear button to remove all numbers from the form. The button doesn't need to be printed when the form is printed. Donna made us a nice matching logo for the Clear button. It's a file named dozerlogo.pdf, and it's in the Chapter 8 folder. Follow these steps:

1. Select the Button tool on the Forms toolbar and draw a button in the lower left corner of the page. The Button Properties dialog box opens.

2. Use these settings:

    - On the General tab, name the button Clear, and under Common Properties, choose Form Field Is Visible, but Doesn't Print.

    - On the Appearance tab, choose No Fill or Border Color; and Text Color Black.

    - On the Options tab, choose the Icon top, label bottom layout. In the Icon and Label section of the tab, type **CLEAR** for the label. Click Browse and locate the file dozerlogo.pdf in the Chapter 8 file. Select the file and click OK. As shown in Figure 8-35, the logo is added to the button.

Note

If you're really ambitious, you can add signatories for Bubba's Brick Laying Company and Bubba's Excavation Company.

3. Click the Actions tab. From the Trigger drop-down list choose Mouse Up. From the Select Action drop-down list choose Reset a Form. Click Close to close the dialog box and set the button.

4. Select the Hand tool and then click the button to give it a try. All the data added to the form is deleted. The final button, shown in Figure 8-36, is a deserving Clear button, since it takes the dirt (old data) out of your way.

Figure 8-36
Click the Clear button
to delete any data
added to the form.

Next up, adding a signature field to the form.

Tutorial: Creating Signature Fields

The engineers that Bubba works with aren't up to speed, and so digital signatures aren't an option. Bubba wants a digital signature field to lock the document down so that any changes in the document can be seen. Remember how to compare documents from Chapter 7.

 1. Click the Digital Signature tool on the Forms toolbar and draw a box at the bottom of the form. The Digital Signature Properties dialog box opens.

2. On the General tab, you can leave the default field name, Signature. At the bottom of the General tab, choose Hidden from the Form Field drop-down list. Check Required as shown in Figure 8-37.

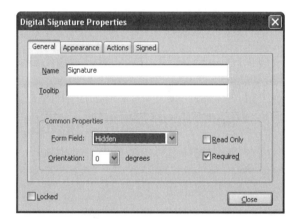

Figure 8-37
Set the digital signature to be a hidden and required field.

3. On the Signed tab, select the Mark as Read-only radio button and select All Fields from the drop-down list as shown in Figure 8-38.

4. Click Closed to close the dialog box and set the field. Click the Hand tool and test the signature field.

You've now seen all the tabs and functions with the different properties except validate and calculate tabs, which only appear in text and combo fields. You'll learn how to use them in the next section on form math.

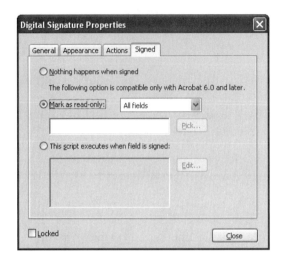

Figure 8-38
Mark the fields as read-only on the Signed tab.

Form Math 101

In an electronic workflow, having forms that constantly perform correct mathematical functions creates major savings. How much time is wasted each year checking and correcting the math in paper forms? Your guess is as good as ours, but it's considerable. In this segment, you're going to work on math. Figure 8-39 shows the continuation sheet, which is page two of the form. We have already added some read-only text fields with the identifying information at the top of the form. You're going to add the other fields, math and validation, to flag overruns immediately. Let's begin!

Figure 8-39
Many of the calculations for the second page of the form are included.

What's in the Form?

Before doing any calculations, here's a quick description of the form itself. The column number, description, and its contents are described in Table 8-4. The final column on the form, Retainage, isn't included in our calculations.

Table 8.4   Structure of Bubba's Continuation Sheet

Column	Label	Content
a	Item number	Tracking number or code
b	Description of work	Text description
c	Scheduled value	Dollar value for item
d	Work completed from previous application	Dollar value for work done previously (total of D and E)
e	Work completed from this period	Dollar value for work done during this period
f	Materials presently stored	Dollar value not included in D or E
g	Total completed and stored to date	Dollar value total of D, E, F
h	Percentage value of completion	Percentage value of G-C
i	Balance to finish	Dollar value to completion, C-G

Tutorial: Completing the Field Calculations

As you can see in Figure 8-39, many of the fields in the table are already complete. There are three columns that require completion and calculations.

Completing the Calculations

You have to do the math for columns *g, h,* and *i,* and then copy the fields, change the math, and create some subtotals. All the fields are created using the Text Field tool.

You use these defaults on all remaining fields:

- Border and background–No color (Appearance tab)

- Text 8 point Helvetica black (Appearance tab)

- Alignment right (Options tab)

- Number format and two decimal places (Format tab)

Total Completed and Stored to Date

Let's start with column *g,* Total Completed and Stored to Date, which is the sum of columns *d, e,* and *f.*

Note

Acrobat 6.0 allows us
alternatively to choose
Simplified field notation
and type in the following:

Sum=d.0+complete.0+
f.0

1. Right-click *g* and select Properties from the context menu to open the dialog box.

2. Click the Calculate tab. Click Value is the Sum (+) of the following fields. Click Pick to open the Field Selections dialog box as shown in Figure 8-40. Scroll through the list and choose these three fields: d.0, complete.0, f.0. Click OK to close the Field Selection dialog box.

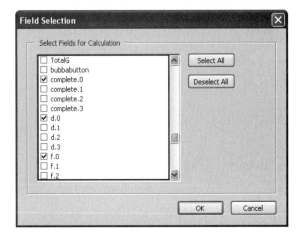

Figure 8-40
Choose the fields to
use for the calculation
from the list.

3. Back on the Calculate tab you see the entries listed in the Value are the sum of the following fields as shown in Figure 8-41. Click Close to close the dialog box and set the field.

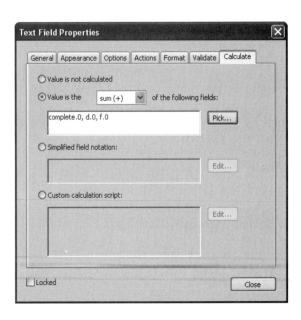

Figure 8-41
The selected values are
listed on the Calculate tab.

Creating Multiple Fields

The first calculation is complete. You need to re-create the same calculations for each of the other items in the column. Earlier in the chapter we described creating multiple copies of form fields. Use that information to create a set of fields for the column.

As a brief refresher, here's how to do it: Using the Text Field tool, select a field, right-click in the field and choose Create Multiple Copies from the context menu. In the dialog box, set the number of field copies to 4 down and 1 across, and then click OK to close the dialog box.

The set of fields are added and numbered as shown in Figure 8-42?

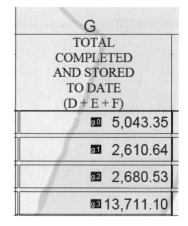

Figure 8-42
Use the Create Multiple Copies process to add fields to the column.

Calculating the Percentage to Completion

Column *h* describes the percentage value of the current completed amount of an item in relation to its scheduled value, expressed as a percentage. The value of column *g* divided by column *c* times 100 yields a percentage.

1. Draw a text field in column *h*. When the field is drawn, the Text Field Properties dialog box opens. Click Calculate.

2. On the Calculate tab, click Custom calculation script and then click Edit to open the JavaScript Editor.

3. Type the code shown in Listing 8-4 into the JavaScript Editor.

Tip

Using Alternate JavaScript Editors

Choose Edit ➤ Preferences ➤ General ➤ JavaScript. On the Preferences tab you can choose an alternative editor and activate the JavaScript Debugger. Many serious forms developers use alternative editors.

Listing 8-4. Code for calculating percentage value of the work completed

```
var a=this.getField("ScheduledValue.0");
var b=this.getField("g");
event.value=b.value/a.value*100;
```

4. Click OK to close the JavaScript Editor. The code is displayed in the Calculate tab as shown in Figure 8-43.

Figure 8-43
The custom JavaScript displays on the Calculate tab.

5. Click Close to close the Text Field Properties dialog box.

6. Select the Hand tool and test the field.

7. Use the Create Multiple Copies process to add more fields to the column.

Be Careful with the Code

When you write the JavaScript for the table, be very careful to type the code exactly as written. That includes the punctuation. In the sample, an extra " was used in the second line of the code, highlighted in Figure 8-44. You see the error is described at the bottom of the JavaScript Editor, in this case, it states there is an unterminated string in line 2.

Figure 8-44
Errors can occur if the punctuation used in your JavaScript isn't typed correctly.

Calculating the Final Balance for an Item

The final calculation takes place in column *i*. The final balance is the difference between the scheduled value and the total completed and stored to date, in other words, the value of column *c* through column *g*.

1. Draw a text field in column *i*. When the field is drawn, the Text Field Properties dialog box opens. Click Calculate.

2. On the Calculate tab, click Custom Calculation Script and then click Edit to open the JavaScript Editor.

3. Type the code shown in Listing 8-5 into the JavaScript Editor:

Listing 8-5. Code for calculating the final balance for the item.

```
var c=this.getField("ScheduledValue.0.0");
var d=this.getField("g.0");
event.value=c.value-d.value
```

4. The code is shown in the JavaScript Editor in Figure 8-45. Click OK to close the JavaScript Editor.

5. Click Close to close the Text Field Properties dialog box.

6. Select the Hand tool and test the field.

7. Use the Create Multiple Copies process to add more fields to the column.

Tip

In Figure 8-45 you see the code is wrapped to the next line. This is because the string has no spaces. The code displays in a single line in the Calculate tab. Regardless of how it displays in an Editor dialog box, the important thing is that it works.

Note

Again, you can use simplified notation instead of the custom JavaScript. The simplified notation is Sum=ScheduledValue. 0-g.0. We were able to get it to work, but if we changed the values of the fields, the sum didn't refresh. We went back to JavaScript.

Figure 8-45
Write the custom
JavaScript in the
JavaScript Editor.

Modifying the Scripts

The fields are created and the parent-child naming added as shown in
Figure 8-46. All field calculations will need to be updated to adjust the
named fields. Otherwise all the fields will calculate the values of the first
item. For example, the second field in column *g* has the calculation
sum=complete.0, d.0, f.0. To change the calculation for the second field,
change the suffix "0" to "1". Modify the set of scripts for the fields in the
three columns.

G	H	I
TOTAL COMPLETED AND STORED TO DATE (D + E + F)	% (G ÷ C)	BALANCE TO FINISH (C – G)
g.0 5,043.35	h.0 3.34	i.0 6,567.97
g.1 2,610.64	h.1 9.07	i.1 24.46
g.2 2,680.53	h.2 2.80	i.2 1,001.77
g.3 13,711.10	h.3 8.08	i.3 2,099.78

Figure 8-46
The completed set
of fields added to the
table are numbered
sequentially when
added to the form.

In the next tutorial, you'll finish the form. There are a few outstanding
details to finish up to make a professional form.

Tutorial: Setting Field Order

Bubba is in trouble in the permanent storm water line item (item 2 on the table, described as Permanent SW Controls.) He is over budget as you can see in Figure 8-47, and will either need to get a change order or eat the $2,099.78 that he is over budget. Just because it appears on the line, doesn't mean it will be paid. You need a column total to see what is going on overall.

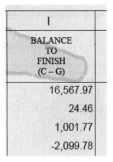

Figure 8-47
Bubba is over budget on one item.

Creating a Column Total

To introduce you to field order, let's total column *g*. Follow these steps:

1. With the Text Field tool, draw a field below the other fields on column *g*. When the Text Field Properties dialog box opens, name the field **TotalG**. Use the appearance and formatting used for the other column fields.

2. Click Calculate. Select Sum from the Value Is drop-down list.

3. Click Pick to open the Field Selection dialog box. Scroll down the list and choose the set of fields in column *g* as shown in Figure 8-48. Pick fields *g.0, g.1, g.2, g.3,* and then click Close to close the dialog box and return to the Calculate tab.

4. The values are listed on the Calculate tab as shown in Figure 8-49. Click Close to close the dialog box and set the field.

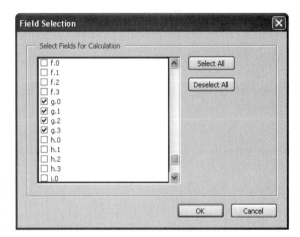

Figure 8-48
Choose the set of fields
from the column to use
for the total value.

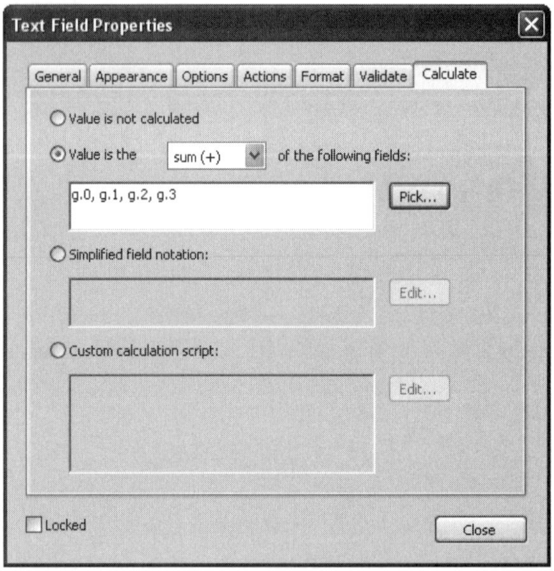

Figure 8-49
The values used for the
calculation are displayed
in the Calculate tab.

Check the Field Calculation Order

When you add calculations to a form, you must make sure they are
done in the correct order or you'll get some strange results. A total must
be made after all the components are calculated. Follow these steps to
set the field calculation order:

1. Select Advanced ➤ Forms ➤ Set Field Calculation Order. The
   Calculated Fields dialog box shown in Figure 8.50 opens. All the

fields in the form that include calculations in their properties are listed in the dialog box.

2. *TotalG* is shown as calculating before *g.2* and *g.3*, which isn't the correct order. Highlight *TotalG* and move it down below *g.3* or move it to the end of the list.

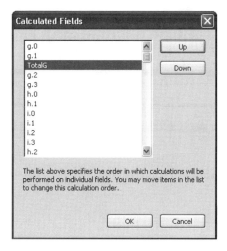

Figure 8-50
Reorder the calculations in the form by moving fields in the list.

3. Click OK to close the Calculated Fields dialog box. Your fields will now be ordered. Save the file and test it again.

Bubba's form is now finished. He has the capability of using the same form for all three companies. If this form were to be used "live" add the fields on page 2 to the list to clear using the Clear button you added on page 1. Your version doesn't include those fields in order to show the calculations using constant values. To see the finished form, open the Bubba's Form done.pdf document in the Chapter 8 folder.

Setting Tab Order

People are accustomed to using the Tab key to move through a form. In Acrobat 5.0 you could use a function to click through the fields in the order you wanted them tabbed. In Acrobat 6.0, there is a different method. Tabbing is based on different structural orders in the form.

Click the Pages tab. Select a page, and right-click to open the context menu. Select Page Properties as shown in Figure 8-51.

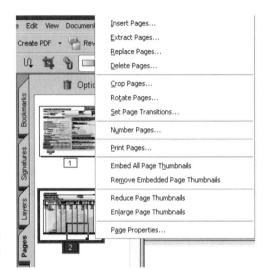

Figure 8-51
Tab Order is accessed from the Page Properties dialog box.

The Page Properties dialog box opens as shown in Figure 8-52. You have four choices. The calculations are done in rows, so select the Use Row Order radio button.

Figure 8-52
Use one of four options to set your form's tab order.

Click Close to close the Page Properties dialog box. Test the form using the Tab key. At this point, the form is complete.

More Forms Information

There are a few last forms items to cover in this chapter. We want to show you the Fields tab and how it works. We also want to mention templates and accessible form fields.

Using the Field Tab

You can view the structure and layout of fields in a document in the Fields tab. Choose View ➤ Navigation Tabs ➤ Fields. Drag the panel's tab into the other panels' tabs for ease of use. The contents of the Fields panel for Bubba's Form.pdf file are shown in Figure 8-53.

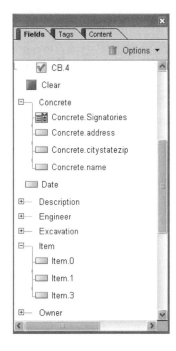

Figure 8-53
The Fields panel for the Bubba's Form.pdf document shows the field types as well as the names.

For any of the listings in the tab, you can select and right-click to access a context menu. As shown in Figure 8-54, this menu's options are straightforward. The Go to Field option highlights the field on the document. The Properties option will open the Field Properties dialog box.

Figure 8-54
You can select and modify a field from the Fields tab.

Form Templates

An Acrobat form can carry hidden pages that are "spawned" as an action. In the spawning process, the form fields take on parent-child naming. This has its place in some workflows. There are some good template examples on the Acrobat 5.0 CD. You can't use templates in Adobe Reader. If you create forms using templates, only those users with Acrobat can work with your forms.

Accessible Forms

Chapter 10 is about accessible PDF documents. Forms require instructions and tabbing order to be considered accessible. You already looked at tabbing order. To add instructions to a field, open the field's Properties dialog box.

In the General tab (Figure 8-55), enter text in the Tooltip field. Make the text descriptive of the field or the instructions for use.

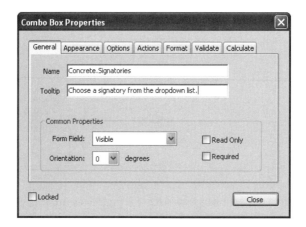

Figure 8-55
Add tooltips to form fields
to provide information
for screenreaders.

When the user works with your form, moving the cursor over the field displays the message in a tooltip frame, as shown in Figure 8-56.

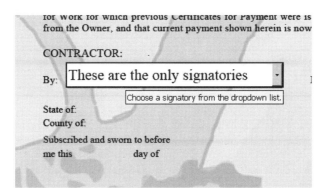

Figure 8-56
The tooltip is displayed when the mouse is moved over the field.

Up Next

This has been more fun that a swamp full of gators. We hope you found it informative and useful. Forms are such useful creations. In this chapter, we covered the basics of building and organizing a form and touched on accessibility issues.

We're serious when we say we covered only the basics. There are so very many forms issues that couldn't be covered here. Other Acrobat features that deal with importing and exporting data and other forms issues are covered in Chapter 15, when you'll look at JavaScript.

Coming up next, you'll look at cataloging and searching documents and collections. Acrobat takes searching information on documents to a new level.

Chapter 9

Searching and
Indexing Documents

Just like the I Can't Believe It's Not Butter commercials, the Acrobat Catalog (Indexes) have an identity problem. It's hard to count the number of times customers have said that the Acrobat Catalog does the same thing as their expensive database.

Indexing: More Than It Seems

All governments and most businesses are legally required to keep minutes of their meetings. These minutes become a record of legal proceedings. Before meetings, a harried clerk has to search through files of the last 10, 20, or 30 years to determine what previous boards had decided. Imagine having to manually search through files of the last 10 years for 24 minutes worth of notes per year so that those at the meeting can determine what the board had decided on accepting private roads into the county system or for board reviews of personnel complaints. Acrobat is a powerful tool that can turn this drudgework into a breeze.

Acrobat 5.0 has some imposing indexing capabilities. With Acrobat 5.0, you can find words or phrases in a file, create an index to search across a number of files, or index collections of files. You can also define and set search functions as well as update and modify indexes. Using some of the navigation tools, you can create impressive ways to maneuver through documents.

Acrobat 6.0 took a major step forward with searching and indexing. Adobe contracted with Lextek International to adapt their Onix search technology to enhance the search capabilities of Acrobat 6.0. Acrobat 6.0's Find function doesn't search only the document you're in; it will let you search a single document, folder, drive, or collection of drives.

The ability to build a catalog still exists in Acrobat 6.0. This feature is especially helpful when you're working with a collection of documents that will be searched numerous times. It's faster than the search of an uncataloged collection of documents. Using commands where the index is associated with a set of documents, the searcher needs less knowledge of searching.

What Indexing Can Be

So what are we looking at here? Lots, actually. Acrobat 6.0 has a command named Adobe Acrobat Catalog. This command creates and manages indexes. In this chapter, you'll go beyond a simple "click the button and make an index" process. You'll also incorporate surrounding building and management issues that affect how the indexed set of documents functions and how indexed files should be handled. You'll look at the following:

- Collecting source material

- Naming and storing the documents in a collection

- Designing the index content

- Creating the index

- Managing the index

And you used to think compiling an index was as simple as knowing your ABCs!

Preparing a Document Collection

As with most things in life, preparation is the key. As you've seen in other chapters, the more factors you take into consideration regarding the intended use of a document, the less time you'll need for time-consuming repairs.

Creating the File Structure

First things first, define the file structure you're going to use. In this chapter, you'll concentrate on creating an index for a number of documents, known as a *document collection*. To create the collection, move or copy files to the same location.

Now that the collection is assembled, turn to the individual documents within it.

Naming the Documents

When you've decided where to house the index materials, look at the individual documents. Some of these issues are fairly straightforward. Some aren't.

Each document must be named correctly and must have document info elements and other metadata added.

MS-DOS Naming Requirements

The safest way to name documents for a collection is with MS-DOS file-naming conventions. The reasons for this are clarity and speed. Acrobat can identify formats of indexed documents, but it will take time to apply the mapping filter when conventions other than DOS are applied. Therefore, the search will be slower. It might even result in inaccurate search results.

Macintosh-Specific Naming Requirements

A number of naming issues are specific to Macs:

- *Using Mac OS with an OS/2 LAN Server.* To make indexed files searchable on all PC platforms, either configure LAN Server Macintosh (LSM) to enforce MS-DOS file-naming conventions or index only file allocation table (FAT) volumes.

- *Using the Mac OS version of Acrobat Catalog to build a cross-platform indexed document collection.* Select Make Include/Exclude Folders DOS Compatible in the Index preferences before building the index. You won't have to change long PDF file names to MS-DOS file names, but you will have to use MS-DOS file-naming conventions for the folder names (eight digits with a three-digit extension).

- *Creating documents that will be searched only by Macintosh users.* Do not use deeply nested folders or pathnames longer than 256 characters.

- *Using ISO 9660 file names with ISO 9660-formatted discs.* In the Macintosh version of Acrobat Catalog, check Log Compatibility Warnings (in the Logging preferences) for noncompliant file names.

- *Indexing PDF documents with long file names that will be truncated for Windows use.* Use either the Windows or Mac OS version of Acrobat Catalog to build or update the index.

Note

This information on Macintosh-specific naming issues was taken from the Adobe Acrobat 5.0 Help file, pages 222–23, a review of the information in the Acrobat 6.0 Help file shows that this information remains consistent.

Completing the Document Information

More information should be added to the document's metadata to allow for broader search access. Document information can be added either in the source application before conversion or in Acrobat after conversion.

The option you choose (or both) depends on how you use your documents. For example, if you're creating a set of Word files that will only be used to convert source material to PDF, it doesn't matter which end of the conversion process you choose. We would most likely add the information in Acrobat, because that is the only location we would be using it. On the other hand, if your source documents will also be used for other purposes, you may want to add the document information in the source documents and then convert to PDF.

Adding Document Information in Source Files

Figure 9-1 shows the Document Properties dialog box from the minutes of a meeting of the Dayton School Board. Your given search will determine what is needed in the document properties.

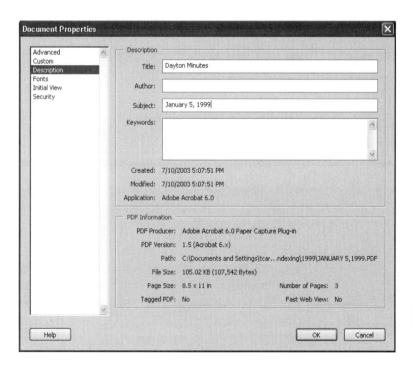

Figure 9-1
Some indexes and searches require additional document information.

Let's go through the dialog box and see what to do. It isn't quite as simple as it looks. You can add whatever you like to the fields, but that won't necessarily make for a good index.

- *Title.* When a search is done, the file name appears in the Search Results dialog box. The title should be descriptive and not simply an alphanumeric string used for file management.

- *Subject vs. Keywords.* Establish a pattern. Consistently use one or the other or both. If you use both, identify keywords in advance for the entire collection so you know what to add here.

- *Author.* This entry identifies responsibility for the document's creation and management. We're responsible for our own work (sometimes to our dismay!). You may use the name of a workgroup rather than an individual in this field.

- *Category.* You can use this field to categorize documents by type.

- *Comments.* Add information to describe the index. When users want to view available indexes, they can select based on the descriptions.

- *Additional Search fields.* Acrobat 6.0 also searches bookmarks, tags, and custom fields as needed.

If the information is added to a source document in Word, the information is automatically transferred when the document is converted to PDF. Speaking of PDF files, you can add the document information directly in Acrobat.

Advanced Document Management

In certain instances, it's appropriate to develop a document management system beyond what you're looking at in this chapter. To give you an idea of what can be done with and around Acrobat, consider these concepts:

- In Acrobat, you can define custom data fields to enhance searchability. This will require custom data fields in the document's properties. This can be used for elements such as document identification in large systems.

- Compile information about a large index system in a readme file. This can include such elements as the scope of the documents, names and locations of folders, search options supported, stopwords used in the indexes, and so on.

- Maintain a list of values for each document (as we described earlier to complete the document information for a file.) This way, you'll have a record of what has been done and used in the past, and you can use it as a frame of reference for ongoing work.

Tip

Working with Fewer Than Thousands of Documents

All kidding aside, it makes sense to coordinate what is going into a set of documents, even if the elements number in the single digits. Again, it all comes down to the value of preplanning. Using a table that lists values assigned to each document is a good way to store overall information as well as maintain consistency. When you've finished the index, store the table in a readme file with the rest of the index materials.

Project Project 9-1: Defining and Constructing an Index from the Meeting Minutes

You worked with a set of minutes in Chapter 4; in this project the minutes are going to be used to build a catalog. In Chapter 4 the minutes were scanned and captured in one PDF document. The document was also bookmarked and named 1999 Minutes captured and bookmarked.pdf.

The set of documents in the 1999 folder in the Chapter 9 folder are split segments from that Chapter 4 1999 Minutes captured and bookmarked.pdf file. Once you've structured a set of documents correctly and have completed all its information, you can build the index using Acrobat Catalog. This same process will create a full-text index of single documents or document collections. A set of the 21 split files is in the Chapter 9 folder in a subfolder named 1999.

Demo: Using ARTS Splitter

ARTS Splitter is a very handy plug-in for Acrobat. You can download a demo or buy the product from PlanetPDF. The set of minutes in the 1999 folder are split portions of the original single document. The minutes files are named by date and have a bookmark to the navigation (interface page). Here's how it was done:

The minutes file was opened in Acrobat. The command Plug-ins ➤ ARTS Splitter ➤ Split This File by Bookmarks was chosen, as shown in Figure 9-2.

This action opens the ARTS PDF Splitter - Split by Bookmarks dialog box. The option was chosen to split the minutes by Level 1 bookmarks. Choose a storage location and run the plug-in. Each file is named according to the bookmark's name.

Once the files were split, their navigation links were tested using the links added in the Chapter 4 project linking the bookmarks to the interface page. As the links worked, the unsplit file was deleted. The folder, 1999, contains a set of 21 files that functions like a single file. A collection provides better search control than one single, long document.

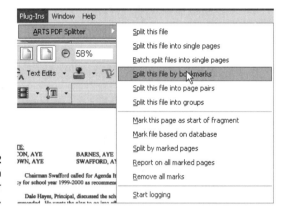

Figure 9-2
You can choose from a variety of options for splitting a document.

Constructing the Index

Let's make an index. Choose Advanced ➤ Catalog to open the Catalog dialog box shown in Figure 9-3.

Note

You cannot select individual files for exclusion. If you have to deselect a file, deselect its folder. Plan ahead and move from a directory any folders that you don't want to include before you start and save yourself time in this step.

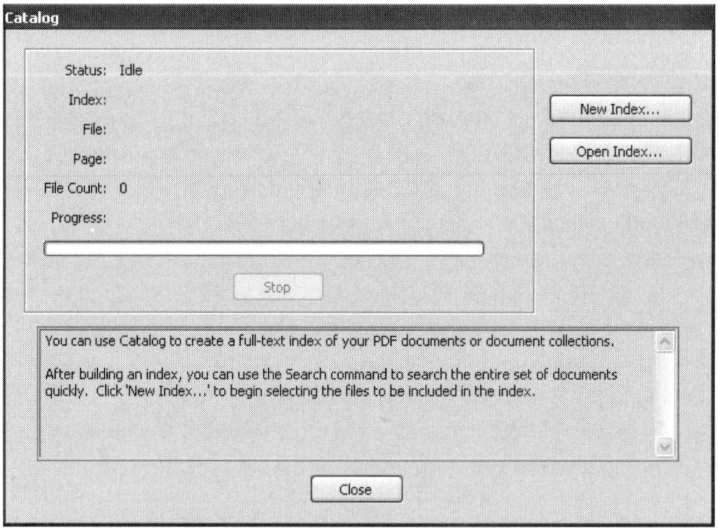

Figure 9-3
Create a new catalog for indexing in the Catalog dialog box.

1. The Catalog dialog box allows you to either create a new index or open an existing index for maintenance. You're going to select New Index, which opens the New Index Definition dialog box as shown in Figure 9-4. You need to give the index a descriptive name that describes what it indexes. You must also define the directories included and list subfolders excluded if necessary.

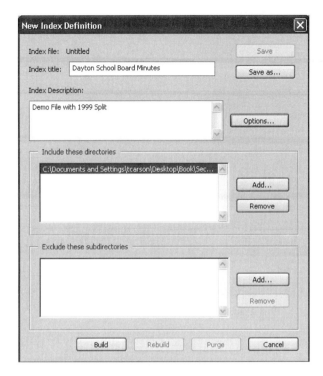

Figure 9-4
Name the file and select directories to start the Indexing process.

2. Click the Options button to open the Options dialog box shown in Figure 9-5. These are the available options and your choices:

- *Do Not Include Numbers.* You aren't going to check this because there might be searches needed for bus stops on HWY 27, for example.

- *Add IDs to Adobe PDF v1.0 files.* There are no version 1.0 files, so you don't need to check this option.

- *Do Not Warn for Changed Documents When Searching.* This one might be worth checking. Any minor changes will cause an alert that unnecessarily concerns searchers.

- Custom Properties opens a dialog box used to define advanced search fields. You won't use any advanced fields in this index.

- Stop Words is a relic from the days when storage space was precious, processing speed was slow, and low transfer rates were the rule. Setting Stop Words can reduce an index file structure by as much as 15 percent, but you lose the ability to search phrases that have these words.

Tip

You can see the Advanced fields displayed in Figure 9-9.

Note

To associate an index with a document, choose Document Properties ➤ Advanced ➤ Search Index.

• Tags are something new to the searching world and quite frankly, we haven't figured out why we need them over other methods yet.

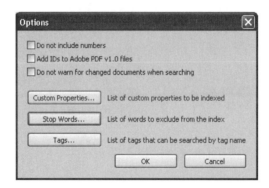

Figure 9-5
The Options dialog box has a wide variety of choices for refining an index.

3. Click OK to close the Options dialog box. It's time to build the index.

Tip

Setting Up Indexes

Determining the way to set up indexes requires considerable thought. In certain instances, we have made indexes for every year or every decade or one index for all years. Indexing by decade and creating one index for the current year may be the best way for minutes. Keeping the current year separate makes it easier to keep the index current.

4. Click Build. You will be asked where to save the file. Click Save As. Once you've specified a storage location, click OK to return to the Catalog dialog box. Consider these points before deciding on a name and storage location:

• Store the index folder on the same disk or server volume as the documents (our recommendation). Change the preference setting to allow different storage locations.

• Do not use ANSI characters with values over 128 or the slash (/) character in the name of the location.

5. Wait until the build completes. The build in Acrobat 6.0 is fast. It took less than one-third the time it takes in Acrobat 5.0, and it didn't take that long in 5.0. Figure 9-6 shows the completed index.

Voilà! All 21 documents containing 52 pages are indexed.

Options for Large Document Collections

Part of the preferences have been moved to Edit ➤ Preferences ➤ General ➤ Catalog as shown in Figure 9-7. You're now able to index on separate drives. This may be important for very large document collections, but you need to be careful how you manage this move. If your index is to be used across multiple platforms, you should force ISO 9660 compatibility on folders. Working with governments and industry, most systems are Windows, and we normally don't check this. Enable Logging is checked by default.

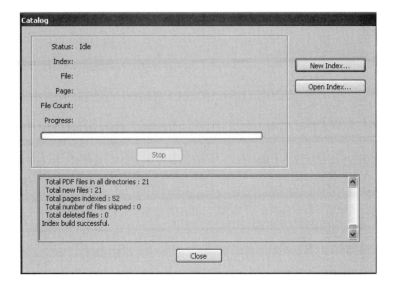

Figure 9-6
Information about the completed index displays in the Catalog dialog box.

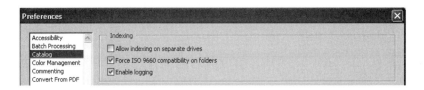

Figure 9-7
Set other Catalog preferences options if you're working with large document collections.

Searching Options

As we discussed in the introduction, Acrobat 6.0 no longer uses the Find function. Find allowed you to search a single document that was open in Acrobat. Figure 9-8 shows the Basic Search options for a document or series of documents. The Advanced Search options are extremely powerful and will be described shortly.

Acrobat 5.0 partially supported Boolean searches, and it was mainly between fields, not words. Acrobat 6.0 has greatly enhanced Boolean searches, but it still doesn't support wildcards (*) and (?). The more common Boolean operators are as follows:

- AND. As shown in Figure 9-8, playground AND construction was used to search for documents containing both words.

Note

Boolean searches cannot be performed on a single document.

- NOT. If playground NOT accidents were the search phrase, you would be trying to eliminate documents containing *playground accidents*.

- OR. In engineering a lot of words like "ground water" become "groundwater" over time. You would want to search ground water OR groundwater.

The uncataloged search works like the old Find function. To search the document you're in, click the In the Current PDF Document button.

Unlike Acrobat 5.0, in Acrobat 6.0 you can click All PDF Documents In and browse to a folder, drive, or even a network. This isn't the fastest search in the world, but it's an option that is new and beats having to read several hundred documents.

Acrobat 6.0's Basic Search includes four searching options. You can use any combination of options. The options include:

- *Whole words only.* Finds the exact word only. When you're searching for band, you don't get husband.

- *Case Sensitive.* Allows searching based on matched cases.

- *Search in Bookmarks.* Allows bookmarks to be included in the search.

- *Search in Comments.* Searches the comments in the documents.

Click Search and the results will soon appear.

Tip

The Sounds Like option from Acrobat 5.0 isn't in Acrobat 6.0.

Using Advanced Search Options

At the bottom of the Basic Search options panel is the Use Advanced Search Options selection. Click the option to open the Advanced Search panel as shown in Figure 9-9.

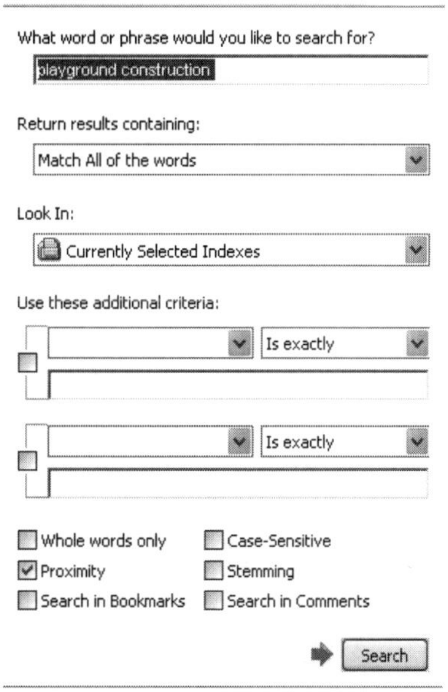

Figure 9-9
Use the Advanced Search options for a single document, collection of documents, or an index to conduct a targeted search.

Like the basic search, advanced searching gives you some options. You can choose to search using these options:

- *Match Any of the Words.* Finds results using any term and is the most general.

- *Match All of the Words.* A powerful search feature when used in conjunction with *proximity.* This allows searches for words that are close, usually resulting in more successful search results.

- *Look In.* Contains your options for where to search. You're allowed to browse to almost any location to which you have access. Two options are as follows:

- *Select Index.* Opens the Index Selection dialog box and allows you to click one or any combination of indexes as shown in Figure 9-10. Click Add and navigate to add any index's PDX file.

- *Currently Selected Indexes.* Searches the indexes selected.

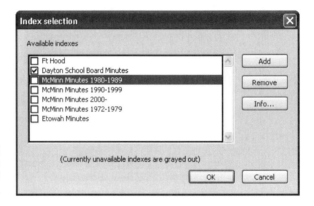

Figure 9-10
Illustrates the ability
to select one of
multiple indexes.

You can add multiple search criteria as shown in Figure 9-11. This really makes Acrobat search options even more powerful. The Multiple Search Criteria option works on cataloged or uncataloged collections. Cataloged searches are really fast! Cataloged or not, the search features turn Acrobat into a powerful document management system.

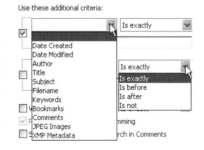

Figure 9-11
You can further target a
search using additional
search criteria. In the
figure, two of the drop-
down lists are shown for
illustration; you can't do
this in the program.

Now that you've looked at searching, it's time to test the index.

Working with the Fast Find Feature

Acrobat has a feature called Fast Find that caches information in PDF files that you use often. This really speeds up searches, but if you have older equipment with small hard drives, you may want to reduce the cache size. Set the cache in the Preferences menu. Choose Edit ➤ Preferences ➤ General ➤ Search. Figure 9-12 shows the Find Fast options.

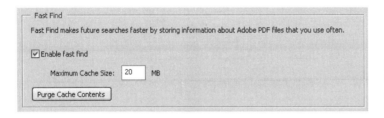

Figure 9-12
Set the Fast Find cache according to the size of your hard drives.

Project **Project 9-2: Testing the Index**

Once you build an index, you should test it by running a search. The Dayton minutes are organized in a manner whereby date, author, and other information is handled by the organization. Minutes are usually searched for ideas or issues like playground construction or street flooding. The words may not be in close proximity to each other, but closeness usually means a positive find. Follow these steps to work with the index:

1. Open the Search panel and attach the index. Click Look In and select Index. The Index Selection dialog box opens. Select Add to browse and select the Dayton School Board Minutes.

2. Select these options:

   • Select Proximity.

   • In Return Results Containing choose Match All of the Words.

   • In What Word or Phrase Would You Like to Search For? type **playground construction**.

As a result of Proximity being selected, any time the words are within 900 words of each other you have a hit ranked by relevance as shown in Figure 9-13.

Figure 9-13
Illustrates the results of
searching the index of the
Dayton minutes.

3. Click Search. The options are applied to the identified document or documents.

4. In the Search Results window, click on the blue highlighted words and the document opens with the word highlighted.

Documents that will frequently need to be searched should be indexed. Indexing is faster and a more organized way to search.

Managing Indexes

Once you've built your index, you still have work left to do. Depending on how you plan to use the material, as components and circumstances change so must the index. Acrobat 6.0 has three methods of managing indexes:

- *Build.* Updates an existing index. Build is quick and works fairly well if there have been few changes. However, lots of changes make the index large and slow to search.

- *Rebuild.* Creates a new index. This can be a problem because it creates a new .pdx, and as a result, the existing listing in the Index selection box is still visible but can't be selected because it no longer exists.

- *Purge.* Removes the existing index and you then rebuild it. In our opinion this is the best tool to complete the task.

Purging and Building Indexes

Have you ever been to a web site that had a bunch of broken links? Of course you have. It's one of the most irritating and annoying web experiences.

Indexing follows the same concept. Although indexes use bookmarks rather than links, the outcome is the same. A "dirty" index has entries for deleted documents and original versions of documents that have since been changed. These entries will be marked as invalid. When an index contains invalid entries, you have to take extra time to search and waste extra disk space to store extra invalid entries. All these factors can lead to incorrect search results and make for a messy situation. The solution? Periodically purge and build your indexes.

Here's how to do it:

1. Select Advanced ➤ Catalog and click Open Index.

2. Browse and select the PDX file for the index.

3. Click Purge. The index file contents will be deleted, but the PDX and folders remain.

4. Now select the PDX file by clicking the name, and then click Open.

5. Click Build.

Acrobat 6.0 can purge and build an index in a small fraction of the time it took Acrobat 5.0. The new "clean" index is ready to go.

Moving Collections and Indexes

Again, there are similarities between an indexed document collection and a web site. Both can be built and tested locally and both can be uploaded to a server for distribution. Both can be stored on disk. Both have dangers in doing this kind of transfer.

The basis for an index is the PDX file. This file contains relative paths between itself and the folders contain indexed documents. After moving a document collection and its corresponding PDX file, you may or may not have to rebuild the index. The index and all portions of the collection must be on the same driver or server volume. If they aren't, moving any component will break the index.

What if you didn't create the indexed collection or didn't store all the files in the same location? A good example is the set of index files for

Tip

When to Purge and Build an Index

Depending on the kind of work you do and the extent to which your documents are modified, you may want to define a purge-and-build schedule.

Tip

Moving Made Simple

Whenever possible, keep the PDX file and its folders containing indexed documents in the same folder. This way, regardless of where and how often the files are moved, the relative paths are always constant. This will prevent rebuilds and headaches.

this chapter's project. If you use the files from the chapter folder, you may or may not find the index functional. Fear not. Follow these steps:

1. Move the indexed documents.

2. Copy the PDX file to the desired folder.

3. Edit Include and Exclude lists if necessary.

We showed you how to set one of the indexing preferences earlier. Let's have a look at more preferences available for indexing and searching, which will wrap up this chapter.

Web Searches

Searching web pages is powered by Google. A web search in Acrobat is essentially a web search engine that only looks for PDF files that meet your search criteria. It's FAST!! Figure 9-14 illustrates searching for PDF files with playground and construction. The speed of the search was impressive. As an interesting side note, the first hit on the search was a document on park construction in San Jose right beside Adobe headquarters.

Figure 9-14
You can search the Web from within Acrobat using Google.

Up Next

In the introduction to this chapter, we tried to convey the idea that indexing isn't dry or dull. We have to stress, though, that it's something that requires a lot of planning and preparation. Unfortunately, it's also something that is often done without enough of the aforementioned forethought.

In this chapter you looked at indexing inside and out. You looked at how to prepare documents, how to create an index, how to store indexes, and how to customize cataloging and searching preferences that correspond with your work environment and needs. Along the way, we discussed how to add some very nice navigation to a set of indexed documents.

Up next you're going to look at the technology to make PDF files accessible to the visually impaired. Acrobat contains built-in technology that allows you to create accessible documents for disabled users as well as those working on small screen devices like PDAs.

Chapter 10

Making Documents Accessible to Everyone

The world is full of information, and everyone has a right to access that information. Here's how to use Acrobat 6.0 to make your information accessible.

What Does "Accessible" Mean?

The idea of user accessibility evolved based on the statements that open this chapter. Consider what can happen when you, the average person, open a document. You scroll down the page, change pages, use the mouse, use shortcut keys, change magnifications, activate links, and so on. If there is video, you can watch it. If there is audio, you can hear it. But what happens if you aren't capable of performing any or all of these functions?

As software and information presentation have become increasingly sophisticated, the need for standards has evolved, as has a greater understanding of what is required to make information accessible. Not only that, but software manufacturers have made methods available for their products' users to create accessible information.

Capabilities

Basically, you're considering two separate but conjoined issues: the abilities of the user and the capabilities of devices.

A user's abilities can be restricted on the basis of movement, sight, hearing, or comprehension. A user might be able to access information only through sight, sound, or touch, or some combination of these three methods.

On the other hand, you also have to consider the capabilities of devices. After all, unless the technology exists for the user to interact with information in a meaningful way, the discussion is pointless. From a device perspective, then, you're looking at two things: screen sizes and interaction methods. Screen size is self-explanatory. Interaction methods may include using keyboard, voice, or assistive devices (such as infrared pointers and the like).

That's what you're starting from. We've stressed that information should be accessible and that the software and devices used for distributing and presenting the information should also comply to standards. Let's have a look at the standards.

Web Accessibility Initiative

The "User Agent Accessibility Guidelines 1.0" (UAAG 1.0) is part of a set of accessibility guidelines published by the Web Accessibility Initiative (WAI) of the World Wide Web Consortium (W3C). The WAI guidelines were designed to present a consistent model for web accessibility in which responsibilities for addressing the needs of users with disabilities are shared (and distributed among) authors, software developers, and specification writers.

Guidelines and Checkpoints

These twelve guidelines state general principles for the development of accessible user agents:

Guideline 1. Support input and output device independence.

Ensure that the user can interact with the user agent (and the content it renders) through different input and output devices.

Guideline 2. Ensure user access to all content.

Ensure that users have access to all content, notably conditional content that may have been provided to meet the requirements of the "Web Content Accessibility Guidelines 1.0" (example: conditional elements include alt tags for images and object tags for embedded elements).

Guideline 3. Allow configuration not to render some content that may reduce accessibility.

Ensure that the user may turn off rendering of content (for example, audio, video, scripts) that may reduce accessibility by obscuring other content or disorienting the user. (example: content such as blinking script, animations)

Guideline 4. Ensure user control of rendering.

Ensure that the user can select preferred styles (for example, colors, size of rendered text, and synthesized speech characteristics) from choices offered by the user agent. Allow the user to override author-specified styles and user agent default styles.

Guideline 5. Ensure user control of user interface behavior.

Ensure that the user can control the behavior of viewports and user interface controls, including those that may be manipulated by the author (for example, through scripts) (example: a script that automatically opens other windows).

Guideline 6. Implement interoperable application programming interfaces.

Implement interoperable interfaces to communicate with other software (for example, assistive technologies, the operating environment, and plug-ins).

Guideline 7. Observe operating environment conventions.

Observe operating environment conventions for the user agent user interface, documentation, input configurations, and installation (example: high contrast color schemes are an operating system convention).

Guideline 8. Implement specifications that benefit accessibility.

Support the accessibility features of all implemented specifications. Implement W3C recommendations when available and appropriate for a task.

Guideline 9. Provide navigation mechanisms.

Provide access to content through a variety of navigation mechanisms, including sequential navigation, direct navigation, searches, and structured navigation.

Guideline 10. Orient the user.

Provide information that will help the user understand browsing context (example: named form field elements).

Guideline 11. Allow configuration and customization.

Allow users to configure the user agent so that frequently performed tasks are made convenient, and allow users to save their preferences.

Guideline 12. Provide accessible user agent documentation and help.

Note

The content of these guidelines and checkpoints is taken from the documents available at www.w3.org/.[1]

Ensure that the user can learn about software features that benefit accessibility from the documentation. Ensure that the documentation is accessible.

An important thing to point out is that these are the guidelines from the W3C. So how are they applicable to Acrobat? If you look at the functionality of the program, its array of outputs, its integration with Internet browsers, and its use of cross-platform readers, creating materials that aren't compliant with the standards is illogical—especially when so much of the work can be done for you using Acrobat tools.

---

1.   Copyright © 2001 by World Wide Web Consortium. All Rights Reserved. See www.w3.org/Consortium/Legal/.

Before we get into the tools, we want to look further at some of Acrobat's elements that play a part in accessible document production.

What Acrobat Can Do?

"Adobe Systems Incorporated is committed to providing solutions that improve document accessibility for users with disabilities such as blindness and motor impairments."[2] Adobe has come through with this commitment in Acrobat 6.0.

General Accessibility Functions

Acrobat 6.0 provides some accessibility functionality as components of the program's structure. The following features don't require any particular modification on your part to use them:

- Keyboard shortcuts

- High-contrast color schemes

- Built-in Read PDF Documents Aloud command and support for other screenreaders

Keyboard Shortcuts

Acrobat 6.0 has more keyboard shortcuts to make it easier for users to navigate a PDF file using the keyboard. Users can cycle through menus, toolbars, navigation panels and most parts of the interface without using a mouse. This also applies when using Acrobat in Internet Explorer.

High-Contrast Color Schemes

Visually impaired users may be able to view a document if a high-contrast color scheme is used—that is, if the amount of contrast between a page's background and its text are in high contrast. Regardless of the color scheme specified in a document by its creator, users are able to override the assigned color scheme and use their own. As you can see in Figure 10-1, this amount of contrast in a document enhances the visibility.

---

2.   Quote from "Adobe Acrobat 6.0 and Accessibility: At A Glance." See www.adobe.com/products/acrobat/pdfs/acro_access_at_a_glance.pdf.

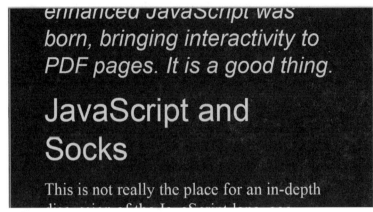

Figure 10-1
A portion of a page after
a high-contrast color
scheme has been applied.
This example also shows
reflowed text.

Here's how to set a high-contrast color scheme:

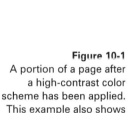

Note
You can also use these
settings to test view any
document in a high-
contrast mode, and then
return to the document
colors by resetting this
preference.

1. With the tagged file open, select Edit ➤ Preferences ➤ General.

2. Select Accessibility from the Preferences list in the left pane.

3. Select Replace Document Colors by checking the box.

4. You have two circle buttons to choose from. The first circle button uses the preferences set in Windows. The second button allows you to set custom colors.

5. Select Text Color and Set Background Colors as shown in Figure 10-2.

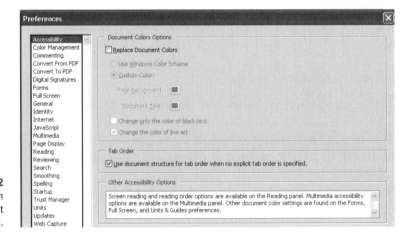

Figure 10-2
You can choose custom
colors for a high-contrast
color scheme.

6. By default Change Only the Color of Black Text and Change the Color of Line Art are selected when you chose to replace document colors.

7. Click OK.

Read PDF Documents Aloud

The Read PDF Documents Aloud command is built into all versions of Acrobat and the Adobe Reader 6.0. Text is synthesized into speech using standard Microsoft Windows and Mac OS X capabilities. Next time you have insomnia, have Microsoft Sam read all volumes of your company's personnel manual to you.

To Read PDF Documents Aloud select View ➤ Read Out Loud.

Screenreader Support

The Acrobat 6.0 family supports assistive technologies by Dolphin Computer Access, Freedom Scientific, GW Micro, and others.

PDFAloud is an interesting new product from textHELP! Systems Ltd. of Northern Ireland. It's designed not for people with visual problems but people with learning problems like dyslexia. Not only does PDFAloud read the document, but it highlights the words as they're read. This is also a tool for situations in which people have low reading skills but must read documents as part of their job.

Now let's look at some of the features and tools you can work with to improve and customize the accessibility features of your documents.

Acrobat's Accessibility Features

Some of the accessible features topics are discussed in other chapters of this book. In order to give you a complete overview of what Acrobat can do, the entire list is collected here:

- Enhanced security settings

- Reflowable text blocks (articles)

- Tagged files

- Tags panel

- Metadata

You'll be looking at some of the specific features later in this chapter.

Enhanced Security Settings

Until Acrobat 5.0, locking a PDF document to prevent the copying and pasting of text meant that the document was inaccessible. As you can see in Figure 10-3, content in Acrobat 6.0 can be made accessible and still have copying and extraction blocked.

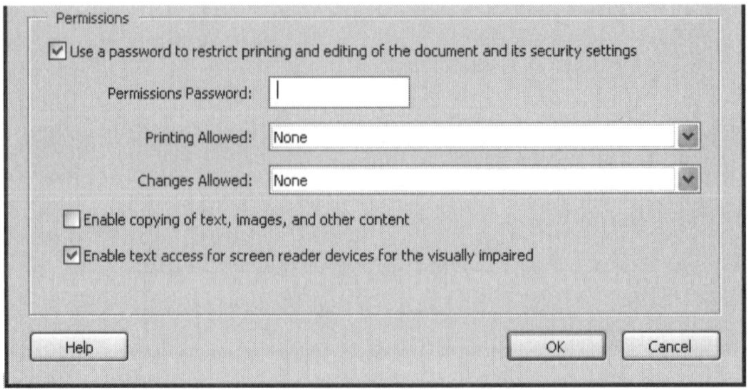

Figure 10-3
You can set specific
security options for
accessible content.

Reflowing Text Blocks

Text that had been reflowed to a user set magnification is illustrated in Figure 10-1. Content is reproportioned based on the zoom factor; a line that has, for example, 12 words on it at normal magnification might contain only 4 words when magnified. When the text reflows at a high magnification, the user can more easily read the content and won't have to scroll the page right and left to read the entire line. Tagged PDF documents may be reflowed. In combination with high-contrast viewing, users with limited vision can more easily read a document.

Tagged Files

You've looked at tagged files in other chapters. You'll look at them again later in this chapter, specifically in terms of how to use them for optimizing accessibility in documents. From the standpoint of making a file accessible, tagged files do the following:

- Allow control over read order.

- Understand paragraph attributes.

- Support alternate text (alt text) descriptions for images.

- Allow accessible interaction with documents (filling in form fields, following links).

- Represent text as Unicode. Unicode presents all characters and words clearly to assistive devices. This text format also distinguishes between soft and hard hyphens, and a word that spans two lines is read as a single word.

Note

Here is an area where engineers and designers have slightly different terminology. Donna refers to text blocks (objects) as articles and a series of articles in a sequence is an article thread. Then reflow reorders content in article sequence. It makes sense—this gray-haired engineer had never heard it described that way.

Tags Panel

We have seen the Tags panel in other chapters. You will recall that it displays the structure of a tagged PDF file. You can revise and edit the palette. As you'll see when you look at the Make Accessible plug-in, you can manipulate the palette to enhance the accessibility of the document.

Document Metadata

Remember this? Data about the data. When a document is manipulated by someone using assistive reading devices, the reader will speak the document's title before it's opened, saved, printed, or closed. If the document isn't titled, the file name is used. Think about some of the strange and awkward-sounding names you give to files. By adding a separate title to the metadata, the user will have a clearer understanding of what the file is about.

One last note on metadata: Adobe has broken metadata into advanced metadata and description metadata. The advanced metadata is shown in Figure 10-4. Dividing metadata into different categories makes the document more readily searchable.

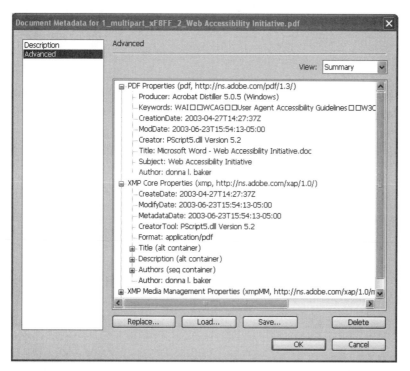

Figure 10-4
You can view the advanced metadata set in the Document Metadata dialog box.

To add information to be stored in the document's metadata, select Advanced ➤ Document Metadata ➤ Description. The dialog box shown in Figure 10-5 opens. Add information to complete the description of the file. Then click OK to close the dialog box.

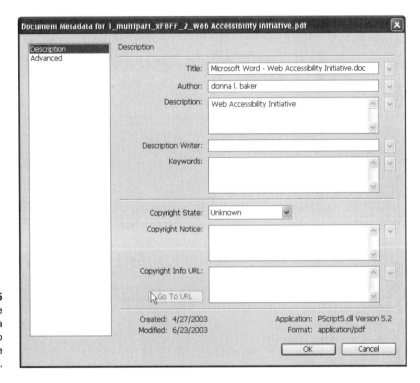

Figure 10-5
Add information to the Document Metadata description dialog box to create more complete metadata for the file.

Now let's have a look at how Acrobat's accessibility tools work.

Note

There are two PDF documents in the Chapter 10 folder that are used throughout this chapter in the tutorials and demos. The files are named nola.pdf and nola tagged.pdf. You can compare the files to see how the different functions work, or use them as a travel guide!

Using the Accessibility Tools

Adobe split the accessibility tools among the four versions of the product. Table 10-1 summarizes the accessibility tools and the appropriate version.

Table 10-1   Accessibility Options Available in Different Acrobat Versions

Tool	Adobe Reader 6.0	Acrobat Elements 6.0	Acrobat Standard 6.0	Acrobat Pro 6.0
Enhanced Keyboard Navigation	X	X	X	X
International Language Support			X	X
Enhanced Accessibility Checker				X
Enhanced Make Accessible			X	X
Accessibility Quick Check	X	X	X	X
Enhanced Structure TouchUp tools			X	X
Read Aloud	X	X	X	X

Making Documents Accessible

What if you have a document created in an older version of Acrobat? Or you have a different type of file that was converted to PDF using Acrobat Distiller? Enter the process of making documents accessible.

Differences in the Program Versions

Make Accessible now only exists in Acrobat 6.0 Standard. Make Accessible is now a part of the program; in version 5.0, it was a separate plug-in.

In Acrobat 6.0 Professional the process isn't even called Make Accessible and a search of the Help manual won't help you find this term. Adobe has chosen to simply call it by what it does: Add Tags to Documents. Having Make Accessible in Acrobat 6.0 Standard and Add Tags to Document in Acrobat 6.0 Professional will cause some confusion. Since this book focuses on the professional user, we're only going to discuss Acrobat 6.0 Professional.

What happens if you try to run the Accessibility Quick Check (AQC) against a file that has no tags? Here's what happens using the nola.pdf file available in the Chapter 10 folder.

When the file is open, choose Advanced ➤ Accessibility ➤ Quick Check. Figure 10-6 shows the results of AQC on an untagged document. AQC just checks to verify that the document is tagged.

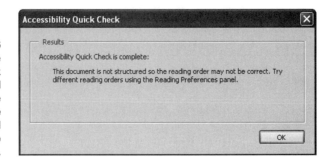

Figure 10-6
Results of running the
Accessibility Quick Check
against the untagged
demo version of the
nola.pdf file states that the
document isn't structured
so it won't necessarily use
a correct reading order.

Tagging and Testing the Document

Now let's tag nola.pdf. To make an untagged document accessible, elect
Advanced ➤ Accessibility ➤ Add Tags to Document. The command will
automatically run. When the process is finished, choose File ➤ Save As
and save the file with another name. Adobe recommends you do this
because the structure of the document is changed after this command is
run and cannot be undone.

Using the Accessibility Quick Checker

Now use the AQC to verify that the document is tagged. Keep in mind
the AQC is a quick check of the document's status and doesn't guarantee
that a document is fully accessible to a screenreader. Figure 10-7 shows
AQC on the nola1.pdf document after you added tags. In reality all the
AQC is doing is determining if the document is tagged.

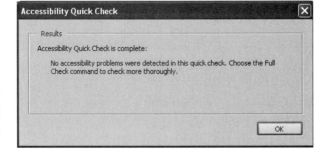

Figure 10-7
Results of running the
Accessibility Quick Check
on the tagged version of
the file states that there
are no problems detected.

Conducting a Full Accessibility Check on a Document

To perform a real check of accessibility you must use Acrobat 6.0 Professional. Choose Advanced ➤ Accessibility ➤ Full Check.

The Full Check command, or the Enhanced Make Accessible command checks the document for noncompliant elements such as missing tags and incorrect or unrecognizable character encodings. Any noncompliant elements will be logged to a file or displayed in an information window.

You can also use this tool as a controller. Run the Full Check and compile a list of problems. Correct the issues and rerun the controller to verify your corrections and amendments. When all the problems have been corrected, your document is ready for distribution.

Tutorial: Running a Full Accessibility Check

You must start with a tagged PDF file, use either the nola.pdf file if you've added tags, or use the nola tagged.pdf file in the Chapter 10 folder. Then follow these steps:

1. Open the file in Acrobat.

2. Select Advanced ➤ Accessibility ➤ Full Check. The dialog box will open with a list of options.

3. Select the options desired. Our selections are shown in Figure 10-8.

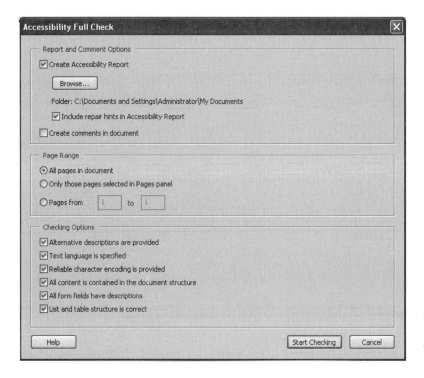

Figure 10-8
Choose reporting and commenting options in the Accessibility Full Check dialog box.

4. Click Start Checking to run the Accessibility Full Check process.

5. The results are displayed in a dialog box as shown in Figure 10-9. As you can see in this image, aside from the <Alt Text> tags, the other issues have been corrected with the tagging process. There are 30 figures in this document that need alternative text to become accessible.

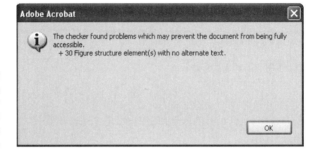

Figure 10-9
The results of running the Accessibility Checker against the tagged version of the demo file shows the alternate text errors.

Showing Issues as Comments

When you set the options for the Checker, you should select Create Accessibility Report, but not Create Comments in Document options. As you can see in Figure 10-10, boxes were drawn around the problem areas. By clicking the Comments tab, you can see each element shows up as a comment. As the problems are fixed, the comments can be checked complete.

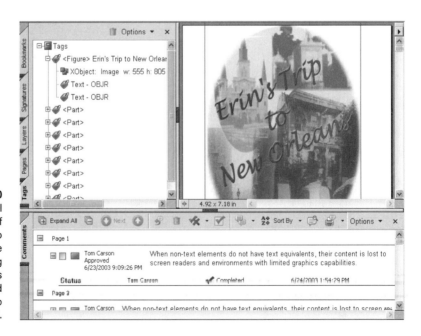

Figure 10-10
After Accessibility Full Check the problems of images with no alternative text are highlighted and clicking on comments shows the problems and allows changes to be documented.

Creating an Accessibility Report

In Figure 10-8, you can see the option to create an Accessibility Report was selected. This function is new, replacing the Create Logfile option in Acrobat 5.0. A report displays when the document evaluation is complete as shown in Figure 10-11. The results are included in an interactive browser-based report.

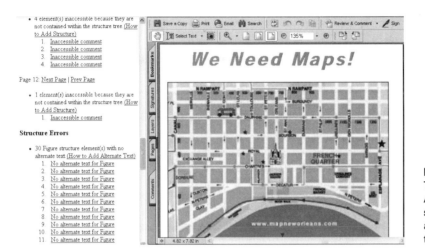

Figure 10-11
The new browser-based Accessibility Report shows both the problems and links to correct these problems.

You've found all the problems, now let's go about solving them. The browser-based Accessibility Report is a tutorial on how to fix the problems. You cannot fix the problems in the browser. You'll notice that the Tags panel is missing in the browser.

Using the Tags Panel

Choose View ➤ Navigation Tabs ➤ Tags to open the Tags panel. Most typical problems can be most easily corrected in the Tags panel. In all instances, once you've located the element in the Tags panel, click it to select it, and then right-click and select Properties from the context menu. Be sure to select the tag, not the description of the element itself. As shown in Figure 10-12, the image only has a size description. The element itself is the <Span> tag.

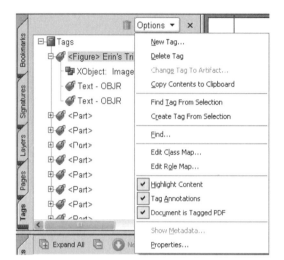

Figure 10-12
Select the tag,
not the description
of the tag's content.

The dialog box displayed varies according to the type of element error.
To add missing alternate text (as shown in Figure 10-12), do the following:

1. Click Properties to open the TouchUp Properties dialog box.

2. Enter the alternate text in the Alternate Text text box of the Tag
   panel as shown in Figure 10-13.

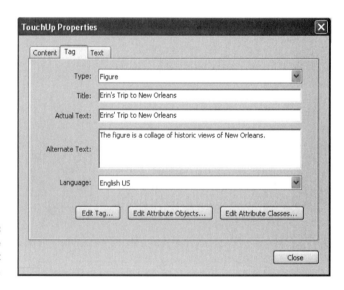

Figure 10-13
Add missing alternate
text in the Alternate Text
area in the dialog box.

3. Click Close to close the dialog box and make the change in the tag.

4. Choose View ➤ Read Aloud and read the page. Here is the proof positive. If it doesn't read right for you, how is a blind person going to understand it?

Interpreting the Tags

Other common errors that can be corrected in the Tags panel include tag type and language. Figure 10-14 shows page 4 of the nola tagged.pdf file. As you can see, it has a heading, two images, one text block, and a graphic.

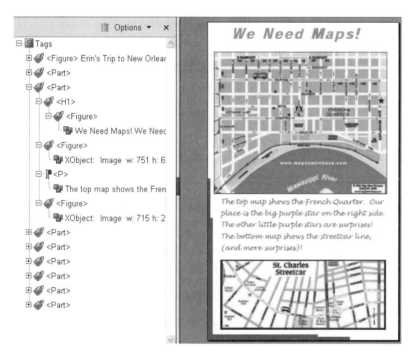

Figure 10-14
Layout of page 4 of the document relates to the tags displayed in the Tags panel.

Figure 10-14 shows the portion of the Tags panel that corresponds to this page (after we've finished the modifications). The highlighted image content was selected from the Accessibility Report menu (shown in Figure 10-11.) The highlight shows the red boxes around the two figures that need alternative text.

To make changes to correct the tag problem:

- We named the part *We Need Maps!*

- We left the <H1> tag as is.

The page reflows in a different way. The two maps will be followed by the text. In the original layout, the maps are separated by the text.

Testing a Document

Testing is the final step in the accessibility workflow. You should test the document using View ➤ Read Aloud. Although you can see the presentation by selecting View ➤ Reflow, this is only a simulation. Only from within a reader will you be able to evaluate the actual reading order and functionality of the document.

Reflowing Tagged PDF Documents

Reflowing. The idea is that in a tagged document, the content can be laid out in such a way as to be readable regardless of the device being used to view it. That is the point of the tags. A tagged document has a highly defined structure. So, whether the reader views it on a handheld device or a large monitor, and regardless of zoom factor, it will be readable and logical.

Here is something else that is interesting. Reflowing in Acrobat is an on-the-fly process. You can't save a reflowed document. You wouldn't want to save a reflowed document. That is because your users will have the document served to them one page at a time and they'll control reflowing as they view your document. Reflowing is simply a viewing option, but you can certainly reflow a document to test it and finesse the layout you've designed.

You can see the reflow of any tagged document by selecting View ➤ Reflow. Leave this view state by selecting another viewing option in the View menu.

Finessing a Layout

We briefly discussed using the Reflow view to see how a document designed with columns would flow on a single page after we added articles to it. We also mentioned that you had a number of options for improving the reflowed layout.

What can you do to tweak a layout? Some touch-up work, using touch-up tools. Specifically the TouchUp Order, TouchUp Text, and TouchUp TextBreaks tools.

Editing Reflow Order

Editing reflow order doesn't change content or the actual structure of a document. Instead, this is a viewing sequence process that overlays the structure of the document. All it does is rearrange the sequence the reader experiences.

Acrobat 6.0 Professional does a much better job of tagging objects and making a file ready for reflow. The file you've been using for this discussion, for example, has images with text wrapping around them for interest. In an on-screen use, however, that may be distracting. Change the reflow to have the image viewed at the end of the paragraph instead. A screen shot of the same file tagged by Make Accessible was used in the last edition and displayed remaining layout errors. The new Advanced ➤ Accessibility ➤ Add Tags to Document process in Acrobat 6.0 did such a good job the example of a problem wasn't there.

In keeping with the new user interface and trying to make actions more uniform the method to edit reflow order had changed. The TouchUp Order tool available in Acrobat 5.0 is gone. To edit the reflow order, follow these steps:

1. Choose View ➤ Navigation Tabs ➤ Content to open the Content panel as shown in Figure 10-15.

Tip

Do You Have to Make a File 100 Percent Compliant?

Not necessarily. We know this contradicts what we said in the Accessibility Full Check discussion, but use your discretion. After all, what you're doing is configuring your document to be used with assistive devices. For example, the Checker might report that the file contains images that don't have alternate text. If these images are just the decorative borders on the page or graphic remnants they are meaningless for someone with vision impairment and wouldn't require alternate text. Similarly, the Check might report that a running header is not part of the structure tree. Again, you could leave this as is, because you don't need this information to be vocalized by a screen-reader. Finally, another common error type is language specification. If language isn't an issue, don't worry about it.

Figure 10-15
Organize the content in a document for alternate reflow using the Content panel.

2. Expand the Content tab tree structure and find the elements you want to reflow in a different order. Change the order of the panel's elements by clicking the content to be moved and drag it like you drag a bookmark. Drag all the ones to be changed.

3. Save the document and then select View ➤ Reflow to test the changes you made.

Consider the Source

Consider this section a giant workflow tip. Rather than having to rework contents of a file once it has been converted to PDF, make some decisions in the source application that will make the file convert smoothly and save time in the long run.

- When using a document that is text-based with added elements, use Microsoft Word 2000 or Word XP. In Acrobat 6 Professional, you can create tagged PDF files directly. (The demo file we used earlier in this chapter was created in Microsoft Publisher and printed to Acrobat Distiller.)

- Use styles for formatting text. These styles can be converted to structural elements when converted to PDF format.

- Use the Table and Column commands instead of simulating tables or columns with tabs.

- Save time required for locating and editing alternate text in Acrobat's Tags panel. Instead, add alternate text in the source program. (In Word, for example, add alternate text by selecting the Web tab of the Properties dialog box.)

- Wherever practical, group a collection of illustrations using the Group command. This will require only one alternate tag and won't affect placement or reflow.

- When converting the file, ensure that Embed Tags in PDF is turned on and Page Labels is turned off in the conversion settings.

Up Next

As you've seen in this chapter, you have many options for making documents accessible. You've seen what Acrobat's design functions provide for accessibility and what makes a document accessible. Then you looked at ways to use Acrobat's tools to evaluate a document in terms of accessibility. You also learned how you can "rescue" a document by changing its reflow structure. Finally, you looked at how to make alterations to the source document and save time after converting to PDF.

In the next chapter, you're going to take a document and plan for output or cross-media publishing. A major power of Acrobat is being able to use a file for multiple purposes.

Chapter 11

Planning and Preparing for Output

So far you've looked at different ways to access and manipulate source information. In this chapter, you'll look at how to create some specific output formats. You'll look at the new PDF Optimizer that replaced PDF Consultant. You'll also look at batch processing. Both PDF Optimizer and batch processing are only available in Acrobat 6.0 Professional.

What If I Want to Make?...

This is where we fill in the blank. So far in this book, we've covered a lot of information—how Acrobat works, how to convert files into PDF format to work with in Acrobat, and how to manipulate and secure the Acrobat documents. We've explained how to comment and edit documents, and we've discussed how to collaborate on documents with others.

This chapter covers a number of interesting types of output. Along the way, you'll look at some more information you'll need to create specific output types.

Just a note before we start. Some output types have a chapter devoted to them because their requirements are specific and because they use different processes. This includes accessibility, forms, and print. In this chapter, though, you'll look at several types of output that you can create using the same source material and variations on the same processes.

Along the way, you'll also look at some processes that we've hinted at or even looked at briefly in earlier chapters, including using the Article feature. Then, you'll look at saving PDF files as different types of web page formats, and you'll conclude with a look under the hood at the metadata of your documents.

Before you delve into any specific output types, we first want to show you PDF Optimizer, which analyzes and optimizes a file.

Using the PDF Optimizer

What a valuable advanced feature found only in Acrobat 6.0 Professional! Regardless of the type of output you're planning, your output will be more efficient and more professional if the output is as clean and focused as possible.

You use the PDF Optimizer to inspect, analyze, and repair documents. PDF Optimizer, which works at the object level, can perform a number of functions. The PDF Optimizer is a multi-tabbed dialog box, and includes numerous optimization options.

The initial options refer to compatibility and space usage:

- *Choose Compatibility*: Acrobat 6.0 has better compression features than Acrobat 5.0 and Acrobat 5.0 has better compression than Acrobat 4.0. Acrobat 5.0 is the default setting and should be used unless you're certain that everyone has Acrobat 6.0.

- *Audit Space Usage.* Indicates how much of the total file weight is attributed to different elements such as images, comments, fonts, and so forth. The values are expressed either in bytes or as a percentage of the entire file's size.

You can choose to modify images and fonts to save space:

- *Downsample Images to the Most Effective for Output Type.* You don't need press-quality images for files heading for web distribution.

- *Enable Adaptive Compression.* Allows you to make a relative choice between higher quality and higher compression.

- *Unembed Unnecessary Fonts.* Determines fonts used in the file and unembeds fonts that may or may not be required depending on what version of Acrobat you chose in the Compatibility field.

On the Cleanup tab, you can modify numerous settings according to the file's content:

- *Object Compression options.* Allows the compression or removal of document structure elements.

- *Use Flate to Encode Streams That Are Not Encoded.* (default).

- *In Streams That Use LZW Encoding, Use Flate Instead.* (default).

- *Remove Invalid Bookmarks and Links.* (default).

- *Remove Unused Named Destinations.* (default).

- *Discard All Comments.*

- *Discard All Form Actions.*

- *Discard All JavaScript Actions.*

- *Discard All External References.*

- *Discard All Alternative Images* (default).

- *Remove Embedded Thumbnails.*

- *Remove Private Data of Other Applications.*

- *Remove Document Structure.*

- *Remove Hidden Layer Content and Flatten All Layers.*

- *Optimize PDF for Fast Web View.*

Let's put this feature through its paces.

Optimizing and Analyzing a Document

We'll use one of the demos Donna designed for this chapter to illustrate how these processes work. Figure 11-1 shows the Document Properties dialog box and the Description feature selected in the window. As you can see, the file is 246 KB. Certainly not a big file, but we're going for concept, not quantity.

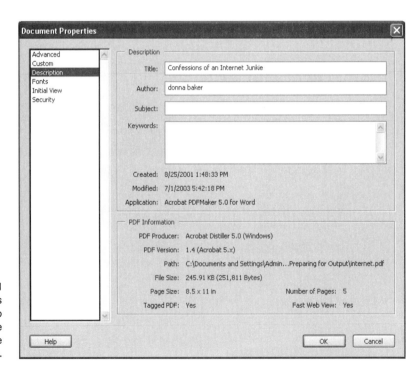

Figure 11-1
The Document Properties dialog box for this demo shows the file size and the program used to generate the original file.

You access the PDF Optimizer by choosing Advanced ➤ PDF Optimizer and then selecting the desired option. Figure 11-2 shows the PDF Optimizer dialog box in the default view. You can choose compatibility options for versions as old as Acrobat 4.0. The newer the Acrobat version, the more PDF Optimizer can do with the file. The Images tab is set for high-quality screen, medium-quality desktop printing.

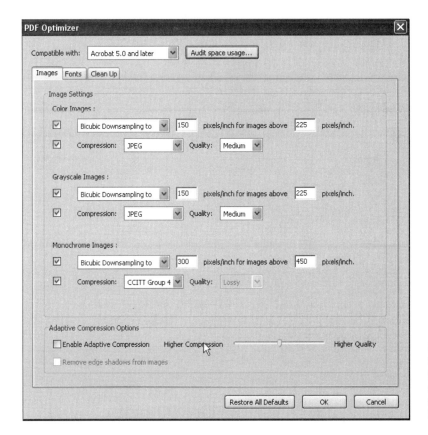

Figure 11-2
Start optimizing a file in the Images tab. The figure shows the default default settings based on Standard Distiller setting.

Audit Space Usage

The Audit Space Usage feature looks at the space based on the different features of the file. Figure 11-3 shows the various categories and the relative space. Over 80 percent of the demo file is images and fonts.

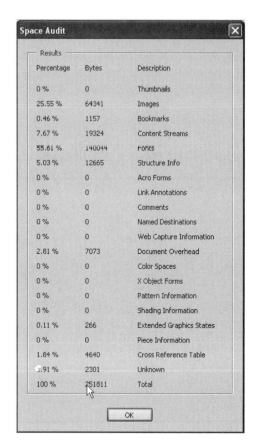

Figure 11-3
You can see the different features of the document and the relative amount of space used listed in the Space Audit dialog box.

Fonts take up almost 56 percent of the document. One of the space-saving features of Acrobat 6.0 is that 41 fonts are now included instead of the 14 that were included with Acrobat 5.0. This means that fewer of the fonts need embedding. The PDF Optimizer shown in Figure 11-4 has determined that Arial-ItalicMT (subset) is the same as in Acrobat 5.0 and will unembed it.

The Clean Up tab is preset to use the most effective compression technology for the chosen compatibility. The Clean Up tab is also set to remove unused bookmarks, links, and destinations. Optimize PDF for Fast Web View also removes duplicate material. Figure 11-5 shows the default settings for cleanup in PDF Optimizer.

Some of the options are entirely dependent on the ultimate use of a document. *Discard All Forms Actions, JavaScript Actions and External Cross References* is appropriate if you're going to use the document in a print environment. *Discard All Comments* may not be appropriate in the print environment if text boxes are used. *Remove Embedded Thumbnails* should almost be a default since both Acrobat 5.0 and 6.0 generate thumbnails on the fly.

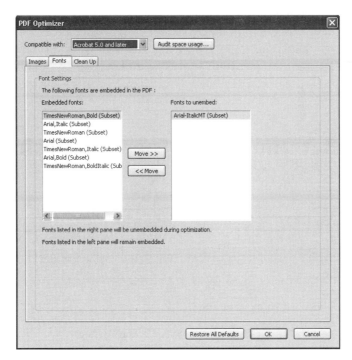

Figure 11-4
The PDF Optimizer lists fonts that can be unembedded on the Fonts tab.

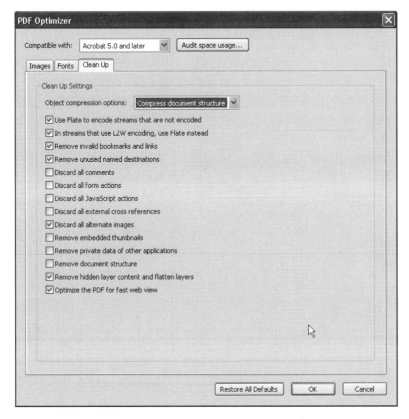

Figure 11-5
You can choose from a wide range of cleanup options.

PDF Optimizer requires that you save the optimized file as another name. After optimizing a check of File ➤ Document Properties ➤ Description shows that the file is now 233.96 KB vs. the initial 245.91 KB or a 5 percent reduction in file size. This shows that Donna created a pretty tight file. Tom, the maker of 3,300-page files, has seen them go from approximately 250 MB to 205 MB or an 18 percent file size reduction.

Batching Files for Conversion

Batching is a way to automate repetitious processes. In the last few years, a number of programs have been released that use JavaScript as a basis for writing custom command sequences. Acrobat 6.0 Professional is part of that illustrious crowd. You can use batching commands on anything from a single document to a collection of documents.

The batching process is composed of three segments:

- Defining commands

- Defining files to execute the commands on

- Defining storage locations for the converted files

Defining the Batch Commands

You can run any of a series of preconfigured commands or create custom sequences. You'll look at both options. To create a new process, select Advanced ➤ Batch Processing. The dialog box shown in Figure 11-6 opens. The window lists the preconfigured commands.

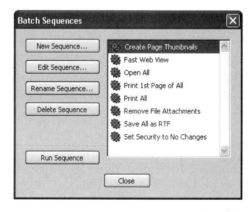

Figure 11-6
Start the batch command process in this dialog box

Follow these steps to define the batch commands:

1. Click New Sequence. A sequence placeholder will appear in the list at the right side of the window.
2. Enter a name for the new command sequence in the pop-up window, and click OK to open the Batch Edit Sequence dialog box, as shown in Figure 11-7.

Tip

Reusing Batch Processes

The Acrobat 5.0 CD included several more batch processes under a folder entitled Batch. You have to copy the files to the Acrobat 6.0/Acrobat/Sequences/enu folder. We haven't tested all these. The one from Acrobat 5 -Set Security to None doesn't work.

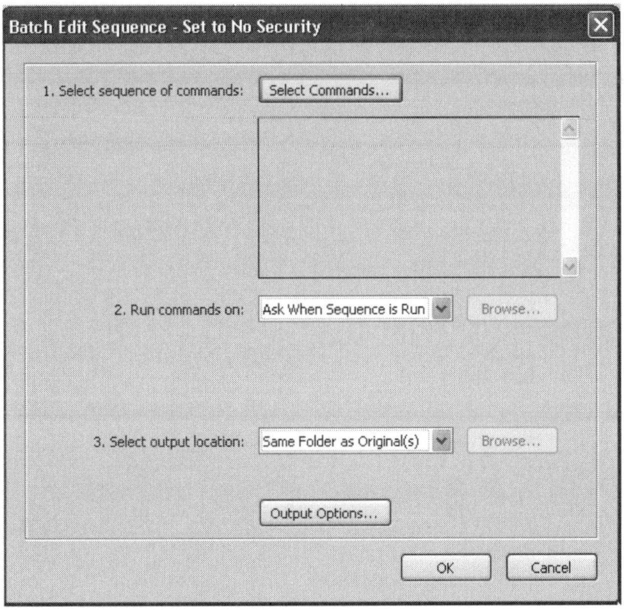

Figure 11-7
The Batch Edit Sequence dialog box houses the information for the command-building process.

3. In the Batch Edit Sequence dialog box, click Select Commands. The Edit Sequence dialog box, shown in Figure 11-8, opens. This dialog box is the heart of the process. Included are a number of commands in the following areas:
   - Comments
   - Documents
   - JavaScript
   - Page
   - Paper Capture

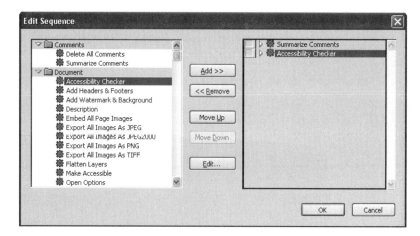

Figure 11-8
Add commands in the
Edit Sequence dialog box.

4. In the Edit Sequence dialog box, configure the commands for the sequence. You can manipulate the content of this window in several ways:

- Select a command from the left pane of the dialog box and click Add. The command will be added to the sequence.

- Delete a command by selecting it and clicking Remove.

- To reorder the list, highlight the command to move, and click Move Up or Move Down.

5. Set options for each command by clicking the command in the right pane and then clicking Edit. For example, as shown in Figure 11-9, you can configure the options for the Summarize Comments command by changing the attributes in the dialog box.

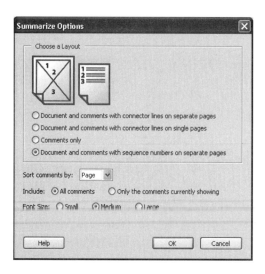

Figure 11-9
Different ways to
summarize comments are
an example of command
configuration options.

6. You can make some commands interactive. Click the white box to the left of the arrow next to the command to activate an interactive mode. This mode pauses the batching process and allows you to configure options before executing the command. For example, look at Figure 11-10. You can see the following:

- You can display the content of each command by clicking the arrow to the left of the command name.

- The sequence of elements in the command is displayed as well as any options.

- The Summarize Comments command has a white box to the left of the arrow. Click the selection box to the left of the command line to make a command interactive. This indicates that the batch process will be paused depending on what settings you use (as shown in Figure 11-10).

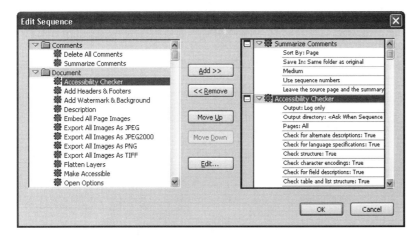

Figure 11-10
You can define a command as being interactive, meaning the batch process pauses depending on your choices.

7. Click OK to finish building the command sequence and return to the Batch Edit Sequence dialog box.

Once you've created a command sequence, it's time to define the target files.

Defining the Target Files

Once you've established a command sequence, the next step is to specify the files on which you want the commands to be executed. The options available are shown in Figure 11-11.

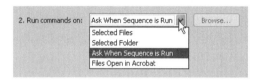

Figure 11-11
Pick the options for
running the command
from this drop-down list.

The drop-down list contains several options:

- *Selected Files.* Select multiple individual files.

- *Selected Folder.* Select all the files in a selected folder.

- *Ask When Sequence Is Run.* Allows you to select different locations and options as the situation requires.

- *Files Open in Acrobat.* Will batch any open files.

The final part of the process is defining storage options.

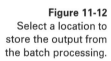

Note

In Windows, the files must all be in the same folder. They may be in different folders if you're using a Mac OS version.

Selecting Storage Options

Storage options include both location and file options. Select a storage location. By default, the files will be saved to their source folder. Other options are to save to a specific folder or to the same folder as the original, or to ask when the sequence is run (again for customized use of the batching process.) These options are shown in Figure 11-12.

Figure 11-12
Select a location to
store the output from
the batch processing.

Define the output options. Hidden beneath the selection list shown in Figure 11-12 is a button named Output Options. Click it to open the dialog box shown in Figure 11-13. The PDF Consultant was run in Acrobat 5.0 as a series of batch processes. PDF Optimizer is now a check box in Output Options.

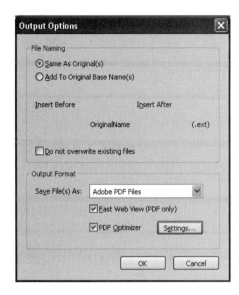

Figure 11-13
Make the final selections for the custom batch commands in this dialog box.

Preconfigured Batch Commands

As mentioned earlier, a number of batch commands are automatically installed with Acrobat. The menu list, which you access by selecting Advanced Processing ➤ Batch Processing, is shown in Figure 11-14.

Figure 11-14
You can choose from a variety of preconfigured batch commands.

As you can see, a number of basic processes can be accomplished quickly. If you look at the list, you'll see that these are all useful ways to save time when performing the same kind of activities on a number of files.

That was quite a whirlwind tour, wasn't it? The best way to appreciate how this feature works is to use it. On that note, a new project is up next.

Project

Project 11-1: Creating a Custom Batch Process for "Article Cleanup"

For this project, you'll construct a custom batch command to run against a magazine article about satellite Internet connections.

The batching processes you'll create here are a custom collection of cleanup and organization processes, and include the following processes as a standard cleanup workflow:

- Delete comments
- Embed thumbnails
- Add page numbers
- Optimize space (PDF Optimizer isn't a sequence, but under output).

What You'll Need

For this project, you'll need the internet.pdf file, which is in the Chapter 11 Projects folder. You'll see that this version of the article has a column layout. This will be important as you work through the projects in this chapter.

If you open the internet.pdf file, you'll notice:

- The thumbnails aren't embedded in the file.
- The text is arranged in columns (we created the columns in Word and converted the file to PDF).

Start the Sequence

To start the sequence, perform these steps:

1. Close all open files in Acrobat. Select Advanced ➤ Batch Processing. In the Batch Sequences dialog box, click New Sequence. Enter the name **Article Cleanup** in the pop-up window, and click OK. As shown in Figure 11-15, the new sequence appears in the list.

Tip

Why Should Thumbnails Be Embedded?

The only reason to embed thumbnails is for someone working with Acrobat 4.0. Acrobat 5.0 and 6.0 generate thumbnails on the fly. A thumbnail is approximately 3 KB in file size. We're doing this for demonstration. You probably won't ever embed thumbnails.

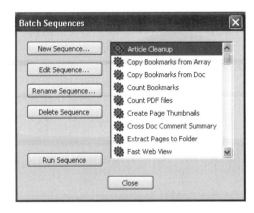

Figure 11-15
Add the new batch sequence to the Edit Sequence list.

2. Click Edit Sequence ➤ Select Commands. The Edit Sequence window will open, as shown in Figure 11-16. Click the names of the commands to be added, and then click Add to move them to the sequence window:

- Delete All Comments

- Embed All Thumbnails

- Number Pages

Note

Only the Number Pages selection has configuration options, as indicated by the arrow to the left of the command line. Leave the default settings.

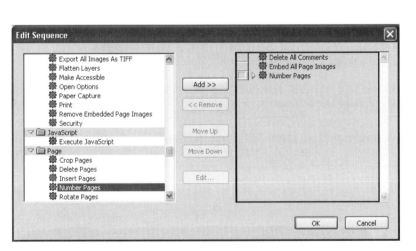

Figure 11-16
Add the commands for the batch to the sequence list.

3. Click OK to close the Edit Sequence dialog box and return to the Batch Edit Sequence - Article Cleanup dialog box. The next step is to define the condition to run the sequence. From the Run Commands On drop-down list, select Ask When Sequence Is Run.

4. The final stages of the process are defining the storage location and output options. As you can see in Figure 11-17, we left the default storage location—that is, Same Folder as Original(s). Since PDF Optimizer is moved under Output Options that will need to be checked there (see Figure 11-13). Click OK to close the Batch Edit Sequence dialog box. Click Close to close the Batch Sequences dialog box.

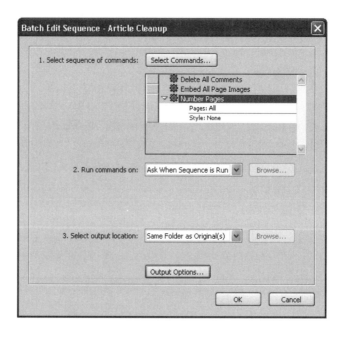

Figure 11-17
Finish selecting the batch sequence options and you're ready to run the script.

Now let's see how it works.

Running the Batch Sequence

Time to run this set of commands.

1. Select Advanced ➤ Batch Processing ➤ Article Cleanup. The Run Sequence Confirmation dialog box shown in Figure 11-18 opens.

2. If necessary, review the contents of the sequence. As you can see in Figure 11-18, the Number Pages command has configuration options (indicated by the arrow to the left of the process's name.) Click OK to run the commands.

3. You'll be prompted for the file to run the batch against. Browse to the file location and click Select. You'll also be prompted when the Number Pages command is reached. Accept the defaults and click OK.

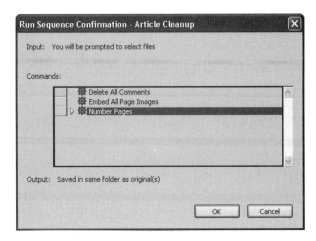

Figure 11-18
Confirm the batch process before the sequence runs.

4. When the sequence has finished, the Warnings and Errors window will open. Review the results, and click OK to close the window.

Now the file is clean, organized, and numbered. You'll use it again later in the chapter.

That has been a batch of information on batches, hasn't it? So far we've looked at processes applied to a document from *outside* the document. Next let's go into a document and look at organizing its content.

All About Articles

Try as we might, using a computer screen to read something just doesn't work the same way as reading magazine or newsletter articles. How often do you read articles that are in several columns, span several pages, and have advertising, images, and other nonarticle information inserted? My guess is regularly. Now translate that concept into reading the same thing on a computer screen.

It's an interesting phenomenon. We let our eyes move through pages and up and down columns and use our fingers to flip pages—without a second thought. It's almost as though our brains are on autopilot. The eye moves up and down the columns and jumps over callouts and images and advertisements until we reach "Continued on p. 79," at which point we flip through the pages to page 79 and continue. Sometimes at the top-left column, sometimes partway down the right column. No big deal.

Tip
Who Would Use This Type of Process?

Again, as we've mentioned throughout this book, think about how you work. If you do a lot of document processing, categorize the types of work you do. For example, the batch process in this project is named "Article cleanup." Depending on what you do on a regular basis, you may have a series of custom batch processes for manuals, brochures, proposals, web pages, and the like. Before building a batch process, review the steps you take to finish a project. Many of these things could probably be incorporated into a batch process. Not only will you save time, but also your output will be more consistent. Learn how to write custom batch scripts in Chapter 16.

On the other hand, if you tried to do the same thing with something on a screen, what would happen? Chaos is my guess. Why? Well, not being a neurologist, I can only hazard a guess. And here it is.

If you consider the mechanics of what you're doing when you read an article on a screen versus when you read a magazine article, there is only one difference. The magazine is a static entity, and your eyes move. When you read something on a screen, it, moves along with your eyes. So rather than commanding your mechanical functions to find the page and the correct location, you have to scroll for it. What's the difference? The simple function is different. After all, we've had centuries to learn how to read a book, and only a few years to learn how to read a screen.

Add to the mix the ability to zoom in and out of a document, and it becomes difficult. After all, if you've zoomed in on the last part of the first column of the first page and want to continue to the second column of the next page, how do you remember where you are? Until we reach the point where on-screen reading is standard operating procedure, it behooves us to distress the on-screen reading experience for our users.

If you built a document using multiple columns, is the solution to rebuild that document if you think it will be read primarily online? *Au contraire, mon ami.* Acrobat has a tool designed just for this purpose.

Introducing Articles

Yes, Acrobat has an article feature. Using linked elements, you configure a path for reading a document regardless of the number of columns or pages it spans, and regardless of the zoom factor being used. This process is used for formatting articles to be read online as is or for use with assistive reading devices.

Articles are linked objects defined in a document. Have you ever spent time on message boards? One way entries can be followed is through threads. A *thread* follows the same topic throughout the content of the board regardless of posting dates or authors. When you follow a thread, you read postings on the same topic. Acrobat's version of an article thread basically follows the same idea of guiding the reader through the material.

As with some of the other structural elements you've looked at, you can either generate article threads before a file is converted to PDF or do it from within Acrobat. You'll look at both of these methods. Regardless of the document origin, Acrobat provides access to an Article panel, which we'll describe later in the chapter.

Creating Articles in a Document

Using text frames, and then linking the text frames together, is a common procedure in desktop publishing programs. When text is entered into the first text frame, overflow spills to the next one, and so on. The same thing happens when you create article threads in Acrobat. In this case, though, the content is already there, and then the text frames are added.

Note

The Chapter 11 folder contains a copy of the document used in this discussion named archer.pdf.

Here's how to define an article in a document:

1. Click the Article tool on the Editing toolbar to select it.

2. Click and drag the pointer crosshairs to define the first box by fencing in the text.

3. When the marquee is complete, release the mouse button, and the text selected is enclosed by an article box.

   The article box is automatically labeled with a two-part label: *<article number>-<sequence>*. For example, the first article defined is labeled 1-1, then 1-2, and so on. As you can see in Figure 11-19, this thread has four defined article boxes.

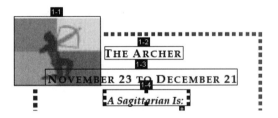

Figure 11-19
Articles defined on a page display numbers and the article box frames.

4. Continue until you have finished. To end the numbering process, press Enter. The Article Property dialog box opens.

5. Each article has its own properties in addition to numbering. As shown in Figure 11-20, you can add a title, subject, author, and keywords in the Article Properties dialog box. Click OK to add the information and close the dialog box.

Note

You can revise the properties by clicking a box to select it and then selecting Properties from the context menu.

If you've made a mistake or want to change anything in the sequence you created, you have to end the process first. Also, in one document you might have more than one sequence. In this case, you also have to end one thread before starting another one.

Figure 11-20
You can add properties
to the articles. At a
minimum, you should
name the article.

Manipulating Articles

Articles can be modified like any other kind of element you add in Acrobat.
You can manipulate the articles themselves as well as the article threads. In
fact, you can delete, insert, combine, move, or resize an article box, and
edit an article's properties. Make sure you have the Articles panel open
to see what you're doing (to display the panel, select View ➤ Navigation
Tabs ➤ Articles). In our example, there are four articles, as shown in
Figure 11-21. To access these functions, click the Article tool on the
Editing toolbar. The articles identified in the document will be displayed.

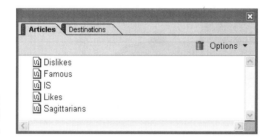

Figure 11-21
Defined articles are listed
in the Articles panel.

Deleting Article Threads and Boxes

Remember that deleting and inserting applies to both the articles and
the threads.

To delete an entire article thread, select the article in the Articles panel
and press Delete. The remaining article threads are renumbered.

To delete a box from an article, do the following:

1. Click the box in the document to select it.

2. Select Delete from the context menu.

3. Select Box from the dialog box. The remaining article boxes will
   be renumbered.

Click another tool to deselect the Article tool.

Inserting an Article Box

You can add an article box to a thread. Here's how:

1. Click the article box located in the flow before the one you want to insert.

2. Click the plus sign (+) at the bottom of the selected box, as shown in Figure 11-22.

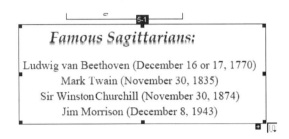

Famous Sagittarians:

Ludwig van Beethoven (December 16 or 17, 1770)
Mark Twain (November 30, 1835)
Sir Winston Churchill (November 30, 1874)
Jim Morrison (December 8, 1943)

Figure 11-22
Use the + indicator
to attach article boxes
to a thread.

3. Click OK when prompted to drag and create a new article box.

4. The new box is inserted into the thread, and all boxes following the inserted one are renumbered automatically.

And that's not all. The boxes themselves are elements that can be moved or resized. If a box is selected, you can drag it to a new location, or resize it by dragging one of the corner handles.

OK, that's quite enough of do-this, click-that. Time to build something.

Project Project 11-2: Threading Your Way Through the Internet Document

For this project, you'll need the same file you used for the first project in this chapter: internet.pdf. It's located in the Chapter 11 folder. In this project, you'll create article threads in the document.

Evaluating the Document

It's always best to start at the beginning. Let's see what's already there to work from. Open the internet.pdf file, and then open the Articles panel.

Tip

Planning an Article Flow

The point of adding articles is to organize a flow for readers who may be using different devices. In order to create a readable document, you have to set a path through the document that makes the content flow from beginning to end.

You can take several different approaches. For example, you may want to add one giant article thread from page 1 to page x. We prefer to organize a flow of articles according to headings.

Click the Article tool to activate the articles in the document. You'll see that four-article threads are preformatted at conversion:

- 1-1 is the graphic on page 1.

- 2-1 is the graphic on page 5.

- 3-1 is the text box on page 2.

- 4-1 is the text box on page 5.

Delete the articles by clicking their icons in the Articles panel and pressing Delete. A confirmation dialog box will pop up. Click OK to delete the articles. The articles that were integrated in the conversion process are of little value in the workflow.

Now you need to add some article threads.

Adding Article Threads

Let's add a series of article threads corresponding with the layout of the document. Figure 11-23 shows the outline for this document from its authoring application, Microsoft Word.

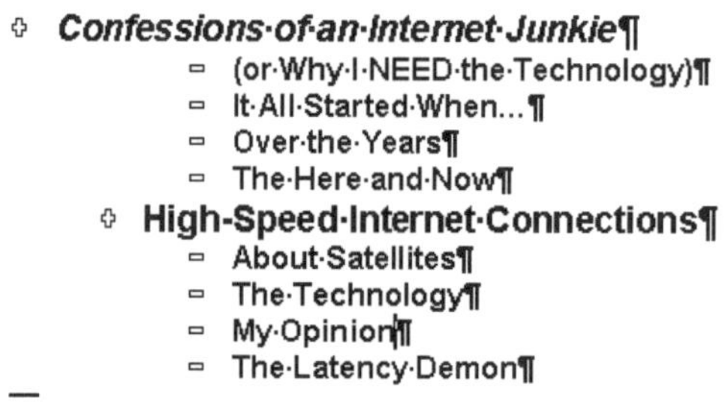

Note

You could leave the articles and attach other elements to them as you come to them, or move their boxes to the correct positions in the sequence and add to them. But it's much simpler and quicker to delete them and start afresh.

- *Confessions·of·an·Internet·Junkie*¶
  - (or·Why·I·NEED·the·Technology)¶
  - It·All·Started·When...¶
  - Over·the·Years¶
  - The·Here·and·Now¶
- **High-Speed·Internet·Connections**¶
  - About·Satellites¶
  - The·Technology¶
  - My·Opinion¶
  - The·Latency·Demon¶

Figure 11-23
Use the original outline from the Word document as a guide for designing threads

There are two first-level and eight second-level headings. This will correspond to 10 article threads. Here's how to build them:

1. Click the Article tool to activate it. Click and drag to fence in the title text. Release the mouse.

2. Click and drag each column in reading sequence. Where you see a text box, click that in sequence as well.

3. Finally, where there are graphics, add them as the last element of the two threads in which they'll appear.

4. Click another tool in the toolbar to deselect the Article tool and end the thread.

5. The Properties dialog box will appear. Enter a name for the thread and click OK.

6. Continue to the end of the document. Save the file.

The structure of each article thread in the document is listed in Table 11-1.

Table 11-1   The Article Threads Added to internet.pdf

Thread	Articles	Page	Instructions/Notes
1	2	1	Two articles, one for titles and copyright, and one for paragraph
2	4	1	Articles for head, each column, and then the graphic
3	4	2	Articles for head, each column, and then the text box
4	5	2/3	Articles for head, each column, and then paragraph-spanning columns
5	4	3	Articles for head, then the callout, and then two columns
6	2	3	Two articles for head and text
7	3	4	Articles for head and column text, then spanning paragraph
8	2	4	Two articles for head and bullet text
9	4	4	Article for head, spanning paragraph, and then the two columns
10	6	5	Article for head, two spanning paragraphs, column text, paragraph under image, graphic, and finally the last text box

Testing the Document

You can test this document's articles either in any of the Acrobat 6.0 family.

1. Click the Reflow tool (in Adobe Reader) or select View ➤ Reflow (in Acrobat).

2. Scroll through the document. You should see that the document flows according to the articles and their sequences.

To make a case in point, we want to end this project with a discussion of Figure 11-24. As you can see in the image, we've shown the article assignment for the last page of this project.

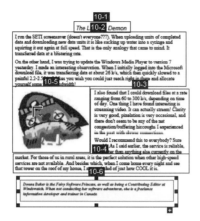

Figure 11-24
Page 5 of the project
displaying a set of articles.

The page has six articles. The way they're assigned is a matter of personal preference to some extent. For example, we could have combined the first two articles, or we could have made the text box at the bottom a separate article. The only thing that should be standard is to have the image last—which we didn't do, by the way, because we wanted to have the image before the author bio text block. The point is, how you work with articles is customized according to both your work habits and what corporate or workgroup requirements may be in place. Many options are available.

Now let's look at another way to distribute output via web browsers—and a new plug-in.

Creating Web Output

Acrobat 6.0 creates web output in several formats just by using the File ➤ Save As command. Use the process to save content from a tagged PDF file as XML, HTML, or plain text.

The plug-in can generate a number of formats. Depending on the intended use of the file, you may need to save a file in more than one version. The plug-in can generate these formats:

- HTML-4.01 with CSS-1.00

- HTML-3.20

- XML-1.00 without styling

Let's have a look at each of these options. In all instances, we've used the same source file to compare the output.

Output in HTML with Style Sheet Information

Sometimes it's extremely valuable to export a formatted document. Think of instances when you're working with different types of documents that use specific corporate templates, colors, and so forth. This export format can save a lot of time. Figure 11-25 shows a partial page layout. We want to point out some of the translation benefits and issues.

LCOME TO MY WORLD...

Actors have been wearing makeup since the dawn of time. Picture ancient man reenacting the thrill of the hunt or an aboriginal ancestor smearing his face with war paint to instill fear in the enemy.

Granted, these people were not standing on a stage but quite often they were using makeup to embellish the movement, attitude and temperament required to get the message across.

One of the best ways to *get into character* before hitting the stage is to watch the growth of that character in the mirror as you create him/her. If that physical character is the product of your search for the entire character - your performance will always be exhilarating.

Y WE NEED MAKEUP

Imagine a performance of the "Wizard of Oz" without makeup. Now, imagine seeing that same performance sitting in the back row of a 2,000 seat concert hall. It doesn't really paint an image of an inspiring, believable performance does it? Here are some reasons why good makeup is so important.

　1. To enhance the color value of the normal face

Under the bright hot lights of the stage, normal colors of the face and hands look shiny, bland and washed out. Properly applied stage makeup will correct those things.

Figure 11-25
The exported HTML 4.01 version of the manual.pdf document converts well from the original PDF with some minor errors.

Look at the main title. The beginning of the title line is missing. And this where a word of caution comes in. Just as you plan different uses for material and design approaches to using content for multiple forms of output, think about such things as templates as well. If we were using this as a one-off process, we would adjust the content of the file. On the other hand, think how tedious it would be to adjust headings constantly every time a page had to be posted, particularly if you were posting dozens of pages a day.

Here's why the initial page title is cut off. In Figure 11-26, we've captured the beginning of the HTML code for the page shown in Figure 11-26.

This output type includes style sheet information (CSS version 1.00). After the opening <head> tag, the first style describes the "Sect" (Section) class, followed by the <h1> class attributes. Here is the issue. If you

```
<!DOCTYPE html
PUBLIC "-//W3C//DTD HTML 4.01//EN" "http://www.w3.org/TR/html40/strict.dtd">
<!--
 Created from PDF via
Acrobat 5.0 SaveAs: 'HTML-4.01 with CSS-1.00'
 Mapping Table version:
21-May-2001
-->
<HTML><HEAD><STYLE type="text/css">
DIV[class="Sect"]
{
 text-align:left;
 margin-bottom:0.00pt;
 margin-top:0.00pt;
 margin-right:0.00pt;
 margin-left:0.00pt;
 text-indent:0.00pt;
 direction:ltr
}
H1 {
 text-align:left;
 margin-bottom:12.00pt;
 margin-top:18.00pt;
 margin-right:6.50pt;
 margin-left:-35.99pt;
 text-indent:0.00pt;
 direction:ltr
}
```

Figure 11-26
A portion of the
HTML content for the
manual file shows the
problem style attributes.

Tip

Why Would I Use This Version if a Newer Version Is Available?

The differences between the two HTML versions aren't so great as to make this an unlikely choice for output. There would be no need for modifying any of the style sheet elements from within a web design program, and pages could be easily converted to web output. Using this form of HTML output would be convenient and would still allow written materials to use the original styles. Of course, in some circumstances that might not be appropriate, but I think it's acceptable in this example—depending on the client!

look at the content of the style, the lines "margin-left:-35.99pt" and "text-indent:0.00pt" are the source of the problem. In order to display the main headings correctly, you have to set the margin-left in the "Sect" to a negative value, or you have to increase the text indent for the body to roughly 36 points to accommodate this.

Now let's look at the layout without style sheet information.

Output in HTML-3.20 Format with CSS Information

The second option you'll look at is output converted without style sheet information. Look at Figure 11-27. You can see that the page layout is simpler. That is, no styles are carried from the PDF document to the HTML version. Unless you have a particular need for the precise layout, however, this might be a better choice for the document you're looking at.

The last option (or perhaps, more correctly, the first option) is XML.

Output in XML-1.00 Format

As Sgt. Joe Friday always used to say, "Just the facts, ma'am." That is the core of XML. Simply the guts of a document, the essence of a file, elegant in its simplicity.

WELCOME TO MY WORLD...

Actors have been wearing makeup since the dawn of time. Picture ancient man reenacting the thrill of the hunt or an aboriginal ancestor smearing his face with war paint to instill fear in the enemy.

Granted, these people were not standing on a stage but quite often they were using makeup to embellish the movement, attitude and temperament required to get the message across.

One of the best ways to *get into character* before hitting the stage is to watch the growth of that character in the mirror as you create him/her. If that physical character is the product of your search for the entire character - your performance will always be exhilarating.

WHY WE NEED MAKEUP

Imagine a performance of the "Wizard of Oz" without makeup. Now, imagine seeing that same performance sitting in the back row of a 2,000 seat concert hall. It doesn't really paint an image of an inspiring, believable performance does it? Here are some reasons why good makeup is so important.

1. To enhance the color value of the normal face

Figure 11-27
The HTML version with style sheet information shows a simpler layout.

Figure 11-28 shows the XML output for the manual.pdf file.

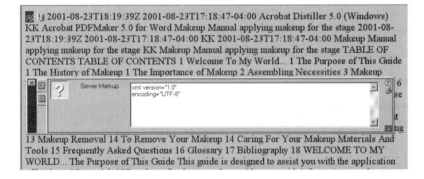

Figure 11-28
The essence of a document is shown in the XML output view.

Visually, there really isn't much to the document. Look at the image, though. After the metadata, beginning with the "TABLE OF CONTENTS" element, everything that must be there is there. That doesn't include things like links or images, which are objects added to a document, not its essence.

When the XML document is viewed in a browser, the tag structure is also included. We've shown a portion of the file, approximately the same view as the other versions, in Figure 11-29.

As an introduction to this section, we referenced XML as the last option for this discussion, but identified it as "more correctly, the first option." Regardless of the HTML/XML format in which you choose to save a PDF file, initially it will be converted to XML and then have the attributes added to it depending on the version.

```
        <TOCI>Bibliography_____11</TOCI>
      </TOC>
    </Sect>
  - <Sect>
      <Heading-1 id="LinkTarget_140">WELCOME TO MY WORLD...</Heading-1>
      <Normal>Actors have been wearing makeup since the dawn of time. Picture ancient man reenacting the thrill of the hunt or
        an aboriginal ancestor smearing his face with war paint to instill fear in the enemy.</Normal>
      <Normal>Granted, these people were not standing on a stage but quite often they were using makeup to embellish the
        movement, attitude and temperament required to get the message across.</Normal>
    - <Shape Alt="">
        <ImageData src="images/manual_b_img_0.jpg" />
      </Shape>
      <Normal>One of the best ways to get into character before hitting the stage is to watch the growth of that character in the
        mirror as you create him/her. If that physical character is the product of your search for the entire character - your
        performance will always be exhilarating.</Normal>
      <Heading-1 id="LinkTarget_145">WHY WE NEED MAKEUP</Heading-1>
      <Style3>Imagine a performance of the "Wizard of Oz" without makeup. Now, imagine seeing that same performance
        sitting in the back row of a 2,000 seat concert hall. It doesn't really paint an image of an inspiring, believable
        performance does it? Here are some reasons why good makeup is so important.</Style3>
    - <L>
      - <LI>
          <LBody id="LinkTarget_147">1. To enhance the color value of the normal face</LBody>
        </LI>
```

Figure 11-29
The browser view of
the manual.xml file
displays the content in
its most basic form.

Previously, as we were describing the content of the XML file, we made a reference to the metadata. Not to confuse the issue, but *metadata* is data about data. We think that deserves some explanation.

Document Metadata

Metadata describes how and when and by whom a particular set of data was collected, and how the data is formatted. Acrobat PDF files use XML-formatted metadata. The metadata is the information you find in a document's properties. Whenever a change is made to the properties, changes will logically be made to its metadata. You cannot change the metadata information directly. Even if you could, it wouldn't then reflect the content of the document accurately.

You can see a document's metadata by selecting Advanced ➤ Document Metadata. The Advanced information window is shown in Figure 11-30.

All the metadata embedded in the document is organized according to different groups of properties. Click the View drop-down list and choose from different viewing options. Select source and you can also see the XML code, as shown in Figure 11-31.

The source code can be copied and pasted (but not changed) from this view window. So why is this important and why is it here? The metadata, as discussed earlier, is information about the information. When a document is converted to any type of HTML, this information will be translated along with it.

Anyone who is familiar with HTML knows that metatags are included in the <head> tags of the file. These serve the same purpose in HTML as information about the document itself. Figure 11-32 shows a portion of the HTML code for the manual.pdf document saved in an HTML 3.2 version. You can see here that much of the information we've shown you in the metadata figures has been translated into metatags.

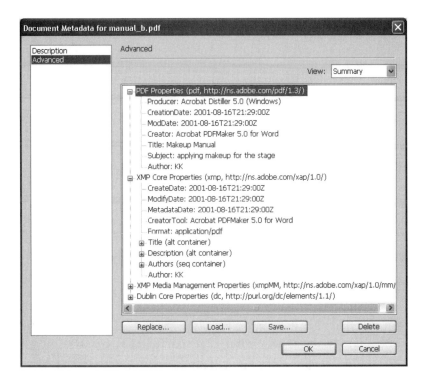

Figure 11-30
You can see the metadata for a document in either descriptive or expanded form

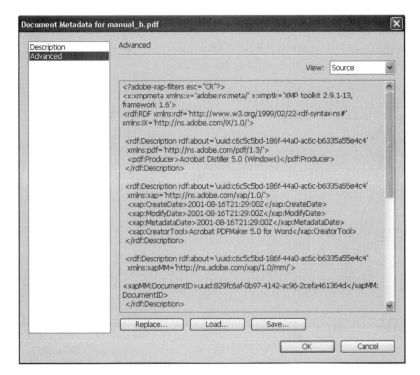

Figure 11-31
The Document Metadata window for the document displays the XML code.

```
<!DOCTYPE HTML PUBLIC "-//W3C//DTD HTML 3.2 Final//EN">
<!-- Created from PDF via Acrobat SaveAsXML -->
<!-- Mapping table version: 28-February-2003 -->
<HTML>
<HEAD>
<META
 name="DC.Title"
 content="Makeup Manual" >
<META
 name="DC.Contributor"
 content="KK" >
<META
 name="DC.Subject"
 content="applying makeup for the stage" >
<META
 name="DC.Creator"
 content="Acrobat PDFMaker 5.0 for Word" >
<META
 name="DC.Date"
 content="2001-08-16T21:29:00Z" >
<META
 name="DC.Date.Modified"
 content="2001-08-16T21:29:00Z" >
</HEAD>
<BODY bgcolor=white text=black link=blue vlink=purple alink=fushia >
<HR>
<UL>
```

Figure 11-32
The <head> tags for the manual.pdf document after saving a version in HTML 3.2 format shows the metadata content has been translated into metatags.

Headers and Footers

We just couldn't end this chapter on such a heavy topic. Acrobat 6.0 has added a couple of real neat features that are fun and powerful.

You have an engineering drawing in the exercises for Chapter 11. The drawing is for Bubba's Center. The drawing doesn't have a title block or page numbers, so you're going to convert it from the DWG (AutoCAD) format.

In Chapter 2 we suggested that you download the free VoloView Express 2.01 viewer from Autodesk. VoloView Express 2.01 will allow you view the 45 layers in this drawing (Adobe Illustrator will also let you view the drawing with layers) and convert them to a PDF. If you have AutoCAD you can convert it with layers intact. If you want to try using VoloView Express 2.01, the instructions are in a sidebar, and the original plan, site.dwg, is in the Chapter 11 folder. A PDF version is included as site.pdf for Mac users or people not interested in converting CAD drawings.

Converting the CAD Drawing

Open the CAD file in VoloView Express 2.01. You may get a warning to download an enabler, you can dismiss the warning and carry on to do the conversion.

Depending on settings the drawing may be small on a large area. You'll take care of that first. Choose Page Setup ➤ ANSI D. On the Drawing Setting tab click Fit Drawing to Page. The drawing will now be 22" × 34".

Choose File ➤ Print to open the Printer dialog box. Choose Adobe PDF for the printer and ANSI D for the paper size. Click Properties and choose ANSI D again for the paper size. Click OK to close the Properties and then click Print Preview. You should have a pretty drawing. Click OK to Print.

Adding Headers and Footers

The CAD drawing does not have a title or page number. Steve Shamblin, the engineer that donated the drawing for this exercise, sanitized it first. Well, it is actually Bubba's new shopping center. Instead of putting an engineering border and title block on the drawing, we will add a title and footnotes. Follow these steps:

1. Headings and Footers are only vertical. Bubba's drawing uses landscape orientation and only has room on the sides. Choose Document ➤ Pages ➤ Rotate ➤ 90⁰ Clockwise.

2. Choose Document ➤ Add Headers and Footers to open the Add Headers and Footers dialog box as shown in Figure 11-33.

3. Insert the text line by line in the Insert Custom Text field. You have control of the font and text size, but not color.

4. Highlight the text and click on the align icons to move the text any of the three text areas.

5. Click OK when finished, but be sure you are finished.

Use the same methods for applying a footer to a document.

Note

The Align icons only move text to boxes, they don't control alignment once in boxes.

Note

Insert Page Number allows you to select a style; Page Range allows you to set the range for that style.

Tip

Once you add headers and footers, you can edit them using the Edit ➤ Undo Headers and Footers command as long as you haven't saved. Once saved you have to edit with the TouchUp Text tool. The only way to edit font color is with the TouchUp Text tool.

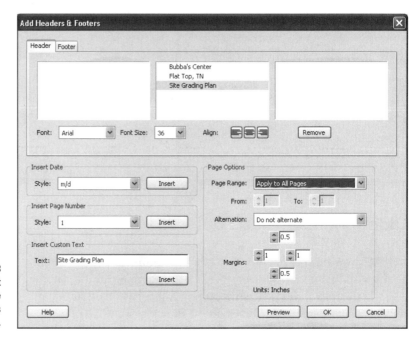

Figure 11-33
The three lines of text
used for the header are
shown in the Add Headers
and Footers dialog box.

Watermarks & Backgrounds

As an engineer, Tom loves backgrounds. He can use his nonartistic taste
and make anything he fancies. I guess there is a lot of Bubba in him.
Bubba really is into branding.

The Chapter 11 folder contains a 23-page specification for earthwork
and stormwater named spec.pdf. We are going to put Bubba's background
on this file. The background is named dozer_bkgd.pdf, located in the
Chapter 11 folder.

Choose Document ➤ Add Watermarks & Backgrounds to open the
dialog box shown in Figure 11-34. Watermarks and backgrounds are
very similar. Backgrounds are placed behind the text or image layer on
the document while watermarks overlay other content. Follow these steps:

1. Click Add a Background.

2. Click Browse. Locate the dozer_bkgd.pdf document and select it.

3. Click All Pages from the Page Ranges options. We want the back-
    ground on all pages.

4. The default alignments are centered. The background uses a land-
    scape orientation and the document uses a portrait specifications.
    Select 90⁰ from the rotation options to make the background
    portrait.

5. Reduce the opacity to about 16 percent. We don't want the background to impact the readability of the document.

6. Click OK to close the dialog box. Save the document.

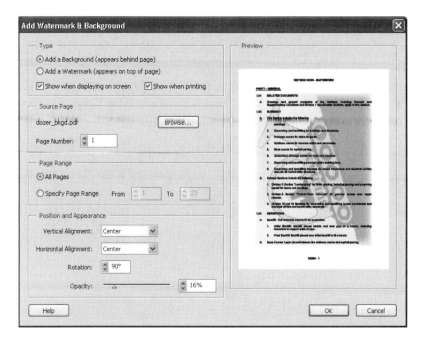

Figure 11-34
Bubba's brand is added through the Add Watermark & Background dialog box.

The Original 23-page PDF file was 140 KB. The dozer_bkgd.pdf document is 119 KB for a total of 452 KB. We put a 119 KB background on 23 pages and the total file is only 452 KB. Isn't Acrobat grand?

Up Next

Hopefully this chapter ended on a bit of a lighter note than the heavy material in the middle. That is the beauty of the software we're discussing in this book. It has an inner beauty along with the cool stuff you can create on the outside. Its inner beauty is characterized by its simplicity. And we do think it's important to understand what is under the hood. It makes the wild and wonderful creations all the more awesome when you know what they're built on.

In this chapter, our aim was to show you a number of types of output you can create from a single PDF document. Rather than showing you one of these and one of those, we concentrated instead on some of the processes and tools at your disposal, and the how and why of using them.

Note

Once saved and closed, there doesn't appear to be an easy way to remove a watermark. You may have to uncheck the Show When Displaying on Screen and Show When Printing option if you no longer want the watermark.

I think it will give you a better sense of what can be done with Acrobat. Not only that, but by using this approach you can better understand how to adapt these processes and tools to your work.

A number of specialized types of output do exist, however. In the previous chapter we looked at making documents accessible for the visually impaired. In the next chapter we go to print and advanced printing and the next eBooks. All these formats are created using the same information.

Chapter 12

Print It!

An international standard has been developed for printing using PDF. Some of the largest printers in the world are specifying PDF as either a preferred or mandatory format for submission. There are reasons for these huge developments. Let's take a look at PDF and printing.

Enhancing Print Workflow

Designers design. Regardless of the medium of choice, all designers understand the advantages of using different programs for vector, bitmap (or raster), and layout production.

For the nongraphics designers, vector is like point angle and distance in trigonometry. Your lines are equations that start at point X_1,Y_1 to X_2,Y_2. and are Z width. Vectors are also like paint by numbers, your computer develops an equation for an area then fills it with a given color. Bitmap or raster images are like the old dot matrix printers and old monitors. There are so many dots per inch across and so many dots per inch down. The computer has to store something for every dot.

PDF uses the best of all worlds. A PDF page is a mathematical description of a space. If inches are your unit and white is the background, a letter-size paper is the rectangular area described by X_0,Y_0 to $X_{8.5},Y_{11}$. Your equation says that the space is white. Other elements are added by vector location. Scalable fonts are a mathematical equation. The computer places a font from a certain font set at a certain X,Y position on the work. PDF actually describes text by the line. Vector graphics are located and described by an equation, unlike raster images. There is computer code for every dot and a high-resolution image has a lot of dots.

The print world is a raster world. The printers you have on your desk advertise so many dots per inch—the more the better. The commercial printing world is also a raster world, but it is a CMYK world instead of an RBG world. We'll discuss these worlds later.

The quicker the feedback, the smoother the review cycle, no matter what type of a designer you are. Acrobat is a very useful tool in this process. What Acrobat can do, in addition to communication, is shorten production cycles and decrease costs. You can use the same format for display, preflight, proofing, editing, archiving, transport, and printing (and for reviewing, bidding, project management, redlining, and long-term maintenance in a nongraphic design environment).

Designer Advantages

Donna hates having somebody touch her work. Look at it, admire it, hate it, make suggestions, but don't mess with the material. Tom has serious legal ramifications to worry about if someone messes with his work and the project goes wrong. Sound familiar? Of course, by using the security settings in Acrobat, you can prevent anyone from modifying your work. But what other advantages are there to incorporating Acrobat into your workflow?

We've compiled a list of benefits. The items in this list are designed to set off those little mental light bulbs. Everyone will have different experiences and backgrounds, but our aim is to offer some points to ponder.

Consider these concepts:

- Proofing is very accurate. Colors can be manipulated to appear as the printed output would. Reviewers can zoom in to a factor of 6400 percent—you can't miss a detail at that magnification. The more accurate the proof, the less chance of proofing error.

- Vector graphics and embedded fonts are always at full resolution. This means you won't have any second-generation quality loss, as would occur from faxing a proof.

- Speaking of graphics, transparency is supported, so layered Illustrator and Photoshop images can be fully integrated.

- In Acrobat 6.0 AutoCAD and Visio layers are supported, and probably will be supported from other programs soon.

- Layouts can be displayed as they'll be printed. Acrobat 6.0 has better support for multiple page sizes, even in the same document. The new Print Colors as Black option in the printer commands for Acrobat 6.0 will solve a lot of the engineering problems with grayscaling of color images to black and white plotters.

- All versions of Acrobat since 4.0 have supported spaces up to 200 inches by 200 inches. This allows the graphics designers to design large posters and billboards and other designers to make high-quality large maps.

- Work can be distributed to many people at once. You can track the review of a document to an entire workgroup, including the client, with one email.

- Matchprints or paper color proofs can be substituted by PDF proofing transfers. This soft-proofing process helps to maintain integrity and saves time and money in this portion of the cycle— you don't have to send a file for printing, review it, and ship it.

- When a proof is signed off, the same PostScript file can be used and the PDF prepress version can be created by changing the Distiller Press settings. This saves time in final prepress delivery (depending on your printing services company).

Once a file is out of your hands, using a PDF-assisted workflow still has its advantages.

The Ripple Effect

The efficiencies of using PDF for production have a ripple effect. For example, because later press deadlines are possible, advertising has more time to adjust for changes in costs or pricing or other corrections, without incurring additional costs for couriers or mailing. Digital distribution is instant. Speaking of instant, from an ad agency perspective, PDF pages can be used as "tear sheets." Emailing the page to the client on the day of publication provides the verification of a traditional tear sheet and speeds up revenue collection.

Project deadlines on engineering projects also can be tighter. Time and money wasted for overnight shipping is gone. Just explain to your customer that an ordinary paper- and courier-based process is costing them time and money, and you'll be surprised at how fast most purchase Acrobat.

Bidding can be handled electronically. Instead of spending the time to print and distribute plans and specs, they're distributed electronically. The cost of printing on engineering jobs is transferred from the designer to the contractor and the contractor can more efficiently control these costs based on what they actually need to print. The contractor also saves money on distributing information to subcontractors.

PDF files maintain corporate identity and branding. PDF files, unlike other less-consistent formats, can be printed exactly as intended. For engineers this is especially true with the new Print Colors as Black option.

What about prepress shops? Whether they are printers or imaging-service bureaus, there are benefits. You can see content and determine immediately if you have the right components including images, fonts, and graphics. And you can do it in composite color. Not only that, but the TouchUp tools will allow you to make last-minute changes without having to redistill the source documents. The new PDF/X settings and compliancy checker will make certain your file is right.

It's an Impressive System

How's that for a buildup? As you would expect, you must deal with a number of issues to make PDF files work for your print output.

In this chapter, you'll examine a number of print-related issues. Remember that regardless of the approach you take to translating a source document into PDF format, the processes will be the same. You'll first look at Acrobat 6.0 Professional and Distiller, then you'll learn how to set some common print output settings. We'll show you how to create watched folders, and you'll examine color settings in Acrobat. Following that is an in-depth discussion on fonts and color issues, and you'll also look at exporting files as PostScript or EPS files.

Acrobat 6.0 Professional and the Print Professional

Adobe didn't call it Professional for nothing. Adobe targeted three markets for Acrobat 6.0: graphics design and print, engineering, and the business forms professionals. The rest of this chapter will be mainly on the features for the print, but engineering and forms will be thrown in where appropriate.

Professional Print features include the following:

- Preflighting. For the nonprint professional this is a checklist type verification that everything is present and correct for high-resolution output.

- Separation Preview. High-quality printing uses color absorption rather than color reflection for printing. Our computer screens use Red, Green, and Blue (RGB) to make the colors. Commercial printers use Cyan, Magenta, Yellow, and K (black) (CMYK). Acrobat 6.0 will make the separations for the four colors and any additional "spot" colors.

- Transparency Flattener Preview. Computer graphics design relies on layers and transparency. These must be flattened and become part of the plates for printing. Acrobat 6.0 allows you to flatten the transparencies and adjust what they'll look like printed.

Note

Printing professionals know these explanations already; they're listed here for other designers and hopefuls.

- Create and Validate PDF/X-Compliant Files. Setting up something to print on a commercial printer is expensive and having to stop the presses can be even more expensive. A committee of print people was formed to develop an International Standards Organization (ISO) standard for PDF files going to printing.

- Overprint Preview (from Acrobat 5.0). Overprint colors are two unscreened inks printed on top of each other. For example, when magenta ink is printed over yellow ink, the resulting overprint is a bright orange color. If overprinting isn't turned on, only the magenta ink would print. Acrobat 5.0 allowed you to see overprint previews.

- Control over Spot Colors. Often a certain spot of color is needed in addition to the CMYK. This has been a problem for printers.

- Enhanced Viewing, Navigation, and Magnification Tools. You now have the Loupe tool, which is like setting a magnifier and moving it around on a big drawing. Split Screen, which is similar to the split screen in Excel, is new, but this split screen can have different magnification in the windows. You can now zoom up to 6400 percent and count the hairs on the gnat's head.

- Rulers with Guides. In addition to the grid, these help with layout.

- Measurement Tools for X and Y Coordinates, Distance Angle, and Area of Elements in the Document. Printer can measure electronically instead of having to print a proof.

Tip
PDFWriter

Adobe developed PDFWriter based on PDF 1.2 (Acrobat 6.0 is PDF 1.5). With Acrobat 5.0 you had to try to load it manually, but some people still used it. It isn't available in Acrobat 6.0. For goodness sakes, don't use PDFWriter or the term Writer. It's old technology that will cause you more problems than it's worth and you risk a lecture from Tom. Also some of the third-party PDF creators still use PDF 1.2.

Distiller plays a major part in getting files ready for print, so you're going to look at Distiller and Distiller's importance in the print workflow.

A Run Through Distiller (aka, Adobe PDF Printer in Acrobat 6.0)

Acrobat Distiller is installed as part of the Acrobat 6.0 installation process. Many programs, especially Adobe programs like FrameMaker and InDesign make their own PDF files. QuarkXPress has licensed the Jaws PDF library from Global Graphics Software to counter the threat from InDesign. This was news on PlanetPDF at the time of publication, stay tuned to see how it works.

Any program with a Print command can print to Distiller. Distiller is its own program, but its functionality is integrated both into authoring programs as a printer option and into Acrobat proper. Whether you convert a file to PDF using PDFMaker or print to Distiller, you'll encounter the same issues.

Let's see what's inside the Distiller box. Before you do, though, here is a summary of some of the biggest features of Distiller 6.0:

- Distiller options for PDF/X1a and PDF/X-3–ISO standards for files for printing.

- Custom Distiller settings can be dropped onto the Distiller window— printers can develop settings for their equipment and they can be emailed to customers.

- Compression panel now Images panel—Text and Line Art compression is no longer an option and is always on.

- Advanced panel now has an option to support Job Definition Format (JDF)—an XML-based file that carries job information to the printer.

- Support for JPEG2000—A new and improved compression standard for color photographs. It's an ISO standard.

The Distiller Interface

This part of the discussion will center on the program itself. You can access Distiller from your desktop by selecting Programs ➤ Acrobat Distiller. The interface, as shown in Figure 12-1, is deceptively simple.

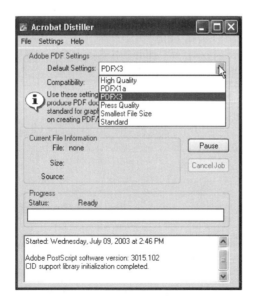

Figure 12-1
Acrobat Distiller is a separate program; although its interface looks simple, it's very powerful.

Each time the program is launched, the fonts table is created; you see the little Acrobat symbol twirling in a circle as the table is built. The Default Settings drop-down list contains the list of settings that Adobe has created and they're suitable for most purposes. The default settings are as follows:

- *Smallest File Size*. You would want your smallest files for the Web or eBooks. Speed and storage size are at a premium.

- *Standard*. This is the setting for the everyday office environment.

- *High Quality*. Is a setting for higher-quality color photos intended for a good inkjet printer.

- *Press Quality*. Is a setting for higher-quality prepress files.

- *PDF/X-1a*. Supports only CMYK (and spot color) workflow. All fonts must be embedded, color management isn't allowed, trapping, output intents, and the Trim box are specified. Transfer functions and halftone screen frequencies aren't allowed.

- *PDF/X-3*. Supports a device-independent color-managed workflow in addition to CMYK and spot colors. Acrobat 4.0 or later compatibility. Trapping, output intents, and Trim box are specified. Transfer functions aren't allowed and halftone screen functions are restricted.

File Settings

With Distiller open select File ➤ Preferences to open the Preferences dialog box. Figure 12-2 was shown earlier in the book, but it's important enough to show again. The Ask for PDF File Destination, the Ask to Replace Existing PDF File, the View PDF When Using Distiller and the Delete Log Files options for successful jobs are unchecked by default. We recommend checking all.

Settings Options

The Settings options are the heart of Distiller. Figure 12.3 shows the various options and you'll explore them all.

Tip

Real-life PDF/X-1a

The *Time* family of magazines accepts (prefers) files in PDF/X-1a format. They have a wonderful web site www.direct2.time.com. There are some good downloads and free publications for your archives They even have Distiller settings for you to drop into Acrobat 6.0.

Tip

If you don't check the Ask for PDF File Destination option, you'll spend unnecessary time searching for files.

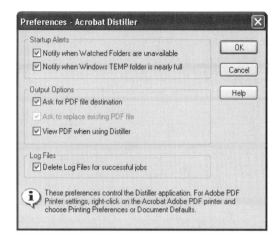

Figure 12-2
Distiller has its own set of preferences for startup, output, and logging.

Font Locations...	Ctrl+L
Watched Folders...	Ctrl+F
Edit Adobe PDF Settings...	Ctrl+E
Add Adobe PDF Settings...	Ctrl+Shift+E
Remove Adobe PDF Settings...	Ctrl+R
Security...	Ctrl+S

Figure 12-3
Distiller's settings options control file processing.

The settings options include the following:

- Font Locations shows all the folders that contain fonts on your computer. Figure 12-4 shows the font location folders. You can add or delete folders. The check box at the bottom may be important to PDF/X-1a users sending material to *Time,* because just like the Visa commercial, *Time* doesn't take TrueType fonts.

- Watched Folders are used to set up a system to look in certain folders on a certain schedule for PostScript files—much more on that coming up.

- Edit Adobe PDF Settings opens the dialog box of the same name with its set of five tabs. Again, more on that coming up.

- Add Adobe PDF Settings allows you to add settings you develop or developed by third parties like your printer. These can be added through the dialog box or dragged to the Distiller panel.

- Security settings are used to set both passwords and encryption as you can see in Figure 12-5. The figure reflects settings for Acrobat 5.0, which allows for 128-bit encryption.

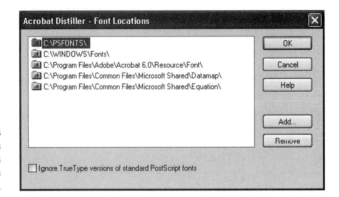

Figure 12-4
Distiller's Font Locations
dialog box describes
the location of fonts on
your hard drives.

Where Have All My Fonts Gone?

Distiller gives priority to fonts embedded in a PostScript file. Then it will search through fonts in assigned folders (PSFonts folder in Windows, System Folder: Fonts on Mac), and Acrobat standard fonts (in the Font subfolder of Acrobat's Resource folder).

Set other locations using Settings ➤ Font Locations. All fonts must be in folders, not in subfolders. The easy solution? Embed the fonts you're using.

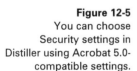

Tip

Setting the security in the distillation process may not be the best idea. Have you ever created a file that you didn't tweak before sending? It takes time to remove security.

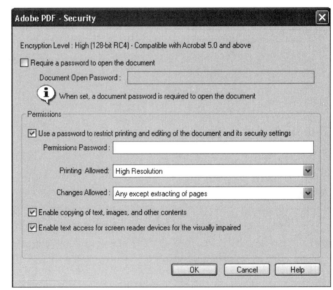

Figure 12-5
You can choose
Security settings in
Distiller using Acrobat 5.0-
compatible settings.

Help!

We can't leave this walk-through without looking at the Help menu. The different Help options for Distiller are shown in Figure 12-6.

Figure 12-6
You can find information on Distiller as well as the *pdfmark Guide* in the Help menu.

Distiller Help Options

As you can see in Figure 12-6 you have several different Help options. We want to point out one file in particular. The *Distiller Parameters Guide* is a 122-page PDF file that covers the Distiller information in this chapter, but to a very great depth. If you're working on a project with complex output requirements, look in this file for more information.

The first listing, *Acrobat Guide*, opens the Help files for Acrobat. The *pdfmark Guide* is a technical programming document. It describes the syntax and use of the pdfmark operator and how to use it for coding purposes. The final option on the menu gives you the Distiller version information.

As mentioned earlier, Distiller can use watched folders. Let's have a look.

Note

Distiller doesn't convert a PostScript file in a watched folder if the file is read-only.

Demo: Setting Up Watched Folders

Distiller can be configured to look in a certain folder on a certain schedule for PostScript files. When it finds a file in the In folder, it converts the file to PDF and moves it to the Out folder. You can have up to 100 watched folders being monitored by Distiller at the same time, and you can create watched folders based on any criteria, such as customer or level of compression.

Here's how to set up watched folders:

1. Open Acrobat Distiller. In the dialog box, select Settings ➤ Watched Folders. The Watched Folders dialog box shown in Figure 12-7 opens.

2. To add folders, click Add. Browse to select the folder, and click OK. The In and Out folders will automatically be added by Distiller, as shown in Figure 12-8. Folders can be added at any level in your directory structure.

Note

Look at the note in the bottom panel of Figure 12-7. Technically, you can set up a watched folder on a network and multiple people can print to the folder to avoid having Acrobat on every machine. While technically feasible, it isn't legal.

Note

To remove a folder, click the name, and then click Remove. The In and Out folders, their contents, and the Folder.JobOptions file must be deleted manually.

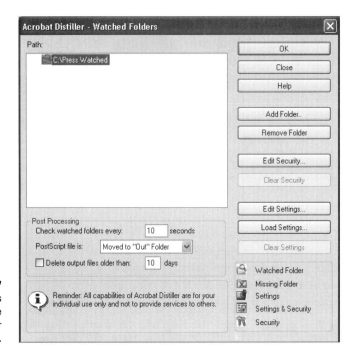

Figure 12-7
Use the Watched Folders dialog box to set up the folder structure; our system has one folder.

Figure 12-8
Distiller automatically adds files to the directory.

Folder Options

We mentioned that you can set the options for the content of the watched folders. These options cover conversion processes, management, and time frames.

1. From the Watched Folders dialog box (shown earlier in Figure 12-7) click Edit Settings to open the Adobe PDF Settings dialog box shown in Figure 12-9. This dialog box contains the same set of options available for creating job options in other areas, such as creating custom job options in authoring programs.

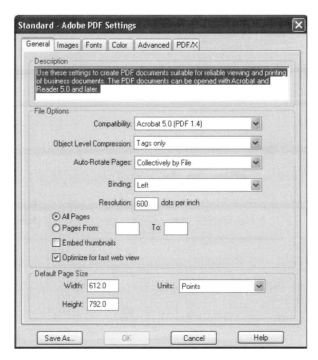

Figure 12-9
You can create a new set of job options to apply to watched folders.

Options for Processing Files

Refer again to Figure 12-7 (the Watched Folders dialog box.) You will see a number of settings below the listing of the watched folders in the Post Processing area of the dialog box. You can set specific options for processing including the following:

- Enter a time in seconds to specify how often to check the folders. The default

- The default is 10 seconds. The value can range from 1 to 9999 seconds.

- Set options for the file after processing. The file can be either moved to the Out folder or deleted.

- Set output file deletion options to clean out the old files on a specified time schedule.

Now that you've looked at Distiller, setting preferences, and creating watched folders. Don't you think it's time to have a look at the particulars of creating print output? Us too.

Print Job Options-PDF/X-1a

PDFX/-1a is a new standard! Let's start there. It will be handy to understand PDF/X when you later test the files for compliance. You all know settings can be tweaked until the cows come home, but they aren't good if they don't work with your printer.

General Settings

Use these settings from the General tab (shown in Figure 12-10):

- Select a compatibility setting of at least Acrobat 4.0. PDF/X was adopted when Acrobat 4.0 was current, making that the level of compatibility.

- Object Level Compression is set to Off.

- Auto-Rotate Pages is used to make pages view correctly on a screen. Select Off to prevent printing problems.

- Clear the Optimize for Fast Web View and Embed Thumbnails options. These options add to file size but have no print output purpose, thus enabling them will lengthen the Distiller process.

- 2400 dpi is required for this high-level print standard.

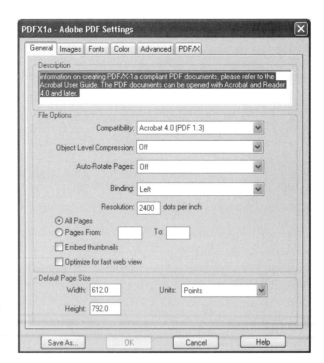

Figure 12-10
Start a oot of PDF/X
compliant settings
in the General tab.

Image Settings

Formerly known as compression options, the Images options set levels of compression for various types of images. The Images tab, with its default settings for PDF/X-1a, is shown in Figure 12-11.

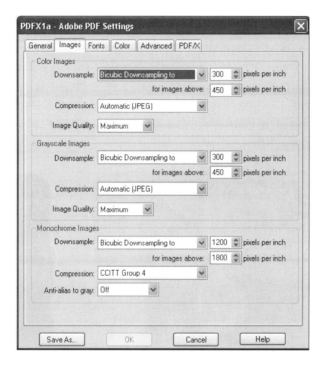

Figure 12-11
The compression options you choose depend on the content of the file.

These are the settings required to print high-quality images:

- The default compression setting is Automatic at maximum quality. This usually results in minimal compression and large file size.

- Compression is done using JPEG and ZIP algorithms. There are five JPEG-quality levels. For imaging output, set the Image Quality drop-down list to Maximum. JPEG is lossy compression; ZIP is lossless, but not as efficient as JPEG. Acrobat 6.0 supports JPEG2000, which is lossless, but it will be a while before most printers can use it.

- Downsampling is often necessary. Images are often digitized at too high a resolution, or they're scaled during layout.

Note

Use 250-300 dpi for contone images for offset printing. *Contone* refers to a type of printer that uses a combination of dithering and printing at different levels of intensity to produce different colors and different shades of lightness and darkness. Contone printers lay down ink using a few different levels of intensity (usually eight). Dithering is required to produce the range of colors our eyes can see.

- If a file will be reused for subsequent work, use bicubic down-sampling. Although it's the slowest, it results in the best quality.

- Target resolutions depend on the screen ruling of whatever imaging process the output is planned for.

- The resolution will be downsampled only if the image's resolution is at least 50 percent higher than the target resolution.

Fonts Settings

The Fonts tab is shown in Figure 12-12. We'll discuss fonts in depth later, but we want to point out some features on this tab. You have two options regarding embedding: You can embed all fonts or only subsets of fonts, and you can also define actions when embedding fails in a document.

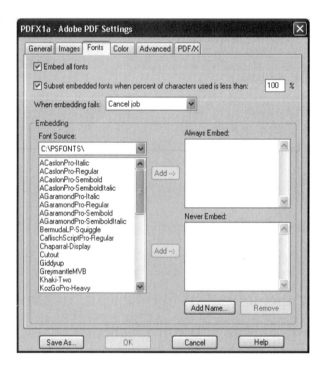

Figure 12-12
Select embedding and subsetting options in the Fonts tab.

PDF/X-1a requires that all fonts be embedded. Some font foundries don't allow their fonts to be embedded in a PDF file. These fonts display a lock symbol on the Fonts tab next to the font's name.

You're given a choice of what to do if embedding fails. With PDF/X you must cancel the distillation. If it doesn't fail now it will fail later.

Color Settings

Next up is the Color tab, shown in Figure 12-13. Much information is coming up in this chapter on color; the figure shows the default settings for PDF/X-1a.

Tip

RGB vs. CMYK Color

If you're creating documents for both the Web and print, use CMYK. CMYK documents convert quite well to RGB. The reverse isn't necessarily true. Converting high resolution PDF images into low-resolution images for the Web isn't a problem.

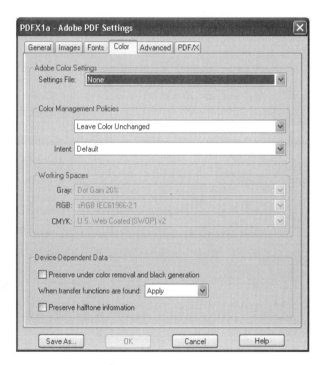

Figure 12-13
Choose color settings that comply with the PDF/X-1a standard.

Advanced Settings

The Advanced tab default settings for PDF/X-1a are shown in Figure 12-14. To be compliant, you need to leave these settings at their defaults.

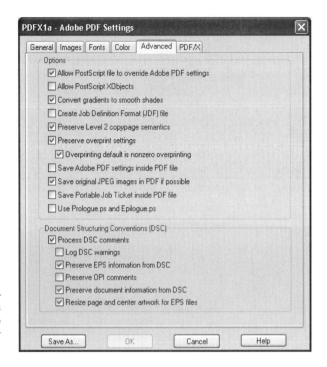

Figure 12-14
Leave the defaults
selected in the
Advanced tab settings for
PDF/X-1a compliance.

The final settings for PDF/X-1a are in the PDF/X tab and include some basic options:

- Choose a compliance level. You can choose from PDF/X-1a or X-3 options.

- Select a response when a job is found to be noncompliant. Again, if the job isn't compliant you must cancel.

- As we mentioned earlier, a PDF/X-1a requirement is that the trim box is specified. The PDF/X-1a settings set a default.

- The PDF/X-1a OutputIntent Profile Name is US Web Coated (SWOP) v2.

We indicated that we'd return to fonts and cover some of these issues in detail. On that note, everything you want to know about fonts is up next.

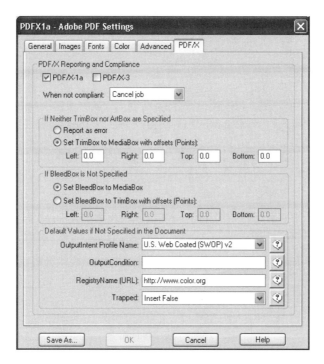

Figure 12-15
PDF/X-1a compliance
settings are selected
by default.

Fonts

Fonts are somewhat of a personal matter. Some designers search for the perfect font (Donna among them). As you've seen, Tom is satisfied to focus on content. Your choice will always depend on the purpose of your document. Regardless of which camp you're in, fonts can be easily embedded into PDF files.

Embedding Fonts

An embedded font means the definition of the font is included in the PDF file. You may create your own settings and embed, subset, or choose not to embed any font depending on your particular requirements.

In general terms, you should always embed fonts for documents heading to print unless the file size is a primary consideration or you're creating screen output. Embedding is useful if you're working in an environment where you characteristically use the same fonts for the same types of work. In fact, you may want to create different custom settings for different types of work, different clients, and the like.

Tip

What About the Base 14 Fonts (Now Base 40)?

The Base 40 fonts aren't embedded by default when you use the Standard Adobe PDF Settings to create documents. This setting shows to be compatible with Acrobat 5.0 and Acrobat Reader.

Tip

**File Size and
Simple Documents**

If you're working with a
basic document, stick to
Helvetica or Times to
minimize your file size.
You don't have to embed
these two fonts—the
document will be viewed
with the system
resources from the
Resources\Fonts folder.

If you have an embedded font, and the user has a font with the same name installed on his system, the file will be read with the user's system fonts, even if they're from a different foundry. The Impact fonts come immediately to mind.

Acrobat tries to simulate fonts not embedded in the PDF and not installed on the computer with Adobe sans MM or Adobe serif MM fonts. It reads the font metrics from the SuperATM database, which is included in the Acrobat installation process. A simulated font uses the same width and has a similar appearance. Simulation works only for relatively normal-appearing fonts. Logically, many decorative or unusual fonts cannot be simulated correctly.

What do you do if you want to ensure the user uses your fonts? You have to subset them.

Subsetting Fonts

Subsetting is different from embedding. Subsetting makes sure each font used is included (subset) in the file. On the Fonts tab, there is a subset setting: Subset at 100%. This setting will ensure that your desired font is actually the one used. Why? It's all in the name. When a subset is embedded, Distiller assigns a unique name to the font derived from the name of the original. This name will never match a font on the host system, and your version will always be used.

Subsetting is especially important for press work. The lower the subset percentage value, the smaller the file size because only the characters used in the file are subset. Another reason for subsetting at 100 percent relates to editing your document in Acrobat. You can use the TouchUp Text tool for small repairs. With a font subset at 100 percent, the entire font is embedded and you can then touch up the text at will. If you subset a font at a lower percentage, only the characters actually used in the document are included.

Note

If you want to test with
the file used in this demo,
look for the nola
tagged.pdf document in
the Chapter 12 folder.

Demo: Keep an Eye on Your Fonts

In Acrobat, you can check what fonts are being used for display. This process requires using two different commands, but it's worth the few minutes it will take you to complete, especially in appearance-critical documents.

Look at Figure 12-16. In this image, you'll see a portion of a page, as well as the tab of the TouchUp Properties dialog box for the heading, selected with the TouchUp Text tool. You can see that the font is HelmetBoldItalic.

Figure 12-16
You can select some text in the document and view its characteristics in detail.

You can check to see what's in your file by selecting File ➤ Document Info ➤ Fonts. As you can see in Figure 12-17, the dialog box lists the fonts in our document, including the HelmetBoldItalic font.

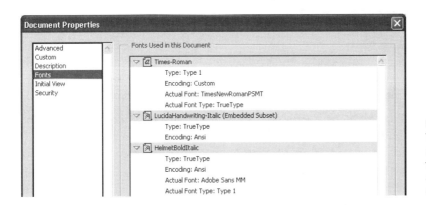

Figure 12-17
The file's document properties describe the fonts used in the document as well as their type and encoding method.

But is this actually what a user would see if the file were shipped elsewhere? No. Here's why. When you check what is actually in the file, the results can be deceptive, unless you set the view options first. Select View, and make sure Use Local Fonts is disabled. Then look at the Document Fonts dialog box again, as shown in Figure 12-18.

As you can see in this dialog box, the Actual Font listed for HelmetBold-Italic is now Adobe Sans MM, meaning that you didn't embed the font correctly. What's the impact of this? Look back at Figure 12-16. As you can see, there is very little difference, so you wouldn't likely redefine and redistill the source document. Whether to redo the conversion or not is a judgment call.

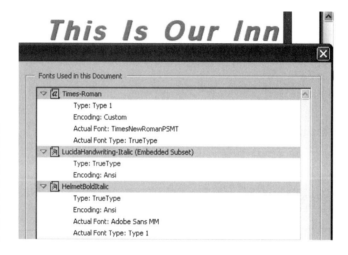

Figure 12-18
The actual fonts used in this document after distribution are different than those that were originally chosen. The most obvious difference in the substituted font is spacing.

Speaking of judgment calls, let's get into color management.

Managing Color in Acrobat

Acrobat provides a number of profiles to use for converting color models in your files. In addition to choosing a color model, you can use the Soft-proofing feature, which gives you a simulation of rendered output.

Note
Acrobat doesn't allow you to save custom CSF files. If you need a custom file, create it in Photoshop or Illustrator. The CSFs used in Acrobat are a subset of the Photoshop and Illustrator versions.

You can choose from a number of common color settings optimized for various workflows and prepress options. Each color settings file (CSF) has associated values for the working spaces and color management engine; these values are preselected. The CSF you choose preselects the other options. A Custom Settings option is available that allows you to edit the Working Spaces settings. Any embedded color information will take precedence over the CSF settings.

Let's look at the components and options available for color in Acrobat.

1. Select Edit ➤ Preferences ➤ Color Management. The dialog box shown in Figure 12-19 opens.

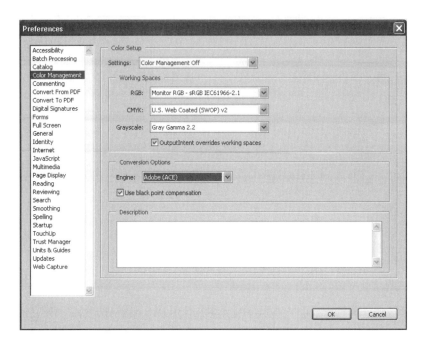

Figure 12-19
You can choose a number of color preferences from within Acrobat.

2. Click the Settings drop-down list and select a Color Management option. The options available are shown in Figure 12-20. When you choose color settings, other options are automatically preselected.

Figure 12-20
The Color Management options allow you to choose from a wide variety of options, which in turn preselect other options.

Using ICC and CMYK Profiles

The International Color Consortium (ICC) defines ICC color as a system used to separate creation from rendering of color information. You use a profile to map source colors into an absolute color space. Then you use other profiles to map out of this absolute color space to destination colors.

The way ICC is converted to CMYK is defined through the profiles and tools that create them. With standard profiles, there is no guarantee that gray text will be constrained to the black channel.

Do you need to use ICC color? Not necessarily. CMYK is the common data path for all PDF color data destined for print. Your primary decision is whether to use the standard CMYK or an ICC-managed workflow. It's simpler to use one or the other. If your files are often received from external sources, preflight and convert them to your internal standards first thing. A standard CMYK workflow is easier to manage, understand, and troubleshoot.

An ICC workflow (specifically CIEXYZ) will result in more reliably reproducible color. It's recommended when using color graphics for multiple purposes, if different printing presses are used, or if you're printing to domestic and international presses because it's device-independent.

Settings Options

As mentioned, when you select any of the settings except for Custom, the other settings are preselected.

- *Color Management Off.* Use this option for video and on-screen output. Documents created with this setting have no profile tags. Using this option emulates behavior of applications that don't support color. You can also use this option when you want to pass through color management information from other non-Adobe applications, such as QuarkXPress. If you're in an Adobe environment, the color management settings (working spaces) should be set the same as in the original program.

- *Emulate Photoshop 4.0.* Use this option if you want to match the color workflow of the Mac version of Photoshop 4.0 or earlier.

- *Prepress Defaults: Europe; Japan; U.S..* Use these options for output under common press conditions in the respective regions.

- *Photoshop 5 Default Spaces.* Use this option if you prefer default color settings from Photoshop 5.0. If you modify any of the RGB, CMYK, or grayscale settings, the Settings selection will change to Custom.

- *Web Graphics Defaults.* Use this option for web-based output.

Note

A ColorSync Workflow (Mac OS only) option is also available that uses the ColorSync CMS with profiles set in ColorSync (version 3 or later). A ColorSync Workflow option is used for work containing a mix of Adobe and non-Adobe applications.

Working Spaces

When you select one of the settings options, the working spaces default according to that setting. Experiment with the settings to see what options are associated with each settings choice. For example, let's say you've chosen the U.S. Prepress defaults. Let's look at the content from the respective drop-down lists. Figure 12-21 shows the RGB options. The Adobe RGB (1998) is the default for the prepress settings.

Figure 12-21
There are several RGB working space settings available.

Choosing the U.S. Prepress settings will set U.S. Web Coated (SWOP) v2 as the default CMYK space (see Figure 12-22). Other CMYK spaces are shown in the drop-down list in the figure.

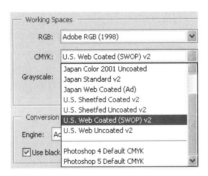

Figure 12-22
The U.S. Prepress option uses U.S. Web Coated (SWOP) v2 as the default CMYK space.

Finally, the grayscale space is set, as shown in Figure 12-23. The default value is a Dot Gain setting of 20 percent.

Choosing any alternatives from the drop-down lists converts the options from a preset to custom settings.

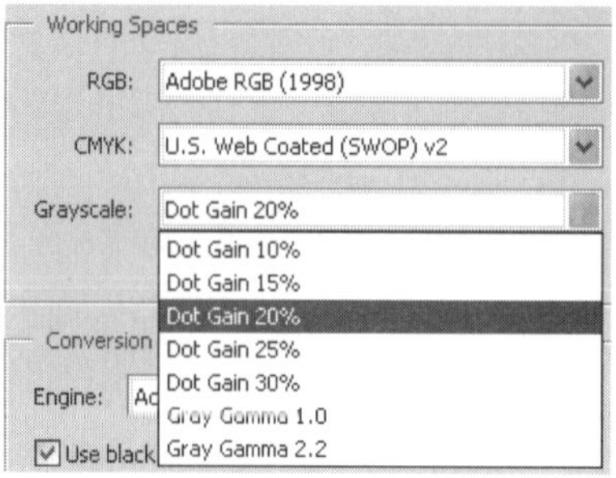

Figure 12-23
The Grayscale space
default setting for U.S.
Prepress options is a dot
gain of 20 percent.

Specifying a Color Management Engine

Acrobat ships with color management engine support. The engine
specifies the system and color matching method. Acrobat uses industry-
standard engines:

- *Adobe Color Engine (ACE).* Uses the Adobe system and engine. This
  is the default.

- *Microsoft ICM (Windows).* This option can be used with Microsoft
  Windows 98, 2000, and XP.

- *Mac OS.* Offers Apple ColorSync, Apple CMM, or Heidelberg CMM.

Any installed third-party color management engines are also displayed.

Black-Point Compensation

Black-point compensation is selected by default. It's used to adjust for
differences in black points when you're converting colors between color
spaces. When it's selected, the full range of the source space is mapped
into the full space of the destination space. In general, leave this option
selected. The only exception is when you're printing to a PostScript
printer using raster image processor (RIP) management.

Once you've selected a set of options, click OK to close the Preferences
dialog box. Remember that whatever settings you've chosen will remain
until you reset the preference again.

Advanced Print Settings

Color management may be either host-based or printer-based. We've
concentrated on document-based color. Let's have a look at the printer

options. These settings are chosen in the Advanced Print Settings dialog box. In addition to color management, you can define such options as tiling and transparency. Let's have a look.

Choose File ➤ Print to open the Print dialog box. Click Advanced at the bottom left of the dialog box to open the Advanced Print Setup dialog box. The dialog box has four different sets of options depending on which settings heading you select in the list at the top left, shown in Figure 12-24. The options also vary depending on the overall settings chosen. The default is the Acrobat 6 Default setting, again shown at the top of Figure 12-24. By the way, if you want to print the document as an image, such as for testing a document for the location of an error, click the Print as Image option at the top of the dialog box.

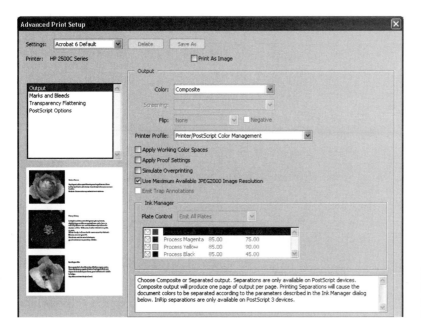

Figure 12-24
Start choosing advanced print options by selecting a settings option.

The options in the Advanced Print Setup dialog box are extensive. In the following sections, we've shown the options available in a figure as well as listed options and their uses in bullet form. Please experiment with the advanced settings. By the way, in order to make life easier for you, if you click a setting in one of the panels in the dialog box, tips and descriptions of the setting are displayed at the bottom of the dialog box.

Output Settings

Tip

Saving Settings

Constructing just the right set of advanced print settings can be a very time-consuming process. You can save the settings once they're perfected. Click Save As in the Advanced Print Settings dialog box, name the file, and click OK. To use the settings, click the Settings drop-down list at the top left of the dialog box as shown in Figure 12-24.

Use the Output settings in the Advanced Print Settings dialog box shown in Figure 12-25 to simulate printing on different printers or to modify settings while printing a document without having to experiment with importing document settings. Your document may be prepared for a particular printer profile, and you can modify the options to print to a desktop printer for evaluation, for example.

- *Composite or Separated Output.* Separations are only available on PostScript printers. Color and grayscale composites are both supported and available from the drop-down list. You can use the composite settings to print a proof of a color-separated document before sending it to press.

- *Screening and Flip Settings.* Available for placing separations only.

- *Printer Profile.* Select an alternate profile from the one included in the document. Use to preview output on a desktop when a job is designed for a press.

- *Apply Working Color Spaces.* Choose this option if you have uncalibrated color objects in your document. The CMYK working-space profile is applied to the objects.

- *Apply Proof Settings.* Uses the CMYK working space as the source for uncalibrated color objects in your document.

- *Simulate Overprinting.* Simulate appearance of overprinted and spot colors using composite colors. Although printing time may be increased, it can be previewed on-screen. Most desktop printers don't support overprinting, but you can preview it by selecting Simulate Overprinting.

- *Use Maximum Available JPEG2000 Image Resolution.* Choose this option to print JPEG2000 images using the highest possible resolution. If you don't select the option and are using JPEG2000 images, the default resolution is used for printing.

- *Ink Manager.* Choose options to control inks. Ink Manager settings apply only to the document print job, and aren't included in the document's information. Ink Manager settings are available only for separations.

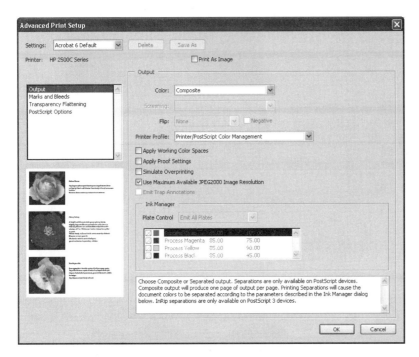

Figure 12-25
Modify the output settings to test output and print to different printers.

Marks and Bleeds

Marks and bleeds are required when you send a document to a press. The marks are used to align color separations and trim pages. Marks are exported in the PostScript component of the document and override embedded settings.

If your source document contained marks, you can use them or choose Marking from within the Advanced Print Settings dialog box. Choose from a single option to select all the marks, or choose specific formats as shown in Figure 12-26.

Tip

You can also choose between Western and Eastern markings, used for printing Asian languages.

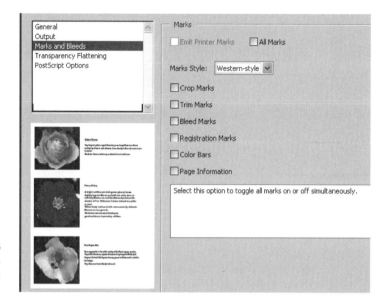

Figure 12-26
Choose print marks as
needed before sending a
document to the printer.

Transparency Flattening

Transparency Flattening is supported by PostScript printers only. Print output doesn't always display the specific detail of a screen image transparency. In order to print transparency accurately, a document is cut into segments, each using specific color levels that combine to simulate a screen transparency. Flattening occurs with any document containing transparent objects or a document that isn't exported to an Acrobat 5.0 or newer format.

To adjust flattening, drag the Raster/Vector Balance slider as shown in Figure 12-27. The higher the setting, the more vector data is exported. Conversely, the lower the setting, the more raster data is exported.

Note

The lowest values on the slider will rasterize all objects. Use it with very complex artwork containing many objects. Highest value ranges will maintain the most vector artwork, but may still rasterize complex artwork. This setting produces the highest-quality output, and generally takes the most time and memory.

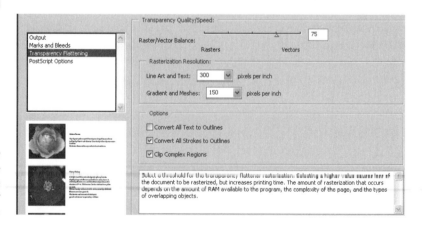

Figure 12-27
Adjust transparency
sliders to export relative
quantities of vector
and raster data.

PostScript Options

Before choosing specific PostScript options, select a policy for controlling when fonts and resources are downloaded as shown in Figure 12-28. You can choose from three settings:

- *Send at Start.* Sends the information on fonts and resources used on more than one page before the first print job starts; the fastest method but the most memory-intensive. Sending at the start.

- *Send by Range.* The information on fonts and resources is sent with the first page that uses them, and then removed as they're no longer needed.

- *Send for Each Page.* Fonts and resources are downloaded with each page.

If you're experiencing memory problems when printing, check these settings. Select other PostScript settings as needed:

- *Emit Undercolor Removal/Black Generation.* Use the undercolor removal (UCR) and black generation functions from the file, not from the printer. This option provides instructions for a PostScript RIP to convert RGB to CMYK with varying degrees of rich black.

- *Emit Halftones.* Use the halftones from the PDF file, not the printer. Having all the same halftoning will minimize moiré on the press. Select this option to preserve halftone information for reproducing special effects for single page output.

- *Emit Transfer Functions.* Use the transfer functions in the PDF file, not from the printer.

- *Emit PS Form Objects.* You can reduce the overall size of a print job by choosing the setting that emits Form XObjects such as page backgrounds. This setting requires a lot of printer memory.

- *Discolored Background Correction.* Correct background tints or discoloration during printing.

Note

You can test the transparency flattening prior to setting up the print settings. Choose Advanced ➤ Transparency Flattener Preview. When the dialog box opens, click Refresh to load the document in the preview window. Adjust settings as needed. Then set the actual settings in the Transparency Flattening panel in the Advanced Printing dialog box.

Note

Click Printing Tips in the Print dialog box. You'll be connected to the Adobe web site for information on troubleshooting printing problems in Acrobat.

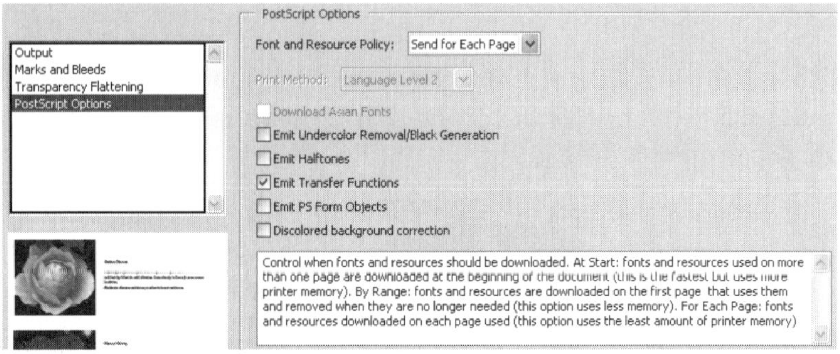

Figure 12-28
Choose PostScript
options for controlling
font and resource
downloads.

Exporting to PostScript and EPS

Choose File ➤ Save As and choose either PostScript or EPS to have more control over these file formats when sending documents for printing or prepress use. The file will be exported with advanced information such as document structuring conventions. Many of the settings are identical to those used in the Advanced Printing dialog boxes. The set of four panels, Output, Marks and Bleeds, Transparency Flattening, and PostScript Options are all included.

Both the PostScript and EPS Save As options include additional general settings for configuring your document. For PostScript files, select a PostScript language level. You must also choose either ASCII or binary output format for the image data. Where possible, use binary output for smaller files. You can choose to convert TrueType to Type 1 fonts, and include comments with the document.

If you choose to save a document as an EPS document, you have similar general settings. In addition to the options listed for PostScript, you can also choose to include a thumbnail preview, and to allow RGB and LAB images in the exported document.

Trapping

You may have noticed that there are no references to *trapping* in the print dialog boxes or discussions. For files being sent to a service bureau, you should declare the presence of trapping information to prevent conflicts. Trapping isn't created in Acrobat but is imported into it with other PostScript file information from your authoring application. With the file open in Acrobat, select File ➤ Document Properties ➤ Advanced ➤ Trapping Key. Select a trapping option, and then click OK.

Soft-Proofing Colors

We mentioned in the workflow discussion at the beginning of the chapter that you can use Acrobat to soft-proof your document's colors, that is, display a simulated output of your document on your screen. Remember that your soft-proof will depend on how good your monitor represents color as well as how it's calibrated. Here's how to do it:

1. Select Advanced ➤ Proof Setup ➤ Custom. The dialog box shown in Figure 12-29 opens.

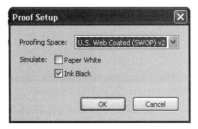

Figure 12-29
Choose a proofing space for soft-proofing your colors.

2. Select a proofing space. You can choose either a profile or None to proof only for Ink Black or Paper White.

3. Select either Ink Black or Paper White Simulation (if you select the latter, Ink Black is selected and grayed out because it's required).

4. Click OK. You can toggle the proof display by selecting View ➤ Proof Colors.

Tutorial: Preflighting a Document

There are several third-party vendors of software that preflight or inspect a file for its validity for printing. Adobe licensed the preflight from Callas Software GmbH. Preflight inspects but it doesn't correct problems.

Let's preflight a file. Donna developed a good file for preflighting called catalog.pdf. It's a CMYK file that isn't PDF/X-1a compliant. You'll find it in the Chapter 12 folder. Open the document in Acrobat, and follow these steps to test it:

1. Choose Document ➤ Preflight. The profiles in your system are loaded and display in the Preflight: Profiles dialog box shown in Figure 12-30.

Note

Ink Black, the default, uses relative colorimetric rendering intent with no black-point compensation. Paper White uses absolute colorimetric rendering intent and simulates the actual color and tone of a document on your monitor.

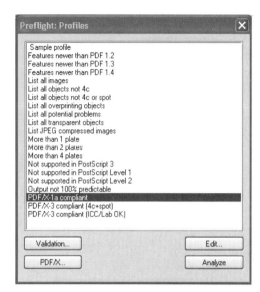

Figure 12-30
Choose a profile for preflighting your documents that allows you to choose different functions and analyze the document against the standard.

2. Click a Profile to select it and activate the Analyze function. Click Analyze to evaluate the file. Figure 12-31 shows the PDF/X-1a compliance report we generated for the file.

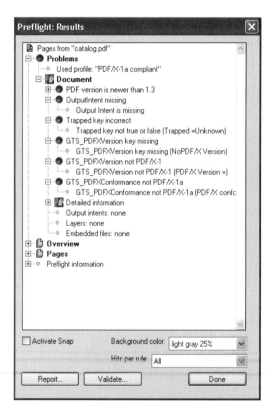

Figure 12-31
The catalog.pdf document is far from PDF/X-1a compliant.

3. After you view the results, click Done and return to the Preflight: Profiles dialog box.

4. This time, click the PDF/X button and the Preflight: PDF/X dialog box opens as in Figure 12-32. You can choose between PDF/X-1a and PDF/X-3.

Figure 12-32
Choose a PDF/X option from the dialog box.

5. You already know the file isn't PDF/X-1a compliant, so click the drop-down arrow and choose Save as PDF/X-1a. As we discussed earlier, PDF/X-1a requires an ICC Output Intent profile. Since we're in the U.S. we select SWOP_CGATS-TR001 to automatically select U.S. Web Coated(SWOP) v2 as shown in Figure 12-33. You can also run three checks in addition to the PDF/X-1a that the printer may require.

6. Click Save. Once you select a storage location, the document is saved and the compliance structures added to the document. You see a Preflight success dialog box like the one shown in Figure 12-34.

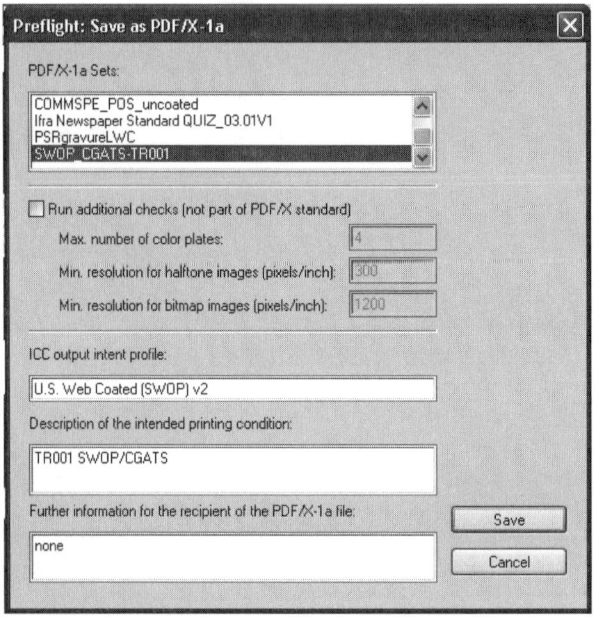

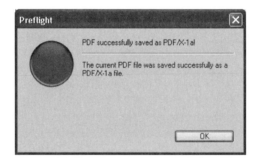

Figure 12-33
You must select an ICC printer profile to use for converting the document to a PDF/X-1a-compliant document.

Figure 12-34
You can convert a document successfully to PDF/X-1a compliance from within Acrobat.

Note

You can also click Report at the bottom left of the dialog box to choose options for reporting the file's generation. Once you finish configuring the document, create a report and have a look.

7. Click OK to return to the Preflight: Profiles dialog box. In the Preflight: Profiles dialog box, click Analyze again to evaluate the document. The results are displayed as shown in Figure 12-35. Click Validate at the bottom of the Preflight: Results dialog box.

8. When the validation is concluded, a message asking Do You Want to Continue? displays in the dialog box as shown in Figure 12-35. Click OK. The message box closes and you return to the Preflight: Profiles dialog box.

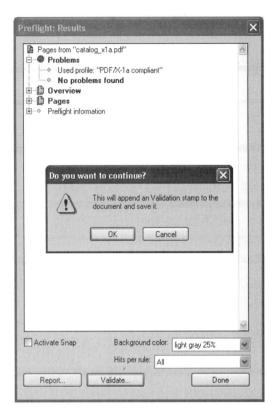

Figure 12-35
When the document is valid, you can add a validation stamp into your document.

9. In the Preflight Profiles dialog box, click Validation and you see the validation stamp placed on your document. Figure 12-36 shows the validation on your document.

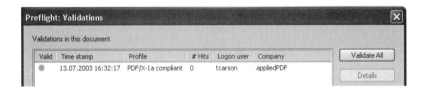

Figure 12-36
You can see the validation stamp and review its contents from the Preflight: Validations dialog box.

Up Next

At the beginning of this chapter, we said that there was much more to this printing process than finding the Print toolbar button. We weren't kidding! As with almost everything in this book, you need a good understanding of what you're designing and a good understanding of the software you're using for designing. From the software perspective, as you've also seen in other chapters, planning in the authoring environment is important to good output.

We gave you our interpretation of print workflows using Acrobat. Then you looked at Distiller and print output options followed by fonts and color. We could only scratch the surface; the important thing to take away from this chapter is that print output is a complex interaction of many different elements. The key to success will be experimentation.

Speaking of experimentation, in Chapter 13 you'll learn how not to print. You're going to investigate eBooks.

All About eBooks

The revolution is here. Have you ever wondered what goes into creating an eBook? Here it is. Find out what it takes to create, format, distribute, and secure eBooks.

The eBook Story

One of the most revolutionary concepts in recent publishing history is the eBook (also known as EBook, e-Book, and eBook). For years, we've avoided reading books on a screen rather than by turning pages primarily because there was nothing "booklike" about reading a document on a screen—no real concept of pages, certainly nothing like turning pages, and as for indexes and tables of contents, they weren't useful either. eBooks and eBook readers are changing that. The increased sophistication of the readers, the capability to create content using Acrobat, and the constantly improving security systems all contribute to eBooks becoming a viable content-distribution method.

As with most developments, you'll find different offerings from all the players in the game. Remember VHS versus beta? Thank goodness an organized body is working toward achieving some sense of unity among the various companies and their readers.

Just as the World Wide Web Consortium (W3C) evolved and developed standards as the Internet developed, so too has the Open Electronic Book Forum (OEBF). This group, conceived in 1998, has developed standards for electronic publishing. The group became the OEBF in January 2000. The specifications for version 1 were released in September 1999, and version 1.2 was released in August 2002.

This group has developed the Open eBook Publication Structure specification. The scope of the standard is to provide specifications for both content and tool providers to develop consistent materials and platforms. The specification is based on HTML and XML.

The specification outlines standards to use for creating eBook content. Using the standards, a publisher can format a title, and the content will be compatible with different readers. If you consider the number of readers on the market now, each using slightly different formatting, you'll see that publishing decisions are made as much on the basis of corporate loyalty as on anything else.

By adopting the standards, however, publishers can distribute works to a diverse audience without reformatting titles for different flavors of readers—or even different devices.

Basically, eBooks come in two varieties: the conventional screen and the handheld device. Dedicated eBook readers are also available. We're waiting for the *Star Trek* series to be developed (so far it exists only in our imagination!).

In this chapter, you'll go through the steps used for a conventional screen, and then we'll show you how to create an eBook for a handheld device. Now, after this historical buildup, let's have a look at what it takes to create an eBook and then build one. The basic stages are as follows:

1. Create a template and format the source material.

2. Convert the file using settings optimized for on-screen use.

3. Add navigational elements.

Creating an eBook Template

An eBook template isn't built in Acrobat. Rather, the template is created in an authoring program. Many of the elements are familiar to anyone who has built word processing or print-layout templates. As with any kind of template, differences exist based on the use of the template. Here, you're trying to optimize the use of the material on-screen, so the elements are a bit different than the usual.

You'll have to use a combination of experience, a good eye, and design sense. If it looks good, and it's legible, it will likely work.

Format the Page Size

Unless you know for certain what page sizes your readers will use, it's best to design to the lowest common denominator—in this case, a page size about 6 × 9 inches, or even smaller.

Note

Remember that readers can use the zoom capabilities in the reader to customize their views.

Set the Margins

In an ordinary document, margins are used to frame the text. The same is true for eBooks. They're used in the same way as ordinary margins—that is, to give the eyes a place to rest and set off the content. Margins also ensure that appropriate spacing exists around graphic elements.

Define Styles

Fonts look different on-screen than in print. Thin strokes are often difficult to read on-screen. So are fonts with heavy strokes. Fonts of 11 to 13 points are the best sizes for on-screen viewing.

Use leading and tracking as required. Try to design pages legible at 100 percent page view. Use tracking instead of kerning where possible. Kerning contributes to file size with little noticeable on-screen impact.

Converting Source Material to eBook Format

Source material for eBooks can come from the same programs as for any other type of PDF file use. In addition, you convert material to PDF format in the same way. For example, in any application you can select Adobe PDF through the Print menu. From within Microsoft Office applications, you can use the Print menu or use the Adobe PDF pull-down menu.

The command features a number of custom conversion settings, including settings for eBooks. Let's have a look at these preformatted settings. We'll also point out some changes we've found useful when creating eBook output. Later, when we discuss handhelds, we'll outline another group of custom settings for that purpose.

eBook Conversion Settings

Select the Smallest File Size setting from the Conversion Settings or Default Settings drop-down list, as shown in Figure 13-1. The other preset settings on this menu are appropriate for other types of projects, but not for eBooks. The Smallest File Size setting is good for eBooks that will be viewed on a desktop or laptop computer, but you might want to create custom settings if you're creating with a handheld device in mind.

Figure 13-1
Use Smallest File Size settings for eBooks that will be viewed on a desktop or laptop.

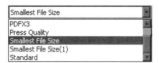

You'll access most of the other conversion settings through the Adobe PDF Settings dialog box, which consists of a series of six tabs.

From the Print menu, access these tabs by selecting Adobe PDF as your printer, then click Properties. From the resulting Adobe PDF Document Properties dialog box, click Edit in the Adobe PDF Conversion Settings area (see Figure 13-2).

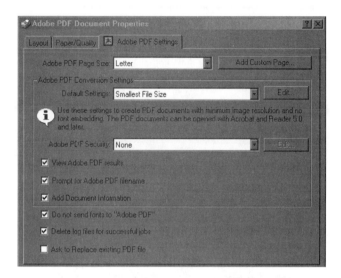

Figure 13-2
You can access custom PDF settings from the Adobe PDF Document Properties dialog box.

From the Adobe PDF menu, access these tabs by selecting Change Conversion Settings. You'll see a dialog box with four tabs: Settings, Security, Word, and Bookmarks (see Figure 13-3). In the Settings tab, click Advanced Settings. You'll come back to the other tabs later.

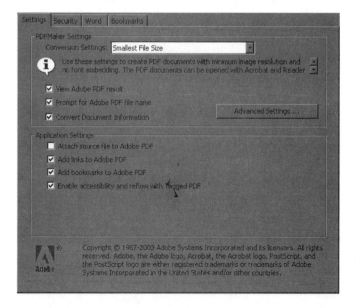

Figure 13-3
You can also change settings from within a document using the Adobe PDF menu.

Adobe PDF Settings Tabs

Choose a number of settings that are useful in creating a good eBook product.

General Settings

Three general settings are important when working with eBooks. Figure 13-4 shows the default settings for eBook conversion.

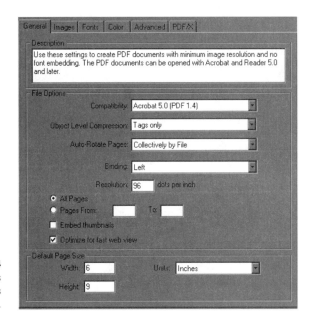

Figure 13-4
Consider three options when choosing settings in the General tab.

First, the Compatibility setting defaults to Acrobat 5.0 (PDF 1.4), which is based on the PDF 1.4 format. Choose your compatibility setting carefully. On the one hand, compatibility with Acrobat 5.0 will make your eBook more user friendly for readers who have not upgraded yet. On the other hand, if you're designing your eBook with Acrobat 6.0 in mind, you're probably taking advantage of some new features like embedding full motion video, which won't be available to readers using version 5. It's your call between Acrobat 5.0 and 6.0, but we don't recommend making your new eBook compatible with any version earlier than 5. Another reason to choose compatibility with Acrobat 6.0 would be if you're designing material for a controlled environment and know that your readers will use Acrobat 6.0 (based on PDF 1.5).

Another setting we want to point out on this tab is the Embed Thumbnails option. If you're designing for readers using Acrobat 5.0 or 6.0, there is no need to select this option, since both create thumbnails on the fly.

Finally, on this tab you also set the default size of the page. This setting may be customized as well, depending on your planned output and type of project.

Image Settings

Now let's look at compression, which is found in the Images tab. Figure 13-5 shows the compression settings. This tab lists parameters for downsampling color, grayscale, and monochrome images. We'll adjust these settings later for handhelds. You can leave the default Smallest File Size settings for an eBook destined for a regular-sized screen.

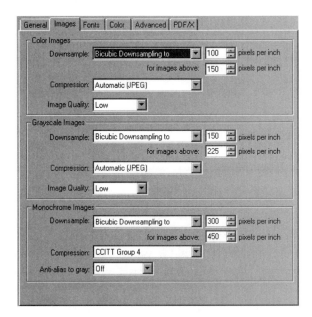

Figure 13-5
Use the default compression settings for images used in an eBook.

Font Settings

Up next is the Fonts tab, shown in Figure 13-6. Depending on the type of output you're creating, you may or may not want to change these settings. For example, with handhelds it's recommended to use Base 14 fonts only. For building a "traditional" eBook, that isn't necessary.

You'll also need to make a choice between embedding all fonts or subsetting embedded fonts. We recommend subsetting. If you choose this option, then when your source document only includes a few characters of a particular font, only those characters will be embedded.

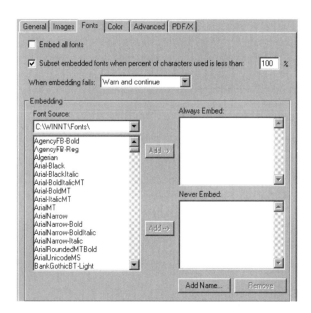

Figure 13-6
Choose the types of fonts
for the eBook depending
on its distribution.

Color Settings

Let's have a look at the color settings next. Figure 13-7 shows the Color tab, with default settings. Depending on what you're creating, you may or may not have a need to alter these settings.

For example, the Settings File option defaults to None. If you're working with full-color images, you'll certainly want to change these options to ensure that the color settings displayed in your PDF file correlate with the color of your original work. The same may apply with overprinting, undercolor removal (UCR), and other print output settings if you allow your readers to print the file.

Advanced Settings

The Advanced tab is shown in Figure 13-8. In general, you can leave the default options, unless you have very specific output or print options in mind. The only option we may be willing to change readily is Save Portable Job Ticket Inside PDF File. If we wanted to store information in a particular version of a document, this would be a useful feature.

The last tab, PDF/X, is only relevant to print projects, so there is no need to change any settings for your eBook project.

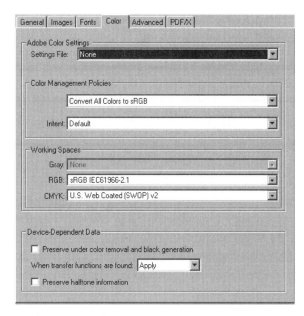

Figure 13-7
Change color settings depending on the type of work you're converting.

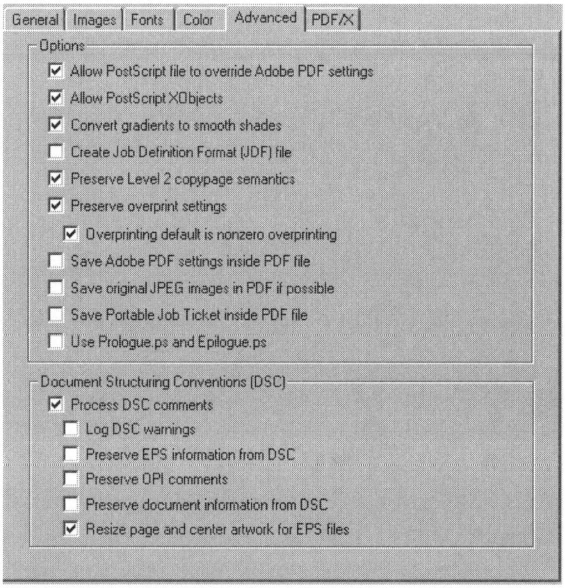

Figure 13-8
Use the default settings in the Advanced tab.

Security, Word, and Bookmarks Tabs

You're almost through with conversion settings. Now, go back to the initial conversion settings screens. Choose Adobe PDF ➤ Change Conversion Settings to open the Acrobat PDFMaker dialog box.

The dialog box opens displaying the Security tab. For now, don't make any changes to the security default settings. You don't need any security on your document until you publish it. You don't want to have to enter a password every time you access your working file, do you?

There's no need to change any defaults on the Word tab, either. On the Bookmarks tab, Convert Word Headings to Bookmarks is already selected. Don't change this default setting, since having a few bookmarks created automatically will save you a little time. Select the heading levels you want converted.

If you've made any changes to the tabs, you'll be prompted to save the changes as a custom job option. Once you've reviewed the settings and made any changes you need, run the macro as usual to convert the file.

Navigation Design Issues

Navigation is a necessary part of digital life. Imagine what it would be like if there were no hyperlinks! Did the world ever really exist before hyperlinks? Sometimes we wonder.

When building an eBook, you can use one of four methods to add navigation: thumbnails, bookmarks, hyperlinks, and pagination. The processes are a bit different for eBooks, however, and you'll have another look at them shortly. Before we get into particulars, we want to talk about using eBook navigation in general. Remember, as with other forms of output, the easier it is for your user to access the material, the more likely your material will be used. But you don't want to overdo it either.

Let's look at three examples: a novel, a technical manual, and a complex business report. All of these examples will need page numbering of some form, but the other navigation aids will depend on the output.

The Novel

Whether or not it's the "Great American Novel," your book will need some logical navigation. Similar to paper books, eBook readers let you bookmark a page. Pagination is going to be key. You may choose to

Tip

Build Several Custom Conversion Sets

As you'll see later in this chapter, there are different reasons to use different settings and types of navigation. If you're working in an enterprise in which you regularly create documents to be used with an eBook reader for different audiences, create specific job options for each. For example, if you create both technical manuals and business reports in eBook formats, you may use thumbnails in one version and not in the other. Create a separate set of options for each variation. It will take a few minutes to create the custom settings, but you'll save revision time each time you use them.

divide the book into a chapter format (for example, 1-1, or Chapter 1, page 1), or you may decide to use simple pagination.

Thumbnails would not be particularly useful for this type of output. The pages are so similar as to be basically useless for visual navigation. Bookmark listings would be useful, with the first pages of each chapter listed. As for hyperlinks, their usefulness would depend on some element, such as bibliographic references, links to publisher outlets for other works by the author, and the like.

A Technical Manual

Suppose you're building an eBook for troubleshooting an electronic device. The odds are good that the manual will contain a mixture of text, lists, tables, schematics, and diagrams. Again, pagination is required, and we would likely lean toward a sectioned format (1-1 or 1-A) for clarity.

This type of eBook would also benefit from hyperlinking within the document as well as linking to external sources of information, such as suppliers. For example, instructions for performing a task could be hyperlinked to schematics or diagrams, which are then linked to spec sheets or other tables of information. Internal hyperlinking from an index may also be practical, depending on the size and complexity of the project.

Bookmarking would be very useful as a navigation reference. Special care would be required in the design of the structure. You might also lay out the bookmark structure differently from the pagination of the document. For example, rather than list the elements in a sequential fashion, you could group the elements pertaining to one process into a nested set of bookmarks.

Thumbnails may or may not be useful, again depending on how the manual is to be used. For example, if the elements were distinctive enough to be visually obvious in the thumbnail view, you might include them as a navigation option.

A Complex Business Document

The key to deciding how to design navigation for this type of output will be the users of the document. If you're designing your project as an internal document only, you may tend to spend less time on visual materials than if it were aimed at external users, such as stockholders. Pagination for an eBook version of this sort of document can easily emulate other forms of output. For example, if a company normally produces a printed report with simple pagination, the same could be used in this format. On the other hand, if the corporate style is to use sectioned pagination, then use the same thing in the eBook format.

The visual components of the project will determine the logic of using thumbnails. For example, in a 60-page prospectus divided into four sections, distinctive designs for the front pages of each section would identify the four section thumbnails. Overall, though, we probably wouldn't use thumbnails in this type of application because there simply isn't enough difference in the material to make the thumbnails visually different.

Bookmarking would be a logical navigation method. For this type of output, we recommend a fairly complete bookmark structure. If you consider a traditional business document, it's usually prefaced by a fairly extensive table of contents. Bookmarks are representative of a table of contents.

Speaking of which, you might also consider adding a hyperlinked table of contents to the document. You can use this approach if you're building a document for a group of people who most often use a traditional type of output, such as a printed report. Although the bookmark structure resembles a table of contents in many ways, for the more traditional user it won't be intuitive. You might want to include a hyperlinked index, again based on the familiarity factor for the less technologically savvy user.

Hyperlinking inside this kind of document might be desirable for linking reference materials to text. For example, summaries of sales can be readily linked to spreadsheets. External hyperlinking would depend on the document's content. For example, you might need to link to external sources, such as suppliers' web sites.

It's interesting to note how the complexity of these decisions increased from the first example to the last. Whereas a novel or similar document generally has one type of content, manuals and complex reports can have many different types of content, and they can be used in very different ways by their readers.

As you can see, deciding which type and how much navigation is required takes a lot of thought. After all, we're discussing design issues, not word-processing details.

Tip

Planning Navigation

Use the information in this section the next time you're planning a large project, even if the distribution isn't necessarily going to be an eBook. Weigh the value of the navigation to the intended user against the size of the additional components in the file. The more tailored the navigation is to users, the easier it will be for them to use the document. That's the hallmark of good design.

Navigation Elements

Now that you've looked at the design aspects of eBook navigation options, let's have a look at the particulars of the different formats. You'll start with the most basic and work up from there.

Page Numbers

How much more basic can you get than page numbers? Regardless of output format, page numbers are basic, and also the most "book like."

Depending on the source material you're converting, the page numbers may not be correct when you correlate them with the thumbnails in Acrobat. This can happen when you're converting a large document, for example, that uses front matter such as a table of contents or summaries. In Acrobat, the pages will be numbered starting at page 1.

Within Acrobat, you can add page numbers or renumber pages according to your layout and style guides. You can use a combination of numbering styles for page ranges as well, so you can simulate a printed document's pagination.

You can renumber pages through the Pages panel. In the Options drop-down list at the top of the panel, select Number Pages. Select either the entire document or portions of it. You can also select different numbering sequences.

Renumbering eBook Pages

When users launch Adobe Reader, a page navigator bar appears that allows them to navigate to any page by choosing the page number. Another option is to display two pages at once. In order to have the pages display correctly in the two-page view, you may have to add blank pages in the PDF file. This will then require renumbering the document, of course. Otherwise, the pages appearing in the reader's navigation bar will not correlate with those on the pages of the eBook itself.

An Adobe eBook can include as many sections, as you might expect to find in a printed book, including the following:

- Front cover

- Inside front cover

- Front matter, such as a copyright page and perhaps a preface or introduction

Note

We're concentrating on Adobe Reader in this discussion. A number of different readers are available; owing to space constraints, however, we can't cover all of them in this book. The design processes will be similar regardless of the reader you're designing for.

- Body pages

- Back matter, such as an index, glossary, or endnotes

- Inside back cover

- Back cover

In practice, some of these sections may be included in the numbering of the body pages, or each section could use a different page-numbering convention. To paginate the document, you'll have to divide it into sections that correspond to each page-numbering convention. For simplicity, we'll divide the book into four sections and show you how to paginate each one. To maintain a smooth flow and to minimize error, start with the cover and work toward the back of the book. As you go through the steps, you'll assume that the document is already open and that the navigation pane is open as well, with the Pages tab displayed.

Numbering the Cover and Inside Front Cover Pages

Don't use numbers for the cover and inside front cover. Adobe recommends using letters for these pages: "C" for the cover, and "c" for the inside front cover. Here's how to do it:

1. From the Pages tab area, choose Number Pages to open the Pages dialog box.

2. Enter **1** in both the Pages From and To fields. In the Numbering portion, select the Begin New Section option.

3. Select A, B, C, . . . from the Style drop-down list. Enter **3** in the Start field. (In this case, "3" refers to the third letter in the alphabet, not to the number.)

4. Click OK.

The front cover is now numbered as you can see in Figure 13-9. Repeat the process for the inside front cover. Again, enter **1** in the Pages From and To fields, because the front cover now is numbered "C," so page 1 is the inside front cover. Choose a, b, c,...from the Style drop-down list.

Now you have the first two pages numbered "C" and "c," and the front matter starts at page 1. If you have a back cover and inside back cover, you can use the same process, numbering these pages "BC" and "bc."

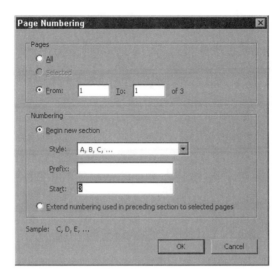

Figure 13-9
Name the eBook in sections using customized numbering.

Numbering the Front Matter

By convention, front matter is numbered with lowercase roman numerals. You can follow the same process in numbering with these changes:

- Enter **1** in the From field in the Pages area and the last page of your front matter in the To field.

- Select Begin New Section, and select the i, ii, iii,...style from the Style drop-down list.

- Enter either **i** or **iii** as the Start page (depending on whether you require counting the cover and inside cover as front matter for paging).

Numbering eBook Content

Again, numbering the content will use the same basic method. How you decide to section the material will depend on the type of document you're working with, however. For a novel, the entire body of the work could easily be paginated as one section. In the case of other types of documents—manuals or reports, for example—it will depend on your requirements and how it makes the most sense structurally.

You'll also be able to define styles for the body of the work. For example, if you're working with a technical manual and want to name the pages according to the section of the manual, break the manual into sections and apply numbering that uses a chapter prefix.

If your book includes back matter (glossary, index, notes), you'll need to decide whether to include these in the numbering style of the body pages or paginate them as a separate section.

Adding Headers and Footers

If your source document doesn't include page numbers, you'll need to use the Header & Footer option, which is accessible from the Document menu. Select Document ➤ Add Headers & Footers (see Figure 13-10).

- Choose the Align option—left, center, or right—that you wish to use.

- Select a font and font size that will be compatible with the formatting of your source document.

- Choose Page Number style, Date style and type any custom text you want to include in your page number. Be sure to click Insert after each selection.

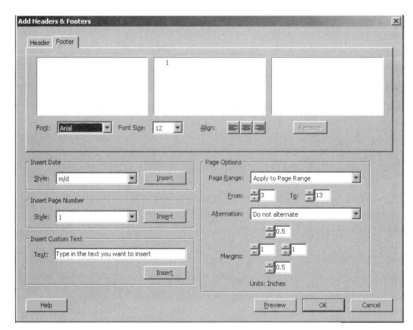

Figure 13-10
Add headers and footers to display numbers on your eBook pages.

Bookmarks

Bookmarks are another "book like" element. Although using bookmarks requires referring to a specific navigation view, the process will seem familiar to the user.

In our earlier discussion of navigation design issues, we mentioned that bookmarking may play a pivotal role in how the user is able to interact with your document. We also mentioned that bookmarking doesn't have to be restricted to a specific table-of-contents layout, but can be added to, depending on materials you want to draw attention to and make available through this navigation tool.

Here's a summary of the bookmark-building process:

1. Open the page you want to bookmark in the document pane, and then open the Bookmark panel.

2. From the Options menu select New Bookmark. Enter a name for the bookmark's label, and press Enter.

In Chapter 6, we described some of the design issues surrounding bookmarking. This is where they come into play. Once you've completed the set of bookmarks for the document, you can rearrange the order for ease of use—for example, to correlate different pages with a topic.

You might also want to use bookmarks as links to actions, such as launching media or changing the zoom factor. Again, this will be a design decision. Adding an action to a bookmark is a smooth process. Select the bookmark, and then in the Options drop-down list choose Properties. Set the action in the Bookmark Properties dialog box.

Thumbnails

Because thumbnails are such a highly visual means of navigation, they may not be valuable with a very nonvisual eBook. In earlier versions of Acrobat, they could increase file size dramatically. Acrobat 6.0 creates thumbnails on the fly, so there is no need to create thumbnails of internal pages.

You'll need thumbnail images of the covers, however, if you're using the Adobe Content Server or other distribution system to serve your eBook. The Adobe Content Server is a system that packages, protects, and distributes Adobe PDF eBooks directly from a web site. Users can purchase products directly through this server system. If you're distributing the file yourself, you won't have to create a cover thumbnail. A thumbnail of the cover is automatically displayed in the Adobe Reader library.

For the Adobe Content Server, create an image of your cover. This image should be in GIF format, 100 pixels wide. It should also have a resolution of 96 pixels per inch. Upload this image to the server for online identification of your eBook.

Hypertext Links

Once upon a time, when the world of hypertext was new, hyperlinks tended to be underlined and in a different color from the rest of the material, like a sign that said "I'm a link, click me." Now that we're all more familiar with the idea of hyperlinking, that style is becoming distinctly passé. And good riddance, we say. This move from blatant display to sophisticated design applies in eBooks as well. eBooks generally don't have overt hyperlink text attributes, which makes the document look more like a printed book.

You might find in some documents that you want to use a fair number of hyperlinks, perhaps to correspond with any hypertext bookmarking you've done. You might also want to differentiate internal hyperlinks by using bookmarks and using external hyperlinks as hyperlinks.

One of the most common eBook uses of hypertext is the table of contents.

Linking a Table of Contents

Wait until your final pagination is complete before linking the table of contents (if you're using one). You can add the table of contents in the source application, but you might run into pagination issues once you've finished working on the file in Acrobat. In addition, Acrobat doesn't provide a simple way to update the fields, as you can in a source application such as Microsoft Word.

You've covered adding these types of links in other chapters. For context, here is the short list:

1. On the table of contents page, select the Link tool and highlight the word that will serve as a link.

Tip

Plan a Table of Contents in Advance

Whether you include a table of contents depends on your intended reader. If you're planning to use one, check the settings in the Conversion Settings dialog box to make sure the Cross-reference and Table of Contents check box is selected on the Office tab. Enabling this option won't necessarily make the output perfect at the other end, but a bit of tweaking will be faster than a major redo. Alternatively, you might want to add links to content without using page numbers. Nothing to fix that way.

2. When the Create Link dialog box opens, do the following:

- Choose the page number to which you want to link.

- Select Zoom/Fit Page.

This dialog box will also let you set the link to open a web page or a new file.

3. Click OK.

4. To confirm the link, choose the Hand tool and click on the linked word.

5. Return to the table of contents page and repeat.

Project Project 13-1: Building the Great American Novel

Well, maybe we don't have the Great American Novel here, but it's an interesting story anyway. In the Chapter 13 folder you'll find alternate versions of both the Word document and the PDF document used for this project. Use the files according to your time and preferences, as follows:

- *book.doc.* The document without formatted sizes.

- *book1.doc.* The document after changing page settings.

- *book.pdf.* The document after conversion.

- *book1.pdf.* The finished document.

You'll start with the raw document book.doc.

Formatting and Converting the Masterpiece

As we described earlier, formatting and converting will require some coordination between the source application and the conversion settings you choose.

1. Open book.doc in Microsoft Word. Change the settings for the document as follows:

- Set the margins to 0.8/0.8/1/1 inches.

- Set the page size to a custom setting of 6×9 inches.

> **Note**
>
> **Thanks to the Author**
>
> My thanks to Terry Dyck for allowing me to use the first chapter of his as yet incomplete novel. You can email him (if you're a publisher—or even if you're not!) at tdyck@skyweb.ca.[1]

---

1. The eBook *Monday* is copyright © 2001 by Terry Dyck.

2. Save the file.

Now you'll need to customize the conversion settings. The default eBook settings are the place from which you should start.

Note

You'll see that we've added a copyright information page before the first page of the chapter, which will serve as the inside cover. We've also added a drop cap for the first page.

1. Select Adobe PDF ➤ Change Conversion Settings. Select Smallest File Size from the Conversion Settings drop-down list. Click Advanced Settings.

2. On the General tab, change these settings (shown in Figure 13-11):

   • Select Acrobat 6.0 (PDF 1.5) from the Compatibility drop-down list.

   • Be sure Embed Thumbnails is cleared.

   • Set the Resolution option to 96 pixels per inch

   • Change the default page size to 6 × 9 inches.

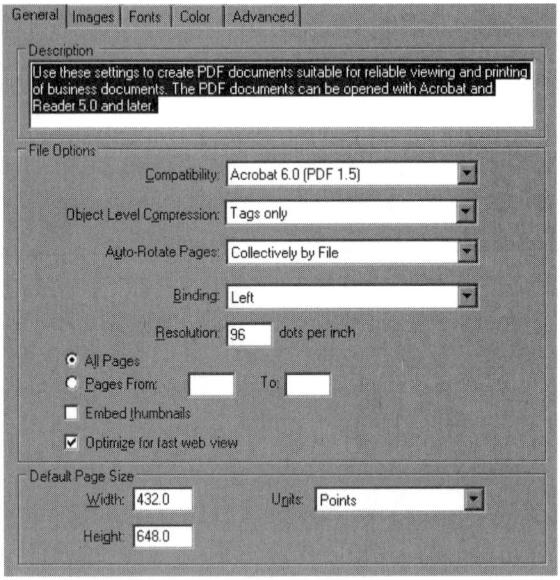

Figure 13-11
Change some general settings to create your eBook.

Note

When you're actually making your eBook, don't customize your security settings until all formatting is completed. Otherwise, you'll have to keep entering a password to format your own eBook.

3. Click the Security tab. As shown in Figure 13-12, make the following permission changes:

   • Select None from the Changes Allowed drop-down list.

   • Select Low Resolution from the Printing Allowed drop-down list.

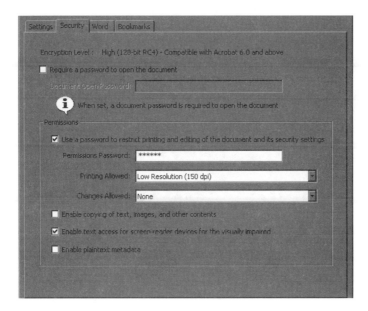

Figure 13-12
Choose security settings after you've finished formatting the eBook.

4. Save the new settings. Click Save As, and save the settings as eBook(1).joboptions.

5. Convert the file.

So far, so good.

Making an eBook

Now comes the fun stuff. You'll need to add a cover, paginate the file, and build some bookmarks—in other words, make it into a real book.

1. Open the document in Acrobat, and then open the Pages panel. Click page 1 (the copyright page).

2. Select Document ➤ Pages ➤ Insert. When the File Select dialog box opens, select cover.pdf from the Chapter 13 folder. The Insert Pages dialog box will open. Select "before" from the Location drop-down list, and select the Page 1 of 12 radio button. Click OK. The cover will be imported into the document. As you can see in Figure 13-13, the layout is correct—that is, the cover is a right-hand page, as is page 1—just like a book.

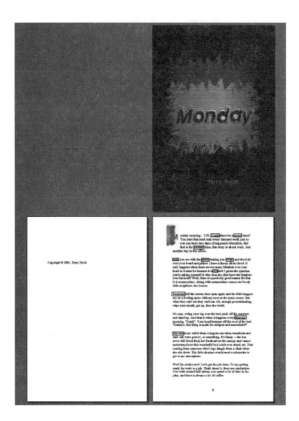

Figure 13-13
Evaluate the finished
book layout in Acrobat.

3. Set the page numbers. Click the cover thumbnail. Select Pages ➤
   Number Pages. In the Page Numbers dialog box, for the selected
   page option, use these Numbering settings:

   • Begin New Section

   • Style: A,B,C,…

   • Start: 3

4. Click OK to close the Page Numbers dialog box. The cover will
   now be named "C," and the page numbers will start from 1 at the
   inside cover.

5. Repeat the numbering process for the inside cover. Substitute "a, b, c,.." for the uppercase numbering used for the cover. The two sides of the cover page will now be named "C" and "c," and the document page numbering will start at 1 with the first page of the chapter—which is what we want.

6. Save the file.

Finishing Details

Now for some bookmarks. This book is so simple, it really doesn't need much in the way of bookmarks. We added three bookmarks, shown in Figure 13-14.

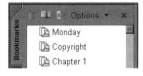

Figure 13-14
Use bookmarks to define important sections of the eBook.

Follow these steps to add the bookmarks for the cover, the copyright info, and the beginning page of the book.

1. Open the Bookmark panel. Select New Bookmark.

2. When the bookmark is added, enter the name. The first bookmark is named **Monday**.

3. Go to the Pages panel and select the cover. With the cover displayed in the Document panel return to the Bookmarks panel and select Set Bookmark Destination from the Options menu. Click Yes to confirm the location.

4. Continue with the other two bookmarks for the copyright page and the beginning page of Chapter 1. Make sure the appropriate pages are displayed in the document pane before setting the destinations.

5. Save the file.

You can see the thumbnail for the book, shown in Figure 13-15, by selecting My Bookshelf.

Tip

Testing with Different Products

Since Adobe Reader is incorporated into Acrobat 6.0 Professional, you might want to keep a separate copy of Adobe Reader and verify your formatting by opening the document in Reader.

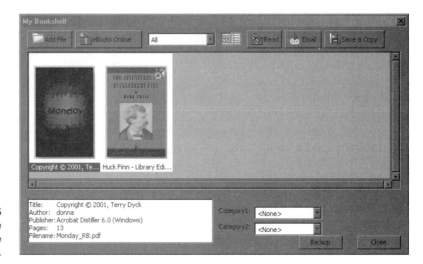

Figure 13-15
The content of the
bookshelf after we
added the book project.

Security and Distribution Options

eBook security has been a hot topic in recent years—and with good reason. We covered security of other formats in depth in other chapters. Here it is again. We suppose you must be getting the message loud and clear by now that Acrobat's security capabilities are valuable, not to mention pervasive. Well, let's look at another security feature. This one is tailored for secure content distribution.

On the one hand, being able to distribute content electronically is revolutionizing publishing. On the other hand, the need for secure distribution is increasing at the same rate. It all comes down to DRM. Consider the lengths music publishers are going to protect their copyrights and discourage free copying. The topic isn't as hot in the eBook world, but the fundamental issue is the same. Do you as the creator of your document want to give unlimited copying rights? Or do you want to manage which rights you sell or give to the user? DRM is how you manage those rights.

And What, Pray Tell, Is DRM?

DRM is *document rights management*. Remember when we discussed adding signatures to documents and sharing trusted certificates with a workgroup? This is the next step. Rather than having the intimacy of sharing a document on which to collaborate, you use DRM to share the finished work with others, in a very controlled fashion.

DRM was handled in Acrobat 5.0 through a plug in from InterTrust Technologies named docBox. Acrobat 6.0 incorporates the same type of functions into the program. DRM let you set access rights that can start and stop on particular days, even at particular times. You can also specify how you want the file to be distributed by establishing recipient rights.

How It Works

The DRM process involves several parts as well as several interested parties. Let's have a look at how this system works from the perspective of these interested parties. To simplify the process, imagine you're an independent writer.

First is the creator: you. You're responsible for two elements that together make up the package: the PDF document you want to distribute and the usage and pricing rules you set on the document. Once the document is configured to an eBook format and you've attached the usage and pricing criteria, your role is complete—as is the package for distribution.

Part two of the process is the server. It's commonly a storefront and processes two separate transactions. The first is the commerce transaction: receiving user payment or identity information and serving the PDF product. The second transaction delivers usage rights to the user.

Part three logically must be the user. The user transfers payment and identity information. If distribution is based only on payment, once payment has been received by the document server, it's downloaded to the user. If distribution is based also on rights, in addition to serving the document, the server site delivers usage rights and receipts to the user (the complexity of this process depends on what rules you, as the creator, have set on the package).

Let's have a look at some of the different ways content is distributed.

How Content Is Distributed

Content is generally distributed in one of three ways. Of course, for each of these areas, infinite combinations and permutations exist. The reason we're including this information is because it's thought-provoking. When you look through the list, you'll see what we mean. The three models are promotional, subscription, and direct-selling.

Promotional distribution is the "free" stuff that isn't always free! However, it's a wonderful way to gain exposure for a particular product. Common types of promotional distribution are time-restricted content (this is common with software), sample chapters with links to retailers to buy the entire product, and free downloads of a product in exchange for completing some sort of survey.

Subscriptions are similar to magazine subscriptions with a few digital twists. For example, you might buy an online subscription, which is commonplace with online newsletters in many industries. You might also find subscriptions that are time-limited. The user buys digital keys to content for specific lengths of time.

The last model is direct-selling. You pay us, and we send you a key that allows you to download our book. Again, there are digital twists. You might have a product that has different pricing, depending on whether you give the user print or save rights, or whether you're selling single or site licenses. You might also have an individual product option that allows the user to customize the content. We can see this being a logical type of product for something such as technical manuals. Different users will have different needs and can download only the components they require.

We've discussed different methods for distributing, but how is it actually done?

Serving the Document

Distributing eBook material for serving to end users requires an intermediary. This server setup controls the permission to access material (supplying and redeeming them) as well as serving the document once a permission receipt has been processed.

A number of companies, including Adobe, will encrypt, store, and serve your documents for public distribution. Many of these companies will do the formatting for your document as well. Interesting, isn't it?

In Acrobat 5.0, DRM was handled by a plug-in, which has been incorporated into Acrobat 6.0. For the eBook buyer, the process is much easier.

There are several different methods of establishing and maintaining security of eBooks. Acrobat calls the process DRM and handles it through a secure server called Adobe Content Server that encrypts eBooks using 64-bit or 128-bit encryption. Comprehensive instructions on setting up DRM fall outside the territory of Acrobat 6.0 and inside the territory of Adobe Content Server.

Note

The Macintosh version of Acrobat 6.0 Professional is supported by Mac OS X version 10.2.2, which is currently available. To purchase and view eBooks, however, you'll need OS X 10.2.4, which wasn't yet available as this book went to press.

DRM Overview

Adobe's version of DRM allows you to set permissions that are permanent, for purchasers of eBooks as well as permissions that will expire after a certain time, so you can loan your eBook from an online library. Earlier versions of Acrobat required eBook users to actively manage the permission certificates that are involved in transferring digital rights. Acrobat 6.0 makes the entire process of DRM transparent to the user.

The first step for the user is activating DRM for every device, including PDAs, that will be used to read eBooks. In Acrobat, choose Advanced ➤ eBook Web Services ➤ Adobe DRM Activator.

Once DRM is activated, what the user sees is a purchase or borrowing transaction that is no different from any other e-commerce transaction. Acrobat 6.0 and the Adobe Content Server handle all the permissions automatically.

Check out books from online libraries according to their particular protocols. Adobe's eBook library process is shown in Figure 13-16. Purchased or borrowed eBooks are stored in the user's My Bookshelf file, which can be viewed by choosing File ➤ My Bookshelf.

Note

Borrowed eBooks appear in My Bookshelf with a Time-out icon next to the thumbnail of the book. The user can click the Time-out icon to view the eBook's expiration date or to return the book. eBooks borrowed from a library generally cannot be sent by email or transferred to other users. Borrowed eBooks can be sent to a mobile device, but cannot be returned from the mobile device.

Tip

Activation requires either an Adobe ID and password or a Microsoft .Net Passport ID and password.

Figure 13-16
You can check eBooks out of online libraries from within My Bookshelf.

You can view an eBook's permissions. Choose File ➤ Document Properties ➤ Security. In the Document Security area of the Document Properties dialog box, select Show Details.

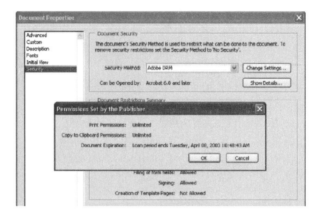

Figure 13-17
View eBook Permissions in the Document Properties dialog box.

Permissions can be transferred securely from one user to the other, with DRM managing the transfer and controlling the transferred rights. The new owner has full ownership rights, while the eBook is no longer accessible to the former owner.

So now you've seen how to format and create an eBook. You've learned how to add and customize navigation. You've also explored how to access a secure eBook using DRM. Let's look at one more topic before leaving this introduction to the world of eBooks: the design of output for handheld devices.

Handheld Devices: A Special Case

There will be times when you know that you'll use the output for a specific document on a handheld device. Or you may want to make a separate version of a document for use on a handheld. You must consider a number of details that will make this process smoother and produce better results.

Source Document Formatting

Like everything else you've considered in this book, understanding the importance of preplanning at the source document stage applies to handheld output as well. When creating the source materials, keep these issues in mind:

- Image display
- Fonts
- Layout

Let's have a look at these features.

Image Display

There is absolutely no need for high resolution or large-scale images for a handheld. That is wasteful, both of time and storage space. Images should be converted to grayscale, resized, and downsampled to target screen size. This will decrease the file size.

Fonts and Layout

Fonts should be scaled back as well, although Acrobat now includes 40 system fonts that are installed on your computer. It's nowhere near the full spectrum of type choices that exist in the wild and crazy world of design, but consider the output device. Not that it's archaic, but it certainly has its own requirements. At this time, this means sacrificing snazzy layouts for content. Since the primary use of handhelds is getting information, we're sure the user would rather be able to read the content clearly and quickly without font-handling issues. Save the fancy stuff for print layouts.

From the layout perspective, set paragraph spacing equivalent to an extra line height. This will clearly separate the paragraphs on the tiny handheld screen.

Before converting the file to PDF, you'll also want to have a look at the conversion settings and make some custom changes.

Conversion Settings for Handheld Devices

Acrobat 6.0 comes with standard eBook conversion settings, entitled Smallest File Size, as discussed earlier. You'll need to make a few modifications for handhelds.

From the source application (such as Microsoft Word), the settings are available by selecting Adobe PDF ➤ Change Conversion Settings. Select Smallest File Size from the drop-down Conversions Settings list, and click Advanced to open the <Job Options> dialog box.

Note

These settings are optimized for Palm OS handhelds. Although these settings are fairly generic, you might have to experiment with them for other handheld systems.

Now make these changes to the settings:

1. On the General tab, in the File Options area, set Compatibility to Acrobat 4.0 (PDF 1.3) or Acrobat 5.0 (PDF 1.4). Remember earlier when we said you should think carefully about whether to choose Acrobat 5.0 or 6.0 compatibility, because of the new features in Acrobat 6.0? Most of those features, like embedded video, still cannot be appreciated with handhelds, so choose Acrobat 4.0 or 5.0 compatibility. Set the resolution to 72 pixels per inch. Leave the other default values.

2. On the Images tab, in the Grayscale Images area, select Bicubic Downsampling, and change the resolution settings to 72 pixels per inch. Make sure the Compression is set to Automatic/Medium Quality.

3. On the Fonts tab, clear all font-embedding options. The handheld will substitute its fonts.

4. On the Color and Advanced tabs, leave the default settings.

5. Save the settings. Click Save As, enter a file name, and click Save.

That, in essence, is how to create a handheld-specific document. You may find that the users of your PDA can readily handle color. In that case, change the settings to reflect the capabilities of the device.

Up Next

This has been a whirlwind tour. In this chapter, we covered the ins and outs of eBooks. We considered source document formatting and custom conversion settings. We discussed navigation design based on the needs and expectations of the user, in addition to the material. We presented you with an interesting book project and walked through yet another security system. Finally, we briefly discussed output for handheld devices.

Up next is a chapter about multimedia and working with different file formats. You'll also take a look at some of the decision-making involved in using PDF versus other types of projects.

Chapter 14

Using Advanced Acrobat Activities

This chapter contains an avalanche of advanced activities that will turn you into a power user. Many of these features like layers are just becoming available and the sky is the limit as they become more widely used and more programs support them.

What You'll Learn

This chapter isn't something that is highly structured in terms of presentation. We've tried to make some sense of how we present things to you. Some of the topics are real discussions, complete with a demonstration, tutorials, and even a project. Other topics are fat workflow tips. Some may elicit the "Ah hah!" response. All are geared toward using Acrobat at a higher level of sophistication.

It Goes Like This

The topics in this chapter share one of two common themes. Either they're about a more advanced use of the software, or they're intended to discuss or show you how to use the software more efficiently. Enhanced efficiency means an advanced use of a piece of software. Here are the topics that are coming up:

- Using PDF files versus other file formats

- Working with video files (a tutorial)

- Working with layers (currently only available from engineering applications, but bet you an RC Cola and a Moon Pie that layers will be everywhere soon)

- Working with destinations (discussion and project)

- Using byte-serving files on the Web

- Reducing file size

Up first is when and how to use PDF files.

Using PDFs versus Other Media Formats

What's one of the key benefits of PDF documents? Rhetorical question. PDF formats are especially conducive to producing documents that are both cross-platform and cross-media.

What does this mean? Basically, you're looking at a format or collection process that will allow information to be used as text and graphics, multimedia, within kiosks, in presentations, and for printing, online and offline. Most of these things can be done with Acrobat. But does that mean they *should* be done with Acrobat?

Your Basic Big Multimedia Piece

Technically, we're referring to project architecture. Consider the types of material you deal with on a regular basis: software installations, marketing pieces, learning materials... the list is endless. Most of these outputs include common structures. How can PDF files be added to the project, how should they be added, and what are the criteria for their use?

A large multimedia project includes these common elements:

- *Installation.* Installation isn't a topic of Acrobat conversation.

- *Introduction.* Many CD pieces launch with an autorun introduction. This is usually highly visual, active content.

- *Navigation.* In addition to the ubiquitous navigation pane, there are many other navigation options—for example, thumbnailing images or video clips, or special panels to control video and talking heads.

- *Content.* The reason for opening the CD in the first place, of course, is content, and it takes virtually unlimited forms. You should consider what is required for the user to use your content. That is, will other plug-ins or extensions be required? This can be a determining factor when you're deciding on one format over another.

Let's see when to use one format or the other.

The Power of PDFs

Many times a PDF file will be the ideal medium for distribution of your work. For example:

- *When you're printing.* You can't beat the PDF format for reliable printed output. With PDF/X it's a standard.

- *When you're using source material from a variety of different authoring programs.* PDFs can be created from virtually any program that can print to Distiller or a PostScript printer.

- *When you're using cross-platform files.* PDFs work well on ISO 9660 cross-platform, formatted CD-ROMs.

- *For security reasons.* PDFs are easily saved with password encryption settings.

- *For interactivity purposes.* Acrobat readily handles different types of actions smoothly and simply. Acrobat 6.0 has greatly expanded this to include various new formats and even embedding movie formats in the file.

The Power of Multimedia

Adobe's Premiere Pro and After Effects and Macromedia's Flash and Director are some of the big guys used for designing multimedia presentations. Depending on the structure of a piece, you may likely use any of the programs. Use these types of programs when the following issues are important:

- *Audio and video synchronization.* Depending on the sophistication, you'll have much better results (use Acrobat to embed files that launch on specific actions only).

- *Lingo programming (Macromedia Director) or Action script (Macromedia Flash).* Use these programs to develop interactive navigation controls and other elements. Again, this depends on the level of sophistication you require.

- *Animation.* We need say no more.

CD-ROM Distribution

In other areas both of this chapter and this book, we've discussed using the Web as a medium for delivering PDFs. That isn't the only option for delivering PDFs, and sometimes it's not even the best option. In several situations, it might be better to publish to CD-ROM. Consider these ideas:

- Suppose you have to deliver large files, movies, executable files, and the like. Internet delivery isn't efficient; CD delivery is. On the same topic, Internet or intranet speeds may be too slow to deliver efficient and quick navigation tools and information.

- How are your users accessing material? If they ordinarily work offline, a CD is much more convenient than finding a laptop connection.

- For highly secure documents, burning a specific number of CDs for distribution will help to control access to your information.

Tutorial: Adding Video to PDFs Efficiently

We've neglected to show you some of the groovy things you can do with Acrobat. Time to change that. And it's a good topic to follow multimedia discussion.

Inserting a Movie into a PDF Document

You can add almost any type of video files to Acrobat 6.0. We'll discuss how to add a movie to a PDF file and offer some tips for using video file formats.

The Chapter 14 folder contains a movie clip named boys.mov. A file named movie.pdf is the basic framework to which you'll add a movie (shown in Figure 14-1). If you set compatibility with Acrobat 5.0, you must insert the movie yourself to ensure that the storage locations for the PDF file and the MOV file are the same. If you set compatibility to Acrobat 6.0 the movie is embedded and you don't have to worry about it getting separated. You can see the finished movie in the file boysmovie.pdf in the Chapter 14 folder.

Note

Acrobat 6.0 has added another layer of thought in the process. Acrobat 5.0 could only use QuickTime movies and they could not be embedded. Acrobat 6.0 plays all documents compatible with Apple QuickTime, Flash Player, Windows Built-In Player, RealOne, and Windows Media Player. You must decide on compatibility (we prefer Acrobat 6.0).

Note

The movie contains two of the most photogenic grandkids in the world. Any Hollywood agents out there are welcome to discuss contracts.

Figure 14-1
The finished Acrobat PDF document plays the movie.

1. Open the movie.pdf file. Click the Movie tool on the Advanced Editing toolbar to select it, and then click and drag to draw a frame on the document page. The Add Movie dialog box shown in Figure 14-2 opens.

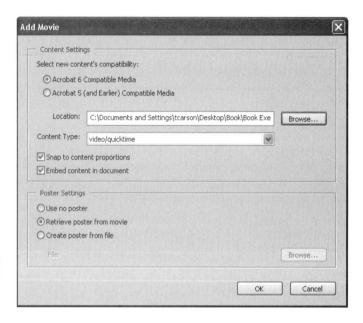

Figure 14-2
Define the properties you want to use to display a movie in a PDF document.

2. In the Content Settings area, select the Acrobat 6.0 Compatible Media radio button, because the file is embedded and you're going to email it. In a few minutes, you'll set it to run on opening.

3. Click Browseselect the boys.mov file from the Chapter 14 folder and click OK to load the movie.

4. Click on the Hand tool and and click the black area inside the frame to watch your movie.

5. Click on the Movie tool and right-click on the movie screen. Click Properties to open the Multimedia Properties box like the one shown in Figure 14-3. The Settings tab is shown by default. Insert alternate text to use for displays with accessibility aids or tool-tips. The selected event is Mouse Up.

6. Click the Appearance tab to set the appearance of the movie box as in Figure 14-4. Since you already had the box, you don't need a visible box.

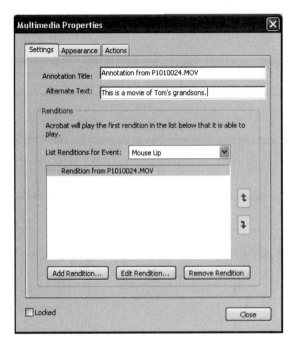

Figure 14-3
The Multimedia Properties dialog box offers numerous features for the movie.

Figure 14-4
Set the box and poster for the movie in the Appearance tab.

7. Click the Settings tab again (shown in Figure 14-3,) and then click Edit Rendition to open the Rendition Settings dialog box.

8. Renditions are much the same as versions. Acrobat sets a version to play with default options. You can set up multiple renditions so if the first option doesn't work the second will run or the third and so on until the media will play on the recipient's computer. A whole new world of choices arises as shown in Figure 14-5.

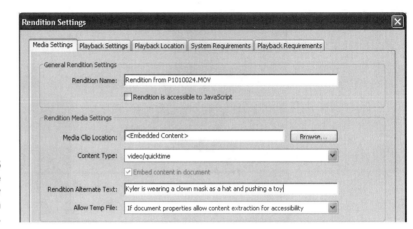

Figure 14-5
You can configure multimedia extensively using the Rendition Settings options.

9. Click the Playback Settings tab to set the volume, player controls, repeat and loop options, and so on. Our choices are shown in Figure 14-6 and include running the clip twice, and displaying controls.

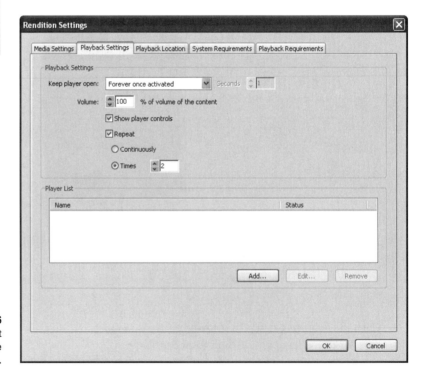

Figure 14-6
The playback settings that allow you to set the options for each rendition.

10. Click the Playback Location tab. Select and format the movie's view. Figure 14-7 shows the options you selected.

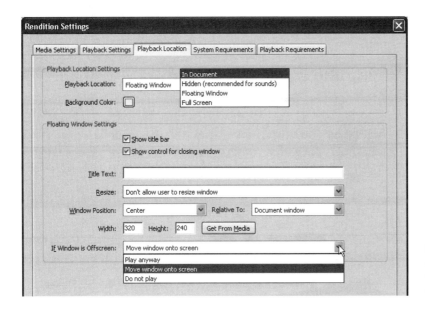

Figure 14-7
Choose options for
Playback Location for
displaying the movie.

The System Requirements tab, as shown in Figure 14-8, allows
you to set specific system requirements for the client. The defaults
will work in most instances, but you may need to make choices
based on deployment.

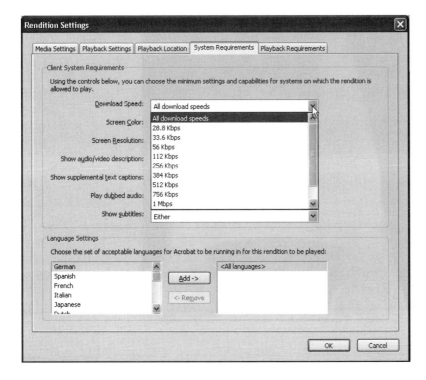

Figure 14-8
Set the system
requirements according to
the method you're using to
distribute your movie.

11. Click OK to close the Rendition Settings dialog box. Save the file and test your movie.

Playing the Movie When the Document Opens

Now we'll show you how to make the movie play when the document is opened. That is done from within the Pages tab. Follow these steps:

1. Open the Pages tab. Right-click the page thumbnail image to open the shortcut menu and choose Properties. The Page Properties dialog box opens as shown in Figure 14-9.

2. Click the Actions tab and select Page Open in the Select Trigger drop-down list.

3. Select Play Acrobat 6.0 Compatible media from the Select Action drop-down list.

4. Click Close and save the document.

It cannot get much simpler than that. People will spend hours looking for this because it has moved.

Figure 14-9
Multimedia is so cool in Acrobat 6.0. Even Tom the engineer can do it.

Layered Documents

Adobe took a major leap forward by including layers in Acrobat 6.0. Layers will open a world of opportunities as more and more graphics programs have the ability to maintain layers.

Currently the only two programs that can generate PDF files with layers are AutoCAD (2000 or later) and Visio.

One of the questions often posed by engineers with Acrobat 5.0 was "will Acrobat support layers in CAD drawings?" Adobe made this a reality by placing a PDFMaker in AutoCAD.

Layers—Should You or Shouldn't You

We're firmly split as to our approach to layers. As a professional engineer, Tom would never release a design drawing with layers active. If a decision were made in a project based on drawings with layers accidentally turned off, it could result in liability issues. From a design perspective, layers open a whole new world of experimentation and communication with the ability to offer layered PDF images using different languages, different images, different content…you get the idea.

Creating a Layered Document

Like Word, Excel, and PowerPoint, Acrobat 6.0 Professional places PDFMaker macros in AutoCAD and Visio. The one difference in the Adobe PDF menu is the Convert All Pages in Drawing command as shown in Figure 14-10. If you select the conversion option, all the layering options are bypassed and a flattened PDF drawing is created.

The PDFMaker macro's default function is to flatten the drawing. The resulting PDF document looks like the original without layers.

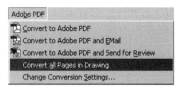

Figure 14-10
The Adobe PDF menu is similar to those in other Office programs with the addition of a Flattening command.

The Chapter 14 folder contains both a Visio drawing named cottage.vsd and the completed document named cottage.pdf. The document was created from the two-layered cottage.vsd drawing in Visio. Follow these steps to create a layered PDF document:

Note

Most options for the layers are controlled from within Visio. The layer's name, visibility, locked status, and whether it can be printed are all controlled in Visio.

1. Click Adobe PDF ➤ Convert to Adobe PDF to open the Visio PDFMaker macro. You can see the interface is quite different than other macros, as shown in Figure 14-11. There are limited options available for the conversion.

Figure 14-11
You can choose either all the layers or specific layers for conversion.

2. Choose Retain All VSD Layers in the Selected Page and then click Next to open an information dialog box, as shown in Figure 14-12. The dialog box states that you're converting and maintaining the layers, and that the PDF document will look identical to the original drawing.

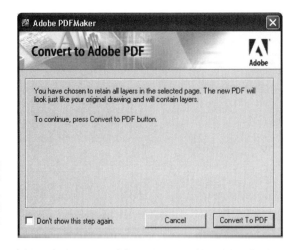

Figure 14-12
Before the PDF document is generated, you're notified about the conversion option you selected.

Selecting Specific Layers

The description of the previous process uses all the layers in the drawing. You can also specify layers for export. If you choose to retain some VSD layers the PDFMaker macro displays the dialog box shown in Figure 14-13.

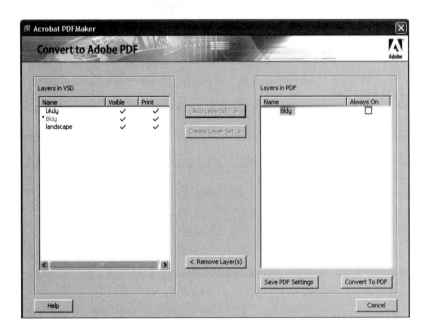

Figure 14-13
You can choose specific layers to retain when exporting a Visio drawing as a PDF.

In the dialog box you can see the drawing layers listed in the left pane. Click a layer to select it, and then click Add Layer to move it to the Layers in PDF listing. Once in the Layers in PDF listing, you can choose to make layers permanently visible by clicking the Always On check box.

Once you've specified the layers for conversion, click Convert to PDF to run the macro.

Displaying the Layered PDF Document in Acrobat

We've converted a simple Visio drawing named cottage.pdf to show you how to work with layers once they've been converted. Open cottage.pdf. The drawing opens with the Layers tab visible as shown in Figure 14-14.

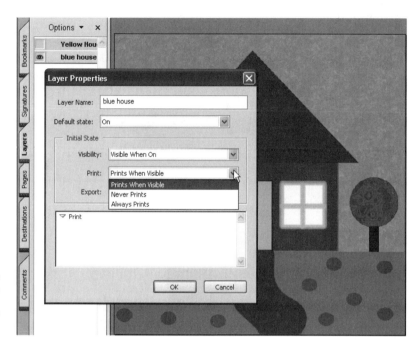

Figure 14-14
Once the document is open in Acrobat, you can toggle layers on and off and choose print options.

The Layers tab conforms to the overall new interface for Acrobat. Right-click a layer and select Properties. The Layer Properties dialog box, also shown in Figure 14-14, displays properties and options you can control. Set the visibility state for the blue house to default as visible. In this file you select the layer to print when visible, since the layer is actually a different picture and not a layer on a background.

Adobe has opened the box on layers and as time goes on the program will give creative and developmental professionals a wide variety of tools.

Working with Destinations

A *destination* is an endpoint for a link represented by text in the Destinations panel. Sounds easy enough. Why is it an advanced feature? Tom probably hates to admit this but he has made some humongous multi-document PDF files and has never made a destination. His workflow has never needed them.

Why would you use a destination rather than a link? When you're linking across documents, a link to a page isn't affected by the additions or deletion of pages in the target document.

Creating and Linking Destinations

Before destinations can be linked, they have to be created and named in the place where they're being housed (the source document). This process can be complex. We have provided a project in order to make using destinations more understandable. But first some general discussion on how destinations work.

For these general instructions, you must have the Destinations panel open. To open the Destinations panel choose View ➤ Navigation Tabs ➤ Destinations. At the lower part of the panel, you'll see a message that reads "Document Not Scanned." You must scan the document each time you open the file when working with destinations. It's akin to setting baselines. To scan a document, right-click the Destinations panel or open the Destinations panel's drop-down menu and choose Scan the Document; you can also click the Scan button at the top of the panel. Once the scan is complete, any destinations in the document will be listed in the panel. If you have no destinations, the message that was previously displayed at the bottom of the panel is replaced with the word *Sorting*.

Using destinations is a three-stage process involving a minimum of two different documents: the source document (where the links are created) and the target document (which houses the links to the source document). You're going to learn about destinations by working through the project.

Keeping Destinations on the Straight and Narrow

Two points to remember: First, the destination names must be unique. Second, decide on a naming convention and stick to it. When working in the target document, or troubleshooting any errors, you'll be able to understand the structure by looking at it in the source document's Destinations panel.

Project Project 14-1: Adding Destinations to a Manual

This project has two phases. First, a set of smaller documents is attached to the table of contents of the main document. In the second phase, elements within the text of the main manual are linked to elements in the glossary.

Tip

Docking a Floating Tab

You should have done this earlier. Tom has been asked this question hundreds of times by students. How do you get the floating tab to dock with the rest of the tabs? (Well that isn't exactly their wording.) You grab the blue vertical stripe on the floating tab and drag it directly under the bottom tag and let loose. Sometimes it may take a couple of tries.

Tip

Why Use Destinations Instead of Regular Links?

The name of the game is efficiency. If you added normal links to pages across documents, the links will be broken if pages are added or deleted from the target document. Destinations, which reside in source documents, aren't affected by changes in target documents. It might take more time to initially create desti-nations. In the long run, however, they can save you lots of time.

Note

The manual used in this project (copyright © 2001 by Kathleen Kotchon) was written and illustrated as a course project by a colleague and friend of Donna's. Kathleen emailed the manual to Donna for her opinion and input. Kathleen has been gracious enough to allow us to use it for source material for this project. Kathleen is a wonderful actress as well as being a great technical writer.

The Chapter 14 Projects folder contains a set of four "raw" files. These files are as follows:

- *manual.pdf.* The main manual document.
- *biblio.pdf.* A bibliography for the manual.
- *FAQ.pdf.* Guess what? An FAQ file.
- *gloss.pdf.* A glossary of terms.

The folder also includes a second set of files, named the same, but each file's name includes "1," as in "manual1.pdf." These four files together make up the completed project.

You'll need the Destinations panel open. Also, select Destinations ➤ Scan Document every time you open one of the files.

Linking the Accessory Files to the Makeup Manual

First, the extra files are connected to the main manual's table of contents. The portion of the table of contents used for the destinations is shown in Figure 14-15.

Glossary	*x*
Frequently Asked Questions	*y*
Bibliography	*z*

Figure 14-15
The table of contents will have files attached to these entries.

1. Open the first target document: gloss.pdf.
2. Set the magnification for the glossary. Click the actual size icon.
3. In the Destinations tab, check the Options drop-down list. Click New Destination to an unnamed Destination as shown in Figure 14-16.

Figure 14-16
Add a new unnamed destination to start the process.

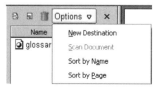

4. In keeping with the new user interface in Acrobat 6.0, setting a destination is very similar to setting the destination of a bookmark. Right-click the destination in the Destinations tab as shown in Figure 14-17. Click the unnamed destination to activate the title and rename it.

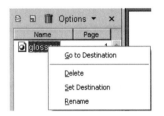

Figure 14-17
Add and name a destination in the target document.

5. Repeat this process for the other two target files:

   • *biblio.pdf*. Name the destination bibliography.

   • *FAQ.pdf*. Name the destination FAQ.

6. Set the magnification to actual size.

7. Save the files.

Build the Links in the Source

Now you have to connect the target destinations to the manual.

1. Open manual.pdf.

2. Set the view mode in the bottom taskbar to Single Page.

3. Add the first link with these properties:

   • Click the Link tool, and then click and drag a rectangle around the *x* page number for the Glossary row.

   • Select Custom Link as shown in Figure 14-18. The Link Properties dialog box opens.

Figure 14-18
Choose a Custom link to
start setting destinations.

4. Click the Appearance tab and choose Invisible.

5. Click Actions. Select Go to a Page in another document and select it. Add as shown in Figure 14-19.

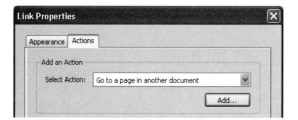

Figure 14-19
Choose the action type
for the destination link.

6. The Go to a Page in Another Document dialog box opens as shown in Figure 14-20. Click Browse and select the project file gloss.pdf.

7. Once the document is chosen, click Use Named Destination, and then click Browse to open the Choose Destination dialog box as shown in Figure 14-21. The named destination "glossary" is listed. Click the destination and click OK to close the dialog box.

8. Click OK and close dialog boxes until the view returns to the manual.pdf document. Save the file and test the link.

9. Repeat the process with the destinations for the other two files.

10. Save the manual.pdf file.

Now you've completed an exercise on destinations. They aren't easy, but have their place.

Figure 14-20
Choose the target document and click Use Named Destination to select the named location.

Figure 14-21
The named destination is listed in the Choose Destination dialog box.

Byte-Serving PDF Files on the Web

Byte-serving starts the view of a file before the entire file is downloaded, one page at a time by default. Depending on the Internet connection speed and the size of the file in question, unless the download is served in chunks, it can take a l-o-o-n-g time to serve an entire document—long enough, of course, for your reader to get bored and surf away.

Preparing the Files

Files should be cleaned, optimized, and saved with the Fast Web View options. Once a document is completed, save a version to be used for online viewing.

Check your Preference settings. Figure 14-22 shows the preferences settings that will optimize your browser display. Select Edit ➤ Preferences ➤ General. Click Internet. As you can see, we've selected all four of the web browser options. In Acrobat 5.0 one of the options was Allow Background Downloading. In Acrobat 6.0 it has taken a neat name change to allow speculative downloading in the background (wonder if a lawyer wrote that).

Figure 14-22
Select all of the web browser options in this dialog box.

While you're in this file-cleaning mode, check for the features that can be deleted from the web-served version. Run PDF Optimizer and remove unused bookmarks, articles, and comments. A major part of our strategy on making documents easy to use is simple navigation.

That completes our trio of time-centric topics. For the grand finale, here are some tips.

Reducing File Size

Sometimes it doesn't matter how big a PDF file is. On the other hand, sometimes it's critical. Consider online files, or ones that are being shared in a workgroup. Although some elements must remain, a good understanding of how to use Acrobat will go a long way toward making file sizes more efficient. Check for these problems before throwing your hands up in disgust or moving to an isolated location without Internet access or indoor plumbing.

The increased processor speed and faster Internet speeds are making some of these less important. Even so, don't become complacent. PDAs are still behind on memory and speed and your files may end up there.

Here is a collection of tips for reducing the size of your files:

- *Embed subsets of fonts rather than the entire font.* To be safe, you can set the percentage at which the entire font is embedded. You aren't going to a printer, therefore you don't need all the fonts. Acrobat 6.0 has 40 fonts with the program versus 14 for Acrobat 5.0.

- *Use the highest compatibility possible.* Acrobat 6.0 has to subset fewer fonts and has better compression algorithms than Acrobat 5.0 and Acrobat 5.0 has better compression that Acrobat 4.0.

- *Watch out for crop marks and prepress information.* Depending on the authoring application you use for creating source files, items such as color bars or crop marks may still be present in the converted file. Remove any of these items before converting the file to PDF. Just cropping once in PDF does not reduce file size.

- *Consider custom PDF creators.* As an experiment, export a source document using different options. If you're using a program with a custom PDF exporting utility, test it. Also create a version using Acrobat Distiller and/or PDFMaker. Check the sizes of the different versions. You may be surprised. Remember that some of the custom creators are based on earlier versions of PDF and may not work as well in a PDF 1.5 (Acrobat 6.0) workflow.

- *Watch those graphics.* Compress objects through Distiller job options. Whenever possible, use vector graphics over bitmaps. Base text on fonts, not bitmaps. Check for downsampling.

- *Periodically use the Save As function instead of Save.* You can use the same name and overwrite the original file. Using Save As will remove deleted objects, optimize the file, and store identical items like backgrounds, which can make an enormous difference in your file size. For example, while constructing our movie.pdf file, we saved it several times, for a final size of 61.6KB. When we used Save As, it dropped in size to 39.5KB—a drop of over 40 percent.

- *Save file size for buttons by attaching actions to pages instead.* Under the Pages panel, right-click on the thumbnail of the page needing an action. Select Page Properties to open the dialog box. Click the Actions tab and in the Select Trigger drop-down list, choose Page Open or Page Close, as shown in Figure 14-23. Going to a snapshot view can also save file size.

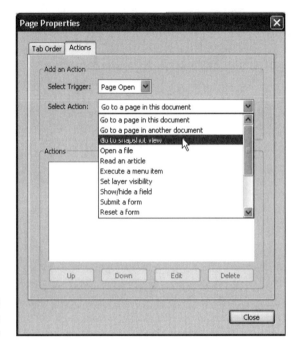

Figure 14-23
Use a snapshot view to
decrease page size.

- *Check the named destinations set in a file.* Each destination is about 100 bytes. If you're using many paragraphs, such as with an index or tables, much of the file size can be attributed to destinations.

Up Next

This chapter is a profusion of different ideas, techniques, and functions. Some of the topics were extensions of previous chapters' content or new timesaving topics. Still others presented ideas and issues rather than any specific technique. As mentioned, many of the concepts presented in this chapter were aimed at taking your use of Acrobat to the power-user level. Although this book isn't a forum for exhaustive discussion of any one topic, we think we gave you enough information to both stimulate your imagination and open other avenues of exploration.

We're going to get into another deep chapter then we will put it all together. JavaScript scares nonprogrammers, but it's amazing how much you can do without being a programmer. Get ready to be amazed.

Chapter 15

About JavaScript

In the beginning, there was Netscape. Netscape Communications created the JavaScript language to make web pages interactive. Then Adobe said, "Let's see what we can do with this language," and Adobe-enhanced JavaScript was born, bringing interactivity to PDF pages. It's a good thing.

JavaScript and Socks

This isn't really the place for an in-depth discussion of the JavaScript language. However, because many of you reading this book haven't ventured too far into code-writing territory, we'll give you the Cook's tour of basic JavaScript. This introduction is important on two levels: first, to understand how we've used JavaScript in other chapters in this book (particularly everything dealing with forms), and second, to give you a foundation to expand your own use of Acrobat JavaScript.

One little story before we go on. This is for the die-hard designers who have never done any scripting or code before. Don't be surprised if it makes no sense to you whatsoever. Several years ago, Donna took four weeks' vacation from her teaching gig to learn JavaScript. The first week was absolutely horrible. Her brain physically hurt. It rebelled. For days she stared at these pages blindly, reacting like a hardcore designer. What did she see? Nothing in the words and letters at all, because she couldn't process it at that level. Instead, she did see how nicely the rows of text lined up, and how the white space made a pattern, and how the repetition of some words and letters made secondary patterns on the page…

So, how did she turn the corner, you may well ask? She used two pieces of cardboard as visual aids in a negative sense—not to enhance her view of what she was reading, but to restrict it to a line-by-line view. She also persisted through the next three weeks, and by the end of the month she could concatenate a string with the best of them. But it still hurt.

The point is, don't sweat it. Either it comes to you, or it doesn't. Give it a chance, though shifting from right-brain to left-brain thinking is no mean feat. Regardless, reading through this chapter may give you incentive enough to try some of these things using the scripts provided. No need to start from scratch in any case, and the results may stimulate you to bigger and better coding efforts.

Tom had not programmed since he programmed in Fortran with a deck of punch cards. You cannot really say that Tom knows JavaScript. He does know enough to keep copies of various scripts that do what he wants and modifies them for the task at hand.

If all else fails, find some cardboard. Those little inserts that come with socks are a good size!

Locating the JavaScript Manuals

The JavaScript manuals for Acrobat 6.0 don't come with the CD for the program and must be downloaded from the Adobe web site. They are in the SDK area of the Adobe Solutions Network for Developers section. The titles are *Acrobat JavaScript Scripting Reference* and *Acrobat JavaScript Scripting Guide.* Download them and keep them handy. There are seven pages of additions to Acrobat 6.0 JavaScript, with many dealing with layers and security. The Acrobat 6.0 SDK is now only available to paying members of the Adobe Solutions Network.

Let's Start at the Beginning

OK, time for some JavaScript. No cardboard required.

JavaScript isn't a programming language per se, but a scripting language. The difference lies in how it works. JavaScript is loosely typed, meaning that objects can be readily converted from one form to another; and its syntax, or phrase structure, is more forgiving to new programmers than a traditional programming language.

JavaScript uses object-oriented programming (OOP) techniques. This type of approach simplifies programming by using three basic concepts: objects, properties, and methods. *Objects* are basically lumps of data with attributes (named values directly associated with them). *Properties* are information about the object. *Methods* perform operations on or with an object.

Data can be accessed through either properties or methods. "Good programming" uses properties as much as possible. For example, consider a rectangle. JavaScript can be written about a rectangle as either a property or a method. As a property, it's written as the "rectangle" property. If a method is used, this is written as a "getRectangle()" method. If you're working with static information, and have a choice between using a property and using a method, use the property. In some cases, the information isn't so straightforward. Where a set of parameters is necessary to obtain the correct information or the information is transitory, you must use a method instead. For example, if the size of a rectangle depends on user input, using a method is necessary.

A real-life example is in order, so let's go shopping. A bit of imagination may be required, but we think it works.

Note

This JavaScript chapter has had minimal modification, except to update it to include interface changes in Acrobat 6.0. This section was reviewed for the first edition by Carl Orthlieb, Director of Engineering, ePaper Solutions at Adobe.

When you have to go to the grocery store, you make a list, which includes eggs, apples, oranges, and peanut butter. The list is an object. You can describe its properties—a torn-off piece of an envelope from the phone bill, written with red pencil crayon. Each word on the paper is also an object, with its own properties—letters, descriptions. You can alter these at will. For example, you decide that your husband needs more fiber in his diet, and add the word "crunchy" to the object "peanut butter."

But are these objects usable in their present state? Well, yes and no. Yes, because you can use them as mental prompts. No, because you really shouldn't eat paper, and it's hard to make omelets with. Therefore, you must employ a method to convert the objects into usable results. That is, you must brave the elements and the humans and make the journey to the grocery store, pick out the items, pay for them, and bring them home. By employing this method, you've converted the written "egg" object into a usable object; that is, you've modified its properties.

Now, more grocery talk. You have the items home, and you have an equivalent collection of objects in your paper bag (paper, not plastic). What do you have now? Four object types—apples, oranges, eggs, and crunchy peanut butter—for the fiber. Again you can look at their properties. First the apples. Golden Delicious. Their properties include the color, size, scent, firmness, and whether or not they have stems. How are their properties accessed? Directly. You can visualize the apple's properties and simply bite into the apple to access all its properties. On the other hand, the eggs, oranges, and peanut butter will require using a method to access their properties—cracking, peeling, or opening the lid. Once the method has been employed, the results can be described.

Now let's convert this all into something written.

Objects and Properties, Apples and Oranges

Just like an apple, a PDF document is an object. Anything on the page is also an object. You identified the properties of the apple, and they can be written like this:

```
apple.color
apple.size
apple.scent
apple.firmness
apple.stem
```

Now, this doesn't give any values to the properties; it just identifies them. You can assign a value to each property as follows:

Note

By the way, because there is more than one apple, egg, and orange, each subset (a group of apples, a carton of eggs) is technically an array. That is, apple1, apple2, apple3 is an array of apples, and so on.

```
apple.color = "yellow";
apple.size = "medium";
apple.scent = "strong";
apple.firmness = "hard";
apple.stem = false;
```

You'll notice that the last property is given a false value. That is because this property description has only two options: true and false. The same could also be used for scent and firmness, but you're choosing a more descriptive route.

Same thing works with a page. Suppose you have added a table to a page. The page is an object and has properties. The table is an object and has properties. Likewise for each cell. Look at this description for a field color, for example:

```
this.getField("Name").fillColor = color.ltGray;
```

This means the table field will be light gray.

What about what you can't see? For example, consider a textbox. Say that this textbox is supposed to contain the user's last name. Because you've learned to name objects in other chapters using a standard method, and have put this method into regular practice, you're in a good position to move from naming objects to using them in Acrobat JavaScript. Let's say the text box is named "Name.Last". The contents of the text box (or its value) is written as

```
this.getField("Name.Last").value
```

> **Note**
> Many objects have common properties. To view a list of these properties, see the *Acrobat JavaScript Scripting Reference* and *Acrobat JavaScript Scripting Guide* described earlier.

Name Your Forms and Fields

Not only is this a good idea from a usability standpoint, but it's also vital to being able to keep all the objects you create in order. Remember that your file names can be organized according to a hierarchy or other understandable naming system, which is really just good practice.

And when we assign a property to that, it becomes

```
this.getField("Name.Last").value="Smith";
```

which means that the content, or property, of this field must be the word *Smith*.

One other thing to note before you go on to methods is the structure of the properties. You can see in the example here that it's arranged in a hierarchical fashion.

Methods

Now let's talk about the eggs. Objects, like eggs, have a certain number of things that can be done to them. Different objects do different things. If you wanted to write methods for cooking eggs, you would write egg.fry() and could enter different options such as egg.fry("scrambled") or egg.fry("overEasy").

In this example, the object is the egg, the method is fry, and the description is the type of frying method used. How is this used? Like this:

```
var breakfast = new Object();
```

Now you have a new object, which is generic and has no properties. You can assign both methods and properties to the object, depending on whether the reference is data or requires calculation, like this:

```
breakfast.favorite = "omelet";
breakfast.quick = "scrambled";
breakfast.calculate = function (a,b) { return a - b; }
```

In these examples, the first two statements create properties and assign values to them. In the third example, you've created a new method for the object by assigning a function to it. This statement means that the breakfast calculation is a function with a value of a "minus b". In the next section, we'll show you what to do with this function.

This is all well and good. You've seen how objects have properties and how methods are employed against these objects. But the real question is, what makes it all go? Answer: events.

Note

Methods and functions are closely related. A function is a piece of code that performs a specific task. A method is a function that acts on a specific object. For example, "starting car" is a function that could be used in a number of situations, but the combination of "starting car" and "navigating to grocery store" would make up the "going shopping" method to be used on the "shopping list" object.

Why You Went Shopping in the First Place

An event had to trigger your fictional trip to the grocery store. In all likelihood, it was the sound of a knife scraping the inside of the peanut butter jar over and over, accompanied by heavy sighs, and then a thunk as the jar hit the recycling bin. This is an event, which triggered a range of activity—find the car keys, drive to the store, and so on. And this was also the last installment of the shopping trip story. From here on in, it's just the facts, ma'am.

JavaScript Events and Functions

JavaScript uses an event model. This means an event is defined to trigger functions to run. The most common events are those involving mouse functions and buttons. Others are used for page and form functions. You'll look at these in more detail further on in the chapter as we discuss specific activities in Acrobat. You've also seen this in action in projects in other chapters.

Speaking of functions, a function can be named at will, because you're defining it yourself, and it's written as follows:

```
function DoIt (variable(s)) {
// what needs to be done
}
```

So what does this mean? Allow me to disassemble this:

1. function: Add this word to indicate you're going to create a function.

   - DoIt: The name we gave to this function.

   - variable(s): There can be more than one. They are sent to the function when it's called. Variables sent to a function are known as *parameters*.

   - { (The left curly bracket, or *brace*): Written at the end of the function's call line, it starts the enclosure of the script that will be executed when the function is called.

   - // What needs to be done: Depends on the function. Here you add statements and declarations.

   - }(the closing brace): This indicates that both the statements and the function are ended.

You have to call the function when you want to use it. Enter the name, variables (parameters), and end the line with a semicolon, like this:

```
DoIt (today);
```

Breakfast Revisited

In the last section, we referred to methods and said the value of a variable can be either a string (the word "omelet") or a calculation. Because this script can accept variables and requires calculation, it's a function. Let's have another look. This is the earlier statement reproduced here for your convenience:

```
breakfast.calculate = function (a,b) { return a - b; }
```

This variable is written to calculate the number of eggs left depending on which variable you choose. For example, you could specify that omelettes take 3 eggs, and scrambled eggs take 2 eggs. If you then said that a carton of eggs contains 12, you can write one more variable that will calculate the eggs remaining in the carton depending on what you cooked, like this:

```
var remainder = breakfast.calculate( 12, 3 );
```

This variable will call the function that you created earlier, and 'remainder' has a value of '9'.

But what if a decision has to be made to do one thing if something happens, and another if something else occurs? Glad you asked. Coming up, your last general topic: making decisions.

Tips on Using Variables

Now a bit on variables. You've used variables to write custom scripts in other chapters, but here are some basic rules for using them:

- Variables have to be declared. They're most often declared with the word "var".

- Variables must start with either a letter or an underscore and are case sensitive.

- When working on a large project, pick a naming convention and stick to it. This will make your life run more smoothly.

- Variable names should describe what they are. Just because you think you'll always remember what something means, don't count on it.

- Establish a pattern of assigning values (or initializing). For the work you're doing in Acrobat, the value of the variables is generally known. So assign the value when the variable is declared. This saves time and frustration later.

- End each variable statement with a semicolon.

- To print characters, enclose them inside quotes. Otherwise, a string of characters is considered a variable. For example, var b = data is a variable, var b = "data" will print the word data.

- Add comments to your code to make it more understandable to yourself and others. Any comments should start with // to differentiate them from something that is to be processed as part of your code.

Decision Making

A common occurrence in all types of programming is decision making. This is referred to as a decision branch. JavaScript uses a common type of if statement, written as in Listing 15-1.

Listing 15-1. Content of a Simple if Statement

```
if (condition) {
do something
} else {
do something else
}
```

You'll look at this in Acrobat specifics later in the chapter. For now, we want to show you a simple example of how this works.

Suppose you have a form. On this form, you're collecting information for marketing purposes. You want to tailor responses to the user based on gender. You want all women to receive one response message and all men to receive another response message when the form is submitted. The script will be written as shown in Listing 15-2.

Listing 15-2. Writing an if Statement

```
var gender=this.getField("gender").value;
if (gender == "female") {
app.alert("Thank you. Ask about our Fashion Specials");
} else {
app.alert("Your form has been submitted.");
}
```

Let me explain this on a line-by-line basis:

1. First of all, you'll have to declare a variable. The content of the gender box on the form will be transferred to a variable named "gender".

2. The response is questioned in the first line of the if statement. Is the gender equal to female?

3. An alert box will be displayed if the question is true; that is, gender is equal to female.

4. If the answer to the question is false, this alert box will be displayed; that is, if gender isn't equal to female.

This concludes our tour of basic JavaScript—very basic JavaScript. We've limited the discussion to those elements you'll be dealing with in the rest of this chapter. We encourage you to consult any of the many JavaScript books and online resources available for further information.

Now, let's finally look at how Acrobat uses JavaScript. Before we get into it, we want to point out that there are differences between JavaScript used in HTML and that used in Acrobat. For example, many common objects and methods aren't part of the core JavaScript language. Instead, they're part of either server-side or client-side scripting. With either use of JavaScript, the code is executed either on the page or through the web server. Similarly, JavaScript for PDF has its own objects and methods, and is executed in either Acrobat itself or Acrobat Reader. For this reason, we heartily recommend that you spend some time with the Acrobat JavaScript Object Specification.

Using JavaScript in Acrobat

In other chapters, we've shown you bits and pieces of Acrobat JavaScript used for particular purposes. You've used scripts for some simple calculations and to navigate through a document. That only scratches the surface. Now let's look at some more real-life, practical uses of JavaScript. Along the way, we'll offer some description and advice, but no more grocery shopping.

Note

At the risk of stating the obvious, in order to have JavaScript run in your documents, you must enable it. If you're having problems with your documents, check your preferences. Select Edit ➤ Preferences ➤ JavaScript, and make sure the Enable Acrobat JavaScript option has been selected.

In some of this discussion, we'll show you how to use dialog boxes within Acrobat to add scripting. In other cases, you'll have to build some scripts. To bring some order to the presentation of how to use JavaScript, we've organized it according to where it's being used—that is, whether you're using it inside a document or outside a document.

Using JavaScript in a Document

You can attach JavaScript to a document in seven different ways:

- With Page Open and Page Close actions
- With Document actions
- With bookmarks
- With links
- With form fields
- At the document level (or top level)
- From the JavaScripts folder on your hard drive

Note

The first option, Page Open and Page Close events, has a sample script to give you a sense of how the process works. In the projects and tutorial coming up later in the chapter, you'll be writing scripts for some of these scripting options.

Let's have a look at these JavaScript options. How and where you access them in Acrobat varies. You'll run through the processes, and then you'll look at some in detail in upcoming projects.

Opening and Closing Pages

First up, using JavaScript with Page Open or Page Closed actions, the script is executed when the page opens or closes. A logical use of this event would be updating a date on the page. If you would like to try this as we explain how it works, open an Acrobat file—any file will do, but save the project files from this chapter for use later in the chapter. The change in interface from Acrobat 5.0 to Acrobat 6.0 changed how these are accessed. A page action involves a page. Pages are under the Pages tab.

To add a Page Open action, follow these steps:

1. On the Pages tab, right-click the page thumbnail you want to apply the action to. Select Page Properties to open the dialog box shown in Figure 15-1.

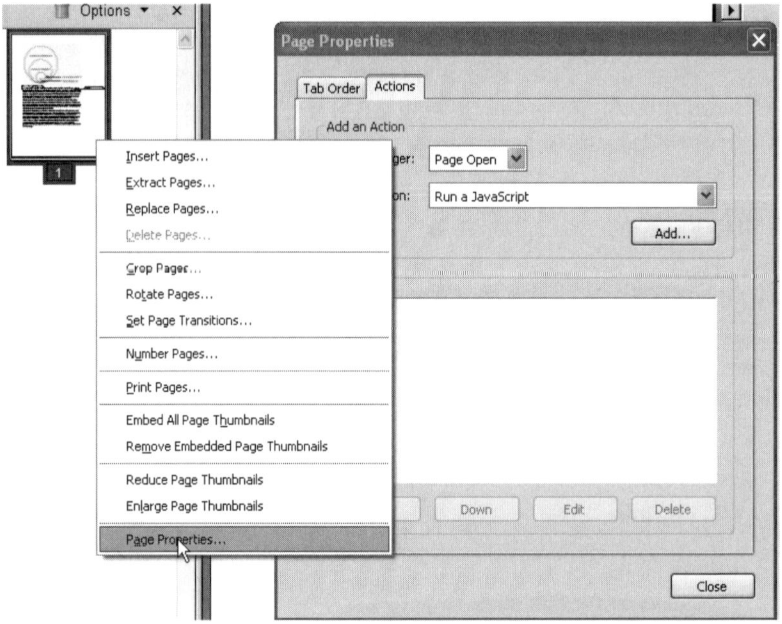

Figure 15-1

Set page properties from
a page thumbnail in the
Pages tab, and choose a
page action from the Page
Properties dialog box.

2. Click the Trigger drop-down list and choose an option. You can choose either Page Open or Page Close (Page Open is selected in this example).

3. Select Run a JavaScript from the Actions drop-down list. Click Add.

4. The JavaScript Editor dialog box opens; write the script, such as:

```
app.alert ("Welcome to my document.");
```

5. Click OK to close the JavaScript Editor window.

6. Click OK to close the dialog box and return to the Page Properties dialog box.

7. Under Actions a Page Open Run JavaScript now appears.

8. Click Close to close the dialog box. Save the file.

To test the script, reopen the file. When it opens, you should see the alert message, as shown in Figure 15-2.

Now let's discuss attaching JavaScript to document actions.

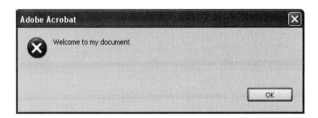

Figure 15-2
The document now displays this alert when it's opened.

Document Actions

Document actions relate to different states of a document, and include the following:

- Document Will Close (when a document closes)

- Document Will Save (before a document is saved)

- Document Did Save (after a document is saved)

- Document Will Print (before a document is printed)

- Document Did Print (after a document is printed)

The states that include "Did" in their names will run the script immediately after the function—either save or print—is completed. Add document actions by following these steps:

1. Select Advanced ➤ JavaScript ➤ Set Document Actions. The dialog box shown in Figure 15-3 will open.

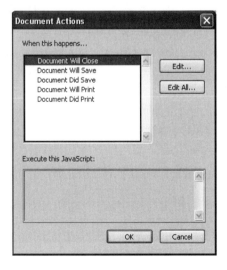

Figure 15-3
Choose a document action from the list in this dialog box.

2. Select the JavaScript action from the list, and click Edit.

3. When the JavaScript Editor dialog box opens, add your script. Click OK to close the dialog box and return to the Document Actions dialog box.

4. The script appears in the bottom window, and a green dot appears to the left of the action's line in the listing, as shown in Figure 15-4. Click OK to close the dialog box.

Figure 15-4
In this example, scripts are attached to the first two options, as indicated by the dots beside their names.

Note

You may have noticed that there is no Delete button on this dialog box. You can delete an action, of course. Select the action from the list at the top of the dialog box and click Edit to open the JavaScript Editor dialog box. Delete the code and click OK. The code is now removed.

You can attach a number of scripts to the same document at this level, and you can view them all in this dialog box. Simply select the action from the list at the top of the box, and the corresponding script will be displayed in the bottom window.

If you click Edit All, the JavaScript Editor dialog box will open, displaying all the scripts attached to the document. More on that coming up shortly. Let's first have a look at bookmark scripts.

Bookmarks

You can add JavaScript to bookmarks by following these steps:

1. Select a bookmark from a document's listing (or add a bookmark).

2. Open the Properties dialog box by right-clicking the bookmark and selecting Properties from the context menu (or select Bookmark Properties from the Bookmarks drop-down list).

3. From the Bookmark Properties dialog box, click Action tab, select Add an Action, and choose JavaScript from the Action drop-down list.

4. Click Edit to open the scripting window.

5. Write or paste in the script, and click OK to close the window.

6. Click Set Action to add the JavaScript and close the Bookmark Properties dialog box.

Attaching JavaScript to links is similar. We'll describe the process for linking next.

Links

Links are commonly used elements for attaching JavaScript. To attach JavaScript to a link, follow these steps:

1. Select a link by clicking on it with the Link tool (in making a new link choose Custom link).

2. Double-click the link or right-click the link and select Link Properties from the context menu. The Link Properties dialog box shown in Figure 15-5 opens.

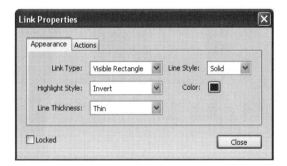

Figure 15-5
Set the link properties on the Appearance tab and add JavaScript on the Actions tab.

3. From the Link Properties dialog box, select JavaScript from the Action drop-down list.

4. Click Edit to open the scripting window.

5. Write or paste in the script, and click OK to close the window.

6. Click Set Link to add the script to the page and close the Link Properties dialog box.

One of the most common uses of JavaScript is with form fields. We've shown you in other chapters how to add JavaScript to form fields, and you'll use them again in a project coming up in this chapter.

Form Fields

We want to give you some general guidelines for using JavaScript with form fields in Acrobat.

- With the Form tool selected, double-clicking a field (or add a new field) opens the Field Properties dialog box.

- From the Actions tab, select run a JavaScript from the drop-down list.

- Depending on the type of field you have defined, there are a number of options for adding scripts.

For Button fields, as shown in Figure 15-6, you can add scripts to any of the six button states listed. Again, as you've seen in other dialog boxes, once a script has been added to an action, it's identified with a dot to the left of the action's listing.

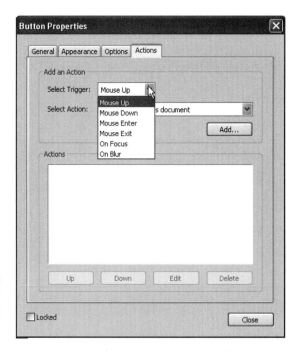

Figure 15-6
Add JavaScript to one of the button states listed in the Select Trigger drop-down list.

For Text fields, you can also add scripts for the same set of mouse events. In addition, with Text fields, you can add Format, Validate, and Calculation scripts. The Format tab is shown in Figure 15-7. For all three tabs, click Edit to add a custom script. More than one script can be added for a single event. Scripts will be executed in the order they're added.

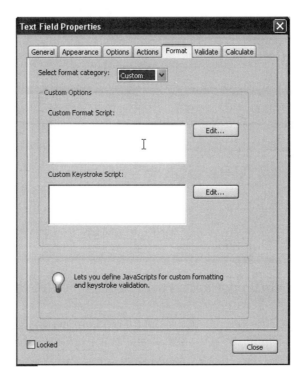

Figure 15-7
You can also write custom scripts for text fields.

Document-Level Scripts

We mentioned that scripts may be added at the document level. This means that scripts added here can be accessed by any other JavaScript in the document. Hence the alternate name, top-level script.

To add a document-level script, select Advanced ➤ JavaScript ➤ Document JavaScripts. You'll return to this topic at the end of the chapter when you look at batch scripts.

The JavaScripts Folder

Finally, we listed the JavaScripts folder. This folder resides on your hard drive. It contains several scripts, which Acrobat calls when they're required. The three types of scripts are as follows:

- Folder level: Stored in the application and user folders

- Console JavaScripts: Primarily used for debugging

- Batch JavaScripts: Used to create and run custom batch scripts

We have some more information on these scripts later in the chapter. We're sure you would like to try some of these processes in a real project, but first we want to touch on some script editing options.

Editing Scripts

Before we get into a project, we want to touch on two features new to Acrobat 6.0. These features are designed for the do-it-yourselfer. Both are quite handy.

Using an External Editor

Note

For Mac users, this feature isn't available.

You can use an external editor program to edit your JavaScripts. By assigning a preference, whenever a script has to be edited from inside Acrobat, your external editor will launch.

Select Edit ➤ Preferences ➤ General ➤ JavaScript. The Preferences dialog box opens as shown in Figure 15-8. Click JavaScript in the left pane to open the preference options. Click External Editor and then click Choose. Browse to the location of your external editor, and click OK. Click OK at the bottom of the Preferences dialog box to make the change and close the window.

Tip

A Warning to Make Your Life Easier

Do not mess with the XML tags! Acrobat uses this tag information to organize the whole works. Although you can freely change anything in the scripts, if you change the tags (anything in < > brackets), Acrobat likely will not accept your changes.

Once the editor preference is set, whenever you edit a JavaScript, Acrobat creates a temporary file and opens it in your editor. In order for the changes to be integrated into your PDF file, you have to save the file. Acrobat is locked when the file is being edited. To return to Acrobat, you must close the external editor first. (Adobe has enhanced the internal abilities of JavaScript editing and the internal editor will work for most users.)

What if you want to see all the scripts you have created in one document? You can do that in the JavaScript Editor as well.

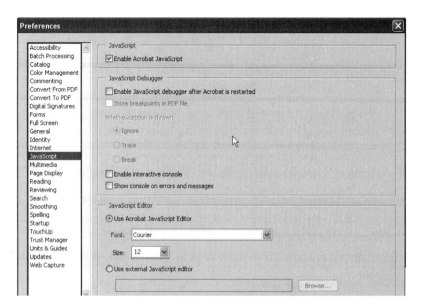

Figure 15-8
You can choose an external editor in the Preferences dialog box.

Editing All JavaScripts in a Document

You can have a look at all the JavaScript you have added to one document. Select Advanced ➤ JavaScript ➤ Edit All JavaScripts. The window shown in Figure 15-9 opens.

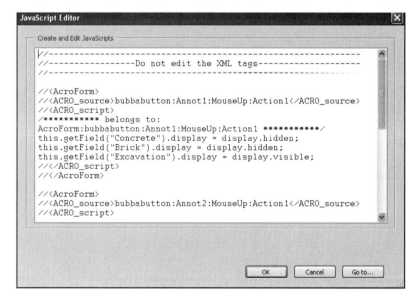

Figure 15-9
The JavaScript Editor dialog box shows all the scripts attached to a file

Let's have a look at some of the features:

- The scripts are organized by XML tag.

- This page has multiple scripted fields. Each of them calls the same top-level script, AcroForm.

- Each script is identified separately and lists the content of the scripts you added to the document at the field level.

- The same feature can be accessed via buttons strategically located in some dialog boxes (for example, the Actions tab in the Form Fields Properties dialog box).

Coming up is a project using JavaScript attached to a document in several different ways.

Project Project 15-1: Brad's U-Park, Part I: A Lot of Parking for a Lot of Money

In other chapters that discussed forms, the focus was on their construction, use, optimization, naming of form fields, and the like. In this chapter, the focus instead is on using JavaScript. You'll add scripts in a number of different ways.

For this reason, the file you need for this project is quite simple. It was designed with tongue firmly planted in cheek. Since what we're doing with it is so serious, it seemed like a good idea to make the material amusing.

The form has two pages. The file, survey.pdf, is in the Chapter 15 projects folder. There is also another file, scripts.txt, which contains the text you will need for the scripts in this project. You can either enter the scripts manually or copy and paste them from this file.

What's on the Form?

As we said, the form doesn't have a lot of content, but it has been constructed to allow for a number of activities. Page 1 is shown in Figure 15-10.

We Need Your Help!

Brad's U-Park

A lot of parking -- for a lot of money

Brad's U-Park has been proud to offer you convenient parking while shopping or working at HighEnd Overpriced Mall. We value all our customers, especially those who choose our services on a regular or daily basis.

A new city bylaw allows us to enforce rules in our lot, including fines for inappropriate driving behavior. In order to improve our services, and to offer you the best possible parking experience, we would like you to complete this survey. Our courteous attendants have helped us prepare a list of the 5 most common complaints we have heard from our customers.

Here's how to complete this survey:

The 5 common complaints are listed below. Please respond to each complaint in two ways -

- how often you encounter this problem on a scale of 1 (rarely) to 5 (regularly).
- how annoying/irritating the problem is to you on a scale of 1 (not very) to 5 (severe).

It is important that you answer these questions carefully. Your totals will be used to determine the cost of fines for parking lot infractions.

When you are done, click the Print button to print the survey. Hand it to your attendant on your next visit. You may also email us with more comments. Click on the Email button.

Click on the Start button to go to the survey page. Thank you.

Figure 15-10
Page 1 of the survey contains text and instructions.

Although the page contains primarily discussion and instruction, you're going to add some scripts to it. On Page 1, you'll do the following:

- Insert an automatic date field at the top of the page.

- Add a Start button, with an action (go to page) attached.

Page 2 is the heart of the survey, as shown in Figure 15-11.

Here are the questions. Click the button indicated for a total; click Reset to start over.

Common Complaints	How Often?	How Annoying?
Drivers who stop in the middle of the lane and block traffic while waiting for a parking spot.		
Drivers who park on the lines, taking up two spots.		
Drivers who park too close to adjacent cars so the other driver must grease up with Vaseline to squeeze into his or her car.		
Drivers who ignore the painted lanes and drive diagonally from one end of the lot to another.		
Drivers who stop in front of a mall exit and wait for passengers to arrive, blocking traffic.		
Your total score is:		

This survey has been sent only to those registered customers who provided us with an email address. Thank you for your participation.

Figure 15-11
Page 2 of the survey form contains the majority of the scripted elements.

You'll add a number of scripts to page 2 by performing these tasks:

- Place an automatic date field on this page as well.

- Add custom field entries to the fields for the survey responses.

- Create a hidden field that displays a grand total defining the user's overall level of irritation once all entries are complete.

- Add several buttons (you can see their finished placement in Figure 15-34).

- Attach a print function to the Print button.

- Attach a document-level script that displays a message after printing.

- Attach a custom script to send email.

All this on one little survey! So let's get to it. Open survey.pdf in Acrobat.

Today's Date Is...

First up, adding date fields. You're going to add a document-level date field to both pages. You aren't going to add two separate fields that require configuring and programming. Instead, by adding two fields with the same name, they also share the same value. You'll make them look different visually.

Follow these steps:

1. Create a text field above the title on page 1 as shown in Figure 15-12.

Figure 15-12
Add the automatic date field to Page 1 in the upper left of the page.

We Need Your Help!

2. The Field Properties dialog box will open once the field has been drawn on the page. Select text from the Type drop-down list, and name the field **date**.

3. Set the appearance of the field:

- Deselect all border options.

- Select Helvetica (or similar) 9pt font

- Select the dark teal text color (from the Color palette, this is the fifth color in the third row).

4. Click the Read-only check box to select it. (This is a calculated field, and the user doesn't interact with it.)

5. Select Format ➤ Date and select the format dd-mmm-yy (for example, 01 Jan 04).

6. Click OK to close the dialog box.

Now that the field has been added and named, you'll attach a document-level script to it. This means that each time the document is opened, the script will be attached to any applicable field it finds. To attach the script, follow these steps:

1. Select Tools ➤ JavaScript ➤ Document JavaScripts. The Document Script dialog box opens. Name the script **date** and click Add.

2. When the scripting window opens, delete the text from the window.

3. Enter this text (or copy the lines of script named "Date" from the scripts.txt file):

```
var d = this.getField("date");
d.value = util.printd("dd-mmm-yyyy", new Date());
```

4. Click OK to close the JavaScript Edit dialog box. The script will now appear in the JavaScript Functions dialog box as shown in Figure 15-13. Click Close to close this dialog box as well.

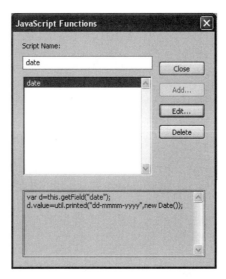

Figure 15-13
The completed document-level JavaScript displays in the JavaScript Functions dialog box.

The script has now been attached. Let's look at it before carrying on. In the first line, you declared a variable "d" (for "date"). The field "date" is bound to the variable. In the second line, the value is defined. The date format is displayed and a new object is created to hold the date object. The date is formatted with the utility object (that is, util.printd).

While you're at it, you may as well add the date field to page 2 as well. Because the field has already been created and configured once, and a script has been created, this process is simpler. When the document is loaded into Acrobat, each field will call and execute the same script.

1. Using the Form tool, click the date field to select it. Copy the field (Ctrl+C or Edit ➤ Copy) or select Duplicate. A Duplicate Field dialog box opens like the one shown in Figure 15-14.

Figure 15-14
The Duplicate field dialog does the same as copying and pasting the field, except you can do multiple pages at once.

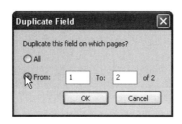

2. Move to page 2 of the survey form. Paste the field (using Ctrl+V or Edit ➤ Paste). If you used the Duplicate tool, then just move it into position at the bottom of the page, as shown in Figure 15-15.

Figure 15-15
The duplicate auto date field moved into place. Notice that the date is showing even though the field is open.

3. Save the file. Test the file by closing and reopening it. You should have the current system date displayed in both text boxes in the chosen format, as shown in Figures 16-16a and 16-16b.

That's it for the date fields. Now back to page 1 to add a button and an action.

(a)   (b)

05-Jul-2003

We Need Your Help!

05-Jul-2003

This survey has
Thank you for y

Figure 15-16
The date displays correctly
in the desired location on
both pages.

No Lights, No Camera—But We Have Action

This is a very simple form, and realistically doesn't require adding buttons for navigation. You've added navigation to other projects in other chapters (see, for example, Project 4.1); but we wanted to briefly include this type of function here to round out the discussion.

Most actions associated with a button should be attached to a MouseUp trigger. Although actions can be attached to other button states, this convention is the most convenient for the user, and also the one most often used professionally.

Follow these steps:

1. Click on the button icon and create a form field in the lower-right corner of page 1. When the Field Properties dialog box opens, name the field **start**.

2. Set these options for the button appearance:

   • Border Color: Dark teal (as in the date text)

   • Background Color: A light beige color (we used a custom color with an RGB value of 255/251/234)

   • Width: Thin; Style: Beveled

   • Text Color: Dark teal; Font: Arial Bold Italic, size 8pt

3. Click Options. Specify these options:

   • Highlight: Push

   • Label: Text only

   • Button Face When: Up

   • Text for Button: Start

4. Click Actions. Select MouseUp from the left pane. Click Add. From the Type drop-down list, select JavaScript. Click Edit.

Note

Acrobat 6.0 can perform this function through the Document ➤ Add Headers and Footers command. It's still good to know how to do it the old-fashioned way.

5. Now attach the script to the button state. In the script window, enter this line of script:

```
this.pageNum++;
```

6. Click OK to close the JavaScript Editor dialog box and return to the Add an Action dialog box.

7. Click Set Action to return to the Field Properties dialog box. A green circle will now appear to the left of the MouseUp listing, indicating a script has been attached. Click OK to close the Field Properties dialog box.

8. Save the file, and then test the button.

The default settings you created with the original file show each page of the survey at full size, so the button's action should display the second page as designed.

That completes the scripts for page 1. Now some more for page 2. You're in button-building mode, and have the default settings in the Field Properties dialog box set for buttons, so let's carry on with the other button actions. Yes, this is out of sequence if you consider the form from top to bottom. From a practical standpoint, however, it makes sense.

Printing the Output

Note

Acrobat 6.0 moved many of the menu items from their locations in Acrobat 5.0. This made the interface easier to use but has caused heart-burn for many forms developers.

One of the simplest things to do is attach menu functions to buttons. Let's do that now, and have the file printed (for the user to hand in to the friendly attendant on his or her next visit to Brad's U-Park). Follow these steps:

1. Create a button field in the lower-right portion of page 2. When the Field Properties dialog box opens, name the field **print**.

2. Use the same appearance options as for the button on page 1.

3. Click Options. Leave the options as set for the last button, add **Print** as the text for the button face.

4. Click Actions. In the Select Trigger drop-down list, select Mouse Up. In the Select Action drop-down list, from the Type drop-down menu, select Execute Menu Item. Click Add.

5. The Menu Item Selection dialog box opens. Select File ➤ Print. As shown in Figure 15-17, the selections will be displayed.

Figure 15-17
Select menu items to attach to buttons through this dialog box.

6. Click OK to close the Menu Item Selection window and return to the Button Properties dialog box.

7. Click Close to return to the Field Properties dialog box. A Mouse Up Run JavaScript will be listed in the Actions box, indicating a script has been attached. Click OK to close the Field Properties dialog box.

8. Test the button. Clicking the button should launch the Print dialog box.

You need to include one more spiffy action before you add the next button.

Telling the User What to Do Next

Let's now attach a document action script. Earlier in the chapter, we outlined a set of document actions, including DocumentDidPrint. Now you'll attach a script to this action and display a pop-up message for the user.

1. Select Advanced ➤ JavaScript ➤ Set Document Actions.

2. Click DocumentDidPrint from the list at the top of the dialog box. Click Edit to open the script window.

3. Enter this script, then click OK to close the script window.

```
app.alert("Thank you. Please give this form to your attendant on
your next visit to Brad's U-Park.", 3);
```

Note

The application alert is required to open an alert window. You can see at the end that we've added the number "3"; this defines the type of alert that is displayed. Leaving it as a default will cause an error icon to display. This will result in the display of an information icon instead.

Note

You have to write this script differently than you would write an alert script for JavaScript used in a browser. The object is an application alert, rather than a generic alert. If you don't include the full name, that is, app.alert, you receive an error message.

4. You'll now see the script displayed in the Document Actions dialog box, as shown in Figure 15-18.

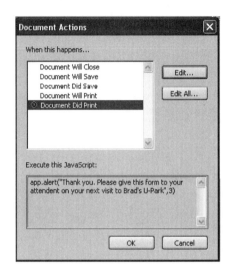

Figure 15-18
The new script is displayed in the Document Actions dialog box.

5. Save the file and test the button. When you click Print, the Print dialog box opens. In order to have the message display, you must click Print. The new message is shown in Figure 15-19.

Now on to more buttons.

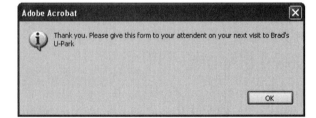

Figure 15-19
An instruction for the user is displayed after the document is printed.

Note

Brad's U-Park is a fictional company (big surprise). The instructions for this project will actually launch your email authoring program, and you'll be ready to send a message addressed to me. Say hi if you like.

There are different ways to send email from a PDF document. You can send a form, send the form data files (FDF) only, or simply launch an external email editor.

In this part of the project, you'll add a button to send the form as an email attachment.

Follow these steps:

1. Create a button form field in the lower-right portion of page 2 to the right of the Print button. When the Field Properties dialog box opens, name the field **email**.

2. Use the same appearance options as you did for the button on page 1.

3. Click the Options tab. Leave the options as set for the last button, and add **Email Us** as the text for the button face.

4. Click the Actions tab. Select Trigger Action Mouse Up from the left pane. Select Action from the drop-down list, then select run JavaScript. Click Add.

5. Now attach the script to the button state. In the script window, enter this line of script:

   ```
   this.mailDoc(true, "yourname@yoursite.com", "", "", "Hi");
   ```

6. Click OK to close the JavaScript Editor dialog box and return to the Form Button dialog box.

7. A Mouse Up Action of Run a JavaScript will now appear in the actions list, indicating that a script has been attached. Click OK to close the Field Properties dialog box.

8. Save the file and test the button. Your email editor should launch, as shown in Figure 15-20.

Figure 15-20
Clicking the Email button launches your email editor.

Note

This script can also be written as follows: mailDoc({ cTo: "dbaker@skyweb.ca", cSubject: "Hi" });.

Note

There are also other ways to send emails using JavaScript. We have included other options in the scripts.txt file. Be careful and test them before you use. Tom left out the comma before Hi!. The JavaScript picked out a person from his address book and added her as a blind copy.

A Quick Look at the Script

Although it isn't really necessary for completion of the projects, we want to show you how the script is built, and how you can add to it.

Mailing a document requires a document method. this.mailDoc refers to the document you're looking at. *true* is a parameter of the method that refers to how the document is handled. *true* means that an email program's interface will be open before mailing; *false* means that the document will be mailed silently, that is, without opening a user interface.

The address follows. The extra sets of quotes can be used to add cc copies to the file. At the end, we have written the word "Hi". This string is the value of a variable that will display the content of the message line in your email editor; in other words, when the email program opens and displays a new message, the subject will be written as "Hi".

Here's how you add a second email address:

1. Reopen the script.

2. Add a secondary address between the first set of double quotes, like this:

   ```
   this.mailDoc(true,"dbaker@skyweb.ca","tcarson@sedev.org","","Hi");
   ```

3. Close all dialog boxes.

4. Test the button. As shown in Figure 15-21, the form will now be sent to both of us.

Figure 15-21
You can easily send a form to a secondary recipient by altering the script.

At this point, we want to end the project and discuss a few more ideas.

Field Calculations

In Chapter 8 we discussed field calculations in some depth. We've added more information, along with the basic process for adding calculations to your document, to make this chapter a more inclusive reference.

Arithmetic Operators

Operators are used to operate on values. Consider this snippet of code from a calculated field:

```
var a = this.getField("amount.0");
event.value = a.value *0.50;
```

What does this mean? In the first line, we've declared a variable, "a". Then we assigned a field object to it ("amount.0"), which is returned by the document getField method.

The use of the event object is dependent on when the script is run. In this case, the script is run whenever a calculation must occur. The script needs to put the value for the calculation event into the value property of the event object. The calculated value is the value of the "amount.0" field multiplied by 0.5.

There are a number of common arithmetic operators you can use. We've listed these, along with examples, in Table 15-1.

Table 15-1 Arithmetic Operators

Operator	Description	Example	Result
+	Addition	6 + 2	8
-	Subtraction	6 - 2	4
*	Multiplication	6 * 2	12
/	Division	6 / 2	3
%	Modulus (returns remainder after division)	7 % 2	1
++	Increment	x = 5; x++;	x is set to 6
--	Decrement	x = 6; x--;	x is set to 5

Calculating Values

Follow these steps to create calculated fields:

1. Create a text field and name the field (for example, Field.1). Acrobat 6.0 automatically names the fields by types and sequential number.

2. To calculate money amounts, click the Format tab and select Number. Choose two decimal places, currency symbol, and separator style.

3. Click the Options tab, enter a default value (use 0), and click OK.

4. Create and name the second field (for example, Field.2). Use the same settings in the Format and Options tabs.

5. Create and name the third field that will be used for calculations (for example, Field.3). Use the same settings in the Format tab.

6. Add a custom script. Click the Calculate tab. Select Custom Calculation Script, and click Edit.

7. When the script window opens, add the calculation script. You'll need three lines for the script:

   • Declare the first variable, whose value is the first field object.

   • Declare the second variable, whose value is the second field object.

   • Populate the event value (remember the value of the calculation event is stored in the field that is being calculated), and perform the calculation.

An example is shown in Listing 15-3.

Listing 15-3. Creating a Calculation Script

```
var a = this.getField("Field.1");
var b = this.getField("Field.2");
event.value = a.value * b.value;
```

Tip

Make It Easier

Rather than build the second or any of a number of fields from scratch, especially a group that shares common settings, select the field or series of fields (hold Shift and click). Right-click the selected forms and select Create Multiple Copies. A dialog box will open to allow you to choose the number of copies. Acrobat 6.0 will automatically renumber the fields sequentially with a parent child number.

8. Click OK to close the script window. The script will be displayed in the Calculate Tab as shown in Figure 15-22.

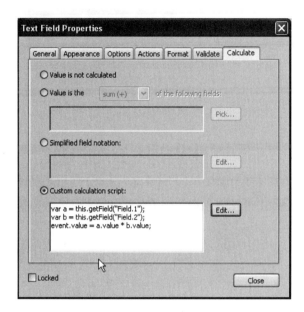

Figure 15-22
Add a custom calculation script to a field.

9. Click OK to close the Field Properties dialog box.

In this example, when the values are entered in both Field.1 and Field.2, the product will be calculated and entered automatically into Field.3.

Comparison Operators

What if you want to create conditional expressions? That is, you want to create an if statement that compares two options and executes one action if the comparison is true and another if it's false. For this effect, you use *comparison operators*. There are six common comparison operators, listed in Table 15-2, and most of them will look familiar from introductory algebra.

Note
If we've dredged up any painful math class memories, we apologize!

Table 15.2 Comparison Operators

Operator	Description	Example
==	Is equal to	9 == 9 returns true
!=	Is not equal to	9 != 8 returns true
>	Is greater than	9 > 8 returns true
<	Is less than	5 < 9 returns true
>=	Is greater than or equal to	9 >= 8 returns true
<=	Is less than or equal to	9 <= 8 returns false

Tutorial: Using Conditions to Manipulate Fields

There are a number of ways you can "lock" a field until a specific condition is met. Most commonly, a field may be hidden or read-only. Regardless of the method used, the user won't be able to interact with the field until the condition is met. We'll show you how this works. It's neat.

To illustrate this process, we've created a simple form in a file called example.pdf, located in the Chapter 15 folder. You can use the file if you would like to follow along. The file includes an example of each of these methods for manipulating the fields. Regardless of the type of manipulation, a value of 25 or greater must be added to the first field in order to activate the second field.

Custom Validation Scripts

In order to be able to see both effects in the same form using the same comparison, we've made a set of corresponding fields. That is, for each condition, there is both a field to enter a value and the field that is being acted upon. The pairs of fields, names, and custom scripts are displayed in Table 15-3 (the scripts are also included in the scripts.txt file in the Chapter 15 folder).

Building the Fields

Now to add the fields and scripts to the form:

1. Create a set of four text fields, named according to the listing in Table 15-3.

Table 15.3 Form Fields and Their Scripts

Field Name	Script	Set Common Properties
hide	var h = this.getField("see.it");h.hidden = (event.value < 25)	None
see.it	None	Form Field is hidden
read	var r = this.getField("do.it");r.readonly = (event.value < 25)	None
do.it	None	Read only

2. Set the common properties of the target fields as described in the table (the common properties are located at the bottom of the Appearance tab in the Field Properties dialog box).

3. Position the fields as shown in Figure 15-23. As you can see in the image, we've added the fields to correspond with each label.

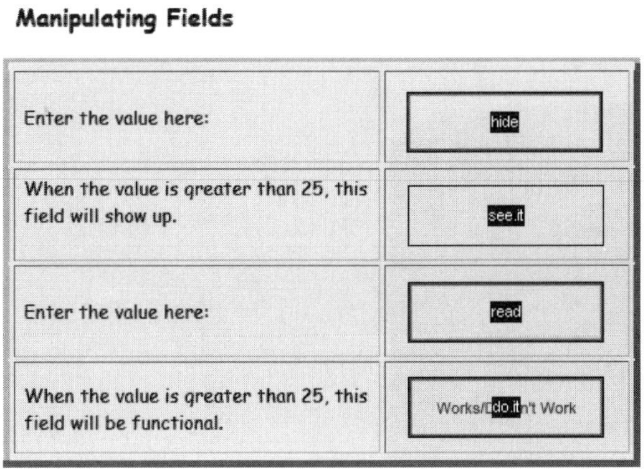

Manipulating Fields

Enter the value here:	hide
When the value is greater than 25, this field will show up.	see.it
Enter the value here:	read
When the value is greater than 25, this field will be functional.	Works/Doesn't Work

Figure 15-23
Add custom fields to the sample table.

4. For each field, double-click to open the Field Properties dialog box. Click the Validate tab, select Custom Validation Script, and click Edit.

5. Add the scripts to the value fields (scripts are in the scripts.txt file). Click Validate, then click Custom Validate Script. Click Edit to open the JavaScript Editor dialog box. Copy and paste the script into the scripting window, then click OK.

6. The custom script will now be displayed in the Validate tab, as shown in Figure 15-24. Click OK to close the Field Properties window.

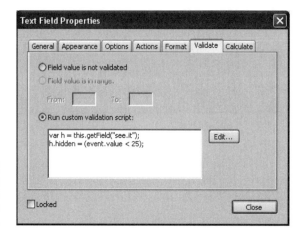

Figure 15-24
Add a custom script to display a hidden field depending on the value entered in another field.

Test the fields. As shown in Figure 15-25, the value entered in the first field is less than 25, so the hidden field stays hidden. On the other hand, the second value field is over 25, so the read-only field can now be manipulated.

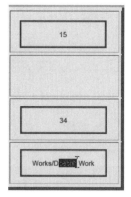

Figure 15-25
Use sample data to test the function of the custom scripts.

One last manipulation topic, and then back to finish up Brad's U-Park, Part Deux. This is a discussion—no file attached.

Restricting Entries

It's common practice to set conditions on a field to make the data more usable. That is, if a certain range of values is possible, you can place conditions that will allow entries only with that specific range.

You may have noticed in earlier screen shots, that there is an option on the Validation tab of the Field Properties dialog box that allows for assigning specific values. However, you have to set some other options before this becomes active. Let's have a look at what is involved:

1. Create a new field. We created a text field named "demo" in the Field Properties dialog box.

2. Click the Format tab. You must use either a number or percentage format. Set the Number Options as shown in Figure 15-26.

Figure 15-26
Select and format the number options to define the allowed entry values.

3. Click the Validate tab. You will see the range option is now available. Click the Value Must Be option, as shown in Figure 15-27. Enter your desired upper and lower range.

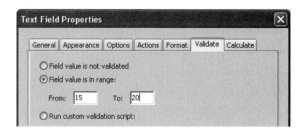

Figure 15-27
Enter the range of entry values allowed for the field

The process is technically complete now, but you can add one more element as well. Click the Options tab to limit the number of characters the user is allowed to enter, as shown in Figure 15-28.

Figure 15-28
Set a character entry
limit in the Options tab.

How does it work? Have a look. In Figure 15-29, we've entered a value outside the defined range. When you move out of the field, the alert message is displayed.

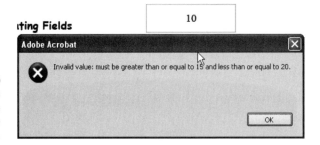

Figure 15-29
An error message
displays when the value
entered is outside the
value bounds of the field.

These processes are fairly simple to use and will result in much more accurate and usable data from your forms (which is the point of creating them, after all). Now, let's get back to that U-Park survey and finish it up.

Project

Project 15-2: Brad's U-Park, Part II: How Irritated Are You?

This project picks up where the last one leaves off. If you've worked through the first project, use your project files. If you chose to start with this project, fear not. In the Chapter 15 projects folder, look for a file named survey1.pdf. That file contains the survey project complete to this point. If you would rather simply follow along with what is going on here, a completely finished version is in the chapter folder as well, named survey2.pdf.

There isn't that much left to do to complete the form. The response fields must be built and value ranges must be assigned to them. There are some total fields to create, and you'll add a hidden field that displays a grand total when the form is complete. Just for good measure, you'll also add a Reset button.

Adding the Response Fields

Acrobat 6.0 has changed the way you do multiple fields. In Acrobat 5.0, you could name the first field and use a suffix .0. Then you would copy the fields and use Shift+keys to incrementally number the fields. That method no longer works, but there is now a feature for creating multiple copies of fields. The Create Multiple Copies of Fields dialog box is shown in Figure 15-30 and the fields themselves are shown in Figure 15-31.

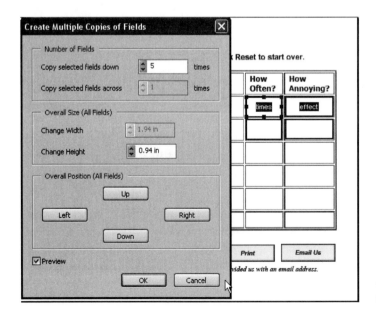

Figure 15-30
Create multiple fields using specific copy commands.

1. Create the first field in each column and name them **times** and **effect**. The Create Multiple Copies of Fields process will number them in sequence:

   - In the Appearance tab, set the text size to 10pt Helvetica, black.

   - In the Options tab, set a character limit of 1 character.

   - In the Format tab, select Number, with 0 decimal places.

   - In the Validate tab, enter a range. Set the lower limit of the range to 1, and the upper limit to 5.

Figure 15-31
Using the copying commands creates a number of duplicate fields.

2. Add the subtotal fields. Name them **TotalTimes** and **TotalEffect**. Each has these properties:

   - In the Appearance tab, set the text size to 10pt Helvetica, black. Set the field as Read Only.

   - In the Format tab, select Number, with 0 decimal places.

   - In the Calculate field, select the middle value option. Select sum from the drop-down list.

Note

We haven't discussed the layout processes for the fields. See Chapter 8 for a discussion on how to make the fields "pretty."

3. Click Pick, and select the entry fields that correspond with each total field. Select the five *times.x* entries for the **TotalTimes**; select the five *effect.x* entries for **TotalEffect**. The *effect.x* entries are shown in Figure 15-32.

4. Save and test the file.

Because the character number is restricted, you can enter only one character. Try entering a number outside the specified range. You will receive a message like the one shown in Figure 15-33.

Last item: Let's add a hidden field that is displayed based on the total values.

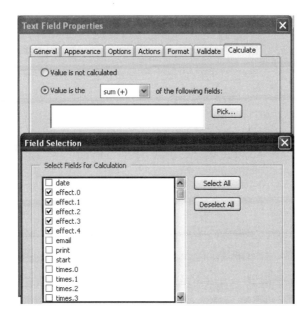

Figure 15-32
Select the fields to be added for the subtotals.

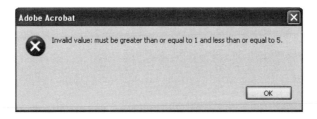

Figure 15-33
Restricting the values to a defined range produces usable results.

Gee, You Sound Upset

It's just sound business. It's one thing to get your customers thinking about your service. It's quite another to ask them how annoyed and irritated they are and then not control the responses. This is a good reason to restrict the possible entry values. If we were severely annoyed about something, even if given a choice of 1 to 5 as possible responses, we would be tempted to enter a value in the millions. This certainly would express my opinion, but wouldn't be helpful from a data-collection perspective.

To finish the project, you'll add two more button fields and two hidden fields.

Adding the Button Fields

You'll add two button fields to finish up the function of the page.

Note

If the respondent's grand total is 50, we could display a message asking the respondent to take the bus from now on. (Kidding, but tempting isn't it?)

1. Hold down Shift and highlight email and print. Ctrl+click and drag the fields to the left to add two more fields. As shown in Figure 15-34, name the fields **reset** and **finish**.

Figure 15-34
A set of four buttons is shown along with the date field. Acrobat 6.0 turns on fields by type, so the date box isn't active.

2. Label the new buttons in the Options tab:

   • Add the label **Reset** to the button field reset.

   • Add the label **Click When Finished** to the button field finish.

As shown in Figure 15-35, if you've added the fields as described in step 1, the default values are the same as the other buttons.

Figure 15-35
The set of four finished buttons use the same appearance characteristics.

The buttons still need some actions, but you'll add actions after adding the hidden fields.

Adding the Hidden Fields

The form still needs two more fields. They're both hidden and will be displayed once the user clicks the field to indicate that the responses are complete.

1. Add a text field. Again, the simplest method is to Ctrl+click and drag one of the text fields to carry over the default settings. The field, named "**total**", is a calculated text field. Locate the field as shown in Figure 15-36 (in the last row of the table).

Figure 15-36
Place the final field in the lower-right corner of the table.

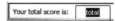

2. Set these properties for the total field:

   • In the General tab, set visibility to hidden, and select Read Only.

   • In the Format tab, select Number, and set the decimal places to 0.

   • In the Calculate tab, select the Value Is the Sum Of option. Pick the fields "**totalTimes**" and "**TotalEffect**".

3. Save the file.

Now back to the buttons to finish this up.

Finishing with Flair

You still have a pair of processes to finish. You'll want to have the totals calculated and displayed. You'll also want an option to reset the form.

1. Click on the Button icon to activate the field. Double-click the finish field to open the Field Properties dialog box. Open the Actions tab, and add this MouseUp action: Show/Hide Field: Show the Total Field.

2. Close the Field Properties dialog box.

3. Double-click the reset field to open the Field Properties dialog box. Open the Actions tab. Add these MouseUp actions:

   • Reset Form: In the Field Selection dialog box, click All, Except, click Select fields, and exclude the Date field.

   • Show/Hide Field: Hide the total field.

4. Close the Field Properties dialog box. Save the file.

Now let's see what you have. Figure 15-37 shows the form with values entered. When the Reset button is clicked, all the values are reset, except for the date. The total value field is also hidden.

Bad Math??

Always check out the calculation order of your form before you post it.

Choose Advanced ➤ Forms ➤ Set Field Calculation Order to open the Calculated Fields dialog box shown in Figure 15-38. Move the fields up and down to the correct order of calculation. If total were ahead of either of the fields in the list, the fields can't be calculated correctly.

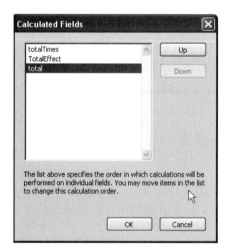

Here are the questions. Click the button indicated for a total; click Reset to start over.

Common Complaints	How Often?	How Annoying?
Drivers who stop in the middle of the lane and block traffic while waiting for a parking spot.		
Drivers who park on the lines, taking up two spots.	5	5
Drivers who park too close to adjacent cars so the other driver must grease up with Vaseline to squeeze into his or her car.	5	5
Drivers who ignore the painted lanes and drive diagonally from one end of the lot to another.		
Drivers who stop in front of a mall exit and wait for passengers to arrive, blocking traffic.		
Your total score is: 20	10	10

06-Jul-03   [Reset]   [Click When Finished]   [Print]   [Email Us]

This survey has been sent only to those registered customers who provided us with an email address. Thank you for your participation.

Figure 15-37
Once you're finished designing the form, test it using different responses.

Calculated Fields

totalTimes
TotalEffect
total

[Up]
[Down]

The list above specifies the order in which calculations will be performed on individual fields. You may move items in the list to change this calculation order.

[OK]   [Cancel]

Figure 15-38
The Calculated Fields box allows the field calculation to be moved to the correct order.

Final Words for Tweakers

There are some other things you may wish to do in this project, depending on your inclination. For example, rather than using any of the automatic scripting options within the Field Properties dialog boxes, you may wish to enter custom scripts.

You may also want to move some of the scripts from the field to the document level. For example, you may want to use messages that ask users to email Brad's if they scored over a certain amount.

Regardless, it's plain to see that there are many ways to use scripting, both within a document as well as within elements of a document. Which brings me to the last major topic of this chapter: using scripts externally to any one particular document.

External JavaScripts

You've had a good look at different types of JavaScript that can be used within a document. These types of scripts are saved with the document. You can also create and use scripts externally—that is, within Acrobat, but not restricted to any one document in particular. Once a script has been written, copy the text file into the Acrobat JavaScripts folder, or into the JavaScript folder in your system directory.

There are three types of external JavaScripts:

- Folder-level JavaScripts. These files are stored in the application and user folders. Acrobat 6.0 uses several folder-level script files, which are read and executed when you start the program. The folder-level files used to run our copy of the program are shown in Figure 15-39. You can see them on your system following this path: Program Files ➤ Adobe ➤ Acrobat 6.0 ➤ Acrobat ➤ Javascripts.

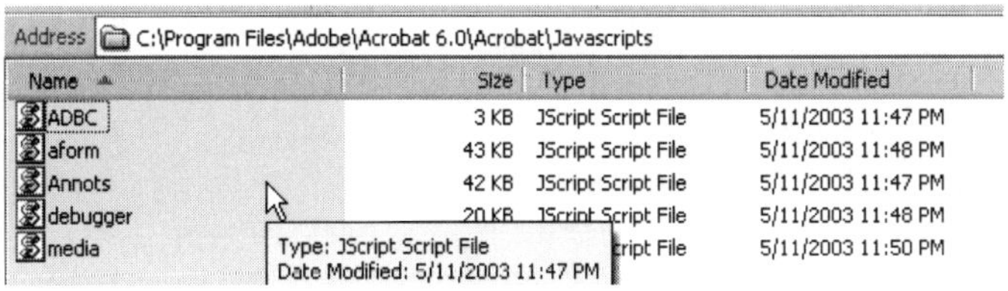

Figure 15-39
Folder-level JavaScripts are located on your hard drive in an Acrobat storage folder.

- Console JavaScripts. For the hardcore developer, enter JavaScripts into the console of the JavaScript Debugger and execute them. We've shown the scripts listed in the console in Figure 15-40. This feature is primarily used for testing and debugging large scripts in Acrobat.

- Batch JavaScripts. The batch sequence feature enables you to create scripts that can be run on any selected files.

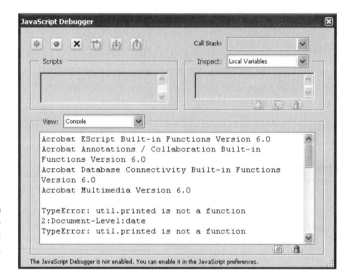

Figure 15-40
The JavaScript Debugger console displays external scripts that are applied to Acrobat PDF documents.

On that note, let's move on to batch sequences.

Creating Batch Sequences Using JavaScript

Batch scripts are a function limited to Acrobat 6.0 Professional. You can also write batch sequences for Acrobat using JavaScript. Although it's beyond the scope of this book to discuss this level of programming in detail, we want to show you some of the possibilities. Also, it helps to round out the JavaScript discussion, and it gives you something to work on when you have nothing else to do!

Basics of Batches

This process picks up where simple batch sequencing using menu items leaves off. Batch Processing is now under the Advanced menu. As before, batching can be performed on files in one of four ways, as you specify through these options:

- Selected Files

- Selected Folders

- Ask When Sequence Is Run

- Files Open in Acrobat

Note

There is a PDF file, named Batch Sequences: Tips, Tricks and Examples, on the Acrobat 5.0 Installation CD that describes batch processing and has bonus sequences. As we suggested earlier in the book, make sure you keep the bonus information from the Acrobat 5.0 disk.

Selected files are those you manually select from your hard drive or other storage area. Selected folders are also manually selected from your hard drive or storage area, and the commands will be run on all files in those folders. Logically, the next option, Ask When Sequence Is Run, prompts you for a file selection when you run the batch. Finally, you can choose to run commands against files you have open.

The drop-down list for assigning the commands is shown in Figure 15-41.

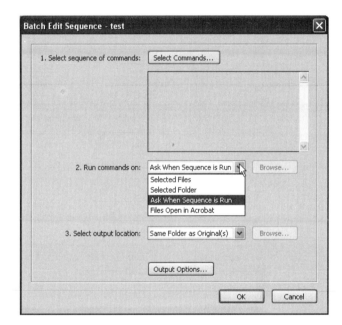

Figure 15-41
Select command options in the Batch Edit Sequence dialog box.

Using Batch File Scripts

The batching information file on the Installation CD includes a section listing problems, solutions, and some sample scripts. We've summarized what is presented in the file in Table 15-4.

Table 15.4   Common Batch File Scripts and Their Uses

Category	Problems and Comments
Bookmarks.	List All Bookmarks. Creates a PDF document that lists the bookmarks in another PDF document. The new document can be saved and printed.
Count Bookmarks.	Counts the number of bookmarks in a specified PDF document.
Gather Bookmarks to Document.	Creates a series of bookmarks in a document open in the viewer that point to selected files (not currently open).

Table 15.4   Common Batch File Scripts and Their Uses (Continued)

Category	Problems and Comments
Copy Bookmarks From Array.	Uses the collection of bookmarks as described in the Utilities section, and inserts them into selected files.
Copy Bookmarks from Document.	Takes the bookmarks from the open document and copies them to each of the selected files.
Insert Bookmarked Pages.	Merges a set of single-page PDF files into one file with bookmarks to each page.
Comments and forms: Insert Stamp.	Inserts a stamp on the first page of each file of a group of selected files.
Insert Barcode.	Inserts a barcode on the first page of each file of a group of selected files.
Cross Doc Comment Summary.	Gathers comments contained in selected files, sorts them by author, and creates a combined report.
Database: Populate and Save.	Uses SQL select criteria for a particular database to populate an open PDF form with data satisfying the criteria, and saves the form to a folder.
Icons: Import Named Icons.	Imports a series of icons into the document currently open.
Insert Navigation Icons.	Inserts a set of navigational icons on each page of each file in a selected set of files.
Pages: Extract Pages to Folders.	Extracts each page of each file from a set of selected files, and saves the extracted pages to a folder.
Security: Change Security to None.	Removes the password protection from selected files. These must be protected with the same password.
Gather DigSig Information.	Writes a report on digital signatures in selected files.
Signature Sign All.	Adds an invisible signature to each file of a group of selected files.
Spell check: Spell Check a Document.	Words that are incorrectly spelled or questionable are marked with an underline squiggle annotation. The annotation contains suggested spellings. Can be used on single or selected groups of files.
Utilities Count PDF Files.	Sets the global variable, global.FileCnt, equal to the number of selected files.
Gather Bookmarks To Array.	Creates and saves a global array of bookmark information from selected files.

Now What?

So you've seen what kinds of issues can be resolved using batch scripts, now you want to know what's next. How do you use them? Where do you put them? Ah, such intriguing questions. Read on.

As we mentioned at the beginning of this section, JavaScript can be applied to any of the sequences as you would apply prebuilt batch commands. Basically, what you're doing is substituting a custom script for any of the scripts supplied with Acrobat. We'll answer the first question in a short tutorial. As for the second question, they aren't put anywhere, as such. They become part of a stored batch sequence, unlike large external JavaScript files that are stored on the hard drive in the folder Acrobat 5 ➤ Acrobat ➤ JavaScripts.

Now back to the first question: how to use a custom batch script.

Tutorial: Creating and Running a Custom Batch Script

For this tutorial, you'll use the 1999 Minutes captured and bookmarked.pdf. document. The file is in the Chapter 4 projects folder. The document is a big file with a lot of bookmarks. Rather than counting the list of bookmarks, you're going to run a little script that will do the counting.

Let's See That Script

The script is shown in its entirety in Listing 15-4.

Listing 15-4. The Count Bookmarks Script

```
/* Count Bookmarks */
/* Recursively work through bookmark tree */
function CountBookmarks(bm, nLevel)
{
if (nLevel != 0)
counter++; // don't count the root
if (bm.children != null)
for (var i = 0; i < bm.children.length; i++)
CountBookmarks(bm.children[i], nLevel + 1);
}
var counter = 0;
CountBookmarks(this.bookmarkRoot, 0);
console.show();
console.println("\nFile: " + this.path);
console.println("The number of bookmarks: " + counter);
```

This script, from top to bottom:

- Names the script.

- Defines the function.

- Not including the root, assesses each bookmark and incrementally adds a number to the counter for each bookmark encountered. In a batch event, this object is the current document being processed by the batch engine.

- Displays the script console and prints two lines: first the path for the file, and then the number of bookmarks.

To complete this process you'll have to create the batch process and then save and run the command.

Creating the Batch Process

You may wish to copy the script from the Batch Script file on the installation CD and paste it into the sequence as you develop it. For your convenience, we've provided a copy in the Chapter 15 folder in a text file named scripts.txt. The script you need is named "COUNT BOOKMARKS SCRIPT," and is the last script in the file.

Batch processes follow similar steps. To create this batch process:

1. Open the batch.txt file in a text editor and copy it. Close the file and the application. Open Acrobat.

2. Create a new batch sequence. Select Advanced ➤ Batch Processing. When the Batch Sequences dialog box opens, click New Sequence and enter a name for the custom sequence. We named ours "count bookmarks." Click OK. This will close the Batch Sequences box, and return you to the Batch Sequences dialog box.

3. As shown in Figure 15-42, the new batch sequence should be selected. Click Edit Sequence.

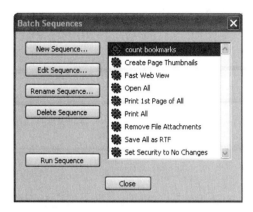

Figure 15-42
The new batch sequence now appears in the listing.

4. The Batch Edit Sequence - Count Bookmarks dialog box will open. There are three steps to complete in order to run our script:

   • Select the commands.

   • Select the files against which to run the commands.

   • Select the output location.

5. Click Select Commands. The Edit Sequence dialog box shown in Figure 15-43 opens. This is where we insert the custom script. Scroll down the list to the Execute JavaScript option. Click Add to move it to the command section.

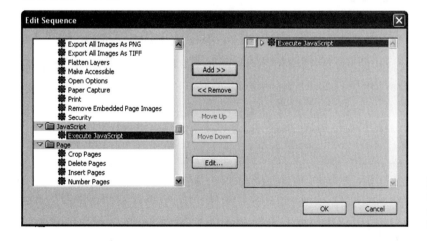

Figure 15-43
Use the Edit Sequence dialog box to select commands for the script.

6. Add the Execute JavaScript command. Click Edit to open the JavaScript Editor dialog box shown in Figure 15-44. Paste the copied script into the script window. Click OK.

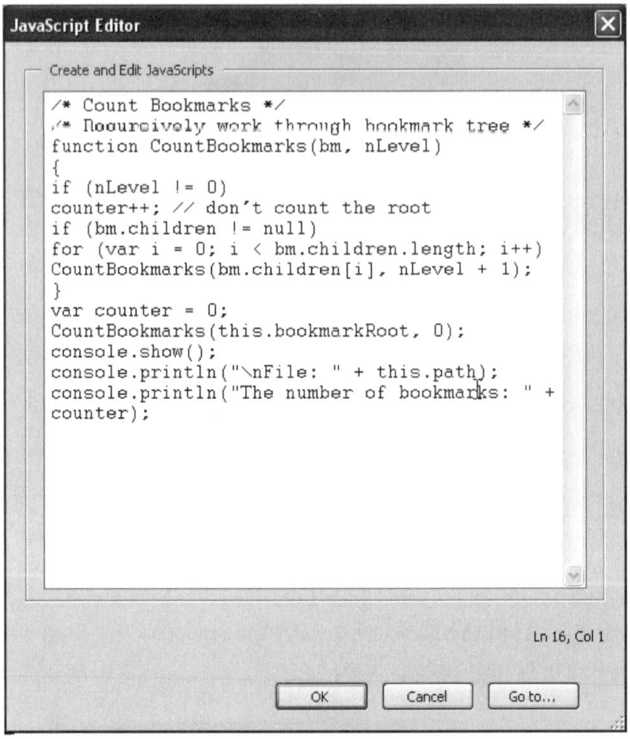

```
JavaScript Editor                                    [X]

  ┌─ Create and Edit JavaScripts ──────────────────────
  │  /* Count Bookmarks */
  │  /* Recursively work through bookmark tree */
  │  function CountBookmarks(bm, nLevel)
  │  {
  │  if (nLevel != 0)
  │  counter++; // don't count the root
  │  if (bm.children != null)
  │  for (var i = 0; i < bm.children.length; i++)
  │  CountBookmarks(bm.children[i], nLevel + 1);
  │  }
  │  var counter = 0;
  │  CountBookmarks(this.bookmarkRoot, 0);
  │  console.show();
  │  console.println("\nFile: " + this.path);
  │  console.println("The number of bookmarks: " +
  │  counter);
  │
  │
  │                                          Ln 16, Col 1

        [ OK ]    [ Cancel ]    [ Go to... ]
```

Figure 15-44
Paste the custom script into the JavaScript Editor script window.

7. Click OK to close the Edit Sequence dialog box and return to the Batch Edit Sequence - Count Bookmarks dialog box.

Now let's set up the files and storage locations.

Finishing the Setup

This is an interesting script. Depending on what type of work you're doing, you have several options. Some scripts will only run on selected files. This script, however, is generic enough that it can run on any option.

At this point, the Batch Edit Sequence - Count Bookmarks dialog box should be displayed. Continuing from the previous section, finish selecting the batch sequence options:

Tip

Is It Worthwhile to Set Up Batch Scripts for Something So Simple?

Depends. If this is something you'll encounter on a regular basis, of course it's worth the 15 or 20 minutes it will take to set up a sequence. On the other hand, there is no point if it's something that will happen once a year on one file.

1. Open the Run Commands On drop-down list, and select Ask When Sequence Is Run. This is the most generic option and will allow you to run this script against anything.

2. Leave the default output location, which is to store output in the same folder as the originals. The final selections for this script are shown in Figure 15-45. As you can see in the image, we've clicked the drop-down arrow to the left of the command line to display the script's name.

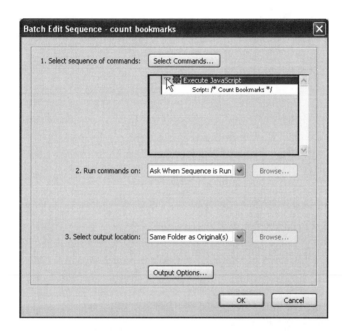

Figure 15-45
The final selections for the batch sequence are listed in the Batch Edit Sequence - Count Bookmarks dialog box.

3. Click OK to close the dialog box and return to the Batch Sequences window.

Now for some action.

Running the Script

Finally, let's do some counting. The Batch Sequences - Count Bookmarks dialog box should be open, as shown in Figure 15-42. Click Run Sequence. The Run Sequence Confirmation - Count Bookmarks dialog box shown in Figure 15-46 is displayed, so you can confirm the batch you wish to run. Click OK.

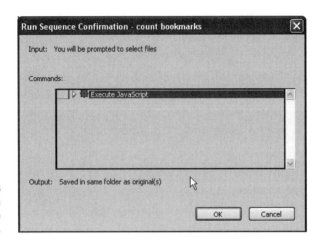

Figure 15-46
Confirm the batch
sequence to execute
before running it.

1. An Explorer window will open for you to select the file to process. Browse to the location of the file you wish to count (we've used the 1999 Minutes captured and bookmarked.pdf file from the Chapter 4 projects folder). Click OK to select the file.

2. The script editing window will open before the file is processed. Click OK to accept the script to be run.

3. When the sequence is complete, the JavaScript Debugger will open and display the information requested by the script, as shown in Figure 15-47. When you have duly noted the number of bookmarks, click Close to dismiss the window.

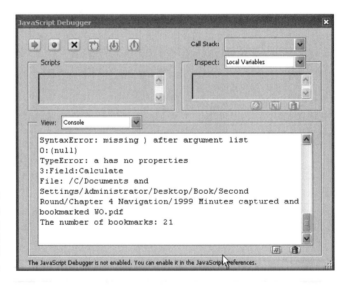

Figure 15-47
The output from the
counting script run
against the 1999
Minutes captured and
bookmarked.pdf file.

This brings the discussion of external JavaScript, and this chapter, to an end.

Up Next

From the JavaScript perspective, there are so many things that we merely touched on or didn't even cover. For example, did you know you can add new menu items to the program using JavaScript? You can. As we've mentioned in this chapter, please spend some time in the Acrobat JavaScript Object Specification.

The next chapter is going to apply some of what you have seen in this chapter to the knowledgebase.

Chapter 16

Putting It All Together

Acrobat is a powerful tool. We have proved that throughout the book. Now, you're going to apply it to some of the subjects.

A Knowledgebase

A knowledgebase is an organized collection of information on a subject. Depending on the subject, a knowledgebase can get really large. Let's say you're working for a city of 70,000. What information is required to run a city? How about its charter, code, and regulations? And don't forget personnel regulations, time sheets, expense reports, and insurance forms. Don't forget the whole lot of property the city owns such as roads, buildings, and utilities. Oh, and who could forget the budgets and audits?

This kind of involved project requires a specific approach. Like other things in life, complex projects and issues are just a bunch of smaller projects and issues. (We usually tell ourselves that when embarking on a large task.) Knowledgebases are truly a lot of small projects that can be managed and distributed among numerous people. Let us show you how to do it.

What You're Going to Do

In this chapter, we'll take you on a step-by-step journey through a mega project. (Tom has an industrial client whose knowledgebase is 30 GB and growing.) First, we'll give you the scenario we're working with, both as the client and as the information developer, consultant, and designer (pick a label.) We've also developed an outline for defining the scope and parameters of this kind of work.

Then, we'll look at the specific elements involved. Basically, the process breaks down into a series of steps:

1. Plan the work to be done.

2. Define the outputs and workflow required.

3. Analyze the available materials for input and define the conversion workflow.

4. Develop conversion processes.

5. Consider collaboration processes and requirements.

6. Build the final assembly.

7. Make distribution decisions.

Before you get into the projects, let's identify the mythical participants in this process: the consultant (you) and the client.

Tip

When undertaking a large-scale project, be like Donna—NOT like Tom. Tom plans everything in his head. It works, but drives everyone else he works with crazy, as they are left out in the dark. Donna develops a plan and gets buy-in and stepwise approval. Tom's is often faster, but Donna's is cleaner.

Project 16-1: Develop the Framework for a Sustainable Knowledgebase

Regardless of the scenario, you are the key to solving issues. Your expertise, objectivity, and skill are what will make something like this work. It takes a plan. Let's start there.

The Story

Etobe City has a problem with information management. Your reputation for helping organize and eliminate paper precedes you. You met with the city management team to develop a plan.

The Planning Process

It's hard to work on a project of any size without a focus. The contents and scope of a plan are of course dependent on the plan itself. Here is the plan used as a guide for the development of this chapter's projects.

Objectives

Objectives define what you'll do. Your objective is to facilitate techno-logical advances in communication within the city, by designing a knowledgebase and supporting materials for different processes as well as instructional materials. You're bound by time and design constraints.

Workflow and Responsibilities

This section defines what has to be done in addition to the design and construction. Responsibilities include information gathering, information design, demos, and consultation with the city's key personnel. Workflow includes the sign-off processes (editing, collaboration, and approval).

Inputs

Inputs tell us what is available. Frankly, we have warehouses full of available information. Etobe City prints tons of materials and spends an incalculable amount of time keeping up with printed information. Every week the city clerk spends hours searching for precedents before each council meeting. The permits process has used paper forms for years and local contractors are tired of spending so much time in line waiting on permits.

Outputs

Outputs represent the deliverables. In this project, there are several different ones, specifically the following:

- Scanned, captured, and cataloged minutes
- New interactive PDF travel form
- Electronic plan review
- Electronic permit system
- Geographic Information System information
- Structure and navigation of knowledgebase, including file structure

So, it's time for the next step.

Tutorial: Information Flow Design

This section is a show and tell. In addition to completing a plan, which is the first step of any project process, it's equally important to understand how information is flowing through a system.

A visual representation of what you understand the situation to be and the changes you're planning—similar to a storyboard—is a very useful tool. To start with, let's establish the current information flow for the two main structures we'll be building.

The Current Situation

Except for word processing for document creation nothing can be classified as streamlined. Everything is being managed the way small cities have managed it for years. Let's look at the city's current information processing structure using a series of information flows.

Minutes

Minutes record the business of the city. First, let's consider the situation as it currently exists. In Figure 16-1, the current status of the minutes searching process is outlined.

Note

There are other elements we haven't included in the project plan because they're beyond the scope of this chapter. Training issues, user guides, and schedules aren't included. Nor have we covered hardware and software purchases and implementations, which we would do in a commercial project.

Historical Minutes Search

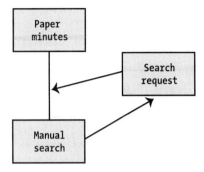

Figure 16-1
You can see the current status of the minutes searching process. The current process involves multiple people and considerable time.

Currently, minutes are legally required to be maintained by all government offices. They're generally maintained on double-sided legal-sized documents in removable binders. Many government offices don't have duplicate copies and problems have been created when fire destroyed the only copies of certain documents. Also, lawyers and others from outside the office often look through the minutes, and they're often not that careful: pages get out of order, notes are made on the pages, and coffee stains mysteriously appear.

The process of searching minutes is labor intensive, time intensive, and inefficient. A commissioner, the mayor, or city manager comes in and asks the clerk, "What have we done about <topic> in the past?" The clerk drops everything and spends several hours searching.

- *Inputs.* Minutes are requested in writing, by telephone, fax, or verbally. The clerk processes the request. For official requests, the clerk must also add customer information and their own identification information.

- *Processing.* The completed request is processed according to city protocol. The clerk may do the searching; alternatively, a records clerk may receive the request and process it in their own internal record-keeping system. Based on the workflow, the clerk may have to transfer the information to several separate documents.

- *Outputs.* The copies of minutes are sent to the requester as faxed or paper copies; receipts may be required from couriers, the requester, and entries made in the processing clerk's record-keeping system.

Time and Travel Expense Form

Employees work using different compensation methods. Many use time and travel expenses. The expense-claim process can be convoluted. We have it mapped out in Figure 16-2. Let's go through it.

Travel/Time Data

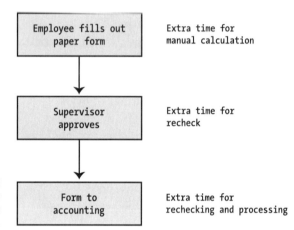

Employee fills out paper form	Extra time for manual calculation
Supervisor approves	Extra time for recheck
Form to accounting	Extra time for rechecking and processing

Figure 16-2
The current expense form process requires numerous steps.

Again, we're looking at significant inefficiencies:

- *Input.* The staff person must manually complete an expense form with employee information, collect receipts, and manually enter the information on the expense form.

- *Processing.* Once completed, the form and receipts are mailed or routed to the appropriate supervisor. The supervisor often time-checks some of the math and determines if the form meets travel procedures. The approved travel is sent to accounting or if it isn't approved, it's returned to the employee for correction. In accounting, the clerk rechecks the math and manually enters the information in the database to create the check.

- *Output.* Check for employee reimbursement and entries into journals.

Plan Review

Tom has extensive experience with plan review. Before the owner and trades can apply for the permits to build a project, the owner (usually the engineer or architect for the owner) submits plans and specifications. The paper plan review process is cumbersome and expensive.

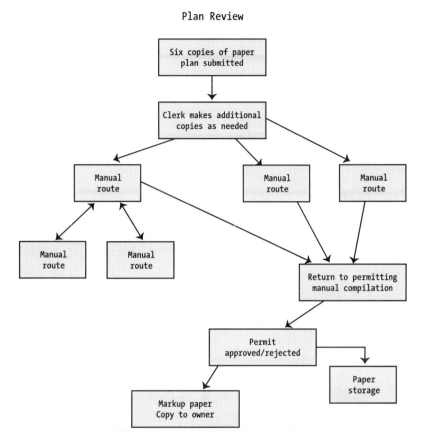

Plan Review

Figure 16-3
The paper plan review process is cumbersome and expensive.

- *Input.* A city often requires six sets of plans, and the city may make more depending on all the necessary reviews. One set of plans and specs can easily cost $100 to produce.

- *Processing.* The clerk manually distributes the plans and specs to all the reviewers, tracks the reviews, and manually brings the comments together for the head of permitting to review. The manager approves or rejects the plans.

- *Output.* A paper copy is returned to the owner and a paper copy is stored for 50 years or until the project is eventually demolished.

Building Permitting

We discussed permitting as part of the intro to Chapter 8. Tradespeople spend a tremendous amount of time going to town and pulling permits. Cities spend a great amount of time and money tracking and storing these permits.

Building Permits

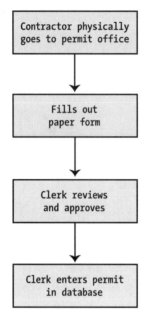

Figure 16-4
A contractor often physically travels to the office to apply for a permit.

- *Inputs.* The contractor physically drives to the permit office and fills out a paper form. The clerk processes the request. For official requests, the clerk must also add customer information and their own identification information.

- *Processing.* The completed request is processed according to city standards. The clerk may or may not be able to grant approval, in which case a supervisory signature is required, entailing an additional waiting time and input. Fees for the permit are also processed.

- *Outputs.* The clerk enters the permit information into the city's database transcribing the paper application. The contractor receives a written receipt and a copy of the permit. Fees collected are sent to accounting for processing.

Geographic Information

Many cities also provide sewer, water, electricity, gas, and other utilities. The information on these utilities is usually in CAD or GIS formats. A city might have a different system for each utility. It's difficult and often expensive to retrieve and share this information.

Why Use a PDF-Based Workflow Instead of an HTML-Based Workflow?

Because that's the subject of another book! Seriously, though, there are significant advantages to using PDF instead of HTML. Once the forms are redesigned, they can be used either online or offline. Many forms are in a legally required format. Acrobat forms are WYSIWYG. The forms look the same printed as they do online.

Forms are easier to update in PDF than in HTML, and the form data format (FDF) data source can easily be updated as well. As you saw in Chapter 15, the JavaScript used in Acrobat forms is different from that which is used in HTML forms, which is an added security feature. Finally, because the forms use JavaScript scripting, server-side scripts can still be used.

Constructing New and Improved Information Workflows

Now let's see what happens when Acrobat is introduced into the mix. First, let's look at the knowledgebase structure. We will improve these processes and add the pieces into the knowledgebase throughout the chapter.

Minutes

You've worked with the minutes in several chapters. Figure 16-5 shows the revamped information flow plan for our city's minutes retrieval process. As you can see, there are a number of differences.

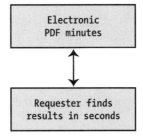

Knowledgebase Minutes

Electronic
PDF minutes

Requester finds
results in seconds

Figure 16-5
The search for minutes is streamlined using a knowledgebase approach.

The most noticeable change is that the hierarchy is flattened. There is no "middleman" in this process, and no processing of any kind. The person needing the information simply clicks on the knowledgebase icon on their desktop, clicks on icons and performs a search of their own. Instead of waiting for a clerk to have time to search, and the time to perform the manual search, it's done in seconds.

Now, let's have a look at the modified time and travel expense-claim process.

Time and Travel Expense

Figure 16-6 shows the modified employee expense process. Again, you can see that the process is simplified considerably. There is less room for error in the programmed form and the supervisor and accounting staff spends less time checking.

A properly designed form will automatically load the database, saving time and errors from manual entry. Another benefit of having the forms on the knowledgebase is that the current form is always available and there is less chance of using an old form.

Travel/Time Data

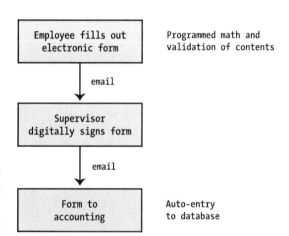

Figure 16-6
Travel and time expense submissions are greatly streamlined using automatic forms.

Using Personal Field Naming

Implementing Personal Field Naming (PFN) for all forms in the system can also save the employees time because fields like name, address, and social-security number can autofill. Adobe had PFN samples and examples on the Acrobat 5.0 CD. There is no mention of PFN in Acrobat 6.0, but it's easy to implement. You simply develop a template with standardized form names and insert a button on the PFN form to export the data to a file. The employee forms have identical fields that populate by pushing a button that imports the data.

Plan Review

An electronic workflow for plan reviewing requires only one copy of the form, and it must be in ePaper format. Figure 16-7 shows electronic submission and Review Tracking using Acrobat 6.0.

Note

An important tool in this process is a scanner. Considering the current inexpensive prices for scanners, it isn't an unreasonable expense, even for hundreds of employees. It will eventually pay off by increased productivity.

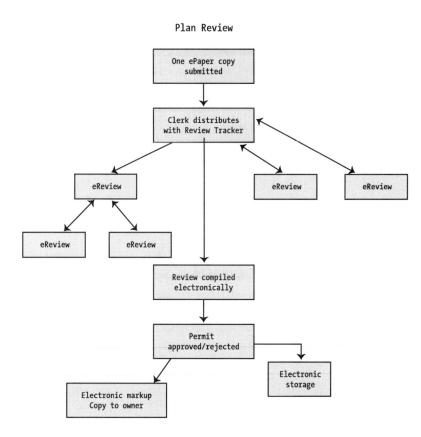

Figure 16-7
Using an electronic review of plans and specs saves time and money.

The submitter emails in one combined set of plans and specs in PDF format, saving up to $600 in printing costs. The clerk initiates a Review Tracking process either over the network or via email, saving time as well as additional printing and distribution costs. The Review Tracker tracks the status of each project as well as the reviewer's input. Instead of manually having to combine the comments, they're automatically entered and sorted.

Note

Cities are being buried in paper storage. An electronic file can be certified and stored. Hundreds of electronic plans and specs can be stored in the same area as one paper set.

Building Permitting

Acrobat forms and Acrobat Approval allow the permit forms to be on the Web, and the contractors can fill out the permit application directly.

The calculations are included in the process. Most importantly, they can email the application rather than going to the office and pulling the permit; the clerk can email the completed permit back. Figure 16-8 outlines the electronic process.

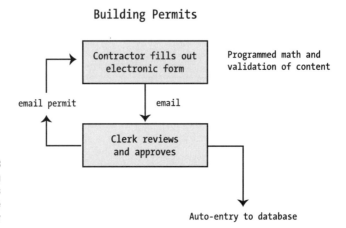

Figure 16-8
An electronic building permit system shortens the processing time dramatically

Tackling the Project Construction

The actual work schedule you decide on is based as much on how you like to work as it is on the approval processes themselves. Incorporate how you work from the initial planning stage. You'll likely have to coordinate your preferences with information gathering, information design, mockups, and approval processes.

The Project Team

Tip

Remember You Are the Consultant

You must be at your diplomatic best to work within a system. If the people on the team buy in to the project it will be a major success. If they balk at the project, your career as a consultant may be short.

In working with your customer you need to develop a project team. In Etobe City you will have an employee from the city clerk's office to handle the minutes. There will be someone from the building inspector's office for plan review and permitting and someone from accounting for the travel form.

A very important person will be the IT member of the team. Without their help with information processes such as drives, folders, and access rights on the networks, you're dead in the water.

Design the Information Content

We know the five areas we're going to work on. We know the players and the desired outputs. We can't stress organization enough. You have to consider many things when building something complex. Only organization makes the project work. After all, your project outputs can be stunning visually, but if they don't work...

We're going to use the format that Tom has used with some of his clients. This by no means is the only way. In fact, it may not even be the best way. It works, but you may come up with something better.

The goal of the project is to have most of the information available through point and click from the desktop. Figure 16-9 illustrates the planned knowledgebase layout. The key, describing read, write, and delete, refers to the rights granted to different groups of users as they interact with the knowledgebase and its forms.

Note

In a large project, you may want to use an alternate route. A large project is one in which you're building an information base from tens of thousands of documents, and as a result, it's possible that hundreds of employees and customers will use the information.

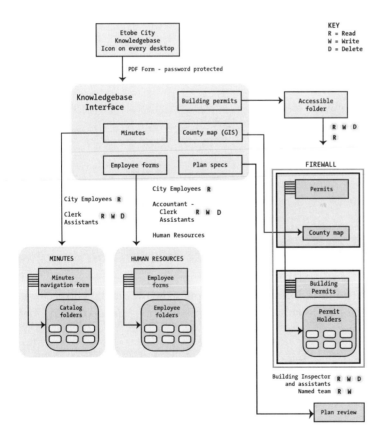

Figure 16-9
The planned knowledgebase describes components as well as rights granted to different employees.

Each employee will have an Etobe City knowledgebase icon on their desktop. The icon links to the Interface page (coming up in the next project.) From here the employee clicks the area they want to visit. They don't realize that they're changing drives and folders.

Here is a summary of the strategy:

- The Interface page is on a common drive that all employees can access.

- The minutes are in a folder for which all employees have read rights. The city clerk and administrative assistant have read, write, and delete rights.

- The travel form is in the Human Resources folder. There is a Human Resources page linked by bookmarks. Only accounting (included in HR), the city clerk, and the administrative assistant have read, write, and delete rights. All employees have read rights.

- Plan review has a folder with a set list of users. The assistant and manager of permitting will have read, write, and delete privileges. The listed users will have read and write privileges. The documents use Acrobat's Review Tracking. The complete documents will be cataloged and stored in this file.

- Building permits is on a folder outside the firewall. Only IT has any rights to this folder. There are no links back inside the firewall due to security. The public will access this folder from the city web site.

- The county map is also outside the firewall for the public to access from the city web site.

Documents for the Projects

Note
You can preview the finished knowledgebase. Download ActiveKB.zip from the Chapter 16 folder. This has the files set up in a demo mode without any security settings.

Although the projects for this chapter are representative of a large knowledgebase, they still include a fair number of files. The files are enclosed in a Zip file, and include a set of four subfolders as well as three other PDF files and one plug-in (the LGIView Zoom-to-Search plug-in.) The files are structured as shown in Table 16-1. Download the files to your hard drive before starting the construction projects.

Table 16-1   Files and Folders Provided for the Knowledgebase Project

Folder	Subfolder	File Name
Human Resources	nil	Human Resources.pdf
	nil	Travel Master.pdf
Minutes	1999	Contains 21PDF documents
	Dayton School Minutes	index1.idx
	Dayton School Minutes	index.idx
	nil	Dayton School Minutes.log
	nil	Dayton School Minutes.pdx
	nil	minutes1.pdf
Permit Forms	nil	Building.pdf
	nil	city permits1.pdf
Plan Review	nil	Etobe City Plan Review.pdf
	nil	Grading Plan. pdf
	nil	interface.pdf
	nil	mcminn.pdf
	nil	You Leaving Network.pdf
	nil	LGIView_Zoom-to-Search.api

Project **Project 16-2: Connecting the Minutes to the Knowledgebase**

Use the interface.pdf file in the Chapter 16 folder, as shown in Figure 16-10. We are going to link the minutes to the interface. You also need the minutes1.pdf file in the Minutes folder.

1. Choose Tools ➤ Advanced Editing ➤ Link Tool.

2. Draw a link box around **Minutes**. When the Link dialog box opens, select Custom. The Link Properties dialog box open. Choose these settings:

   • Under Appearance select Invisible.

   • Under Action select Go to a Page in Another Document. Select Add to and browse to minutes1.pdf in the minutes folder. Select First Page and OK. This sets the link.

Note

You can review linking in Chapter 8.

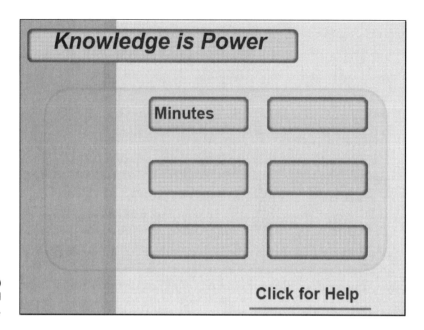

Figure 16-10
Link the minutes to a label
on the interface page.

3. Now go to the minutes1.pdf page. From the Minutes page, create a link to return to the Interface page. Draw the link around ".back" at the bottom of the Minutes page, shown in Figure 16-11. Use the same settings as in step 2 and set the Interface page as the linked page.

Council/Commission Minutes

1970	1980	1990	2000
1971	1981	1991	2001
1972	1982	1992	2002
1973	1983	1993	2003
1974	1984	1994	2004
1975	1985	1995	2005
1976	1986	1996	2006
1977	1987	1997	2007
1978	1988	1998	2008
1979	1989	1999	2009

... help   ... back

Figure 16-11
Link from the year on the
Minutes Interface to
minutes' document.

4. The next link is from the minutes.1 pdf page to the January 5, 1999 minutes file. Draw the link box around "1999" on the minutes1.pdf page and use the JANUARY 5,1999.PDF document (in the 1999 subfolder within the Minutes folder) as the linked document. Use the same settings as in Step 2.

In the JANUARY 5,1999.PDF document, the bookmark back to the navigation system is already in place, as you can see in Figure 16-12.

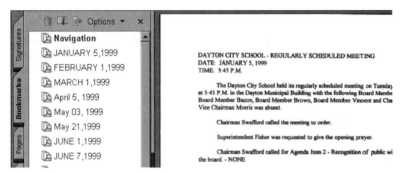

Figure 16-12
The navigation pane back to the minutes interface is already in place.

Test the links. Click Minutes on the Interface page, go to the Minutes Interface page, click 1999 to open the minutes for the first meeting of the year, January 5,1999. Then click Navigation in the bookmarks list to return to the minutes interface, and finally click back to return to the interface.

Project **Project 16-3: Adding a Search Function**

You're going to set an index to attach when the minutes interface opens. You're also going to program the search to open with the minutes attached and ready for searching. You work with the minutes1.pdf document, the minutes interface page.

1. Choose File ➤ Document Properties ➤ Advanced. Click Browse to open an Explorer window. Select the Dayton School Minutes.pdx document in the Minutes folder. Click OK to load the index in the Document Properties dialog box, as shown in Figure 16-13. Click OK to close the Document Properties dialog box.

Note

In Chapter 9, you made a link from the navigation pane to the interface, then split the 1999. pdf file. Once you found out that the links in the split files worked, you deleted the unsplit file. Well, Tom didn't plan ahead. The link should have been to the minutes1.pdf. As a result, there is a new catalog in the Minutes folder.

Figure 16-13
Attach the index
created for the minutes
to use automatically
for searching.

Note

Depending on your
system, you may or may
not be able to use the
supplied index file. If you
receive error messages,
create the index yourself.

2. Open the Pages tab. Right-click the minutes1.pdf page thumbnail and choose Page Properties from the shortcut menu. The Page Properties dialog box opens.

3. Click the Action tab. Select Execute a Menu Item from the Actions drop-down list. Click Add as shown in Figure 16-14.

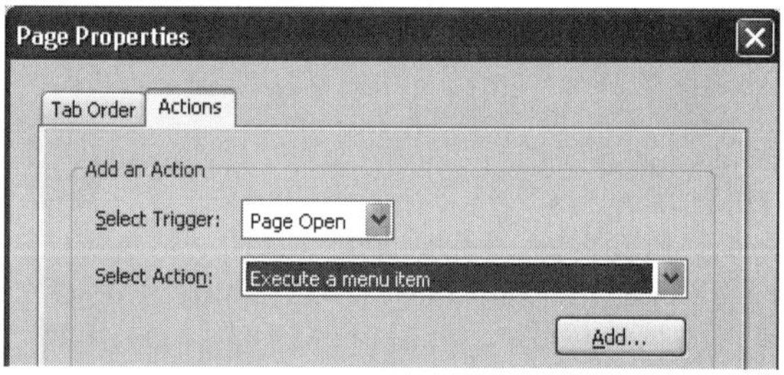

Figure 16-14
Add an action to the page
to load a command when
the page opens.

4. From the Menu Item dialog box, click Edit, and select Search as shown in Figure 16-15.

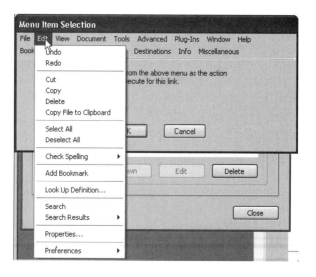

Figure 16-15
Select the Search
menu item to attach it
automatically to the page.

5. Click OK to close the Menu Item Selection dialog box, and then click Close to close the Page Properties dialog box.

6. Save and close the document.

Open the interface and click the Minutes link. The Minutes Interface page opens and the Search panel also opens. The index is displayed as shown in Figure 16-16. Setting the index to auto open simplifies the process for the user.

Note

Track the minutes through the book—we scanned and captured them in Chapter 3; linked and bookmarked them in Chapter 4; and cataloged them in Chapter 9.

Figure 16-16
Associate an index using a page action to make the searching process automatic for users.

Potential Document Issues in this Type of Project

Initially, the city wants to go back 30 years. There is even talk of going back to the beginning, which would be an onerous task. These minutes are in oversized bound books with very neat handwriting. You'll have to shoot them with a good digital camera. Right now you won't be able to perform Optical Character Recognition (OCR) on them, but maybe in five years. You do have a problem. They used a dot matrix printer for a year and a half and from experience you know that you won't be able to capture these documents.

Project Project 16-4: Using the Travel Reimbursement Form

Earlier, we wrote a long chapter on Forms. We aren't going to make you create a new form in this chapter. In the Human Resources folder, we've attached a rather good travel form. You're going to attach it to the knowledgebase. You're going to make buttons to the Human Resources page to connect it to the interface. Human Resources made their own design, which always happens when you don't have tight control on a project.

Tip

Pretty vs. Simple

Since an engineer and a graphics designer are writing this book, the question has surfaced more than once about pretty vs. simple. Tom just has to put his two cents in. The interface pages are pretty—no doubt about it. But how are we going to make the fancy numbers when we add minutes? Tom makes a table in PowerPoint with black numbers in the boxes. After converting to PDF, he uses the Text TouchUp tool and makes them blue as that year is added. It isn't as pretty, but it works.

1. Open the Interface page (interface.pdf).

2. Click on the Button Forms tool and draw a box in the box under minutes. In the Button Properties dialog box, use these settings:

   • Leave the default settings on the General tab.

   • On the Appearance tab, set No Fill and No Color; Text blue Font Arial, bold 8pt.

   • On the Options tab, choose Label Only, and type **Employee** for the label.

   • On the Action tab, choose Go to a Page in Another Document. Select the Human Resource.pdf document in the Human Resource folder.

3. Click OK to close the dialog box and set the button.

4. Test the interface again using the Human Resources documents. The Travel Master.pdf form is accessible through the Travel Form link as shown in Figure 16-17.

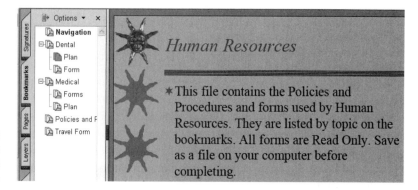

Figure 16-17
Link to the travel form from the Human Resources interface.

Future Developments with the Travel Form

The travel form contains calculations math in the form. When the employee completes and signs the form, the form fields become read-only. The employee will email them to her supervisor who approves them and then forwards them to accounts payable. The ultimate plan would have the form load the accounts payable database.

Other Components: Plan Review, Permits, and Maps

Note

Human Resources already has bookmarks made for its different topics. Click the travel form link shown in Figure 16-17 to see the completed Travel Master document.

The remaining elements for the knowledgebase are available in the Chapter 16 folder.

Plan Review

In Figure 16-7 you saw the new flow for plan review. Instead of all the paper copies, one electronic copy is submitted, it's loaded on the network, and then it's linked to a bookmark on the Plan Review page. The assistant initiates a plan review with the Review Tracker like you did in Chapter 6. Once the plan is reviewed and approved, the bookmark is moved to the Permits Storage listings.

By using the Review Tracker and ePlans, plans get posted at least one day sooner, thus consolidating the comments is instantaneous and tracking down the tardy is super simple.

Once construction is complete, the files are moved to the Permit Storage folder and the document metadata is filled in like we've discussed so many times. With the Catalog and Search functions, the files can be retrieved in seconds.

Note

We've put the rest of the links in and are going to explain what happens next. We have the knowledgebase in a folder named ActiveKB.zip in the Chapter 16 folder. Unzip the knowledgebase file and make a link from your desktop to interface.pdf in the unzipped folder. Figure 16-20 is the completed interface.

Permit Forms

We've spent a lot of time discussing the amount of time it takes to fill out building permits. We've put the building permits outside the firewall and made them available for the public. Figure 16-18 shows the Permits page, city permits1.pdf, and the bookmarks to the permits. Users can fill the forms out as shown in the instructions. We could even go back into Chapter 15 to get the JavaScript to create a button to automatically open and address the email. The city is looking at setting up a digital signature handler, but it isn't there yet.

Once the permits are returned, the metadata fields are set, and the files are stored in the Permit Storage folder. Again, with the Catalog and Search functions the files can be retrieved in seconds.

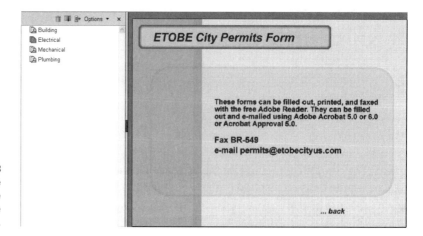

Figure 16-18
The user exits the knowledgebase to use the permits form in the publicly accessible files.

County Map

Note

There is a Zoom-to-Search plug-in for you to place in Acrobat. Install the file to this location: C:/programs/adobe/acrobat6/acrobat/plug-ins.

An interactive map of the county is in the knowledgebase named mcminn.pdf. Use the plug-in in the Chapter 16 folder to work with the map.

You can search the drawing once the plug-in is installed. Test the search. Type **Tom** in the Search field on the Search panel. As shown in Figure 16-19, there are three roads in the county that have Tom in their name.

Figure 16-19
With the Zoom-to-Search plug-in you can find text on maps.

Layton Graphics

The technology for Geographic Information Systems (GIS) in PDF is being developed by Layton Graphics of Marietta, Georgia. This map is 76" × 67" and is completely searchable. Layton has developed the technology to convert AutoCAD and MicroStation drawings to PDF as well as embed latitude and longitudes. They also are converting Environmental Systems Research Institute (ESRI) information to PDF. Governments and utilities use this information to publish engineering information in an electronic format that is inexpensive and easy to use.

A field technician with a laptop can search thousands of drawing in seconds to find a piece of equipment, an intersection, or other information. Database information is embedded in the PDF. By clicking on a power pole, all the equipment on the pole is shown as well as other utilities on the pole and the customers affected by an outage at that pole. As an engineer this technology is very exciting.

The Big Question

Have we achieved the aims of this exercise? We think so. We didn't spend much time discussing collaborative processes as the knowledgebase was being developed. Rather, we concentrated on how to build the materials with the minimum amount of effort and the maximum amount of usability. While we covered them in the introductory tutorials in this chapter, we didn't think it would be a useful exercise to go through adding comments and markups; that has been covered in several chapters and projects. The completed interface for the project is shown in Figure 16-20. You can see the links correspond to the areas identified in the flowchart shown in Figure 16-9.

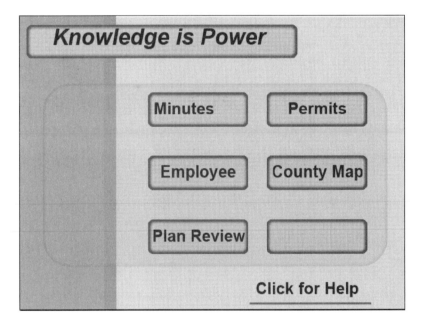

Figure 16-20
The completed interface shows the links to different elements that correspond with areas described in the project's flowchart.

What about security issues? We haven't locked any of the files used in this chapter. You should include appropriate restrictions on access to both the forms and the content of the knowledgebase files.

Happy Trails to You, Until We Meet Again!

At this point we've basically covered Acrobat from front to back. For many of you, we've covered more than enough material to make a difference in your workday. This, of course, is one of our primary goals. By including this comprehensive project chapter, we hope we've also shown you how to use the power of the program in a number of ways.

We aren't through. Check the Apress web site for our book or our web sites for new information as we find it. Cheers!

Donna and Tom

Appendix A

References and Further Information

This appendix contains a list of URLs referenced in this book as well as other sources of information you may find useful in your work.

Here are some sites that will give you more information on specific areas of this book's content.

Adobe Sites

You may access these areas directly, or from the main Adobe Acrobat site:

- Downloads for Windows and Macintosh:
  www.adobe.com/support/downloads/main.html

- User to User Forum/Macintosh:
  www.adobeforums.com/cgi-bin/webx?14@@.ee6b2ed

- User to User Forum/Windows:
  www.adobeforums.com/cgi-bin/webx?14@@.ee6b2f2

- Adobe Acrobat Expert Center:
  studio.adobe.com/expertcenter/acrobat/main.html

- Acrobat Support Knowledgebase:
  www.adobe.com/support/products/acrobat.html

- Adobe Acrobat Certification Exam Information (Adobe Certified Expert Program): partners.adobe.com/asn/training/acehowto.html

Information Sites

Here are some popular PDF sites:

- Planet PDF: www.planetpdf.com. This site has lots of information on PDF issues, uses, and third-party extensions.

- Seybold Reports: www.seyboldreports.com. Seybold concentrates on media publishing technologies, including PDF, and hosts the Seybold Seminars conferences, which include PDF conference days.

- Creativepro.com: www.creativepro.com. This site offers articles, issues, and reviews for designers.

- Publish.net: www.publish.net. A network site to all manner of things graphic: news, information, tips, and third-party extensions.

- PDFzone: www.pdfzone.com. This is the PDF site of Publish.net.

- Time Magazine Publishing: www.direct2.time.com. This is a great resource for high-end printing.

- CrossMedia magazine: www.crossmediamag.com. Neat magazine dedicated to CrossMedia publishing.

Organizations

Major organizations offering insight and information exchange including the following:

- ACM SIGGRAPH (computer graphics organization): www.siggraph.org

- The IEEE Computer Society International Professional Bodies for IT Professionals: www.computer.org

- Association for Information and Image Management (AIIM): www.aiim.org

- International Digital Enterprise Alliance (formerly Graphic Communications Association): www.idealliance.org

- Society for Technical Communication: www.stc.org

- PDFConference is the premier PDF conference held twice yearly. The spring meeting is near Washington, DC and the fall conference is in the Southwest: www.pdfconference.com.

Acrobat Plug-ins

Acrobat 6.0 comes with numerous plug-ins as well as several third-party plug-ins. Here's a rundown on their installation and use.

Adobe Plug-ins Included with Acrobat 6.0

Many plug-ins are available for Acrobat 6.0. There are no requirements on your part to have this set of plug-ins installed; they will autoinstall with a typical install setting when you're loading Acrobat from your installation CD. Basic information about the plug-ins is included in Table B-1.

Table B-1   Installed Plug-ins

Plug-in Name	File Name	Description and Information
Acrobat Accessibility	Accessibility.api	Allows assistive technology like screenreaders to work with Acrobat.
Acrobat PDDom	PDDom.api	Structure and content toolkit for accessibility and repurposing.
Acrobat Public Key Security	PPLite.api	Provides public key signing and encryption.
Adobe DRM	ebook.api	Enables features for obtaining and reading documents protected with Adobe DRM technology.
Catalog	Catalog.api	Creates a full-text index of a document or document collection. Also provides a search function. Uses Onix full-text indexing and retrieval toolkit.
Comments	Annots.api	Allows users to mark up online and offline documents with Acrobat.
Convert2AdobePDF	DistillerPl.api.	Allows opening PostScript files as Adobe PDF.
Database Connectivity	ADBC.api	Allows users to interact with databases using JavaScript.
Digital Signature	DigSig.api	Provides users with a generic PDF digital-signing process that can integrate with other signing plug-ins.
ECMAScript	Escript.api	Allows PDF documents to take advantage of JavaScript.
External Window Handler	EWH32.api	Allows users to view PDF files in a web browser.
Flattener View	FlattenerView.api	Flattener Preview allows previews of Flattener settings.
Forms	AcroForm.api	Enables users to work with electronic forms in Acrobat.
Highlight Server	Hls.api	Allows users to view search highlights from web searches in PDF files in a web browser.

Table B-1   Installed Plug-ins (Continued)

Plug-in Name	File Name	Description and Information
HTML2PDF	HTML2PDF.api	Converts HTML to PDF files (known as the Web Capture feature).
Image Conversion	ImageConversion.api	Allows users to open and save image formats as PDF; allows for image extraction.
Image Viewer	ImageViewer.api	Allows viewing of multimedia slideshows.
Internet Access	IA32.api	Creates Internet access in Acrobat.
LegalPDF	LegalPDF.api	Provides legal warnings on digital signatures.
Make Accessible	MakeAccessible.api	Converts untagged to tagged PDF for accessibility and reflow.
Multimedia	Multimedia.api	Allows users to author and play back movies and sound.
PaperCapture	PaperCapture.api	Converts static image PDF to live searchable text with Optical Character Recognition.
PDFConsultant and Accessibility Checker	Checkers.api	Optimize PDF and check accessibility.
Picture Tasks	PictureTasks.api	Allows users to export, edit, and print digital pictures.
Preflight	Preflight.api	Examines documents for detailed preflighting and checks compliance with PDF/X standards.
Reflow	Reflow.api	Enables users to reflow the content of a page to fit a window's width.
SaveAsRTF	SaveAsRTF.api	Saves PDF file content as Rich Text Format (RTF) for export.
SaveAsXML	SaveAsXML.api	Filters for saving tagged documents as XML, HTML, or plain text.
Search	Search.api	Provides the back-end for providing search services. Uses Onix full-text indexing and retrieval toolkit.
Search5	Search5.api	Provides back-end for catalog to use indexes created by earlier versions of the catalog. This uses the Verity full-test search engine.
SendMail	SendMail.api	Adds a button to the toolbar to send the current document as an email attachment.
Separation Preview	SepsView.api	Separation Preview mode allows you to preview separations.
SOAP	soap.api	Allows connectivity to web services through SOAP Protocol.
Spelling	spelling.api	Allows spell-checking of form fields and comments.
TablePicker	TablePicker.api	Allows user to select a table and copy to the clipboard or save in a variety of formats.
TouchUp	TouchUp.api	Allows users to perform touch-up editing of content and document tags.

Table B-1   Installed Plug-ins (Continued)

Plug-in Name	File Name	Description and Information
Updater	Updater.api	Manages lists of updates to Acrobat and Adobe Reader.
Web2PDF	WebPDF.api	Facilitates the Web Capture feature's functions.
Weblink	Weblink.api	Allows users to link to web pages from PDF documents.
XFA	XMA.api	XML Forms Architecture (XFA) extensions to Acrobat forms.

Other Plug-ins Used in This Book

Adobe has a wide variety of Readers for PDF files and more are being developed. You can find information at www.adobe.com/products/acrobat/readstep2.html.

- *Splitter.* Formerly a separate plug-in, Splitter has been merged with another product to become ARTS Split and Merge Lite/Plus. An Adobe Acrobat plug-in for splitting and merging batches of PDF documents that comes in two different versions—Lite and Plus, the split functionality lets you split one or more PDF documents based on page groups, page ranges, bookmarks, and page marks. The merge functionality lets you quickly sort and then combine a collection of PDF documents. The functions we used are only available in Plus. Find out more at www.aroundtable-solution.com/arts_split_and_merge.asp.

- *ARTS PDF Tools.* An Adobe Acrobat plug-in for performing repetitive tasks. ARTS PDF Tools is a set of tools and commands that allow you to customize how you use Acrobat. Copy and share tools across workgroups. The Flattener tool was what Tom used to flatten Free Text to the base layer. Find out more at www.aroundtablesolution.com/arts_pdf_tools.asp.

- *LGI Zoom-To-Search.* An Acrobat plug-in developed by Layton Graphics of Marietta, GA. LGIView Zoom-to-Search is part of a suite of plug-ins for Acrobat and Adobe Reader. The plug-ins are primarily for use in the engineering and geographic information system area. They include plug-ins to go to latitude and longitude in a set of hundreds of drawings, and the ability to select an area from a master map and print all the submaps as a set. Layton develops server base products that take thousands of CAD or GIS drawings and make them into easy-to-use, smart PDF files. Rather than developing proprietary viewers, Layton uses PDF and Acrobat. These products are primarily used in utilities and governments. Find out more at www.layton-graphics.com.

- *PDFAloud.* Don't confuse this plug-in with Read PDFAloud in Acrobat 6.0. This plug-in, developed by the Northern Ireland company, textHELP Systems Inc., is designed for people with dyslexia and reading disorders. This product highlights the words as they are read and the user can control the speech and other features. Find out more at www.texthelp.com.

Other Plug-ins to Consider

There are hundreds of plug-ins; we've used the following listed here:

- *ARTS PDF Stamper.* A flexible tool for applying stamps and watermarks to PDF documents. Use ARTS PDF Stamper to apply any combination of text, image, and PDF stamps to one or more PDF documents. The latest version features a new user interface, support for PDF file stamps, additional dynamic text options, and the ability to preview your stamps prior to applying them. You can read more at www.aroundtablesolution.com/arts_pdf_stamper.asp.

- *ARTS PDF Bookmarker.* An Adobe Acrobat plug-in for adding, editing, building, replacing, and deleting bookmarks across one or more PDF documents. ARTS PDF Bookmarker helps you use bookmarks more effectively, thereby providing you with a simple way to make almost any PDF document more usable and easier to navigate. Find out more at
www.aroundtablesolution.com/arts_pdf_bookmarker.asp.

- *ARTS PDF Search.* A powerful PDF searching tool for Adobe Acrobat and Adobe Reader that lets you index, publish, and search large PDF document collections on the Web, intranets, networks, CDs, and DVDs. The COM interface lets developers integrate ARTS PDF Search into custom PDF applications, including web applications. Find out more at
www.aroundtablesolution.com/arts_pdf_search.asp.

- *ARTS PDF Workshop.* A tool for managing PDF document collections. ARTS PDF Workshop lets you view and update the properties of batches of PDF documents, including document info (title, author, subject, and keywords) as well as document open options and security. Read about it at
www.aroundtablesolution.com/arts_pdf_workshop.asp.

Index

Symbols and Numbers

D